The
Greatest
U.S. Marine Corps
Stories Ever Told

The
Greatest
U.S. Marine Corps
Stories Ever Told

UNFORGETTABLE STORIES OF COURAGE, HONOR, AND SACRIFICE

EDITED BY IAIN C. MARTIN

WITH AN INTRODUCTION BY COL. JOSEPH H. ALEXANDER USMS (RET.)

THE LYONS PRESS
An imprint of The Globe Pequot Press
Guilford, Connecticut

The Lyons Press is an imprint of The Globe Pequot Press.

10 9 8 7 6 5 4 3 2 1

Printed in the United States of America

ISBN 978-1-59921-017-9

The Library of Congess Cataloging-in-Publication Data is available on file.

The Marines' Hymn

From the halls of Montezuma
To the shores of Tripoli,
We fight our country's battles
In the air, on land, and sea.
First to fight for right and freedom,
And to keep our honor clean,
We are proud to claim the title
Of United States Marines.

Our flag's unfurl'd to every breeze
From dawn to setting sun;
We have fought in every clime and place
Where we could take a gun.
In the snow of far-off northern lands
And in sunny tropic scenes,
You will find us always on the job -
The United States Marines.

Here's health to you and to our Corps
Which we are proud to serve;
In many a strife we've fought for life
And never lost our nerve.
If the Army and the Navy
Ever look on Heaven's scenes,
They will find the streets are guarded
By United States Marines.

Contents

Acknowledgments

I would like to thank my friend Donald K. Allen, author of *Tarawa: The Aftermath*, for sharing his research and narratives of his travels to Betio and Guadalcanal. I am also indebted to him for his introduction to Col. Joseph H. Alexander who kindly agreed to write the introduction for this book and assist with the editorial process. The series editor, Tom McCarthy and I are most grateful for his contributions to the project.

The task of an editor is never an easy one. Creating a single volume of the best literature on the Marines is a daunting task, yet with the resources at hand the book represents some of the finest writing on the Corps to be found. Nineteen of the twenty-four chapters are first person accounts. Readers may ask about the many Medal of Honor recipients whose acts of courage are at the heart of many great stories, yet this book is not about them. A few are told in passing; however, the emphasis of this collection tells the story of the Marines as a whole. Selections were made for their historical and narrative merits that best represent the events of that time. It goes without saying, to capture all of the great stories about the Marines, it would take endless volumes.

At the time of this publication, the Marines are seeing combat in Iraq and Afghanistan, as well as defending the United States from other posts around the world. I wish to dedicate this book to the men and women of the United States Marine Corps for their selfless dedication to their country and fellow Marines.

—Iain C. Martin, April 2007

Introduction

COLONEL JOSEPH H. ALEXANDER, USMC (RET.)

Marines take their history seriously. Their inspiration begins at Boot Camp, where drill instructors teach neophyte Leathernecks a special blend of history, traditions, myths, and legends. The centuries-old system seems to work. Young men and women continue to graduate from basic training at Parris Island or San Diego with an ingrained obligation to honor all Marines who have preceded them. You never let your fellow Marine down; you never let the Corps down. No matter where you go after Boot Camp, you carry with you the indelible image of some nameless veteran of the "Old Corps," hands on hips, staring at you appraisingly, judging your performance. That consciousness becomes as much a part of a Marine's combat kit as his rifle or fighting knife.

Marines are warriors as well as historians. If they seem brash and downright aggressive, it's because their mission for hundreds of years has required them to be "First to Fight," to sail into harm's way at the earliest storm warning, land forcibly, fight outnumbered and out-gunned, close with the enemy, and win. Such embedded aggressiveness spawns a distinctive warrior ethos in all Marines, "the long and the short and the tall." Stories of their predecessors' sacrifices and achievements comprise part of that ethos. Over time each Marine develops his or her own favorite story, hero, or battle. Indeed, one sure way to provoke a heated discussion among any gathering of Leathernecks is to introduce a definitive list of "the best Marine Corps stories of all time."

Iain Martin has done his work well. Few Marines will object to the 23 stories he has selected to represent the first 231 years of Marine Corps history. Others will decry the exclusion of their favorites. Perhaps this begs the case for a second volume—even a trilogy.

Readers who are not Marines will be well served by these selections. There is no better way of absorbing America's history than that as seen through the eyes of her Marines. Such readers might also benefit from understanding in advance who the Marines are and what they do.

As a short primer, Marines are a global, expeditionary force-in-readiness. They operate from the sea in partnership with the U.S. Navy—and have since 1775. Marines fight as a combined arms team—ground forces, aviation, and logistics support merged into a single-task force. One in every four Marines serves in an aviation outfit. Every Marine—air or ground, man or woman, officer or enlisted—is a rifleman. No Marine is a non-combatant. The Navy provides all the surgeons, hospital corpsmen (field medics), chaplains, and dentists for the Marines. Twenty-three of these Navy men have earned the Medal of Honor while supporting Marines in combat. The Marine Corps, with the highest ratio of enlisted men to officers of the armed forces, places unique emphasis on NCO leadership. Tough training and shared hardships forge the Marines' warrior spirit. "Marines are happiest when they are miserable," observed ABC News chief White House correspondent Martha Raddatz after a dozen trips to Iraq, "and even happier when I am miserable, too."[1]

The Marines' motto *Semper Fidelis* ("Always Faithful") is both a work ethic and an unspoken bond that no Marine will be left behind. Graphic photographs of the 1st Marine Division battling its way to the sea from North Korea's Chosin Reservoir in 1950 with its own dead strapped to jeep fenders and howitzer barrels attest to that promise made good.

General Charles C. Krulak, the 31st Commandant, said that the Corps contributes two principal things to America: "We make Marines, and we win battles." Other truths are implicit in the statement. The Marines may win battles, but it takes all the armed forces, and indeed the entire nation, to win wars. Secondly, although the Marines have suffered their share of defeats —Penobscot Bay, Bladensburg, Manassas, Fort Sumter, Wake Island, and the Chosin Reservoir come to mind—not all defeats turn out to be a net loss. Certainly the Marines' lionhearted defense of Wake against an overwhelming Japanese landing force—or the five-day defense of Toktong Pass in "Frozen Chosin" by Fox Company of the 7th Marines—inspired the nation during the darkest of days. "Retreat, hell!" snapped Marine General Oliver P. Smith to reporters at Hagaru-ri, "We're just attacking in another direction!" Thirty-two years earlier, Captain Lloyd Williams replied in kind to a dispirited French officer's suggestion the Marines join his retreat from the German advance on Belleau Wood, growling "Retreat, hell! We just got here!"

Iain Martin's selection and thoughtful frame-setting of these great stories enables the reader to put on a well-worn pair of Marine "boondockers" and march progressively through American history, literally "From the Halls of Montezuma to the Shores of Tripoli," as proclaimed in the opening stanza of the Marines' Hymn. The stories provide first-hand combat accounts by troops on the ground, pilots in the air over the battlefield, or such intrepid war correspondents as Stephen Crane at Guantanamo Bay, Robert Sherrod at Tarawa, Pulitzer-Prize winner Ernie Pyle at Okinawa, or Molly Moore with the Marines crossing the Saddam Hussein Line to liberate Kuwait. Readers will become acquainted with Lieutenant Presley O'Bannon, who led his Marines on a wild, 600-mile expedition across the Libyan Desert on a hostage-rescue mission to Tripoli; Corporal Miles Oviatt, who received the Medal of Honor for manning his 9-inch gun on the sloop *Brooklyn* under murderous fire from the Confederate ironclad *Tennessee* at Mobile Bay ("Stand fast, men!" he boomed over the din –"*Stand fast!*"); Sergeant John Quick exposing himself to Spanish fire in Cuba to wig-wag urgent signals to the Navy gunship to cease firing on friendly troops; or the storied Gunnery Sergeant Dan Daly, one of only two Marines to receive the Medal of Honor twice, leading his men through the fire-swept wheatfields at Belleau Wood, yelling, *"Come on, you sons-of-bitches, do you want to live for ever?"* The great stories continue: Captain Joe Foss, one of the Marines' greatest fighter aces, dueling Japanese Zeroes over Guadalcanal; "Red Mike" Edson, the legendary Raider, leading the rock-ribbed defense of Henderson Field from a brigade of Japanese jungle fighters; the unique Navajo Code Talkers fighting their way through every Pacific campaign, confounding Japanese eavesdroppers who could never decipher their ancient language nor their special code; Carlos Hathcock, known to the enemy as "White Feather," one of the greatest Marine snipers in history, stalking and shooting a North Vietnamese general from 800 yards away; the helicopter pilots and flight crews who ran a daily gauntlet of anti-aircraft fire to resupply besieged Khe Sanh and its surrounding hilltop outposts in the fourth year of the Vietnam War.

Not all the struggles and achievements of the Marines resulted in battle streamers for their flag. Offering full acceptance and equality to African-Americans and women in the middle decades of the 20th century was a painful, often glacial process that took years to instill. Both achievements are great stories in their own right.

The Iraq War created a fresh generation of combat stories. Jay Kopelman's *From Baghdad with Love* provides a promising start.

Many discerning readers consider Eugene B. Sledge's haunting personal narrative *With the Old Breed at Peleliu and Okinawa* to be the definitive enlisted account of frontline combat in World War II, ranking in impact with the Civil War's *The Red Badge of Courage* and World War One's *All Quiet on the Western Front*. Sledge was a doctor's son from Mobile, sensitive and observant, who grew impatient with an officer candidate program at Georgia Tech to volunteer for duty as a rifleman with the 5th Marines in the western Pacific. Sixteen years after publishing his book, he contributed a final introspective essay, "The Old Breed and the Costs of War," which is included in this anthology. His reflections offer a strong antidote to anyone who would glorify war.

No anthology can include all books and essays that otherwise could qualify as "The Greatest Marine Corps Stories." Readers who seek additional stories of this genre might consider, for World War I, John W. Thomason's *Fix Bayonets;* for World War II, Gregory ("Pappy") Boyington's *Baa Baa Black Sheep,* George B. Hunt's *Coral Comes High,* and Richard Tregaskis' *Guadalcanal Diary;* for the Korean War, Joseph Owens' *Colder Than Hell: A Marine Rifle Company at Chosen Reservoir,* and Edwin H. Simmons' superb monograph *Frozen Chosin: U.S. Marines at the Changjin Reservoir;* for the Vietnam War, John Miller's *The Bridge at Dong Ha* and the Pulitzer Prize-winning book by Lewis B. Puller Jr. (son of the legendary "Chesty" Puller), *Fortunate Son;* and for the Marines' more recent engagements in Lebanon, Afghanistan, and Iraq, Eric Hammel's *The Root: The Marines in Beirut, August 1982–February 1984* and Nathaniel Fick's *One Bullet Away.*

The Greatest Marine Corps Stories Ever Told is a superb treasury of Leatherneck history, and I salute Iain Martin and series editor Tom McCarthy for their hard work and tough choices.

Semper Fidelis...

JOSEPH H. ALEXANDER
Author, *The Battle History of the U.S. Marines: A Fellowship of Valor* and *Utmost Savagery: The Three Days of Tarawa.*

An American Flag on Foreign Soil

RICHARD ZACKS

The inauguration of President Thomas Jefferson brought with it America's first foreign war with the Barbary States of the North African coast. Since the United States lost the protection of the French navy in 1783, American merhant ships in the Mediterranean came under attack of the Moslem kings of Algiers, Tunis, and Tripoli who demanded tribute from the new government. When he became president, Jefferson made good on his promise to end the payments to the Barbary kings, a sum that had totalled as much as twenty percent of the government's annual revenue. The Pasha of Tripoli and his allies responded by declaring war on the United States.

The recommissioning of the American navy in 1794 allowed the President to take the fight to the enemy and protect American interests. Congress never voted on a formal declaration of war, but it did authorized the President to instruct the commanders of American warships to seize all vessels and goods of the Pasha of Tripoli "and also to cause to be done all such other acts of precaution or hostility as the state of war will justify." As part of this measure Jefferson assigned William Eaton, a former Army officer and Consul to Tunis, a secret mission to overthrow the rulers of Tripoli by launching an overland attack with the support of a small detachment of U.S. Marines under the command of U.S. Marine First Lieutenant Presley O'Bannon, and a motley force of Arab, Greek, and Berber mercenaries. With them was the deposed leader of Tripoli, Hamet Karamanli, who they intended to restore to power.

In the following chapter, Richard Zacks describes the climactic assault on the city of Derna by Eaton's forces with the support of Captain Issac Hull and the U.S.S. *Argus* on April 27, 1805, from his best selling work *The Pirate Coast*.

> There is but one language which can be held to these people,
> and this is terror.
>
> —William Eaton

★   ★   ★   ★   ★

William Eaton Rolled Up the pants leg of his homemade general's uniform and walked out into the surf off Bomba beach. With the sun glinting off his epaulets, he waited for the American boat coming ashore.

"All was now rejoicing and mutual congratulation," wrote Midshipman Peck. The sight of the two-masted *Argus* brought elation that morning to the weary Americans, lifting them from the prospect of starvation or massacre to granting them yet another chance to pursue their unlikely mission.

Eaton and the midshipman stepped aboard the longboat; a dozen sailors rowed them out to the USS *Argus*, anchored safely offshore. "I enjoyed the pleasure of embracing my messmates," later recalled Peck, "and sitting down to a comfortable meal which I had not enjoyed for near 40 days."

Eaton was thrilled to see Hull again, who throughout had remained his steadfast advocate. Hull, like Eaton, hailed from the Massachusetts/Connecticut region with family members residing in both states. At fourteen, he had gone to sea as a cabin boy, and when shipwrecked at sixteen, he had saved his captain's life. Now thirty-two years old, Hull was known as an adept seaman, with an uncanny knack of squeezing every ounce of speed out of any vessel. "He was a rough boisterous captain of the sea," noted a contemporary, adding, "his manners were plain, bluff and hearty." Hull, like Eaton, did not suffer fools gladly. He could be "ruffled on sufficient occasion," added the observer.

Beyond Hull's welcome, Eaton was greeted by a long letter from Commodore Barron. Given Barron's lukewarm support of his mission, Eaton no doubt unfolded the document with trepidation. Within moments, he was calmed. "I cannot but applaud the energy and perseverance that has characterized your progress through a series of perplexing and discouraging difficulties," Barron had written on March 22. (Actually, too ill to write, he had dictated the words to his secretary.)

Barron noted that he had instantly ordered military supplies and food to be loaded onto the *Hornet* and *Argus* to be rushed to Eaton, as well as the ample sum of 7,000 Spanish dollars. But Barron, in this note, was not uniformly supportive. He wrote that he deeply opposed the Convention that Eaton planned to sign with Hamet. (Barron didn't know that Eaton had already signed it.)

"I reiterate to you . . . my dissent from any guarantee . . . [that] the United States may stand committed to place the exiled prince on the throne." By way of clarification, Barron stressed that the United States was helping Hamet to help himself . . . and that if Yussef offered honorable terms of peace, the United States must be free to accept them and "then our support of Hamet must necessarily be withdrawn." In stark terms, he described Hamet, "as an instrument to an attainment."

Obsessive Eaton weighed the mixed message, and he decided not to waver. He planned to capture Derne, Bengazi, then Tripoli. Though it's clear from later letters that Eaton understood Barron's calculated use of Hamet, he deeply opposed that approach. Eaton's world featured Good and Evil; and Yussef by enslaving American sailors was Evil.

At 6 p.m., the crew of the *Argus* rowed a feast ashore for the weary troops. Eaton remained on board that night, eating well and drinking well and no doubt regaling his messmates with the tales of faithless Tayyib and the Bedouin women's love of brass buttons. In the morning the sailors in the *Argus* longboat rowed him ashore.

That afternoon, the *Hornet* sloop arrived, carrying the bulk of the supplies. Over the course of the next two days, the sailors rolled and hoisted 30 hogsheads of bread, 20 barrels of peas, 10 tierces of rice (approximately 3,000 pounds total), 10 boxes of oil, 100 sacks of rice, one bale of cloth, and 7,000 Spanish dollars into longboats and rowed it all ashore. The army's thirst requirements were not ignored. The *Hornet* offloaded one hogshead (63 gallons) of brandy and two hogsheads of wine. Since, in theory, only the Christian troops drank liquor, and since that contingent totaled 75 men, each soldier—in a fair appointment—could look forward to about two and a half gallons.

The troops, having survived the long march, spent three days lolling about, recuperating, eating, drinking. O'Bannon played his fiddle; the drummer avoided anything martial. Eaton, in his tent, finalized attack plans as best he could from his perch in Bomba about forty miles from the battle site in Derne.

A turbaned messenger arrived from the Moslem camp with yet another rumor that Yussef's army had reached Derne with 500 men. Eaton complained in notes to Hull that this fact—if true—made his need for field artillery even more acute, and that he was disappointed the *Congress* hadn't arrived with the promised fieldpieces. "Besides the terror that Cannon impress on the undisciplined Savages we have to dispute with, they will be our best resort against the Walls of Derne," he wrote.

Eaton then requested that he be allowed to borrow two of the *Argus*'s 24-pound carronades. (Carronades were short-barreled guns that launched a heavy shot for a short distance.) He also asked for four barrels of musket gunpowder, balls and flints, and as many muskets as could be spared. Eaton warned the carronades might have to be abandoned in case of retreat.

As to the specific plan of attack, he wanted his forces to reach the eastern hills overlooking Derne and then attack from there; he hoped that the navy would come close enough to shore to blast out the town's batteries. Eaton waxed optimistic, especially if he could afford to buy the loyalty of the local Arabs. "I find them like the rest of mankind, moved by the present good . . . Cash will carry them . . . with this the Gates of Tripoli may be opened."

On the days leading up to battle, many soldiers cannot avoid thoughts of mortality. Eaton confronted his own possible death. "Of the effects I leave on board, in case I see you no more," he wrote to Hull, "I beg you will accept my cloak, and small sword, as marks of my attachment; the Damascus Sabre, which you will find in my chest, please give to Capt. James Barron, it is due to his goodness and valor, I owe it to the Independent integrity of his heart; my Gold watch chain give to [my stepson Eli] Danielson; every thing else please deliver over to Mr. Charles Wadsworth my Executor." (Conspicuously absent is any sentimental mention of his wife.)

Two other men also sent letters to Captain Hull, both requesting permission to fight alongside Eaton. Lieutenant Presley O'Bannon wrote that he was "unwilling to abandon an Expedition this far conducted." Midshipman George Washington Mann asked to go onshore and replace Midshipman Peck. Mann labored to avoid insulting his commander. "I am actuated by . . . a wish to contribute generally by my services to the Interest of my Country." Captain Hull granted both requests, and allowed Eaton in addition to keep his six U.S. Marine privates and one sergeant.

All this while, Hamet and his followers, and the hired sheiks and the Bedouin, camped away from the Christians. Swarthy teenage boys hut-hutted their camels to fertile pastures to graze. The more devout prayed five times a day. So close to open enmity but a week earlier, the two allies kept a safe distance.

Before Hull gave any reply to Eaton's tactical letter, the *Argus* suddenly disappeared from port. Eaton could only assume—and hope—that Hull had seen a sail and taken off in pursuit. Then the next day, heavy clouds darkened the sky, and a storm hit the coast. Eaton in the rain was left wondering whether Hull would be able to rendezvous with him for the up-coming combined attack at Derne. But he had more pressing matters: moving an army the final leg to the battlefield.

The Gulf of Bomba sits ringed by mountains. The army, which had marched down along the coast to relax, now had to hike back up to head west to Derne. High cold winds mixed with rain soaked the troops as they marched ten miserable miles on Tuesday, April 23, up over rocky terrain. They camped in a ravine, within a mile of natural fresh water "springing from the top of a mountain of freestone, near Cape Ras el-Tin," as Eaton recorded in his diary. In the distance could be seen cultivated fields. Hamet sent a herald throughout the various camps to announce. "He who fears god and feels attachment to Hamet Bashaw will be careful to destroy nothing. Let no one touch the growing harvest. He who transgresses this injunction shall lose his right hand." By forbidding plundering, Hamet was trying not to alienate the local peasants who might rally to his cause.

The Americans, after so long in the desert, had finally reached a cultivated region. In antiquity, these lands bloomed with diverse crops; wealthy Romans squabbled over vacation homes. "Marched fifteen miles over mountainous and broken ground, covered with herbage and very large and beautiful red cedars—the first resemblance of a forest tree we have seen during a march of nearly six hundred miles." The mixed troop camped in a valley along a stream. Eaton estimated them to be "about five hours march from Derne."

A messenger arrived with news that the governor of Derne had fortified the city to repel any attack and that Yussef's army would probably reach Derne before them. Another messenger reported that no American ships could be seen off the coast, since that harsh storm of the previous day. Eaton, with his typical bullheadedness, recommended haste, a quick march double time to Derne. the turbaned allies reacted differently. "Alarm and consternation seized the Arab chiefs, and despondency the Bashaw," recorded Eaton. "The night was passed in consultations among them at which I was not admitted."

At 6 a.m., before dawn, the drummer pounded out a general wake-up call; everyone hustled about, striking their tents; Eaton promptly gave orders to prepare to march. The European mercenaries and the American Marines in uniform lined up. The followers of Hamet also lined up but in the opposite direction. Sheik Tayyib and Sheik Muhammed guided the 300 cavalry slowly back toward Bomba. The Bedouin merely refused to move and remained in camp.

Eaton's babysitting duties had commenced again. By now, he realized that the sheiks felt no overarching loyalty to Hamet or to the overthrow of Yussef. They were Moslem mercenaries on a sliding pay scale, which slid upward as the dangers increased. Eaton began with encouragement, shifted to reproach, and ended up promising $2,000 to the sheiks. They agreed. At 2 p.m. the Hamet-Eaton horse reached a hill overlooking Derne. The general was finally looking at his first target.

The easternmost town of any importance in the kingdom of Tripoli, Derne had a population of around five thousand. Nestled in a *wadi* (valley) of incredible fertility, the local crops included fig, pear, peach, orange, peas, tomatoes, cucumbers, pumpkins, jasmine, and sugarcane. Derne was famed for its honey and its unusual butter, concocted of butter and mutton fat and prized for Middle Eastern stews. The town's limestone buildings piggybacked on much older dwellings, with most of them having entrances on the second floor, reached by grapevine-trellis-covered staircases. In the summer, the local inhabitants likes to sit on their stoops under the shade of the grape bunches. Unfortunately, for a place with so much to export, the harbor was miserable, shallow, pocked with reefs and exposed to high winds from the north and east. One traveler reported it unusable for seven months of the year, from February to August.

Eaton, along with Hamet, surveyed the target. From the hilltop, through his spyglass, he observed that a battery of eight cannons, probably nine-pounders, pointed seaward, guarding the harbor. To the northeast of the town, he saw residents building up some temporary breastworks, while to the southeast, the walls of old buildings blocked access. Eaton also noted a "ten-inch howitzer" mounted on the terrace of the governor's palace. Spies told him that in town the inhabitants had fortified their terraces and knocked loopholes in their walls for shooting. They also said that because the governor of Derne "could bring 800 men into battle, and he possessed all the batteries, breastworks and seaboard, we should find it difficult to dislodge him . . . besides Yussef's army was just at hand." In addition, no American ships had arrived.

Eaton looked at Hamet. "I thought the Bashaw wished himself back to Egypt."

The following morning, at 8 a.m., Easton ordered the Christian soldiers to build big bonfires in hopes the smoke signals would alert the American ships to their location. Without field artillery or ships, the attack would be foolhardy, even by Eaton's standards. In the meantime, he sent a letter under white flag of truce to the governor of Derne.

Sir, I want no territory. With me is advancing the legitimate Sovereign of your country—Give me a passage through your city; and for the supplies of which we shall have need you shall receive fair compensation—Let no differences of religion induce us to shed the blood of harmless men who think little and know nothing.—If you are a man of liberal mind you will not balance on the propositions I offer.—Hamet Bashaw pledges himself to me that you shall be established in your government.—I shall see you tomorrow in a way of your choice.

—William Eaton

The governor's response arrived quickly:

My head or yours.

—Mustifa

At 2 p.m. a distant sail was spotted. At 6 p.m. Lieutenant John Dent, captain of the *Nautilus,* sent a boat ashore, rowed by U.S. Navy sailors in crisp blue and white. "You will please send a large party down early in the Morning for the field pieces & ammunition, which I am afraid you will have some difficulty getting up the hill." Dent added he was ready to send over any supplies that Eaton might want. "Make my respects to O'Bannon & all your Brave followers & wishing you all the Success you so fully deserve."

After so many months at a slow pace, events were coming quickly to a head. General Eaton decided that, with Yussef's army on the march toward Derne, he must order an immediate full-scale attack for the following day, Saturday, April 27.

The next morning, at 5:30 a.m., the Americans spotted three more ships hovering near the 14-gun *Nautilus.* Hull had arrived in the 18-gun brig *Argus* towing a lateen-sailed prize, while Lieutenant Samuel Evans showed up in the pip-squeak 10-gun sloop *Hornet,* which had formerly been a Massachusetts merchantman named *Traveller.*

The *Argus,* days earlier, had indeed spotted a ship and captured it. The vessel was flying Ottoman colors but carried mostly Tripolitan passengers on board, including a gunboat captain and several leading citizens of Bengazi. The cargo included gunpowder bound for Tripoli. Though Hull admitted he didn't know whether Barron considered the whole coast under blockade, he decided he would keep the vessel as a prize.

The *Argus* carried long guns capable of firing 24-pound shot; the *Nautilus* sported stubby carronades hoisting 12-pound balls, and the *Hornet* carried brass cannons throwing 6-pound balls.

At 10:30 a.m. a longboat began ferrying the brass fieldpieces ashore to a spot east of Derne. The men rowed in close to the shore, only to discover that cliffs lined that whole section of the coast and that even the best place would require hauling the heavy gun up an almost twenty-foot-sheer cliff. While another boat looked for an alternative, the men hoisted up nine barrels of gunpowder, 200 bags of musket balls for grape filler, and 150 rounds for the fieldpiece as well as the rammer and wadding. (A bag of musket balls is a cannon's equivalent of bird shot, delivering a lethal spray at the enemy.)

The fieldpiece was a problem. The weight is not listed, but a good guess might be 1,500 pounds, to be hoisted from a rocking boat up a cliff and over the edge. The men, using ropes and horses and struggling for several hours, finally lugged up one fieldpiece. Eaton decided that it would take too long to haul up the other, so he left it to be carried back to the *Nautilus*.

The three U.S. Navy ships began to sail to take their positions outside Derne harbor.

Eaton readied the army. The Christians and Moslems would have separate missions. Eaton with his small force would tackle the governor's main defense. Hamet and his hundreds of robed riders would circle around back of the town to try to capture an old castle to the southwest of town. They hoped to meet at the governor's mansion. The navy would try to take out the shore battery, then plunk balls into the town.

At 2 p.m. General Eaton along with Lieutenant O'Bannon, leading an attack force of 7 U.S. Marines and 26 Greek recruits as well as 24 European mercenaries to handle the fieldpiece, advanced on the southeast corner of Derne. Hundreds of men opposed them, shooting up from a fortified ravine, protected by earthworks. The fieldpiece rained big balls and sprays of musket balls down upon the enemy.

Upon the start of gunfire, the brave little *Hornet* sailed to within one hundred yards of Governor Mustifa's battery of nine-pounders and spit out a relentless barrage of grape and balls from its brass six-pounders. The *Nautilus* stood about a half mile from shore and lobbed its 12-pound balls over the *Hornet* and toward the battery and the town. Anchored a bit farther out was the *Argus*, at the right distance to shoot its 24-pound shot.

Hamet's troops—more than 1,000 men—galloped downward, green

Moslem flags streaming, and quickly took the largely undefended old castle on the hill at the back of the town, but then they remained there, stock still in that safe zone.

Eaton's French-Maltese-Sicilian artillery team learned the niceties of their new weapon on the run; they mastered it quickly, but their speed of reloading was diminished when the crew accidentally fired away the only rammer.

The three ships kept up constant fire on the enemy's shore battery on the ramparts above the harbor. The *Hornet,* located within pistol shot, repeatedly tacking, braved especially heavy fire. At one point, a shot from the Derne battery snapped the halliards that held aloft the large American flag in the stern. From war immemorial, there has been an almost mystical disgrace to losing one's national flag, to having it captured or seeing it lowered. It is the symbolic embodiment of the will to fight. Lieutenant Blodget scooped up the immense flag, fifteen feet long, and climbed the ratlines amid a torrent of musket fire. Just as he nailed it to the main masthead, he was hit with a musket ball near his hip, which miraculously "lodged in his watch while in his fob," according to an eyewitness account. He escaped injury as did the flag, which now caught the breezes.

The *Hornet* sprayed jagged grapeshot on the shore battery. The navy men kept up such a constant barrage that the brass six-pounders pulled the plants out of the deck. The turbaned gunners tried to remain brave as ball after heavy ball from the *Nautilus* or *Argus* plowed up the earth nearby. After three-quarters of an hour, the governor's gunners abandoned the battery and rushed to join the governor's troops defending the southeast section of town.

Eaton and O'Bannon had approximately one hundred soldiers, including seven U.S. Marines perched on the hill to the southeast of town. The total enemy force was estimated at close to one thousand, well entrenched, firing their muskets from behind bulwarks.

At around 3:30 p.m., Eaton came to a grim conclusion. "The fire of the enemy's Musketry became too warm and continually augmenting. Our troops were thrown into confusion and undisciplined as they were, it was impossible to reduce them to order." The British infantry, fighting against Napoleon, was famous for its unflappable lines of muskets. This hodgepodge European-American unit was verging on chaos and retreat.

Eaton made a desperate decision; a charge. His hundred against their thousand. The men attached bayonets. He gave the signal. The drummers pounded the skins.

Eaton and O'Bannon in full uniform led the charge down the hill into the teeth of the enemy. A polyglot war cry rose from the throats of the attacking men: English, French, Italian, Greek, Young Scot Farquhar raced near the front, as did the U.S. Marines. The men poured downward toward the earthworks, completely exposed during this rumble down the hillside. The enemy could squeeze off target-practice shots at them, but only one round or possibly two before the attackers would reach them. Eaton's goal was to descend quickly enough to fluster the enemy. He had had little choice; the firefight had been going badly.

The Americans and Europeans poured forward. U.S. Marine Private John Wilton was instantly killed by a shot to the heart. Another marine, Edward Steward, crumpled, as did several of the Greeks. A pair of marines— David Thomas and Bernard O'Brian—were also hit. Maniacal Eaton, at the very front, suddenly spun to the ground. He grasped his left wrist; a musket ball had torn through the wrist and exited the other side. Blood poured out, staining his general's coat, splattering in the dust of the dry *wadi*. O'Bannon and Mann kept on charging with the 75 men, and Eaton quickly gathered himself, somehow wrapped the wound, and continued forward.

With this determined force coming at them, the men of Derne fired off another round, but then most of them didn't dare to try to reload; they scattered from the earthworks to the safety of the nearby houses. A bayonet can skewer a man before a scimitar can do any harm.

Twenty-nine-year-old O'Bannon, along with twenty-one-year-old Mann, as well as the few U.S. Marines and Greeks zigzagged through the shower of musket fire from the loopholes in the buildings. They fought and raced to the abandoned battery and fort in the harbor.

Captain Hull observed the action through his spyglass on the *Argus*, a half mile offshore. "At about half past 3, we had the satisfaction to see Lt. O'Bannon and Mr. Mann, midshipman of the *Argus,* with a few brave fellows with them, enter the fort, haul down the Enemy's flag, and plant the American ensign on the walls of the Battery."

This marked the first time the American flag—then fifteen stars and fifteen stripes—had ever been planted in battle on foreign soil outside of North America. Eaton and the Marines never explained their rationale, but it's *unlikely* that Thomas Jefferson ever envisioned that his reluctant permission to allow Eaton to aid Hamet would lead to an American flag flapping in conquest over a city in Tripoli. Whatever Jefferson might have thought, the sight greatly stirred the emotions of the handful of hardened men who witnessed the accomplishment.

The soldiers who captured the fort labored hard to turn the heavy guns and point them upon the town. They discovered that the enemy in its haste to retreat had left a round loaded, primed, and ready to go. Around this time, Hamet Bashaw and his cavalrymen advanced into the southwestern end of town. And now the allied forces pinned the defenders between two streams of gunfire as the navy ships kept lobbing balls into the town, creating chaos.

With the tide of battle turning, the Bashaw and his men cantered through the narrow streets, harassing the enemy. They took possession of the governor's palace, and the cavalry chased the fleeing enemy. As Eaton later described it: "They held safe positions to catch fugitives until the doors of the Enemy were open'd for plunder, when they became at once brave & impetuous." The governor of Derne first took refuge in a mosque then somehow slipped into the harem of one of the town's leading citizens and claimed the ancient rights of sanctuary. Most of the defenders of Derne tried to hide their weapons and slip back into civilian life.

By 4 p.m. Eaton claimed the town as captured. Hull sent a boat ashore to bring more ammunition and carry off the thirteen Christians wounded, including U.S. Marine Bernard O'Brian. At 5:30 p.m. Easton went aboard the *Argus* to have his wound dressed; it was described as "musket ball through the left wrist," in other words, a metal ball of at least three-quarter inch in diameter had passed through just below the wrist joint. (Eaton would never regain full use of the arm.)

The time of recuperation for Eaton and the other Christian wounded, however, would be brief. A spy reported that Yussef's troops were within fourteen hours' march of the town. The doctor bandaged Eaton's arm and made the general put it in a sling, which was draped next to his shiny epaulet. Eaton later complained he could no longer wield his rifle. (In this era, the rifle, with its longer range and accuracy, was replacing the cumbersome musket.)

Eaton allowed himself one night aboard the *Argus*. The next day bright and early, the New Englander began orchestrating the town's defenses. He set up his own headquarters under the American flag in the small fort by the harbor battery. Someone, probably Eaton, dubbed it "Fort Enterprise"—a telling name that brings to mind hard work and boldness. Eaton, with help from his engineer, colorful Jean Eugene, repaired the ramparts and the fort and set about permanently pointing the cannons into the city. He placed barricades in various spots in the city to create ambush points. The guns were cleaned and repaired. Nine-pound cannonballs were neatly stacked nearby. Local reports estimated that about one-third of the quite perturbed populace remained secretly loyal to Governor Mustifa Bey, then holed up in the sheik's harem.

After consulting with Eaton, Hull decided that he would send off the *Hornet* to Malta, both for repairs to its sheered planks and, equally important, to inform Commodore Barron of their victory. In four years of war against Tripoli, this easily ranked as the United States' greatest victory.

Eaton, still weak from his wound, set about the pleasant task of relaying their good news. "We are in possession of the most valuable province of Tripoli," he announced. Eaton recounted the battle in vivid blow-by-blow detail and begged the liberty to praise O'Bannon, Mann, and the commanders of all three navy vessels for their courage and competence. He recommended them all for reward or promotion.

★   ★   ★   ★   ★

Lieutenant Presley O'Bannon had the honor of being the first American to raise the flag over foreign soil. The Pasha of Tripoli, fearing siege from sea and land, sued for peace after the capture of Derna. Legend has it that Hamet Karamanli presented Lt. O'Bannon with his personal Mameluke sword as a gesture of gratitude following the attack. Marine Corps Commandant Archibald Henderson adopted the Mameluke sword in 1825 as the standard for Marine Corps officers, a tradition that continues to this day.

Gamble of the Marines

RAYMOND J. TONER

John Marshall Gamble is a legendary hero of the Marine Corps. At the age of twenty-one, the newly commissioned Second Lieutenant Gamble took command of the Marines of the frigate *Essex*. On October 22, 1812, under the command of Captain David Porter, the *Essex* sailed to the coast of Brazil for her second wartime cruise. In January, unable to run the British blockage to return home, Porter took the *Essex* into the Pacific to attack British whalers. The *Essex* succeeded in capturing three British ships, one of which, the *Greenwich*, was given to Lt. Gamble to command. Gamble was, and most likely will ever be, the only Marine officer to command an American warship. Shortly afterwards, Gamble and a crew of fourteen men engaged the British whaler *Seringapatam* and forcing the enemy to surrender. Naval Captain Raymond J. Toner describes the action from his book, *Gamble of the Marines*.

> A ship without Marines is like a garment without buttons.
> —Admiral David Porter

* * * * *

The fierce midday sun of the equator poured down on the blue Pacific. Three ships, in line abreast, stood along their courses under easy sail. Astern, to the south, lay the dim shape of Albemarle, one of the Galapagos Islands.

The largest of the three ships, the *Essex*, was disguised to look like a whaling ship. Any experienced seaman, however, would have known by the trim set of her sails, the smart appearance of her boats, and the sleek lines of her hull that she was a man-o'-war.

The smaller ships were true whalers with rugged, simple lines. Each

1 3

had a brick try-works amidships where whale blubber was boiled, or "tried," to extract the precious oil.

The man-o'-war *Essex* was a United States frigate of thirty-two guns. The smaller ships, the *Greenwich* and the *Georgiana*, were formerly British whalers but had been captured and were now prizes of the *Essex*. The three had set sail from Albemarle Island to search for other British whalers reported cruising to the northward.

On the windward side of the *Greenwich* quarterdeck stood her prize master, Lieutenant John M. Gamble, United States Marine Corps, Marine officer of *Essex*. He was twenty-three—a young man in a young nation's service.

Gamble's face above the white ruffles of his neck-cloth and the high collar of his uniform was deeply suntanned. His features were regular and his mouth was firmly set. Brown eyes peered through deep-set lids. His legs were widespread to ride with the ship's lift and roll.

The upward tilt of Gamble's chin and the straight line of his back showed his pride in the *Greenwich*, his first command. For an officer of the Marines to command a naval ship was an unheard of thing. But Gamble had been lucky.

The *Essex* had captured so many ships of the British whaling fleet that her commander, Captain David Porter, U. S. Navy, could spare no more experienced officers to command his latest prizes. As a result, he had placed Gamble, the *Essex'* Marine officer, in command of the *Greenwich* when she was captured on May 29.

From his position near the stern, Gamble watched the members of his prize crew as they went about their tasks along the decks. He looked aloft to see that all sails were drawing properly.

"Sail ho!" came the cry from the masthead lookout.

Gamble snatched the speaking trumpet from the binnacle chest beside him and called up. "Where 'way?"

"Three of them, sir," came the reply. "One dead ahead, the other two broad on the larboard bow."

"*Essex* is making signals, sir," reported the quartermaster, who was watching the frigate through a long glass.

"Let me have the signal when you have it decoded," Gamble replied.

Turning to his second-in-command, he said, "Pipe all hands to handle sail, Mister Wilson."

The lookout's hail brought all hands tumbling up on deck. Even before the boatswain's pipe ceased to shrill, the sail handlers were swarming up the shrouds and laying out along the yardarms to loosen and set sail.

Under the added press of sail the *Greenwich's* deck began to heel. The wind blowing through the taut rigging took on a sharper sound. Her blunt bow, never designed for speed, rose and fell in a smother of foam, sometimes sending spray flashing over the bulwarks to wet the windward side of the forecastle.

"Ease her off a quarter point, helmsman!" Gamble shouted through the speaking trumpet. "We're starving her too much. We're already to windward of the *Essex* and all the strange sail."

Turning to his second-in-command, Gamble said, "I intend to engage the largest ship, Mister Wilson. We have a better chance of overhauling her than does *Essex*. Crowd on every bit of sail the ship will carry."

"*Essex*' message decoded, sir." The quartermaster touched his finger to his forehead in salute and pointed to the page of a signal book.

The signal read, "Engage closest ship."

Gamble nodded and smiled. He had sailed with Captain Porter long enough to know that he could expect bold action. He raised his long glass to observe the ship they were chasing.

She was definitely the largest of the strange ships. All three, now aware that they were being chased, had put themselves before the wind and were crowding on all sail. The *Essex*, with her greater spread of sail, had hauled ahead of her consorts toward the center ship of the three that lay ahead.

After a half hour's chase, it was clear that the *Greenwich* was rapidly overhauling the stranger. Because she was much to windward of the other ships when the chase began, the *Greenwich* was able to run down with a following wind on her starboard quarter.

The strangers, realizing that they could not outrun the frigate *Essex* before the wind, had chosen to beat to windward. This not only slowed them; it shortened the distance the *Greenwich* had to run.

After more than three hours of chase, the *Greenwich* was nearly within long range of the nearest stranger. Gamble gave the order to "Beat to General Quarters." Men eagerly triced up the gun ports and ran out the broadside guns.

The *Greenwich* carried only five guns to each broadside. Even so, Gamble had barely enough crew to man the guns of one broadside.

"*Essex* is hove to, sire. The ship she was in chase of has hauled down her colors," the quartermaster reported.

"Good!" Gamble replied. "But it will be some time before *Essex* can beat to windward to help us."

Gamble noticed with pleasure that under the capable direction of Lieutenant Wilson all was ready for the attack. The tense excitement of a ship about to go into battle was seen in the faces and actions of the men standing at their stations at the guns. They often peered through the open ports to sight the chase and glanced aft to watch their commander.

Gamble, too, was excited. For the first time he felt the great responsibility of command. He knew that he must not let the enemy captain outmaneuver him. He had to justify the confidence Captain Porter had shown by placing him in command of a ship.

Now the Marine officer raised the long glass and studied his opponent carefully. He saw that she was pierced for six guns to each broadside. That gave her two more guns than the *Greenwich*. She also seemed to be somewhat larger and carried a greater spread of sail. Gamble knew that if the *Greenwich* had not been to windward, she could never have overhauled the stranger.

Suddenly Gamble noticed that the enemy ship's headsails had begun to flutter. He could see her sail handlers tailing out on the weather braces. From the peak of the gaff English colors suddenly broke in the wind. At the same instant the lookout hailed, "Chase is coming about, sir!"

"So! They've decided to give us a fight before the *Essex* can come to our aid," Gamble thought. He seized the speaking trumpet and shouted to Lieutenant Wilson at his station near the foremast.

"Mister Wilson, man the larboard battery! I intend to round up and give them a broadside while her head is in the wind! Aim for her bulwarks! Hold your fire until I have the ship steady on her course!"

With a shout the men leaped to the guns of the larboard broadside. They adjusted the quoins and blew on the slow matches.

Gamble felt a momentary surprise that he knew so well what was happening. It was as though he were again watching the diagramming of single ship actions the officers so often discussed in the *Essex'* wardroom. He could predict what the stranger would do, and he knew what he must do to prevent her from gaining a windward position.

Gamble was tempted to round up and fire his broadside, but he did not. His opponent was almost into the eye of the wind. "Just a little longer now," Gamble said to himself, "and I'll be able to give them a raking broadside at closer range."

The quartermaster and helmsman, both manning the wheel, watched Gamble intently. The few sail handlers who could be spared from the guns stood ready to handle sheets and braces.

"Bring her head to north-northeast and let me know when you are steady on course!" Gamble called. "Trim braces and sheets as necessary."

The *Greenwich's* wheel spun in answer to Gamble's order. The shrill of the boatswain's pipes passing orders to the sail handlers rose above the sound of water rushing along the *Greenwich's* lee side and the creak of her running rigging.

"Steady on nor'-nor'east, sir," sang out the helmsman.

"All right, lads," shouted Gamble, "when you have her bulwarks in your sights, fire!"

Gamble tensed, expecting an immediate response, as though he had given an order to musketry fire. The deck was responding to the motion of the sea with a moderate roll and pitch. The guns of the broadside were not yet bearing on the hull of the chase. At last one gun roared, followed in an instant by the other guns of the broadside. White gunpowder smoke swirled about the decks to make a dense haze that hid the other ship briefly.

At first Gamble thought that the entire broadside had missed. The enemy ship had passed the eye of the wind and was paying off on the larboard tack. Then as the gunsmoke cleared Gamble saw the smashed bulwark. Two of the *Greenwich's* solid shot had raked the entire length of the other ship.

"Stand by to tack ship," Gamble shouted, "Ready about!" He turned and motioned with his hand to the helmsman to spin the wheel. As he did so, he heard a loud rushing sound that became a high whistle, then faded.

"Enemy fired his broadside, sir," reported the quartermaster. "No damage as I can see."

Gamble nodded, intent on the handling of the ship. "They fired their windward broadside," he reasoned. "If we can come about and steady on a course before they reload, I can hit with my starboard broadside."

Gamble turned his head to give the order to man the starboard broadside. He noted with satisfaction that Lieutenant Wilson had foreseen his order. The big naval officer, his red face streaked with powder, was stripped to his shirtsleeves. He was directing the loading of the last gun of the broadside. The remaining gun crews crouched by their guns, awaiting the command to fire.

After what seemed like an eternity, the *Greenwich's* head passed the eye of the wind. She began to pick up headway as she laid off on the larboard tack, running to the windward and almost parallel to the other ship.

"Steady as she goes, sire," sang out the helmsman.

"Fire when she bears!" commanded Gamble.

Scarcely were the words out of his mouth when the decks of the *Greenwich* shuddered under the recoil of all five guns of the starboard battery. Gamble noted that Lieutenant Wilson was working furiously with the gun crews to reload the battery. Under his expert direction the men were sponging the bores and ramming home the solid shot.

Again it was difficult to see how much damage they had inflicted on the other ship. Gamble saw a flash of flame and the plume of gunpowder smoke as one or two enemy guns fired. Then the ship was lost to sight as the second broadside roared from *Greenwich's* starboard side.

Realizing that Lieutenant Wilson and the gun crews needed no further attention, Gamble turned to keeping the enemy on bearing and his own ship as steady as possible. After the *Greenwich* had fired two more broadsides, Gamble noticed that the enemy was wearing ship—that is, placing his stern instead of his bow to the wind. The ship thus took the wind on the opposite tack.

This was a dangerous maneuver. Evidently the Britisher had had all the fighting he wanted and was not trying to make a run for it down wind. Gamble saw at a glance what an opportunity this presented.

"Mister Wilson, hold your fire! Load all guns of the larboard battery. I shall come about, and when they present their stern to us we'll give them a raking broadside." Turning to the helmsman, Gamble ordered, "Steady as you go."

"Steady as she goes, sir," replied the helmsman calmly.

Gamble braced his long glass against the mizzen shroud to keep the enemy in constant view. He noted that some of her braces had been shot away and that she moved sluggishly. He forced himself to hold back the order to come about. The range must be closed further to do more damage. The minutes dragged on as the *Greenwich* closed the distance between herself and the other ship.

Raking broadsides are devastating when they hit. But a raking target is narrow because it presents either bow or stern, hence the need for close range.

"Ready about!" shouted Gamble. "We have her where we want her, lads. Hold our fire, and keep her in your sights."

The *Greenwich* responded readily to her rudder and headed into the wind. The sail handlers on the forecastle backed the headsails into the wind to make the ship's head pay off more readily on the new tack.

"Keep her full and by," Gamble called to the helmsman, who nodded and shifted his glance to the courses and topsails as they were trimmed to greatest advantage on the new tack.

"Full and by, sir," the helmsman finally called.

Gamble had kept the other ship in the field of his long glass. Her stern was not presented almost squarely to *Greenwich's* larboard broadside. Turning toward the gun crews, Gamble raised his arm, "Fire!"

This time the damage inflicted by the *Greenwich's* broadside could be seen at once. The enemy's mizzen-topmast swayed at an awkward angle, then crashed down on the quarterdeck. The entire bulkhead on the starboard quarter was stove in. A gun lay overturned on its carriage.

The *Greenwich's* crew gave a loud cheer as the red flag with the Union Jack in its quarter came fluttering down from the mizzen gaff of the chase. Gamble ordered all sail shortened and the main yard braced aback to heave to.

Suddenly a loud shout rose from the gun crews. Gamble spun about and put his glass on the enemy. To his amazement he saw that the other ship, after hauling down her colors, had crowded on all sail and was heading toward open waters between the *Essex* and the *Greenwich*.

"Mister Wilson," Gamble ordered through the speaking trumpet, "pipe all hands to make sail. Sheet home everything the ship will carry."

The standing and running rigging of the *Greenwich* creaked and groaned under the greatest press of sail she had ever carried. Whalers are designed for sea-keeping qualities and for rendering whale blubber into oil. They are not made to carry guns. They are not intended to make the speed a man-of-war needs. Gamble was pleased to notice that for all her sturdy lines, the *Greenwich* was not sluggish.

The *Essex*, under a press of sail, was rapidly closing the gap through which the British ship was trying to escape. The sun was already low.

Shortly after sunset the stranger saw no chance to escape. Not wishing to risk a broadside from the frigate, she bore up and lay hove to.

A boat set out from the *Essex*, carrying a prize crew. As it pulled across the open waters between the ships, a signal fluttered from the frigate's signal halliards.

Gamble smiled as he lowered his long glass. No need for the quartermaster to decode this signal's meaning. Turning to the boatswain's mate, Gamble said, "Pass the word that *Essex* has signaled *Greenwich*, 'Well Done.' "

★   ★   ★   ★   ★

The *Essex* would go on to capture thirteen prize ships in the Pacific before being trapped in the neutral waters at Valparaiso by two British frigates. Critically damaged by bad weather during an escape attempt, she was eventually attacked and forced to surrender after fires broke out on deck, forcing fifty of the crew to abandon ship.

John Gamble was later captured by the British in the Sandwich Islands following a mutiny by his prize crew. He survived imprisonment and reached New York in August 1815, where he was promoted to major and later lieutenant colonel. He retired from the Marine Corps in 1834.

The Battle of Bladensburg

Americans best remember the War of 1812 for the writing of "The Star Spangled Banner" by Francis Scott Key, as he witnessed the British siege of Fort McHenry guarding the port of Baltimore on September 13-14, 1814. It is not as widely remembered that three weeks earlier, the British landed an army in Maryland, marched on Washington after a brief engagement with a confused and poorly led American defense, and put the government to flight and the major public buildings to the torch. Yet it was this stand outside Washington, on the fields near Bladensburg on August 24, where the Marines continued to earn their reputation as tenacious warriors. Revolutionary war hero Commodore Joshua Barney led a mixed force of 400 Marines and sailors from his vanquished Chesapeake gunboat flotilla called into action in support of the militia defending the capital. Standing at the center of the third and final line of defense they encountered the full might of the veteran British regiments sent against them as other American units fell back in disarray. In the following chapter, Captain Joshua Barney describes the engagement in his report to the Secretary of the Navy.

> The first and second line of the Americans having been dispersed, the British, flushed with success, pushed forward to attack the third . . . The gallant Colonel Thornton, soon confronted Barney, in the center, who maintained his position like a genuine hero, as he was. His 18-pounders enfiladed the Washington Road, and with them he swept the highway with such terrible effect that the enemy fled off into a field, and attempted to turn Barney's right flank. There they were met by three 12-pounders and Marines, under Captains Miller and Sevier, and were badly cut up. They were driven back . . . leaving several of their wounded officers in the hands of the Americans. Colonel Thornton, who bravely led the attacking

21

column, was severely wounded, and General Ross had his
horse shot under him.

—Benson J. Lossing
Commodore Joshua Barney to the
Secretary of the Navy Farm at Elk Ridge,
29 August 1814

★ ★ ★ ★ ★

This is the first moment I have had it in my power to make a report of the proceedings of the forces under my command, since I had the honour of seeing
you at the camp at the "Old Fields." On the afternoon of that day, we were informed that the enemy was advancing upon us. The army was put under arms,
and our positions taken; my forces on the right, flanked by the two battalions
of the 36th and 38th, where we remained some hours; the enemy did not make
his appearance. A little before sun-set general Winder came to me, and recommended that the heavy artillery should be withdrawn, with the exception of
one 12 pounder to cover the retreat. We took up our line of march, and in the
night entered Washington by the Eastern Branch bridge. I marched my men,
&c. to the marine barracks, and took up quarters for the night, myself sleeping at commodore Tingey's, in the navy yard. About 2 o'clock general Winder
cam to my quarters, and we made some arrangements for the morning. In the
morning I received a note from general Winder, and waited upon him, he requested me to take command, and place my artillery to defend the passage of
the bridge on the Eastern Branch, as the enemy was approaching the city in
that direction. I immediately put my guns in position, leaving the marines and
the rest of my men at the barracks, to wait further orders. I was in this situation when I had the honour to meet you, with the President and heads of departments, when it was determined that I should draw off my guns and men,
and proceed towards Bladensburg, which was immediately put into execution.
On our way, I was informed the enemy was within a mile of Bladensburg—
we hurried on. The day was hot, and my men very much crippled from the
severe marches we had experienced the days before, many of them being without shoes, which I had replaced that morning. I preceded the men, and when
I arrived at the line which separates the district from Maryland, the battle began. I sent an officer back to hurry on my men; they came up in a trot; we took
our position on the rising ground, put the pieces in battery, posted the marines
under captain Miller, and the flotilla men, who were to act as infantry, under
their own officers, on my right, to support the pieces, and waited the approach

of the enemy. During this period the engagement continued, and the enemy advancing, our own army retreating before them, apparently in much disorder. At length the enemy made his appearance on the main road, in force, and in front of my battery, and on seeing us made a halt. I reserved our fire. In a few minutes the enemy again advanced, when I ordered an 18 pounder to be fired, which completely cleared the road; shortly after, a second and a third attempt was made by the enemy to come forward, but all were destroyed. They then crossed over into an open field, and attempted to flank our right; he was there met by three 12 pounders, the marines under captain Miller, and my men, acting as infantry, and again was totally cut up. By this time not a vestige of the American army remained, except a body of five or six hundred, posted on a height on my right, from whom I expected much support, from their fine situation.

The enemy from this period never appeared in force in front of us; they pushed forward their sharp shooters; one of which shot my horse under me, who fell dead between two of my guns. The enemy, who had been kept in check by our fire for nearly half an hour, now began to out-flank us on the right; our guns were turned that way; he pushed up the hill, about two or three hundred, towards the corps of Americans stationed as above described, who, to my great mortification, made no resistance, giving a fire or two and retired. In this situation we had the whole army of the enemy to contend with. Our ammunition was expended; and, unfortunately, the drivers of my ammunition wagons had gone off in the general panic. At this time I received a severe wound in my thigh; captain Miller was wounded; sailing master Warner killed; acting sailing master Martin killed; and sailing master Martin wounded; but to the honour of my officers and men, as fast as their companions and messmates fell at the guns, they were instantly replaced from the infantry.

Finding the enemy now completely in our rear, and no means of defence, I gave orders to my officers and men to retire. Three of my officers assisted me to get off a short distance, but the great loss of blood occasioned such a weakness, that I was compelled to lie down. I requested my officers to leave me, which they obstinately refused; but upon being ordered they obeyed, one only remained. In a short time I observed a British soldier, and had him called, and directed him to seek an officer; in a few minutes an officer came, and on learning who I was, brought general Ross and admiral Cockburn to me. Those officers behaved to me with the most marked attention, respect and politeness, had a surgeon brought, and my wound dressed immediately. After a few minutes conversation, the general informed me (after paying me a handsome compliment) that I was paroled, and at liberty to proceed to Washington or Bladensburg; as also Mr. Huffington, who had remained with me, offering me every assistance in his power, giving orders for a litter to be brought, in which I was carried to Bladensburg; captain Wainwright, first captain to admiral Cochrane, remained with me, and behaved to me as if I was a brother. During the stay of the enemy at Bladensburg, I received every marked attention possible from the officers of the army and navy.

My wound is deep, but I flatter myself not dangerous; the ball is not yet extracted. I fondly hope a few weeks will restore me to health, and that an exchange will take place, that I may resume my command, or any other that you and the President may think proper to honour me with.

★   ★   ★   ★   ★

The British Army advanced into Washington on the night of August 14 unopposed, eager to avenge the American destruction of York, Ontario in April 1813. General Ross kept his men under strict orders that only the major public buildings were to be destroyed. Only quick action by the President's wife Dolly Madison and some brave government servants and clerks, were some of the nation's most treasured documents and artifacts saved. The gallantry of Joshua Barney and his Marines inspired a legend that General Ross spared the Marine Corps Commandant's home from destruction as a gesture of respect. The burning of Washington galvanized American resistance. By September, more than 15,000 volunteers converged on Baltimore to fight the British. General Ross was felled on September 12 by American sharpshooters in a skirmish on the road to North Point near Baltimore. Joshua Barney would pass away in December 1818 from complications due to the wound suffered at Bladensburg.

Dispatches from the Mexican War

GEORGE WILKINS KENDALL

In September of 1847 General Winfield Scott moved his army against the defenses of Mexico City. His adversary, Mexican General Antonio Lopez de Santa Anna had deployed most of his army south of the capital. Scott thus planned to make his attack from the west against the formidable defenses of the fortress Chapultepec on a hill before the gates to the city and its approaches guarded by a series of defenses named El Molino del Rey. After the destruction of these positions on September 8, General Scott prepared his final assault on Chapultepec on September 13. He ordered the third division under Major General Gideon J. Pillow to attack west up the hill, while the fourth division under Major General John A. Quitman was assigned to advance from the southeast.

With Quitman's force was a small number of Marines from the brigade that reinforced the fourth division, handpicked as part of a 250-man storming party under the command of Major Levi Twiggs. They would lead a charge up the hill fighting hand-to-hand as they went, to place the American flag over the fortress by 9:30 that morning. Witnessing these events was George Wilkins Kendall, a reporter for the New Orleans *Picayune* who accompanied General Scott's headquarters throughout the campaign. In the following chapter, he describes the action to take Chapultepec and the San Cosme Gate from his battlefield dispatches. While he makes no direct mention of the Marines, he provides one of the best first-hand accounts of the battle in which they played a central role.

> Quitman's storming-parties . . . the first of these, furnished
> by Twiggs's division, was commanded in succession by Cap-
> tain Casey, 2d infantry, and Captain Paul, 7th infantry, after
> Casey had been severely wounded; and the second, originally

under the gallant Major Twiggs, Marine Corps, killed, and then Captain Miller, 2d Pennsylvania volunteers. The storming-party, now commanded by Captain Paul seconded by Captain Roberts, of the Rifles, Lieutenant Stewart, and others of the same regiment, Smith's brigade, carried the two batteries in the road, took some guns, with many prisoners, and drove the enemy posted behind in support. The New York and South Carolina volunteers (Shield's brigade) and the 2d Pennsylvania volunteers, all on the left of Quitman's line, together with portions of his storming-parties, crossed the meadows in front, under a heavy fire, and entered the outer enclosure of Chapultepec just in time to join in the final assault from the west. . . . No scene could have been more animating or glorious.

—General Winfield Scott
Tacubaya, September 10, 1847

★　★　★　★　★

We have accounts from Mexico, brought in by Frenchmen and other foreigners, to the effect that Santa Anna's loss at El Molino was much more severe than anyone here had anticipated. They say that during the afternoon of the 8th no less than 1500 wounded men came into the city, while the number of killed was over 600. The slaughter from the batteries of Col. Duncan and Capt. Drum must have been terrific. Santa Anna, it is said, would have laid all the blame of the defeat upon Gen. León, but that officer, unfortunately for him, died. He has since torn epaulets from the shoulders of Col. Miguel Andrade, commander of the celebrated regiment of Hussars, accuses him of everything, has thrown him into prison, and denied him all communication. He must have some one to break out upon.

Everything looks quiet today, but the Mexicans are busily employed in fortifying at every point. At Chapultepec they can be seen at work, while they are also repairing the damage done at El Molino and other points on that line. On the Piedad road they have strong works, while at the Niño Perdido and San Antonio Abad entrances to the city they are also fortifying with the greatest vigor. [1] Gen. Pillow's division, as also Col. Riley's brigade, attached to that of Gen. Twiggs, occupy the village of La Piedad and neighborhood, in plain sight and in fact under the guns of the enemy. Gen. Worth remains here in Tacubaya, but he is sending all his sick and wounded to Mixcoac, out of the range of the guns of Chapultepec. No one knows what point will be first attacked, but this question will soon be determined. The next blow struck will be hard, and all hope decisive. It must read strange, the story that some 7 or 8000 men have set themselves down before a strongly fortified city of over 200,000 inhabitants, with an army of at least 25,000 men to defend it; but the tale is a true one and the proud capital of Mexico must fall.

Yours, Etc.,

> G. W. K.
> *Daily Picayune*, October 14, 1847
> Tacubaya, September 11, 1847

A small party of us have just returned from a ride over to La Piedad, the headquarters of Gen. Pillow. Gen. Scott was there, as also were some of his principal officers, holding a council as to the best mode and point of attack.[2] The result of their deliberations is not known, but it is thought that the infantry will have some respite after their hard labors, and that all the heavier cannon recently captured from the Mexicans will be employed in sending their own balls back at them. With their own guns, and those brought up by Gen. Scott, at least fifty pieces of heavy calibre can be opened at any one point—enough to demolish any work the Mexicans have constructed in time incredibly short, and give them a lesson they will not soon forget.

From the Puente del Hermita, which has been destroyed by the Mexicans, they can plainly be seen at work on several fortifications between the roads of San Angel and San Antonio de Abad. These works are but little more than a half a mile from the city, which is also in plain view. Shortly after we left, the enemy opened with two of their heavy guns upon our pickets or engineers, and continued the fire for near an hour. I cannot learn that they did any injury. On our return to Tacubaya we found that Maj. Sumner and Col. Duncan had had a little brush with the enemy's lancers near the battleground of El Molino. Capt. Ruff, with his company of Mounted Riflemen, drew a large party of the Mexican cavalry immediately within the range of one of Duncan's guns, when one or two discharges sent them scampering off in every direction. Only one man was wounded on our side, but it is known that the enemy lost several in the skirmish. They opened with one heavy gun from Chapultepec on our men, but did no harm other than frightening the inhabitants of this place half out of their wits.

Lieut. Burbank, who was mortally wounded at El Molino, died

yesterday, and Capt. E. Kirby Smith this afternoon of wounds received at the same time. Lieut. Col. Dickenson, shot badly in the ankle at Churubusco, is also dead. All were gallant officers, and their loss is much regretted.

I have already mentioned the execution of nineteen of the deserters captured on the 20th August at Churubusco. Gen. Scott has just signed the death warrant of thirty others, taken at the same time, and they will suffer the same fate in the course of a day or two.

From various movements, there is certainly strong reasons to believe that Gen. Scott will open a heavy fire upon Chapultepec tomorrow morning, from not only his own siege guns but from those captured from the enemy. Whether it is a feint to draw the Mexicans to that point and weaken other defences, is not known.

Yours, Etc.,

G. W. K.
Daily Picayune, October 14, 1847
Tacubaya, September 12, 1847

At early daylight this morning a heavy cannonade was opened upon the stronghold of Chapultepec, which was increased during the day as additional siege guns were placed in position. The Mexicans returned the fire with great spirit at intervals during the day, but with little effect other than dismounting one of our guns—I cannot learn that a man has been killed at any of the batteries. Several of the Voltigeurs, while skirmishing with the enemy's sharpshooters at the foot of Chapultepec, were wounded, but none of them severely. A 10 ½-inch mortar was opened upon the place during the afternoon, and as several shells have been seen to fall and explode directly within the enemy's works, it is certain that great damage has been caused. A firing of heavy guns has also been heard in the direction of La Piedad, showing that the Mexicans have been diverted in that quarter.[3]

At dusk this evening several loads of scaling ladders were sent down towards the foot of Chapultepec, and the movements of our infantry and other light corps would indicate that the strong works upon the crest are to be stormed early tomorrow. A large portion of the entire army will be brought to the struggle, and it is thought the contest will be terrible. I have little time to write.

Yours, Etc.,

G. W. K.
Daily Picayune, October 14, 1847
City of Mexico, September 14, 1847[4]

Another victory, glorious in its results and which has thrown additional lus-
tre upon the American arms, has been achieved today by the army under
Gen. Scott—the proud capital of Mexico has fallen into the power of a mere
handful of men compared with the immense odds arrayed against them, and
Santa Anna, instead of shedding his blood as he had promised, is wandering
with the remnant of his army no one knows whither.

The apparently impregnable works on Chapultepec, after a desperate struggle, were triumphantly carried—Gens. Bravo and Monterde, besides a host of officers of different grades, taken prisoners; over 1000
non-commissioned officers and privates, all their cannon and ammunition,
are in our hands; the fugitives soon were in full flight towards the different
works which command the entrance to the city, and our men at once were
in hot pursuit.[5]

Gen. Quitman, supported by Gen. Smith's brigade, took the road
by the Chapultepec aqueduct towards the Belén gate and the Cuidadela;
Gen. Worth, supported by Gen. Cadwalader's brigade, advanced by the San
Cosmé aqueduct towards the garita of that name. Both routes were cut up
by ditches and defended by breastworks, barricades, and strong works of
every description known to military science; yet the daring and impetu-
osity of our men overcame one defence after another, and by nightfall
every work to the city's edge was carried. Gen. Quitman's command, after
the rout at Chapultepec, was the first to encounter the enemy in force.
Midway between the former and the Belén gate, Santa Anna had constructed a strong work; but this was at once vigorously assaulted by Gen.
Quitman, and aided by a flank fire from two of Duncan's guns, which Gen.
Worth had ordered to approach as near as possible from the San Cosmé
road, the enemy was again routed and in full flight.[6] They again made a
stand from their strong fortifications at and near the Belén garita, opening
a tremendous fire not only of round shot, grape and shell, but of musketry;
yet boldly Gen. Quitman advanced, stormed and carried the works, although at great loss, and then every point on this side of the city was in
our possession. In this onslaught two of our bravest officers were killed—
Capt. Drum and Lieut. Benjamin.

Meanwhile Gen. Worth was rapidly advancing upon San Cosmé. At
the English burying ground the enemy had constructed a strong work. It
was defended by infantry for a short time, but could not resist the assault of
our men—the affrighted Mexicans soon fled to another line of works
nearer the city, and thus Gen. Worth was in possession of the entrance to San
Cosmé. As his men advanced towards the garita, the enemy opened a heavy

fire of musketry from the house tops, as well as of grape, canister and shell from their batteries, thus sweeping the street completely. At this juncture the old Monterey game, of burrowing and digging through the houses, was adopted. On the right, as our men faced the enemy, the aqueduct afforded a partial shelter; on the left, the houses gave some protection; but many were still killed or wounded by the grape which swept every part, as well as by the shells which were continually bursting in every direction. About 3 o'clock the work of the pick-axe and the crow-bar, under the direction of Lieut. G. W. Smith, of the Sappers and Miners, had fairly commenced, and every minute brought our men nearer the enemy's last stronghold. In the meantime, two mountain howitzers were fairly lifted to the top of one of the houses and into the cupalo of the church, from which they opened a plunging and most effective fire, while one of Duncan's guns, in charge of Lieut. Hunt, was run up under a galling fire to a deserted breastwork, and at once opened upon the garita. In this latter daring feat, four men out of eight were either killed or wounded, but still the piece was most effectively served. The work of the Miners was still going on. In one house which they had entered, by the pick-axe, a favorite aide of Santa Anna's was found. The great man had just fled, but had left his friend and his supper! Both were well cared for—the latter was devoured by our hungry officers; the former, after doing the honors of the table, was made a close prisoner. Just as dark was setting in, our men had dug and mined their way almost up to the very guns of the enemy, and now, after a short struggle, they were completely routed and driven with the loss of everything. The command of the city by the San Cosmé route was attained.

During the night, Gen. Quitman commenced the work of throwing up breastworks and erecting batteries, with the intention of opening a heavy cannonade upon the Cuidadela with the first light this morning. At 10 o'clock at night, Gen. Worth ordered Capt. Huger to bring up a 24-pounder and a 10-inch mortar to the *garita* or gate of San Cosmé, and having ascertained the bearings and distance of the grand plaza and palace, at once opened upon those points. The heavy shells were heard to explode in the very heart of the city. At a little after midnight Major Palacios, accompanied by two or three members of the municipal council of the city, arrived at Gen. Worth's headquarters, and in great trepidation informed him that Santa Anna and his grand army had fled, and that they wished at once to surrender the capital! They were referred to the commander-in-chief, and immediately started for Tacubaya; but in the meantime the firing upon the town ceased.[7]

At 7 o'clock this morning, Gen. Scott, with his staff, rode in and took quarters in the national palace, on the top of which the regimental flag of the gallant Rifles and the stars and stripes were already flying. An immense crowd of blanketed *leperos*, the scum of the capital, were congregated in the plaza as the commander-in-chief entered it. They pressed upon our soldiers, and eyed them as though they were beings of another world. So much were they in the way, and with such eagerness did they press around, that Gen. Scott was compelled to order our Dragoons to clear the plaza. They were told, however, not to injure or harm a man in the mob— they were all our friends!

About five minutes after this, and while Gen. Worth was returning to his division near the Alameda, he was fired upon from a house near the Convent of San Francisco. Some of the cowardly Polkas, who had fled the day previous without discharging their guns, now commenced the assassin game of shooting at every one of our men they saw, from windows, as well as from behind the parapets on the *azoteas* or tops of the houses. In half an hour's time, our good friends, the *leperos*, in the neighborhood of the hospital of San Andres and the church of Santa Clara, also commenced discharging muskets and throwing bottles and rocks from the *azoteas*. I have neglected to mention that just previous to this Col. Garland had been severely wounded by a musket, fired by some miscreant from a window.

For several hours this cowardly war upon our men continued, and during this time many were killed or wounded. It was in this species of fighting that Lieut. Sidney Smith received his death wound. The division of Gen. Twiggs in one part of the city, and Gen. Worth in another, were soon actively engaged in putting down the insurrection. Orders were given to shoot every man in all the houses from which the firing came, while the guns of the different light batteries swept the streets in all directions. As the assassins were driven from one house, they would take refuge on another; but by the middle of the afternoon they were all forced back to the barriers and suburbs. Many innocent persons have doubtless been killed during the day, but this could not be avoided. Had orders been given at the outset to blow up and demolish every house or church from which one man was fired upon, the disturbances would have been at once quelled. As it is, I trust that the lesson the rabble and their mischievous leaders have received today may deter them from future outrages.

On entering the palace Gen. Scott at once named Gen. Quitman governor of Mexico—a most excellent appointment. Some wag immediately proclaimed aloud in the plaza as follows: "Gen. John A. Quitman of Mississippi, has been appointed governor of Mexico, Vice Gen. Jose Maria Tornel, resigned—*very suddenly!*" It seems that the valiant Tornel ran off at any early hour, and his magnificent house has been converted into a hospital for our wounded officers.

Yours, Etc.,

G. W. K.
Daily Picayune, October 14, 1847

★　★　★　★　★

At the urging of city officials, Santa Anna withdrew some 12,000 troops from the city to Guadalupe Hidalgo shortly after midnight. A delegation of city officials were at Scott's headquarters near Chapultepec by 4 a.m., requesting terms of capitulation; Scott refused to grant any concessions. It is a legend in the Marine Corps that officers and noncommissioned officers wear the scarlet stripes on their blue dress trousers, which are now referred to as "blood stripes," to commemorate the Marines' bloodshed at Chapultepec. The capture of Chapultepec is immortalized in the first line of the Marine Corps Hymn "From the Halls of Montezuma, to the shores of Tripoli."

A Civil War Marine at Sea

MILES M. OVIATT

Miles M. Oviatt was a Marine corporal who served as a gunner aboard the sloop U.S.S. *Brooklyn* when it saw action at Mobile Bay against the Confederate coastal forts and the ironclad C.S.S. *Tennessee* on August 5, 1864. Despite severe damage to his ship and the loss of several men in his crew, Oviatt stayed with his gun during the two-hour duel with the enemy warship leading to her eventual surrender. For his actions that day, Oviatt was awarded the Medal of Honor on December 31, 1864. The following passages are taken from Oviatt's diary as he describes the preparation for battle and eventual combat against the C.S.S. *Tennessee*.

> Damn the torpedoes! Full speed ahead!
> —Admiral David Glasgow Farragut

★   ★   ★   ★   ★

Friday, July 15th

Papers from New York arrived today bringing news of the sinking of the *Alabama*[7] by the U.S.S. *Kearsarge*. Called all hands to muster and read the same, then gave three cheers for the *Kearsarge*.

Wednesday, July 20th

Got up anchor and ran over to Pensacola and commenced coaling. Passed the monitor *Manhattan* on her way to join the fleet. Manned the rigging and gave three cheers.

Wednesday, July 27th

Finished taking on coal and provisions. Got out our sheet cable and put on the starboard side to protect the boilers. Put iron plate around the top for sharp shooters and men at the howitzers and made a devil to rake up torpedoes.

Thursday, July 28th

Ran back to our station off Mobile and came to anchor about 10 a.m. The *Manhattan* lays at anchor inside of Sand Island in smooth water.

Tuesday, Aug 2nd

Preparations are still going on to prepare the fleet for the coming engagement. Nearly all have been to Pensacola and got supplies and coal. There are three ironclad monitors inside of Sand Island, two of them are double turreted from New Orleans. Are daily expecting the *Tecumseh* from New York. P.S. She arrived on the 4th, at 4:00 p.m.

1864, Friday, Aug 5th

At three this morning all hands were called and got breakfast. Took the *Octorara* along port side and lashed her fast. At 5:00 a.m., got up anchor and formed in the line of battle, we taking the lead of the wooden fleet. The monitors which were at anchor inside of Sand Island started about the same time and engaged Fort Morgan, but they did not reply till we had got within range. The first shot from the fort, at 6:50 a.m., was directed to us but fell a little short, striking the water on the starboard bow and ricocheted over the bow. We immediately replied with our 100-pound rifles on the bow, which at first fell short, they being the only guns that could be brought to bear at the time. The firing soon became very rapid and was responded to with equal vigor. When abreast the fort, the monitor *Chickasaw*, stopped and we were compelled to stop and back about the length of the ship. While doing so, the *Hartford*, next ship to us, ran past. The *Richmond* came next and tried to follow the example of the *Hartford* and get past to a place of safety, but did not succeed.

About 7:30, the monitor, *Tecumseh*, struck a torpedo and went down almost instantly while going after the rebel, *Tennessee*. At 9:00 a.m. had passed the forts and came to anchor inside the bay out of range of the forts. Her ram came out as we passed and tried to run into our starboard quarter, but by superior speed, we avoided her, and she swung round and ran for the *Lackawanna*, but she avoided being run into. The ram went across her bow, then came too and gave her a broadside. We had just come to anchor when the Ram came on again, steering for us. As she approached, the small vessels between us and her got up anchor and left. But still she kept on intending to run us down. But when within a quarter of a mile, we got under way, came around and gave her a broadside. But they might as well been left in the guns for the affect they did. The *Manongahela* came around head onto the ram and ran against her with all force but without any apparent damage to the Ram, but smashed her fore-fort in and gave her a few shots with her 200-pound rifle. The *Lackawanna* and *Hartford* struck her next but with no better effect. We was underway to strike her, when the *Hartford* ran in ahead of us, and not having the ram's broadside to her, she struck her near the bow and slid off. Finally, the monitors came around and set to work but a good ways off and gave her the contents of their heavy guns which, together with the wooden vessels, began soon to tell on her. And it was seen that her firing was less frequent than at first. Our 100-pound rifle on the forecastle carried away her smoke stack, and the 60-pound rifle cut the rudder chain which left them in rather a helpless condition. And the monitors got round and sent some telling shots into her steam.

When the Rebel rag came down, a white one was sent up in its place. Our loss was fourteen killed and thirty-to-forty wounded. The *Brooklyn* was struck fifty-nine times, thirty-nine in her hull, four in the main mast, rest in her rigging, came to anchor the second time at 10:10. The stations were as follows: The monitors, *Tecumseh, Chickasaw, Winnebago*, were to go first. *Brooklyn* and *Octorara, Hartford* and *Metacomet, Richmond* and *Port Royal, Lackawanna* and *Seminole, Manongahela, Ossipee, Oneida*. The *Metacomet* took the Reb steamship *Selma*. Her armament was six rifles.

In the afternoon, the monitors went up to Fort Powell. At 11 o'clock, the Rebs left the fort and blew it up. In the afternoon, sent down a flag of truce asking leave to send our wounded to *Pensacola*, which they granted provided the vessel would return as we were all considered as prisoners.

Aug 6th, 1864

Sent men to take possession of Fort Powell and sent a flag of truce to demand the surrender of [Fort] Gaines, but they refused to surrender and in the afternoon, sent the monitors down to bombard the fort. Their firing was very brisk on our side, but was not answered by the Rebs very briskly.

Sunday, Aug 7th, 1864

The Admiral sent down a flag of truce to demand the surrender of Gaines today, but was refused again. At 3:00 p.m. they sent off a flag of truce requesting Farragut to accept the surrender instead of giving it to the Army as he requested. But he refused and gave them till next morning at 8:00 a.m.

Monday, Aug 8th, 1864

At 8:00 this morning, the fort hoisted the American flag. We took possession at 12:00 a.m. and fired a salute of twenty-one Guns and the *Hartford's* Marines in Fort Powell. We took 850 Prisoners, 50 or 60 guns and ammunition, and six months provisions for the garrison.

Saturday, Aug 13th

Our boats have raked several torpedoes out of the channel between Fort Morgan and Gaines of very large size, some containing from 50 to 60 pounds of powder. We have also been landing troops over in rear of Fort Morgan so that the present force must be at fifteen or sixteen thousand men.

Monday, Aug 22nd

General Granger having his ten thousand troops in rear of Fort Morgan and guns in position ready for a bombardment. Accordingly at 5:00 a.m., we got up anchor and ran down and commenced the bombardment, till 11:00 a.m. when we were ordered to hold off. The monitors kept up the fire till dark, then left it to the land batteries to continue the fire through the night. Which they did with a spirit which was anything but agreeable to the Rebs, "judging by myself." At 8:00 o'clock the fort took fire, which gave our men a better chance to see where to fire, which was still burning in the morning.

Tuesday, Aug 23rd

At daylight a flag of truce was seen flying from the fort. Two monitors and a gunboat were sent down to see what was wanted. They found out that

Page was willing to come to terms. He was informed that nothing but unconditional surrender would do, so he accepted. At 2:00 p.m. we took a formal possession. They had destroyed the carriages, spiked the guns, broke up and burned their small arms and swords and provisions and wet all of the powder. Even Old Page, himself, had no sword to give up. All the vessels fired a salute of twenty-one guns. We took from five to six hundred prisoners. Page has since been court-martialed for destroying everything and acquitted honerably.

Wednesday, Aug 24th

The monitors, *Chickasaw*, and *Sebago*, went up within a few miles of Mobile and engaged the batteries. They report Mobile on fire.

Thursday, Aug 25th

Went down to the fort to take one or two guns on that had been ashore previous to the bombardment. Two boats crews from the *Galena* went to buoy the monitor *Tecumseh*, then commenced to drag the channel for torpedoes. They hooked onto five which were attached to each other and in getting them out on the beech, one exploded killing three men and wounded eighteen more, which they brought aboard us to take to Pensacola. General Granger commenced taking the troops off again today, and carried through Grants Pass.

Friday, Aug 26th, '64

Got under weigh and left for Pensacola. At 11:00 a.m. called all hands to bury the four men that died last night from injuries received by the explosion of the torpedo. Arrived at Pensacola at 4:00 p.m. and made preparations for some slight repairs before leaving for home.

★ ★ ★ ★ ★

The U.S.S *Brooklyn* was struck forty times by enemy fire and suffered eleven men killed and forty-three wounded during the battle. Oviatt would survive the war and complete his four years of service in the Marine Corps in 1866 with the rank of sergeant. He returned to his home in Olean, New York where he later married and continued to serve in a volunteer cavalry unit. He passed away from ill health on November 1, 1880.

Marines Signaling Under Fire
at Guantanamo

STEPHEN CRANE

Stephen Crane's *The Red Badge of Courage*, written in 1895, depicted the American Civil War from the viewpoint of the common soldier. The novel won for the author international fame and a job as a war correspondent that took him to Texas, Mexico, Cuba, and Greece. He returned to Cuba in 1898 to report on the Spanish-American War. The following chapter is a dramatized reworking of Crane's reporting of events he witnessed as U.S. Marines defended their positions from Spanish counterattacks at Guantanamo Bay.

> Courage is the first of human qualities because
> it is the quality, which guarantees the others.
>
> —Aristotle

*   *   *   *   *

They were four Guantanamo Marines, officially known for the time as signalmen, and it was their duty to lie in the trenches of Camp McCalla, that faced the water, and, by day, signal the *Marblehead* with a flag and, by night, signal the *Marblehead* with lanterns. It was my good fortune—at that time I considered it my bad fortune, indeed—to be with them on two of the nights when a wild storm of fighting was pealing about the hill; and, of all the actions of the war, none were so hard on the nerves, none strained courage so near the panic point, as those swift nights in Camp McCalla. With a thousand rifles rattling; with the field-guns booming in your ears; with the diabolic Colt automatics clacking; with the roar of the *Marblehead* coming from the bay, and, last, with Mauser bullets sneering always in the air a few inches over one`s head,

3 8

and with this enduring from dusk to dawn, it is extremely doubtful if anyone who was there will be able to forget it easily. The noise; the impenetra-
ble darkness; the knowledge from the sound of the bullets that the enemy
was on three sides of the camp; the infrequent bloody stumbling and death
of some man with whom, perhaps, one had messed two hours previous; the
weariness of the body, and the more terrible weariness of the mind, at the
endlessness of the thing, made it wonderful that at least some of the men did
not come out of it with their nerves hopelessly in shreds.

But, as this interesting ceremony proceeded in the darkness, it was
necessary for the signal squad to coolly take and send messages. Captain Mc-
Calla always participated in the defence of the camp by raking the woods on
two of its sides with the guns of the *Marblehead*. Moreover, he was the senior officer present, and he wanted to know what was happening. All night
long the crews of the ships in the bay would stare sleeplessly into the blackness toward the roaring hill.

The signal squad had an old cracker-box placed on top of the
trench. When not signaling, they hid the lanterns in this box; but as soon
as an order to send a message was received, it became necessary for one
of the men to stand up and expose the lights. And then—oh, my eye—
how the guerillas hidden in the gulf of night would turn loose at those
yellow gleams!

Signaling in this way is done by letting one lantern remain station-
ary—on top of the cracker-box, in this case—and moving the other over to
the left and right and so on in the regular gestures of the wig-wagging code.
It is a very simple system of night communication, but one can see that it
presents rare possibilities when used in front of an enemy who, a few hundred yards away, is overjoyed at sighting so definite a mark.

How, in the name of wonders, those four men at Camp McCalla
were not riddled from head to foot and sent home more as repositories of
Spanish ammunition than as marines is beyond all comprehension. To make
a confession—when one of these men stood up to wave his lantern, I, lying
in the trench, invariably rolled a little to the right or left, in order that, when
he was shot, he would not fall on me. But the squad came off scathless, despite the best efforts of the most formidable corps in the Spanish army—the
Escuadra de Guantanamo. That it was the most formidable corps in the Spanish army of occupation has been told me by many Spanish officers and also
by General Menocal and other insurgent officers. General Menocal was Gar-
cia's chief-of-staff when the latter was operating busily in Santiago

province. The regiment was composed solely of practicos, or guides, who knew every shrub and tree on the ground over which they moved.

Whenever the adjutant, Lieutenant Draper, came plunging along through the darkness with an order—such as: "Ask the *Marblehead* to please shell the woods to the left"—my heart would come into my mouth, for I knew then that one of my pals was going to stand up behind the lanterns and have all Spain shoot at him.

The answer was always upon the instant:

"Yes, sir." Then the bullets began to snap, snap, snap, at his head while all the woods began to crackle like burning straw. I could lie near and watch the face of the signalman, illumed as it was by the yellow shine of lantern light, and the absence of excitement, fright, or any emotion at all on his countenance, was something to astonish all theories out of one's mind. The face was in every instance merely that of a man intent upon his business, the business of wig-wagging into the gulf of night where a light on the *Marblehead* was seen to move slowly.

These times on the hill resembled, in some days, those terrible scenes on the stage—scenes of intense gloom, blinding lightning, with a cloaked devil or assassin or other appropriate character muttering deeply amid the awful roll of the thunder-drums. It was theatric beyond words: one felt like a leaf in this booming chaos, this prolonged tragedy of the night. Amid it all one could see from time to time the yellow light on the face of a preoccupied signalman.

Possibly no man who was there ever before understood the true eloquence of the breaking of the day. We would lie staring into the east, fairly ravenous for the dawn. Utterly worn to rags, with our nerves standing on end like so many bristles, we lay and watched the east, the unspeakably obdurate and slow east. It was a wonder that the eyes of some of us did not turn to glass balls from the fixity of our gaze.

Then there would come into the sky a patch of faint blue light. It was like a piece of moonshine. Some would say it was the beginning of daybreak; others would declare it was nothing of the kind. Men would get very disgusted with each other in these low-toned arguments held in the trenches. For my part, this development in the eastern sky destroyed many of my ideas and theories concerning the dawning of the day; but then I had never before had occasion to give it such solemn attention.

This patch widened and whitened in about the speed of a man's accomplishment if he should be in the way of painting Madison Square Garden with a camel's hairbrush. The guerillas always set out to whoop it up about this time, because they knew the occasion was approaching when it would be expedient for them to elope. I, at least, always grew furious with this wretched sunrise. I thought I could have walked around the world in the time required for the old thing to get up above the horizon.

One midnight, when an important message was to be sent to the *Marblehead*, Colonel Huntington came himself to the signal place with Adjutant Draper and Captain McCauley, the quartermaster. When the man stood up to signal, the colonel stood beside him. At sight of the lights, the Spaniards performed as usual. They drove enough bullets into that immediate vicinity to kill all the marines in the corps.

Lieutenant Draper was agitated for his chief. "Colonel, won't you step down, sir?"

"Why, I guess not," said the grey old veteran in his slow, sad, always-gentle way. "I am in no more danger than the man."

"But, sir ——" began the adjutant.

"Oh, it's all right, Draper."

So the colonel and the private stood side to side and took the heavy fire without either moving a muscle.

Day was always obliged to come at last, punctuated by a final exchange of scattering shots. And the light shone on the marines, the dumb guns, the flag. Grimy yellow face looked into grimy yellow face, and grinned with weary satisfaction. Coffee!

Usually it was impossible for many of the men to sleep at once. It always took me, for instance, some hours to get my nerves combed down. But then it was great joy to lie in the trench with the four signalmen, and understand thoroughly that that night was fully over at last, and that although the future might have in store other bad nights, that one could never escape from the prison-house which we call the past.

At the wild little fight at Cusco there were some splendid exhibitions of wig-wagging under fire. Action began when an advanced detachment of marines under Lieutenant Lucas with the Cuban guides had reached the summit of a ridge overlooking a small valley where there was a house, a well, and a thicket of some kind of shrub with great broad, oily leaves. This thicket, which was perhaps an acre in extent, contained the guerillas. The valley was open to the sea. The distance from the top of the ridge to the thicket was barely two hundred yards.

The *Dolphin* had sailed up the coast in line with the marine advance, ready with her guns to assist in any action. Captain Elliott, who commanded the two hundred marines in this fight, suddenly called out for a signalman. He wanted a man to tell the *Dolphin* to open fire on the house and the thicket. It was a blazing, bitter hot day on top of the ridge with its shriveled chaparral and its straight, tall cactus plants. The sky was bare and blue, and hurt like brass. In two minutes the prostrate marines were red and sweating like so many hull-buried stokers in the tropics.

Captain Elliott called out:

"Where's a signalman? Who's a signalman here?"

A red-headed "mick"—I think his name was Clancy—at any rate, it will do to call him Clancy—twisted his head from where he lay on his stomach pumping his Lee, and, saluting, said that he was a signalman.

There was no regulation flag with the expedition, so Clancy was obliged to tie his blue polka-dot neckerchief on the end of his rifle. It did not make a very good flag. At first Clancy moved a ways down the safe side of the ridge and wigwagged there very busily. But what with the flag being so poor for the purpose, and the background of ridge being so dark, those on the *Dolphin* did not see it. So Clancy had to return to the top of the ridge and outline himself and his flag against the sky.

The usual thing happened. As soon as the Spaniards caught sight of this silhouette, they let go like mad at it. To make things more uncomfortable for Clancy, the situation demanded that he face the sea and turn his back to the Spanish bullets. This was a hard game, mark you—to stand with the small of your back to volley firing. Clancy thought so. Everybody thought so. We all cleared out of his neighbourhood. If he wanted sole possession of any particular spot on that hill, he could have it for all we would interfere with him.

It cannot be denied that Clancy was in a hurry. I watched him. He was so occupied with the bullets that snarled close to his ears that he was obliged to repeat the letters of his message softly to himself. It seemed an intolerable time before the *Dolphin* answered the little signal. Meanwhile, we gazed at him, marveling every second that he had not yet pitched headlong. He swore at times.

Finally the *Dolphin* replied to his frantic gesticulation, and he delivered his message. As his part of the transaction was quite finished—whoop!—he dropped like a brick into the firing line and began to shoot; began to get "hunky" with all those people who had been plugging at him. The blue polka-dot neckerchief still fluttered from the barrel of his rifle. I am quite certain that he let it remain there until the end of the fight.

The shells of the *Dolphin* began to plough up the thicket, kicking the bushes, stones, and soil into the air as if somebody was blasting there.

Meanwhile, this force of two hundred marines and fifty Cubans and the force of—probably—six companies of Spanish guerillas were making such an awful din that the distant Camp McCalla was all alive with excitement. Colonel Huntington sent out strong parties to critical points on the road to facilitate, if necessary, a safe retreat, and also sent forty men under Lieutenant Magill to come up on the left flank of the two companies in action under Captain Elliott. Lieutenant Magill and his men had crowned a hill which covered entirely the flank of the fighting companies, but when the *Dolphin* opened fire, it happened that Magill was in the line of the shots. It became necessary to stop the *Dolphin* at once. Captain Elliott was not near Clancy at this time, and he called hurriedly for another signalman.

Sergeant Quick arose, and announced that he was a signalman. He produced from somewhere a blue polka-dot neckerchief as large as a quilt. He tied it on a long, crooked stick. Then he went to the top of the ridge, and turning his back to the Spanish fire, began to signal to the *Dolphin*. Again we gave a man sole possession of a particular part of the ridge. We didn't want it. He could have it and welcome. If the young sergeant had had the smallpox, the cholera, and the yellow fever, we could not have slid out with more celerity.

As men have said often, it seemed as if there was in this war a God of Battles who held His mighty hand before the Americans. As I looked at Sergeant Quick wig-wagging there against the sky, I would not have given a tin tobacco-tag for his life. Escape for him seemed impossible. It seemed absurd to hope that he would not be hit; I only hoped that he would be hit just a little, little, in the arm, the shoulder, or the leg.

I watched his face, and it was as grave and serene as that of a man writing in his own library. He was the very embodiment of tranquility in occupation. He stood there amid the animal-like babble of the Cubans, the crack of rifles, and the whistling snarl of the bullets, and wig-wagged whatever he had to wig-wag without heeding anything but his business. There was not a single trace of nervousness or haste.

To say the least, a fight at close range is absorbing as a spectacle. No man wants to take his eyes from it until that time comes when he makes up his mind to run away. To deliberately stand up and turn your back to a battle is in itself hard work. To deliberately stand up and turn your back to a battle and hear immediate evidences of the boundless enthusiasm with which a large company of the enemy shoot at you from an adjacent thicket is, to my mind at least, a very great feat. One need not dwell upon the detail of keeping the mind carefully upon a slow spelling of an important code message.

I saw Quick betray only one sign of emotion. As he swung his clumsy flag to and fro, an end of it once caught on a cactus pillar, and he looked sharply over his shoulder to see what had it. He gave the flag an impatient jerk. He looked annoyed.

★　　★　　★　　★　　★

Stephen Crane returned to England in 1899 due to ill health. He set about publishing a collection of poems, *War is Kind,* before his death from tuberculosis at the age of twenty-eight the following year. His haunting tales of childhood, *Whilomville Stories,* and a collection of his stories from Cuba, *Wounds in the Rain,* were published later that year.

Miracle at Belleau Wood

ALAN AXELROD

Belleau Wood is one of the most crucial battles ever fought by the United States Marine Corps. The German victory over Russia in 1917 freed almost sixty divisions for the western front. In March 1918, the Germans launched a massive surprise attack on the British lines west of Cambrai with the goal of splitting the French and British armies as they advanced towards Paris. By May the Germans had come within fifty miles of the French capital at Cantigny and Chateau-Thierry where they encountered the 2nd and 3rd Divisions of the U.S. Army including the 4th Brigade of U.S. Marines attached to the 2nd Division. The American forces were tasked with counterattacking the German onslaught in order to save Paris. Belleau Wood was heavily defended by entrenched elements of five German divisions. The 4th Marine Brigade was sent forward to advance across an 800-yard field covered by German machine guns to assault the woods. The following chapter from Alan Axelrod's *Miracle at Belleau Wood* describes the event that has gone down as legend in Marine Corps history.

> Retreat? Hell, we just got here.
> —Marine Captain Lloyd Williams

★   ★   ★   ★   ★

Five in the afternoon, Belleau Wood, France, June 6, 1918. No bugles, *Tribune* correspondent Floyd Gibbons would write. No flashing swords. Just a general advance through fields of wheat toward a former hunting preserve, tangled, overgrown, and now transformed into one big machine gun nest. Gibbons, as well as the 6th Regiment's Colonel Albertus Catlin, remarked on the beauty of the marines advancing toward the wood in perfect rank and file, as if on parade, a gloriously doomed march into "a veritable hell of hissing bullets," a "death-dealing torrent," against which the marines bent their heads "as though facing a March gale."[1]

That is how many of the marines began the attack, in the orthodox "advance in line of sections" they had learned so painstakingly under French tutelage. It was a style of advance born of a very human desire to impose order on chaos, to ward off confusion with method. It did not work for long.

Against Benjamin Berry's 3d Battalion, 5th Marines, who had to advance across the most extensive stretch of open wheat field—some 400 yards of it—the German fire was longest and hottest. "The headed wheat bowed and waved in that metal cloud-burst like meadow grass in a summer breeze. The advancing lines wavered, and the voice of a sergeant was heard above the uproar: 'Come on, you _____! Do you want to live forever?'"[2]

Correspondent Gibbons had heard this cry, too, or so he reported. In his 1918 memoir, *And They Thought We Wouldn't Fight,* Gibbons wrote of how, when he was a boy, he read "Hugo's chapters on the Battle of Waterloo in 'Les Misérables'" and conceived his "ideal of fighting capacity and the military spirit of sacrifice." In Hugo's classic, an old sergeant of Napoleon's Old Guard, facing annihilation at the hands of the English, refuses the call of his enemy to surrender. "Into the very muzzles of the British cannon the sergeant hurled back the offer of his life with one word. That word was the vilest epithet in the French language. The cannons roared and the old sergeant and his survivors died with the word on their lips. Hugo wisely devoted an entire chapter to that single word." Today, Gibbons continued, "I have a new ideal . . . I found it in the Bois de Belleau."[3]

A small platoon line of Marines lay on their faces and bellies under the trees at the edge of a wheat field. Two hundred yards across that flat field the enemy was located in trees. I peered into the trees but could see nothing, yet I knew that every leaf in the foliage screened scores of German machine guns that swept the field with lead. The bullets nipped the tops of the young wheat and ripped the bark from the trunks of the trees three feet from the ground on which the Marines lay. The minute for the Marine advance was approaching. An old gunnery sergeant commanded the platoon in the absence of the lieutenant, who had been shot and was out of the fight. The old sergeant was a Marine veteran. His cheeks were bronzed with the wind and sun of the seven seas. The service bar across his left breast showed that he had fought in the Philippines, in Santo Domingo, at the walls of Pekin, and in the streets of Vera Cruz. I make no apologies for his language. Even if Hugo were not my precedent, I would make no apologies. To me his words were classic, if not sacred.

As the minute for the advance arrived, he arose from the trees first and jumped out onto the exposed edge of that field that ran with lead, across which he and his men were to charge. Then he turned to give the charge order to the men of his platoon—his mates—the men he loved. He said: "Come on, you sons-o'-bitches! Do you want to live forever?"[4]

The Battle of Bunker Hill gave us "Don't fire until you see the whites of their eyes," the sea-going duel between John Paul Jones's *Bon Homme Richard* and HMS *Serapis,* "I have not yet begun to fight," the siege of a San Antonio mission turned fortess, "Remember the Alamo," and the Battle of Belleau Wood, "Come on, you sons of bitches! Do you want to live forever?" Along with Captain Lloyd Williams's earlier "Retreat, hell! We just got here," they were the most celebrated utterances to emerge from marine throats in World War I, and they became hallowed words in annals and lore of the Corps.

The declaration was universally attributed to "Gunnery Sergeant" Dan Daly, but nobody has been found who actually heard him say it. Catlin's memoir implied that the sergeant (Catlin does not name him) was attached to Berry's battalion, and Gibbons, who accompanied elements of that unit in its attack on Belleau Wood, implies that he was even within earshot. But Daly, 44 years old, had shipped out to France as *first sergeant* (a full rank above gunnery sergeant) of the 73rd Machine Gun Company and, at Belleau Wood, was attached not to Berry's battalion, but to Sibley's, which attacked Belleau Wood south of Berry's position and formed part of the American center along this entire front. Daly's platoon was on the outskirts of Lucy-le-Bocage when it was either completely pinned down by fire from Belleau Wood or wavered in its advance—sources vary on this—whereupon Dan hefted over his head a bayonet-tipped Springfield, and made his deathless declaration. Daly later told a Marine historian that "What I really yelled was: For Christ's sake, men—COME ON! Do you want to live forever?" But, accurately or not, the lore of the Corps has chosen to remember it as "Come on, you sons of bitches."[5]

Dan Daly was a real marine, who really did fight at Belleau Wood, coming to that battlefield already having received the Medal of Honor twice, once for single-handedly defending the Tartar Wall in the Boxer Rebellion of 1900 and again for defeating 400 Caco bandits with just 35 marines in the Haitian campaign of 1915. John A. Lejeune, who would succeed George Barnett as Marine Corps commandant after World War I, pronounced Daly the "outstanding Marine of all time."[6] Short and slight, standing five-six and weighing 132 pounds, Daly repeatedly refused offers of a commission throughout his career, protesting that he would rather be "an outstanding sergeant than just another officer." Unassuming, he remained single his entire life and retired from the Corps on February 6, 1929, with the rank of Sergeant Major. In civilian life, he became a guard in a Wall Street bank and died quietly, at 65, on April 28, 1937, in his Long Island home.

A real marine in a real battle, Daly really did say something that ended with the rhetorical question, "Do you want to live forever?" That the versions of the legend surrounding Daly and his battle cry vary in various details does not diminish the reality on which the legend is based. Both Catlin and Gibbons seized on the phrase, changing its location a bit and, in Gibbon's case, even claiming to have heard it personally, for much the same reason that the marines marched against Belleau Wood in the elaborately choreographed line of sections formation: to impose order on chaos, to make sense of it, to extract some greater meaning from it. Even the minor error that all versions of the story share—"demoting" Daly from first sergeant to gunnery sergeant—is significant in the effort to mythologize this aspect of the battle. For while the first sergeant outranks the gunnery sergeant, it is the "gunny" that is the archetypal marine non-com, perceived as the rugged, tough-love layer of command closest to the grunts.

Without such patterns and stories, the "Battle" of Belleau Wood threatened to emerge into posterity as what Catlin admitted "it has been called"—nothing but "an exaggerated riot," a slaughter, full of sound and fury, signifying—just what?[7]

Even under fire, legends endure far longer than a line of sections. "The ripping fire grew hotter," Catlin wrote. "The machine guns at the edge of the woods were now a bare hundred yards away, and the enemy gunners could scarcely miss their targets. It was more than flesh and blood could stand." Berry's "men were forced to throw themselves flat on the ground or be annihilated, and there they remained in that terrible hail till darkness made it possible for them to withdraw to their original position." Henry Larsen, Berry's adjutant, reported to brigade after the battle: "three platoons 45th Company went over. Only a few returned," and Catlin wrote: "Berry's men did not win that first encounter in the attack on Belleau Wood," which was another way of saying that not a single one of Berry's marines even reach the edge of the woods, and 60 percent of the battalion became casualties.[8] Among these was Major Benjamin Berry himself. Floyd Gibbons was there when it happened—and he was more than a witness.

Gibbons, with Berry and many of his men, was making his way down a wooded slope, midway down which was a sunken road, littered with French bodies and "several of our men who had been brought down but five minutes before. We crossed that road hurriedly knowing that it was covered from the left by German machine guns." Gibbons, Berry, and the marines came to a V-shaped field, "perfectly flat and . . . covered with a young crop of oats between ten and fifteen inches high." On all sides of the field were dense clusters of trees. Gibbons and the others could hear the machine guns. "We could not see them but we knew that every leaf and piece of greenery there vibrated from their fire and the tops of the young oats waved and swayed with the streams of lead that swept across." After giving orders to follow him at 10- to 15-yard intervals, Berry "Started across the field alone at the head of the party. I followed." The woods around the field "began to rattle fiercely," and Gibbons could see "the dust puffs that the bullets kicked up in the dirt around our feet." Berry was well beyond the center of the field when he turned toward Gibbons and the other men: "Get down everybody."[9]

He did not have to repeat the order. "We all fell on our faces. And then it began to come hot and fast," the volleys of lead sweeping the "tops of the oats just over us." As Gibbons "busily engaged [in] flattening [himself] on the ground," he heard a shout. "It came from Major Berry. I lifted my head cautiously and looked forward. The Major was making an effort to get to his feet. With his right hand he was savagely grasping his left wrist. 'My hand's gone,' he shouted."[10]

In some ways what really had happened to him was worse. Berry's hand had not been shot off, but a bullet had entered his left arm at the elbow, passing down alongside the bone, "tearing away muscles and nerves to the forearm and lodging itself in the palm of his hand. His pain was excruciating," causing him to stand up as he gripped his arm. Gibbons called to Berry: "Get down. Flatten out, Major," knowing that "he was courting death every minute he stood up." Berry in turn called over to Gibbons: "We've got to get out of here. We've got to get forward. They'll start shelling this open field in a few minutes." Gibbons replied that he was crawling over to him. "Wait until I get there and I'll help you. Then we'll get up and make a dash for it."[11]

Gibbons crawled, pushing "forward by digging in with my toes and elbows extended in front of me. It was my object to make as little movement in the oats as possible."[12]

And then it happened. The lighted end of a cigarette touched me in the fleshy part of my upper left arm. That was all. It just felt like a sudden burn and nothing worse. The burned part did not seem to be any larger in area than that part which could be burned by the lighted end of a cigarette.[13]

A bullet had had gone through the bicep of the upper arm and come out the other side. Gibbons looked down at his sleeve and could not even see the hole where the bullet had entered.

Then the second one hit. It nicked the top of my left shoulder. And again came the burning sensation, only this time the area affected seemed larger.[14]

Feeling surprisingly little pain, Gibbons continued to craw toward Berry.

And then the third one struck me. In order to keep as close to the ground as possible, I had swung my chin to the right so that I was pushing forward with my left cheek flat against the ground and in order to accommodate this position of the head, I had moved my steel helmet over so that it covered part of my face on the right.

Then there came a crash. It sounded to me like some one had dropped a glass bottle into a porcelain bathtub. A barrel of whitewash tipped over and it seemed that everything in the world turned white. That was the sensation. I did not recognize it because I have often been led to believe and often heard it said that when one receives a blow on the head everything turns black.[15]

Gibbon asked himself, "'Am I dead?' . . . I wanted to know . . . . How was I to find out if I was dead? . . . I decided to try and move my fingers on my left hand. I did so and they moved. I next moved my left foot. Then I knew I was alive."[16]

Floyd Gibbons's left eye had just been shot out of his head, along with part of his skull. With his remaining eye, he watched Major Berry "rise to his feet and in a perfect hail of lead rush forward and out of my line of vision."[17] Despite his wound, Berry continued to command, led his men in destroying a German machine gun nest, and later received the Distinguished Service Cross from General Pershing. Gibbons, with his fellow journalist Hartzell (who was unwounded), remained in the oat field for three hours, until 9:00 p.m., not daring to move until they judged it was sufficiently dark to risk crawling back to the American position. After a series of agonizing

stops at various forward dressing stations, Gibbons was loaded into an ambulance and evacuated to a hospital. Astoundingly, he was on his feet and
once again covering the war within ten days of having been wounded.

If the line of sections advance, in all its archaic formality, failed to
work for long, in some places it did not work at all. The poverty of communications and the level of confusion were so profound on the afternoon of
June 6 that some units never even formed up to join the "parade." They were
not aware of the attack until after it had actually begun.

A Lieutenant Gordon, commanding a platoon in one of Berry's
companies, was standing—*standing*—at the periphery of the wheat field
"watching the shells as they dropped along the edge of the woods across the
wheatfield." He was talking with a friend, who remarked of the shelling, "I
wonder what this is about. . . . They must have something spotted over there."
Several minutes passed before Captain Larsen ran up to Gordon and his
friend. "Get your platoons ready immediately," he shouted. "You should have
started across with the barrage." Gordon later remarked:

> This was the first information we had received regarding an attack and did
> not know one had been planned. No objective was given as to where it was
> to stop and no maps had been distributed; the only thing we were sure of
> was the direction and we knew that.[18]

Attacking from Lucy-le-Bocage, well south of Berry, Sibley's 3rd Battalion,
6th Marines was, in Catlin's words, "having better luck." Catlin thrilled to the
sight of these men "sweeping across the open ground in four waves, as
steadily and correctly as though on parade." As if to justify on some pragmatic
terms the ostentatious grandeur of this procession under fire, Catlin explained: "They walked at the regulation pace, because a man is of little use
in a hand-to-hand bayonet struggle after a hundred yards dash." The obvious response to this observation would have been to ask the colonel just
how much use a dead man was. But who could have dared such imperti-
nence as Catlin looked on. "My hands were clenched and all my muscles taut
as I watched that cool, intrepid, masterful defiance of the German spite." He
saw "no sign of wavering or breaking."[19]

> Oh, it took courage and steady nerves to do that in the face of the enemy's
> machine gun fire. Men fell there in the open, but the advance kept steadily
> on to the woods. It was then that discipline and training counted. Their
> minds were concentrated not on the enemy's fire but on the thing they had

to do and the necessity of doing it right. They were listening for orders and obeying them. In this frame of mind the soldier can perhaps walk with even more coolness and determination than he can run. In any case it was an admirable exhibition of military precision and it gladdened their Colonel's heart.[20]

Interviewed in October 2003, upstate New Yorker Eugene Lee—at age 104, then the nation's "oldest living marine"—recalled the grim journey across the wheat field Catlin watched from afar. "They split us out into formation. They had the first wave go so far. They kept on firing in the woods there. The next wave would come and jump over them and they'd go so far, and would fire till they got in the edge of the woods."[21] The object of this leap-frog advance was to allow the first wave to cover the farther advance of the second wave, and the second to cover that of the third, and the third to cover the fourth as it finally reached the woods. Once the fourth had been delivered to the objective, the marines of the preceding waves—those who survived—would follow it in. Lee was in the third of the four human waves.

Unlike Berry's men, many of Sibley's, who had much less open field to traverse, made it to Belleau Wood. Yet their entry into the objective was somehow anticlimactic. Catlin wrote that the "Marines have a war cry that they can use to advantage when there is need of it. It is a bloodcurdling yell calculated to carry terror to the heart of the waiting Hun. I am told that there were wild yells in the woods that night, when the Marines charged the machine gun nests, but there was no yelling when they went in." Catlin also noted a report that the marines "advanced on those woods crying 'Remember the *Lusitania!*' If they did so, I failed to hear it." Quite rightly, he observed that this did not "sound like the sort of thing the Marine says under the conditions." In fact, so far as he could observe, Catlin did not believe "a sound was uttered throughout the length of those four lines. The men were saving their breath for what was to follow."[22]

Having written of this wordless entry into Belleau Wood, an entry bought at the price of many dead and wounded, the colonel of the 6th Marine Regiment feared that he had "given but a poor picture of that splendid advance." True, there "was nothing dashing about it like a cavalry charge," yet it was nevertheless "one of the finest things I have ever seen men do." Catlin fully appreciated that these marines "were men who had never before been called upon to attack a strongly held enemy position." What lay before them was a "dense woods effectively sheltering armed and highly trained opponents of unknown strength." Indeed, within the depths of this dark space "ma-chine guns snarled and rattled and spat forth a leaden death. It was like some mythical monster belching smoke and fire from its lair." Yet these marines, the vast majority entirely new to combat, marched "straight against it . . . with heads up and the light of battle in their eyes."[23]

Months after the battle, Private W. H. Smith, recovering from wounds in the Brooklyn Naval Hospital, related to Catlin what it had been like marching into Belleau Wood. He said that there "wasn't a bit of hesitation from any man. You had no heart for fear at all. Fight—fight and get the Germans was your only thought. Personal danger didn't con-cern you in the least and you didn't care." Smith explained that he and about 60 others had gotten ahead of the rest of the company. "We just couldn't stop despite the orders of our leaders." Reaching the edge of the woods, they "encountered some of the Hun infantry," and then "it be-came a matter of shooting at mere human targets." At first, it was almost easy. The marines fixed their rifle sights at 300 yards and, "aiming through the peep kept picking off Germans. And a man went down at nearly every shot." But then the enemy "detected us and we became the objects of their heavy fire."[24] Colonel Catlin, who had no field telephone, "felt obliged to see what was going on." He took his stand on a "little rise of ground protected by a low line of bushes about 300 yards from the woods." The position was near a road, the point at which the left flank of Thomas Holcomb's battalion made contact with the right flank of Berry's battered battalion. "The shelter trenches did not cross the road," so Catlin was fully exposed as he watched the advance through his binoc-ulars. "Bullets," he recalled, "rained all around me, the machine gun crews near me forming a target for the Germans." The "racket of rifle and ma-chine gun fire and bursting shrapnel and high explosives" was "like the continuous roll of some demoniacal drum, with the bass note of the heavy guns that were shelling Lucy." Through his binoculars, Catlin watched "a number of our brave lads fall" as the German machine gun-ners made sure to aim low, sweeping the ground, thereby "catching most of the men in the legs." Those who were thus disabled "lay right in the line of fire and many of them were killed there on the ground" whereas those "who were able to stand and keep going had the best chance." Some of these men "went through the whole fight with leg wounds re-ceived during the first ten minutes."[25]

Vivid as his perceptions of battle were, Catlin was not destined to be an eyewitness for long. "Just about the time Sibley's men struck the woods a sniper's bullet hit me in the chest. It felt exactly as though some one had struck me heavily with a sledge. It swung me clear around and toppled me over on the ground. When I tried to get up I found that my right side was paralysed." Catlin's French interpreter, Captain Tribot-Laspierre, a "splendid fellow who stuck to me through thick and thin" and who had been "begging me to get back to a safer place," instantly came out of his cover and rushed to Catlin's side. "He is a little man and I am not, but he dragged me head first back to the shelter trench some twenty or twenty-five feet away."[26] Like Gibbons on Berry's side of the attack, Catlin, on Sibley's, was more fascinated than horrified by the sensations of being wounded. "I have heard of men getting wounded who said that it felt like a red-hot iron being jammed through them before the world turned black," but nothing of the kind happened to Catlin. "I suffered but little pain and I never for a moment lost consciousness." Nor did he think of death, "though I knew I had been hit in a vital spot. I was merely annoyed at my inability to move and carry on."[27]

The colonel took a peculiarly professional and analytical interest in the circumstances of his wounding, concluding that it had been a "chance shot and not the result of good marksmanship, for the bullet must have come some 600 yards." It passed "clean through" Catlin's right lung, "in at the front and out at the back, drilling a hole straight through me." Catlin related that ballistics experts calculated that a "bullet fired at short range—less than 500 or 600 yards—twists [so that] when it strikes an obstacle it wabbles." Catlin therefore reasoned that had he been shot at close range, the bullet would have "torn a piece out of my back as big as my fist." However, had the bullet been fired from a range greater than about 600 yards, it would have been "already wabbling, and would have made a big hole in the front of my chest and perhaps would not have gone clear through." Because the holes going in and out were both small, Catlin concluded that he had been shot from a range of about 600 yards, "and I am thankful" for that.[28]

Catlin calmly sent word of his wounding to the command post, ordering his second in command, Lieutenant Colonel Henry Lee, to assume command of the 6th Regiment. Forty-five minutes elapsed before the regimental surgeon, Dr. Farwell, came, under heavy fire, to Catlin's side. Farwell had brought stretcher bearers with him, but heavy shelling prevented immediate evacuation, and when gas shells began to detonate nearby, the stretcher men put a mask on the colonel. "I never knew before how uncomfortable one of those things could be. It is hard enough for a man to breathe with a lung full of blood without having one of those smothering masks clapped over his face." What gave Catlin comfort was the sound of the fire gradually receding, which told him that "Sibley's men were advancing." However, when the firing grew louder on the left, he "knew that Berry's outfit was being beaten back."[29]

At length, the pace of the shelling eased, and four men raised Catlin's stretcher to their shoulders. "Carrying a 215-pound man on a stretcher over rough country under fire is no joke," Catlin observed, "but they got me to Lucy," thence to an ambulance, and on to hospitals at Meaux and Paris.[30] The colonel remained hospitalized until July 22, when he was sent home on leave.

In Catlin's absence, the men on Sibley's left flank, most of them, clawed their way into Belleau Wood, via its southwestern hook. On contact, the combat was a combination of close rifle fire and fierce bayonet work. Both the U.S. Army and the Marine Corps administered bayonet training, and soldiers and marines made ample use of the bayonet in the "Great War"—more, certainly, than they had in any previous conflict. Yet U.S. Army soldiers tended to dread the weapon, whereas marines, at least in the attack, reveled in its use. In a war fought to such a great extent by the weapons of high technology—high-explosive artillery, gas, the machine gun, the airplane, and even the tank—it was as if marines craved contact at its most warrior-like. The isolated German outposts in the southwestern end of Belleau Wood fell prey to the marines' bayonets, but the terrain, with its tangle of undergrowth, soon broke up the cohesiveness of the attacking units. Isolated and slowed, Captain Dwight Smith's company of Sibley's marines, after they had penetrated a few hundred yards into the woods, made easy marks for the German machine guns. The machine gun fire became so intense that the attackers were deflected northward from their due-eastward push.

Another of Sibley's companies, led by Lieutenant A. H. Noble, followed Dwight Smith's men into the woods, desperately trying to maintain contact with the lead company, but failing to do so amid the rugged terrain and the outpouring of machine gun fire. As if shivered and split by the stream of fire, the left flank of Noble's company sheered off to the north—just as Smith's men had done—but the right flank, advancing along the ravine at the southern tip of Belleau Wood, continued due east. This flank consisted of two platoons, one under Lieutenant Louis Timmerman and another under a lieutenant named Hurley. The attack on the woods, which had begun in parade-order "line of sections," increasingly broke up within Belleau Wood itself. Yet, in doing so, it did not falter or flag. Instead, as companies divided into platoons and platoons into sections and sections into fire teams or even individual marines, the fragmented fight only intensified.

In Timmerman's case, his platoon soon lost contact with Hurley's, and then the sections of the platoon itself lost contact with one another. Marines set up machine gun positions within the woods wherever they could. This was necessary, of course, but it also added to the confusion of this most chaotic combat. Timmerman and the men who were still with him passed one marine machine gun company, so he naturally assumed that the machine gun fire he heard to his rear was coming from them. In fact, what he heard was the sound of German machine gunners pinning down all of Smith's company along with Sibley's other two companies and the two sections of Timmerman's own platoon that had veered to the north. Unaware of this, Timmerman just kept going. In their advance, they stumbled across a German outpost. The marines and the enemy were equally surprised, but it was the Germans who gave up, and Timmerman sent back the prisoners under a single man while he and the others kept moving.

That's when Timmerman got his second surprise. He was suddenly shocked to discover that he had broken through to the east side of Belleau Wood, finding himeself at a point slightly to the north of the Bouresches.

Just before the attack, the company commander, Lieutenant Noble, had passed on to his platoon commanders the orders he had received. They were for the platoons on the right flank to move through Belleau Wood and capture Bouresches. Like all neophyte lieutenants, Timmerman was anxious to follow orders, and he assumed everyone else was, too. Finding himself and the two platoon sections with him—about twenty marines in all—on the east side of Belleau Wood, and entirely unaware that the rest of the marines in the southern end of the woods were being held down and held back by *German* machine guns, Timmerman experienced a moment of panic. It was not panic born of an awareness of the actual situation: that he and twenty other marines were alone in enemy territory, separated from the rest of their unit by a dense woods exploding in hostile fire. Instead, it was panic born of the fear that everyone else had made it through Belleau Wood before him and that *he* was behind in the assault on Bourseches.

Sending one wounded private—a marine named Henry—to the rear, Timmerman deployed his two sections into a line of skirmishers, sent a Corporal Larsen and Private Swenson ahead as scouts, then led his men along the ravine they had followed through the woods until they reached a wheat field. On the other side of this field, about 200 yards away, was Bouresches. As with the wheat fields on the western face of Belleau Wood, this one (as pictured in Timmerman's diary) "was thrashing to and fro with machine gun bullets."[31]

Timmerman watched as Larsen and Swenson reached "a sort of mound of earth parallel to our line of advance." They signaled a halt there, and Timmerman advanced his men to the mound. Suddenly, he "noticed that we were coming under fire from all directions," despite being "sheltered from the enemy in front."[32]

Who was firing from the rear?

It was a profoundly disorienting moment. After no more than a minute, however, the disorientation blossomed into disbelief as Private Henry—the wounded marine Timmerman had sent to the rear—"came running back yelling something." Timmerman could not make out what Henry was trying to say, so signaled for him to come over. What he was saying was that "the woods in back of us were full of Germans." At first, the lieutenant simply did not believe him. After all, "we had just come through there." But the sight, sound, and sensation of "the bullets kicking up dust and landing all around our side of the barricade" made an instant believer out of him.[33]

Clearly, Timmerman realized, he and his two sections—now reduced from twenty to "about fifteen" men—could not long stay behind a mound that offered no shelter. Timmerman yelled to his marines, ordering them back into Belleau Wood. "Luckily I hit the edge of the woods just where the Germans were."[34]

There were seventeen German privates and two non-coms manning a pair of machine guns in a patch of low ground that led off from the ravine. The machine gunners were second-line troops, and they did not expect a swarm of marines to descend on them from the *east*. In the lead, Timmerman kick the faces of the first two Germans he encountered, knocking both unconscious. The others, confronted with the marines' bayonets, threw down their weapons and laid themselves prostrate before the attackers. Some tore open their uniform blouses, baring their chests, as if to say in a language that required absolutely no translation, *We are unarmed!*

At this point, a sergeant from Hurley's platoon broke through Belleau Wood with a couple of marines. Timmerman put his prisoners into their custody and instructed them to take them to the rear. Still under the unshakeable conviction that most of the other marines had broken through the woods and were already attacking toward Bouresches, Timmerman could not afford to be encumbered by POWs. He further assumed that capturing the machine gunners had put an end to German resistance in the south end of Belleau Wood. He therefore resumed his interrupted advance and returned to the mound. This time, machine gun fire opened up from the town, then also from his left flank, coming from a rise just fifty yards off. To this was added fire from Timmerman's left rear as well. "I faced around and saw Swenson lying dead with a bullet hole through the forehead." Timmerman shouted to "Open fire to the right" and pointed "toward the hillock where a terrific fire was coming from." No sooner had he done this than he himself was hit in the left side of the face. Timmerman "fell forward thinking, 'I've got mine,'" believing that a bullet had ripped through under his eye. He lost consciousness momentarily, but then "felt better." Although "I was covered with blood I realized I had not been dangerously hit." Nevertheless, Timmerman's "men were dropping around there" and so "I told them to follow me" and, once again, they "ran back for the shelter of the woods."[35]

Lieutenant Louis Timmerman had begun the advance on Belleau Wood commanding a platoon of 50 marines as part of a company of some 200. This mass of men broke apart inside the woods, leaving Timmerman with fifteen men on the other side. By the time he retreated back to the eastern perimeter of Belleau Wood, shot through the face, he commanded just six marines. They hunkered down in the German machine gun position they had captured minutes ago. Only now did it occur to him that Belleau Wood had neither been taken nor even traversed—at least not by very many of the marines who had entered it. Beyond these realizations, the lieutenant knew only that the battle, which had been ahead of him in Belleau Wood when Belleau Wood had been ahead of him, was now ahead of him in the little town of Bouresches. But the battle was also on either side of him and, not least of all, it was raging yet in the ruined tangle of trees, rocks, and ravines that now lay behind him.

$\star$ $\star$ $\star$ $\star$ $\star$

American victories at Chateau Thierry and Belleau Wood brought an end to the last major German offensive of World War I. The Marines and the Army's Third Infantry Brigade secured the forest by June 26 after a vicious close quarters engagement that became a hallmark for Marine aggressiveness, marksmanship, and tenacity. The victory earned the Marines a reputation as America's fiercest and most effective warriors, placing them among the world's preeminent fighting elite. The French renamed the wood "Bois de la Brigade de Marine" (Wood of the Marine Brigade) in honor of the Marines' tenacity. The French government also later awarded the 4th Brigade the Croix de Guerre. Legend has it that Germans who faced the Marines at Belleau Wood nicknamed the Americans *Teufelhunden,* the "Devil Dogs."

Henderson Field

JOE FOSS WITH DONNA WILD FOSS

Guadalcanal stands out in American history as one of the greatest military campaigns of World War II. The Japanese had occupied the island, the southern most of the Solomons, during the opening months of the war. Construction of an airfield that would allow the Japanese to threaten the critical sea-lanes to Australia was under way. In August 1942, the Americans landed the First Marine Division to capture the airfield and begin a campaign that would lead the Allies northwards through the Solomons towards the Japanese bastion at Rabaul. Key to all the major campaigns of the Pacific Theater was airpower. The possession of the field at Guadalcanal (renamed Henderson Field after Marine Major Lofton Henderson, killed in action at the Battle of Midway) allowed the Marines to challenge the Japanese at sea and in the air as they counterattacked to regain the island. One of the Marine aviators to fly from Henderson Field was Joe Foss, executive officer of VMF 121 deployed to Guadalcanal in October 1942. In the following chapter, he describes his arrival to the island and his first combat against the Japanese.

> In the deep dark days of the early '40s when America needed a hero, Joe Foss was there . . . he became that hero that spurred an entire nation into a resolve that we would win the Second World War and make the world a safer place.
>
> —Bill Janklow

★ ★ ★ ★ ★

The island of Guadalcanal was a rude shock for a guy from the plains of South Dakota. Graceful flying fish skimmed the turquoise coastal waters, and man-eating sharks infested the coral reefs below. Rushing streams zigzagged through the jungle floor of the island. Sleepy crocodiles sunned themselves on muddy riverbanks, while brightly colored birds of every species fluttered among the branches. It was a tropic paradise plunged into war.

Since we landed on the island right after a bombing raid, however, it looked more like what the Australians called it—"a bloody stinking hole." We also arrived during the rainy season, which lasted from November to March. Actually there were only two seasons: wet, hot, and steamy, and wetter, hotter, and steamier. Between the rain and the humidity nothing ever dried out, including us. I'd never seen so much rain and mud in my life.

A writer for *Life* magazine would extol, "Guadalcanal is an exciting place . . . botanically, meteorologically and zoologically speaking. . . . There are butterflies the size of birds and spiders that spin webs as thick as chewing gum."[1] All I knew was that there were mosquitoes as thick as termites in a woodpile. I'm allergic to mosquito bites anyway, and these buggers were the sticking kind. They'd swarm over your face so thick you had to wipe them off, and before you were done, they'd be covering the other side of your face. I think they even got hooked on the repellent we used.

Two battles were raging over Guadalcanal when we arrived: one between American and Japanese troops, and the other between forces within the American military who disagreed fiercely over the wisdom of supporting the Guadalcanal campaign. While some wanted to strengthen our position, others wanted to pull out entirely. Those of us doing the fighting were caught in the middle, poorly equipped and often confused by the actions of our superiors.

Scavenged from divisions all over the Pacific, the men on Guadalcanal were mostly a mixture of experienced misfits—career soldiers with little hope of promotion—and raw recruits. So far, despite inferior equipment and support, they had held their ground and beaten the odds, surprising both Japanese and Americans. Salty veterans provided the seasoning the untested soldiers needed and gave them a sense of Marine tradition and honor that couldn't be taught in boot camp. But it became increasingly clear that they could not endure without reinforced air power. The first wave of pilots and planes to follow the infantry landing had suffered high losses, and rapid reinforcements were needed if the ground forces were to survive.

There was no consensus, however, that such reinforcements should be sent. From the beginning, Vice Admiral Robert L. Ghormley, chosen to execute the campaign, considered holding Guadalcanal a futile impossibility, and circumstances combined to complicate the already poorly planned effort.

In Wellington, New Zealand, the longshoremen's union went on strike just before the campaign began; they refused to load materials needed for the front, leaving soldiers with only days of ammunition. When the food they carried in their ration packs ran out, the men were forced to subsist on anything they could raid from the Japanese positions they captured. Elsewhere, sixty U.S. Merchant Marine vessels, on the advice of their union, refused to deliver supplies and ammunition without an impossibly extravagant hazard bonus, although they were already earning more than those who were actually targets of the Japanese attacks.

Available pilots and planes in other Pacific regions were held back from Guadalcanal by commanders who would not give up their forces to what they considered a suicide mission. Eventually, many historians would accuse at least one admiral of desertion in the face of battle for the cavalier failure to support the Marines on the beleaguered island.

The Yanks on Guadalcanal were hard-pressed to decide who we resented more, the unions or our own brass. We did agree that we hated the Japanese most of all and were willing to pay the price to win if we could get the air support we needed. Our precarious situation inspired numerous songs and poems, recited and sung wherever Marines gathered to swap scuttlebutt. One raunchy ballad began, "Say a prayer for your pal on Guadalcanal."

The men of VMF-223, the fighter squadron we were replacing, had been on Guadalcanal for six weeks, hanging on to Henderson Field and fighting the Japanese for control of the rest of the island. Many of the men were sick with malaria and trembling with exhaustion, and I wanted to let these guys know how much I appreciated them for proving that American pilots could hold out against greatly superior Japanese odds. I also wanted to pick up any tips they could give, so I talked to as many as possible as they prepared to leave. I was particularly impressed by Major John Smith and Captain Marion Carl. Smith and Carl, along with Major Robert Galer, had been labeled "The Three Flying Fools of Guadalcanal." All told, the three of them shot down forty-six Japanese planes and were decorated by Admiral Nimitz, Commander of the Pacific Fleet.

The enemy believed they could take the island back from the Allies like a piece of cake and move on to Australia and New Zealand. These guys had stopped them cold, and now it was our turn.

One of the first men I met after I landed on Guadalcanal was First Lieutenant Ben Finney, a Marine I'd gotten acquainted with shortly before we shipped out for the South Pacific. Outside of the skipper, Finney, already in his forties, was the only officer in the squadron older than I was, and we hit if off immediately. I'd already made something of a reputation for myself as a joker and raconteur, but I was an amateur compared to old Finney. Seeing his mug among the palms was a welcome sight.

Finney was descended from an old and once wealthy aristocratic Southern family whose ancestors had emigrated from Ireland. Ben used to joke that he came from the wrong part of two countries: the north of Ireland and the south of the United States. Some said he'd managed to go through life without working a day. Actually he just made work look like play. He'd been an actor, a film producer, a screenwriter, and a skillful investor and entrepreneur. A veteran of World War I, where he had served in France, Finney had later returned and almost single-handedly turned the Riviera into "the" place to be. His closest friends included F. Scott and Zelda Fitzgerald, Ernest Hemingway, Harpo Marx, Alexander Woolcott, Noël Coward, Cole Porter, William Powell, Ronald Coleman, and Charlie MacArthur. He hobnobbed with bootleggers, movie stars, politicians, royalty, and practically anybody else who was part of the "lost generation." Finney managed to spend much of his life on the most luxurious private yachts in the world, attested to years later in his autobiography, *Feet First*.[2]

Soon after Pearl Harbor, Ben interrupted his society lifestyle to reenlist in the Marines. This was not easy, since he'd been given a Purple Heart and a disability discharge in 1919. In his own words, he "began to feel that the Corps took a dim view of taking on a 'retread.'" But nothing deterred old Finney, and through some rather bizarre circumstances he ended up being ordered to Guadalcanal as a ground installation officer for our unit, where he found himself in the middle of some of the most torrid action of the war.

Finney didn't know what a ground installation job was, but he did his best. He always said, "I was moved from a job I knew little about to one that I knew nothing about."

Finney was an anachronism. Besides being a veteran of the last war, he always looked like he was going to lunch in Beverly Hills—a decided contrast to his bearded, scruffy compatriots. The skipper didn't know what to do with this debonair, middle-aged, nonflying officer who'd been assigned to our unit.

"Well, I do need a ground installation officer," Duke finally said. "You're in charge of everything from security to where we put the tents."

That would turn out to be one of the best decisions the skipper ever made.

Approximately ten ground Marines were required to keep each pilot in the air, so our squadron numbered well over four hundred when we were fully operational. A dive bomber outfit had arrived on Guadalcanal the same day we did, commanded by Eddy Miller, my former instruments instructor from Pensacola. Both squadrons were assigned living areas in a palm grove jungle between the landing strip and the beach. A few yards away was the latrine—a shallow trench with a log slung over it. The bathtub was the Lunga River, complete with an endless supply of running water and an occasional crocodile audience.

Miller's unit quickly set up their tents, stowed their gear, and went walking about, checking the area and gabbing with the veterans, but we didn't get off that easy. Finney put us to work digging foxholes near our tents.

Due to alternating rain and blazing sun, the ground had baked to ceramic hardness, and once we got below the crust, we hit coral. But Finney insisted that we shouldn't burrow into the softer ground. If dirt was easy to excavate, he said, it was because water tended to pool there during the rains. During an attack, a foxhole brimming with rainwater and mud was about as much use as a second tail on a tomcat.

While we slaved and sweltered away in the suffocating heat and humidity, interrupted by the frequent torrential downpours that sent rivers running through our tents, we heard lots of smartass comments from the bomber squadron, which we returned in kind.

By the end of the day we were all physically exhausted but emotionally exhilarated to be in the center of the action. As daylight faded we could hear the mortars and small arms fire announcing that the nightly struggle for the perimeter had begun. The vets had warned us about "Millimeter Mike" and "Pistol Pete," nicknames for the Japanese artillery fire and the enemy gunners located somewhere up in the hills above Henderson Field. At the moment, they controlled those hills and could lob a shell into the base at any time. They pestered the airfield nightly with rocket and mortar fire.

Then there was "Maytag Charlie," who flew nightly raids over the field in a plane with unsynchronized twin-engine props that made a peculiar grating sound like an old gas-engine washing machine. Probably more than one pilot flew this nightly nuisance mission and possibly more than one aircraft, but to us he became one and the same. Usually Charlie made one pass over the field, dropping bottles that whistled like bombs. Just to make it interesting and keep us awake, however, he occasionally lobbed the real thing blindly into our dark camp, and he did score some direct hits.

We quickly learned that a whistle meant an incoming bomb or shell, which meant you jumped for cover, and even then you weren't entirely safe. Not long after we arrived I was standing talking with four other Marines when the familiar descending whistle sounded—the whistle dropped in pitch as the bomb or shell Doppler shifted toward you. There were two bomb craters nearby, so I jumped into one with another solider, and the other three men leaped into the other one. When the deafening explosion passed, and with ears still ringing, I crawled out of the pit and looked for the other Marines. The shell had scored a direct hit on their foxhole and cut the heads off all three.

Throughout most of my first night on Guadalcanal shells streamed above our tents in both directions as Japanese ships in the channel targeted our artillerymen on the island, who returned the fire. Twice we had to hit our foxholes—the ones Finney had driven us so hard to finish that first day. The veterans of the island struggle, who enjoyed their sardonic one-upmanship, assured us that the night's shelling was "light."

I was up at 4:00 the next morning, but didn't make my first combat mission until that afternoon, flying escort for dive bombers on a run up "the slot." The Solomon Islands, of which Guadalcanal is a part, are an archipelago that stretches over four hundred miles in a generally straight line northwest from San Cristobal at the bottom to Bougainville at the top. Running through the middle of the chain of islands is a long, thin trench of ocean we called "the slot," down which the Japanese attacking forces came with bitter regularity. My eight-plane flight flew high cover that first day and kept a sharp lookout for Zeroes. We didn't spot any, but the bombers located a Japanese destroyer and scored a direct hit, sending a mushrooming explosion of fire and smoke high into the sky.

The next day, October 11, we scrambled to intercept twenty-eight Japanese bombers and twenty-one Zeros that were rapidly approaching Henderson Field from their base on Bougainville Island, to the northwest. These attacks, I would soon learn, were an almost daily routine. For some reason, this time the enemy miscalculated and dropped their bombs two miles behind their own lines, probably killing many of their own infantrymen. They turned and headed back to their base, but not before our squadron downed two bombers and one Zero. The dogfight ended almost as quickly as it had started, and I didn't get close enough to fire a single shot.

That night there was a terrific naval engagement off Cape Esperance at the northwest hump of the island. Sleep was impossible. By morning heavy oil and debris covered the surf while the Navy picked up swimming sailors— Americans and Japanese. The light cruiser *Boise*, armed with only small six-inch guns, had sunk six enemy ships in only thirty minutes, earning itself the title of "The One Ship Navy." The Japs lost two heavy cruisers, one light cruiser, and three destroyers. We lost one destroyer and 107 officers and men from the *Boise*. Despite their heavy casualties, the Japanese did succeed in landing thousands of troops on the island.

The third morning, October 12, we took off before dawn, heading up the slot, again escorting dive bombers going in to chase off Japanese ships still in the area following the previous night's battle. Just off the coast of New Georgia we spotted two Japanese destroyers. My flight went in first to divert the antiaircraft fire away from our torpedo planes, and our attacking bombers scored a square hit on one of the destroyers and sank a cruiser. We returned to Henderson without a scratch.

After a relatively quiet night when we actually got some sleep, we returned to the air to intercept twenty-two approaching enemy bombers, but they changed course and we never fired a shot. A scant two hours later we got the call, "Eighteen bombers headed yours," which meant a second flight of eighteen enemy bombers had been sighted on a direct course toward Henderson Field.

We scrambled and climbed high and to the left of the big bombers and spotted six Zero escorts off to the right. I led my men along the edge of some clouds, hoping the Zekes would not see us. The old adrenaline was pumping now, as I sensed the real thing closing in. I just wanted one good shot at a Zero. Just give me one.

Suddenly I spotted my wingman, Greg Loesch, in close, waving urgently and pointing upward.

I smiled and waved acknowledgment. "I've already seen them," I yelled. In my excitement I didn't notice that my radio wasn't working.

Just then Loesch dived out of formation. I looked around and saw that all my men had scattered. Then a shower of fiery tracers sprayed over my head.

Hell. Loesch hadn't been waving with excitement. He'd been trying to warn me. At that moment a crazy little jungle raced through my head:

Zero and me,
Down in the sea,
You really should flee!

That bird came by like a freight train and gave me a good sprinkling, but I knew I had him. I pulled up and gave him a short burst, and down he went. *Glad to get rid of that one!* I thought. *That's one less Zero we have to worry about.*

I felt charged with electricity—my hair standing on end and my mouth dry as cotton. I'd just gotten my first Zero. Straining against my lap belt to stand as erect as possible in the cramped cockpit, I yelled a victory war whoop at the top of my lungs.

Busy celebrating, I failed to see the three Zekes lining up on me—until I found myself in the midst of streaming tracers.

"Got to head out of here, fast!" I said aloud. I jammed the stick forward and went into a screaming dive from 22,000 feet. I'd read that a Zero couldn't follow such a dive; its wings would come off trying to pull out. Well, whoever wrote that was a fiction writer, because those boys just kept on my tail, pumping lead!

Two shells entered my fuselage. Dark, smoky oil spewed out the right oil cooler. With its lubrication pouring into the air, the high-speed engine froze almost instantly. Clouds of smoke replaced oil, pierced by tracers from the three planes on my tail.

When the engine seized, the reduction gear between the propeller and the engine was wrenched off and the prop became a free agent, causing extreme vibrations. Between the wind shrieking through the holes in the canopy and the rotating prop with its ruined connections, the noise level was deafening. And if that wasn't enough to get my attention, through the side of the canopy I stared wide-eyed at a gaping hole in my wing where a 20 mm cannon shell had exploded. I could see the ocean through it.

In an almost vertical dive, picking up airspeed rapidly, violent vibrations set in, and sharp pressure and pain began to build in my ears. I knew other pilots in the same situation had suffered burst and hemorrhaged eardrums. Mine held, but it was a wild ride.

When the earth took up most of my field of vision, I pulled back on the stick with all my strength, hoping the tail assembly was still functional, and leveled out just over the ground. Streaking dead stick just above the trees, I headed for the field, at the same time worrying about keeping as much distance as possible between myself and the closing Zeros.

It was just about then I asked myself, *Why did I ever leave the farm? Sitting on a plow, staring at a horse's tail, is a whole lot safer than this!*

By now I was only 150 feet off the ground, my pursuers hot on me, still sending sizzling streamers in my direction. I was coming in much too fast—150 knots when 90 was considered the maximum for a safe landing—but if I slowed down they'd blast me out of the sky. The piercing, penetrating racket increased, and the vibrations were unbelievable. The vacuum flaps designed to slow the plane refused to deploy at 150 knots. Only the landing gear that I had dropped was slowing me down.

In a desperate attempt to line up with the runway, I side-slipped the Wildcat. It set down, hitting hard, but kept upright. I managed to turn forty-five degrees into the palm grove and was fortunate enough to go bumping down the only row between the palm trees that was clear of barrels or trenches. When I finally came to a stop, I just sat there thinking, *The score is tied—I'm ready to be a farmer again.*

The antiaircraft batteries surrounding the field did a good job of chasing away my pursuers, and the next thing I knew, an ambulance with red lights flashing and siren screaming was racing to the scene.

I climbed out of my plane, flustered, embarrassed, and mad as hops. I'd bagged my first Zero, but I'd also made a boob of myself, which almost cost me my life. My bad mood didn't last long though. When the rest of the squadron got down, the young bucks swarmed around yelling congratulations and beating me on the back.

"Congratulations, skipper!"

"Boy, you got one of the sonsabitches."

They went on and on, looking up to the old man, and that charged my battery up again. The further I got from the actual fight, and the more I was thinking, *Boy, I really am good.*

Actually, though, I learned two important lessons that day. I had been indelibly reminded that I had to stay alert to stay alive, and no one ever caught me asleep at the switch again or so intent on an attack that I failed to keep looking around. In fact, from then on I looked around so much that the guys soon started calling me "Swivel-neck Joe."

The second lesson was a result of what happened to Lieutenant Bill Freeman, a drawling engineer from Bonham, Texas. Separated from Duke Davis's flight, Bill had dived alone into a V formation of bombers and shot down the leader, which made him an easy target for every side gunner in the group. Fortunately, he squeezed through without being shot down and survived to share his rather obvious discovery: Always start an attack at the rear of a formation and move progressively forward.

That night, huddled in the meager shelter of a shallow, muddy foxhole, bombarded by enemy fire, all I could think about was the plane I'd shot down, its pilot, and the war. *Why was I here and what was I doing?* After all my eagerness to enter the fray, I had suddenly experienced the real thing. I'd killed and almost been killed.

Suddenly I wasn't so sure about this war business. Then I thought about the attack on Pearl Harbor, and I got upset all over again. The Japanese were our enemies, and they had some ideas I didn't like. They wanted to do away with our great country, and I liked America. And that's when I finally realized, for real, that if I didn't do my part in the war, I wouldn't have a farm to go back to.

After that first night I never again thought about putting my tail between my legs and running back to the farm. I was where I was supposed to be, come what may, and I accepted it.

★   ★   ★   ★   ★

Joe Foss and VMF 121 were withdrawn from combat in January 1943 with seventy-two enemy aircraft destroyed to their credit. Twenty-six of those belonged to Joe Foss making him one of America's top aces. He was awarded the Medal of Honor by President Roosevelt in May the same year and he appeared on the cover of *Life* magazine. After the war Foss helped organize the South Dakota Air National Guard and went back to active service with the United States Air Force during the Korean War as a Director of Operations and Training for the Central Air Defense Command. He would go on to serve two terms in the South Dakota legislature and in 1955 serve as state governor. He passed away in 2003.

The Battle of Bloody Ridge

J O H N   B .   S W E E N E Y

Henderson Field on Guadalcanal was key to the success of the Allied campaign to gain a foothold in the Solomon Islands in the summer and fall of 1942. American airpower flying from Henderson made any Japanese attempt to reinforce and supply their soldiers a costly endeavor. It was essential for the Japanese to storm the American lines and recapture the airfield to regain their dominant position throughout the region. The 6,000-strong Japanese 35th Infantry Brigade, under the command of Japanese Major General Kiyotaki Kawaguchi, was deployed to Guadalcanal in response to the American landings of August 7. On the night of September 12, the Japanese launched a full-scale night assault from the jungles against the American perimeter from the west, east, and south.

In their way was a low-lying set of hills and ridges from which the Americans defended the precious airfield beyond. With his forces still deployed to repel an invasion by sea, Major General Alexander Vandegrift entrusted the defense of the ridgeline to the 1st Raider and 1st Parachute Battalions under U.S. Marine Corps Colonel Merritt A. Edson. John B. Sweeney commanded the 1st Platoon, Company B of the 1ˢᵗ Marine Raiders that night on the ridge. In the following chapter, he gives us a firsthand look at some of the toughest fighting that took place on Guadalcanal.

> Bastogne was considered an epic in the ETO. The 101st Airborne was surrounded there for eight days. But the Marines on Guadalcanal were to be isolated for over four months. There have been few such stands in history . . . the First Marine Division . . . all but abandoned by the vessels which brought them there, reduced to eating roots and weeds, kept on the line though stricken by malaria unless the temperature reached 103 degrees, dependent for food and ammo on the destroyers and

fliers who broke through the blockade, always at great risk, they fought the best soldiers Tokyo could send against them, killed over twenty thousand of them, and won.

—William Manchester

★　　★　　★　　★　　★

On 7 August 1942, I landed on Tulagi with the 1st Raider Battalion commanded by then-Col "Red Mike" Edson. At the time I was a captain and commanded the demolition platoon. The next day I became commander of the 1st Platoon, Company B. On the night of 9 August, the Navy lost a number of ships and men in the Battle of Savo Island near Guadalcanal. It looked like Maj. General Alexander A. Vandegrift's 1st Marine Division was going to have to fight the Japanese without the full support of the naval task force. During the latter part of August, Edson's Raiders were ordered to move from Tulagi to Guadalcanal, along with 2d Battalion, 5th Marines (2/5) and the 1st Parachute Battalion.

We left for Guadalcanal on 30 August. Initially Edson's Raiders were placed in division reserve with Col Edson having operational control of the 1st Parachute Battalion. Over the next 2 weeks we were called upon to participate in various operations, to include a raid on Savo Island on 4 September, where we found no Japanese, and a well-orchestrated raid on Tasimboko on the early morning of 8 September, where we found plenty of evidence of Japanese activity, to include the capture of ammunition, food, beer, cigarettes, and boxes of maps and documents detailing Japanese plans for attacking Henderson Field. In the process, we killed at least 29 Japanese soldiers, losing 2 of our Marines killed and 6 wounded in action.

We spent the next day at the Lunga River, which was turned into a combination shower room and laundry. It was then we learned that Red Mike would be moving us the next day—10 September—to a rest area along a ridge just south of Henderson Field. It was felt that there would be less likelihood at that location that we would be harassed by shelling from enemy ships.

Defensive Action, 10-12 September

We marched to our new positions carrying our "home" and personal belongings on our backs. Heavier equipment, to include tents, was loaded on trucks. We were in position by mid-afternoon on 10 September. Company A was positioned on the Lunga River. Company C occupied a frontline position upstream with its right flank on the river and its left flank on the edge of a lagoon that formed a natural boundary between it and Company B. Our company occupied the southernmost tip of the ridge, and my platoon constituted the right flank at the edge of the jungle. The left edge of the line tied into Company B of 1st Parachute Battalion.

Some of the trucks brought forward concertina and barbed wire that we erected along the forward positions. In addition, we were busy digging foxholes and positioning our light machineguns. Col Edson set his forward command post (CP) up on Hill 120 just behind our forward positions.

As the troops went about their duties in the vicinity of Hill 120, we noticed the arrival of several jeeps of 11th Marines artillerymen. Then-Col Pedro A. Del Valle had moved his 3d Battalion with its twelve 105mm howitzer tubes closer to the ridge in direct support.

In the late afternoon of 10 September, both galleys were operating for Companies A and C near the Company A position on the river. We were served two hot meals that afternoon and evening, and then everyone settled down for the night, except for listening posts in the company positions. The only interruptions came when the usual shelling took place around midnight from the Japanese ships making their nightly visit. Things were fairly quiet until noon on the 11th when we heard air raid warnings throughout the perimeter. Japanese planes ignored the airfield this time and dropped a string of bombs along the main axis of the ridge hitting several of the bivouac areas as well as some of our Company B Marines constructing defensive positions.

On the afternoon of 11 September several patrols went into the jungle scouting out the Japanese movements. These patrols continued to report disquieting information that large, organized groups of Japanese were cutting trails through the rain forest to the east and south, safely hidden from aerial observation. They estimated the strength of the columns to be about 3,000 to 4,000. Additional patrols on the morning of 12 September convinced Red Mike that an enemy force was close by and led by Japanese Maj. General Kiyotaki Kawaguchi, the commander the Raiders had missed at Tasimboko.

Throughout the 12th, the Raiders and the paratroopers were feverishly working on their defensive positions. Double-apron barbed wire was being erected in open areas along the main ridge. In the jungle, Company C Marines hung strands of barbed wire from tree to tree and cut fields of fire through the undergrowth in front of machinegun positions.

That evening around 2130, the Japanese cruiser, *Sendai*, and three destroyers started a bombardment after a Japanese plane dropped a flare over Henderson Field. The searchlight from the *Sendai* illuminated the ridge as though it were daylight. In fact, it was so bright that I felt the ship's skipper could see me moving on the ridge.

After the bombardment ended, enemy flares were fired in front of Company B and Company C positions. The flares were quickly followed by the sounds of enemy soldiers moving through the undergrowth in front of Company C. There followed a vicious firefight, including several banzai charges, as the enemy encircled Company C's forward platoons, ultimately forcing their withdrawal back on the ridge.

During all of this action in the low-lying jungle between the ridge and the Lunga River, Company B's forward rifle units held their positions. Although the night of 12 September was a tense and sleepless one, not a shot was fired in our sector. It was an eerie and exhausting experience—each man in his foxhole fully expecting to see Japanese soldiers charging out of the jungle to his front at any moment.

The Fight to the Finish

Around noon on the 13th, Edson had Companies A and D press a counterattack along the Lunga near Company A's position and into the jungle forward of the ridge. Efforts there were unsuccessful, and in the early afternoon Red Mike withdrew Company B and the paratroopers to a new position just forward of Hill 120. At division the decision was made to move 2/5 to reinforce the Raiders, but they didn't arrive at the ridge until dusk, so the decision was made to effect the relief in the morning.

At the time Edson made the decision to withdraw the forces back up the hill, he also told me that I was the new commander of Company B". . . as of now!" The former commander, Maj Nickerson, had been evacuated that morning with bleeding ulcers. He also told me to have Company B occupy ". . . and hold!" a position on a nose of the main ridge just 100 yards or so forward of Hill 120. A deep, grassy ravine separated the two locations. The small ridge and ravine sloped off into the jungle. Within the new defensive positions there were gaps between company positions as well as between platoon positions because the distance from the ridge to the river was considerable—about 1,000 yards—all in thick jungle. In effect the Raiders established platoon strongpoints (later we referred to them as speed bumps) reinforced with Company E machineguns. There was no time to erect protective wire.

Major Brown, the battalion operations officer, led our 2d Platoon into position on the extreme right flank of the company position. I placed the understrength 1st Platoon (24 Marines plus a machinegun section) into the jungle flat to the east where they were positioned about 200 yards from the ridge astride a trail generally parallel to the ridge. I placed the understrength

3d Platoon (20 Marines plus a machinegun section) in the center along a small ridge. There was no company reserve.

I placed my command section—myself, 1st Sgt Brice Maddox, Cpl Gann, and a new replacement private first class messenger a few yards to the rear of the frontline on the reverse slope. As the foxholes were being dug and the positions hardened, the only communications we had was a hand-held walkie-talkie radio. As it turned out, wire communications never was established. Although the walkie-talkie was ineffective in the jungle, it performed well in open terrain, especially when Edson was operating from Hill 120— as he was doing most of that night.

Edson returned to the Company B CP at about 1730 to scan the ridge and jungle to the south with his binoculars . . . Red Mike's face was grim. His ever-present messenger/runner, Cpl Walter Burak, was close by. As Edson prepared to go, he turned to me and said, "John, this is it. We are the only ones between the Japanese and the airfield. You must hold this ground." Then he and Burak departed around 1800.

Shortly after dark the Japanese attacked, attempting to exploit the gap between our 2d Platoon and the Company D engineers on the right flank. At 1930 the 1st Platoon was almost cut off and overrun. In both cases, individuals and squads were scattered as they worked their way back to the reserve position on Hill 120. During this time, the artillery had been firing preplanned barrages forward of the frontlines.

Meanwhile the 3d Platoon was confronted with sporadic rifle fire together with a few enemy hand grenades that caused no casualties. The paratroopers on the left and the Company D engineers on our right also received sporadic firing and probes, but nothing like the assault on the center of Company B.

Col Del Valle's howitzers went into action with preplanned concentrations when the battle erupted on our company right flank. The initial impact areas were well forward of the action, but as it turned out they did extensive damage to a Japanese battalion in an assembly area preparing to attack Hill 120. In addition, the defensive actions of Company B's 2d and 3d Platoons disrupted and dispersed the Japanese battalion that had been forming for the attack up the ridge.

At about 2100 seven Japanese destroyers cruising off Lunga Point began a 30-minute bombardment of the airfield. At the end of the shelling, the ground attackers fired what appeared to be a mortar from the vicinity of our former company CP—just 200 yards forward of Hill 120's final defensive position. The round, trailing sparks, hit on the forward slope of the hill where it burned brightly for several minutes, causing dry kunai grass in the vicinity to catch fire.

The incendiary round served both as a signal for the Japanese to renew their attack and as a marker to identify their objective and allow them to regain their sense of direction. During the attack, Raiders from both the 1st and 2d Platoons were scattered and ended up as lonely, scared individuals or in small groups. Those lucky enough remained intact as a squad. The goal of all was to reach Hill 120, which was already in a "last-ditch" defensive mode.

One of those individuals was PFC Edgar Shephard, who was wounded as the Japanese rushed through the position. PFC Frank Whittelsey had dragged Shephard to temporary safety in the underbrush. Whittelsey was killed moments later. With Whittelsey's death, Shephard was on his own. He crawled through the jungle toward the rear, stopping only when onrushing Japanese came close. Slowly and painfully he made his way through the old galley and bivouac area where he was pulled to safety. Pharmacist's Mate Karl Coleman found Shephard and patched up the three bullet holes through his left upper arm, his chest—leaving a punctured right lung—and his right shoulder. He was evacuated the next day to the division field hospital and then back to the States. He recovered and rejoined the 1st Marine Division in time for landings at Cape Gloucester, Peleliu, and Okinawa

At the height of the battle, I was in radio communications with Red Mike. He had an 11th Marines forward observer (FO) with him. 1st Sgt Maddox, with my command group, got on the radio with the FO and walked the howitzer rounds along the ridge blunting the ongoing Japanese attack.

About 2230 two red flares arced above the 3d Platoon position and impacted on Hill 120. The whole area was made plain to the oncoming Japanese gathering at the jungle's edge. Edson, near his forward CP on Hill 120, did not want to use the radio, so he ordered the reliable Burak to get a message to me. Burak crawled out to the frontline, cupped his hands and yelled, "John Wolf! This is Burak. Do you hear me?" I heard him and recognized him, so I answered in the affirmative. Burak continued, "Red Mike says it's OK to withdraw!" That was a welcome message! I had the first sergeant work with the FO to lay down a covering barrage in front of our company position, and then in 5 minutes I had him lead the men to where the road cuts across the ridge and await further orders.

I prepared for the withdrawal by moving along the defense line to inform the squad leaders of the imminent move. I then pulled my Raiders back to the reverse slope of the spur as the enemy raked the position with rifle and machinegun fire. Miraculously, none of our Marines were hit. After lobbing the few remaining hand grenades we had, my Raiders went down through the waist-high kunai grass in the ravine to the faint road east of Hill 120. As we moved, the artillery let loose a hellacious barrage that rolled across the spine of the ridge and into the adjoining jungle not more than 100 yards forward of the abandoned position.

Up along the ridge, both the paratroopers of Company B and my Raiders of Company B intermingled. Noncommissioned officers finally got the Marines sorted out around midnight. A withdrawal at night is often an invitation to a headlong flight, but the Marines of both units kept disciplined. Once I had my troops in position astride the dirt road, we remained in place until daylight. A few stragglers moving along the road were stopped and added to the defensive positions.

Red Mike moved on to meet with Capt Henry Torgeson, the new commander of the 1st Parachute Battalion. He told "Torgy" to counterattack to regain the left flank position and to tie in with the Raiders defensive line on Hill 120. Torgeson took charge of regrouping his Company B and moved toward the front. The counterattack by two understrength companies, launched after midnight, sputtered initially and then gained momentum urged on by Torgeson. The nearly exhausted and bloodied paratroopers soon succeeded in checking and then throwing back the renewed Japanese assault on the left, including the recently vacated spur extending off the ridge. This fighting was particularly heavy and costly to both the enemy and our paratroopers.

Edson had returned to his forward CP and called the division CP to report that he had withdrawn to his final defensive position. At the time, 2/5 was poised to afford relief at dawn. There were to be several more banzai charges at the Raiders during the remainder of the night, but they were stopped by a combination of rifles, machineguns, Browning automatic rifles, bayonets, and knives.

Near dawn Kawaguchi's bid for the airfield slowed and then stopped. Torgeson's paratroopers evicted the Japanese from the left flank. Henderson Field was safe. The battle for "Bloody Ridge" was essentially over. At about 0400, companies of 2/5 began to slip through to stiffen the ridge. At daylight, the remainder of 2/5 relieved the ridge defenders. Soon after, Edson asked for an airstrike to be conducted, and three P-400s caught a large number of Japanese soldiers in the open beyond Hill 100.

By 0800 many Raiders were on the reverse slope of Hill 120 smoking cigarettes, awaiting word to return to the coconut grove. By 1200 we were all back in the bivouac area near the coconut grove. The ridge was now being called "Bloody Ridge" or "Raiders' Ridge." But finally it became known as "Edson's Ridge."

Casualties

There have been disputes over the number of casualties suffered by both sides. In his seminal book, *Guadalcanal* (Random House, 1960), author Richard Frank places the number of combined Raider and paratrooper casualties at 263 with 59 either killed in action or missing. Frank admits that the number of Japanese casualties is hard to assess, but through records research, he believed that the numbers could well have exceeded 800 killed or missing.

We found PFC Whittelsey while out on patrol on 16 September, and we buried him where he had fallen—". . . 1,000 yards south of Henderson Field, just forward of the front lines on Lunga Ridge . . ." as reported in the terse language of the Muster Roll. The jungle held his remains for 47 years. In 1989 a native farmer dug up the remains uncovering some bones and a dog tag with the name Frank R. Whittelsey. After confirming the identity of the remains, PFC Frank Russell Whittelsey finally returned home. On Memorial Day, 25 May 1992, in the presence of dozens of relatives, childhood friends, and comrades-in-arms, his ashes were interred with full military honors near the graves of his parents in Pittsfield, MA. *Requiescant in pace*—Rest in peace!

Afterthought

In composing this story about my experiences during the battle of Bloody Ridge, I have had a renewed appreciation, not only for this experience, but also for the many times I have had other moments to confirm my decision to enlist in the Marine Corps in February 1941 and follow a career with a special group of America's best—the Marines!

★   ★   ★   ★   ★

Captain Sweeney was awarded the Navy Cross for his leadership during the battles of September 12-14 and survived the war. Col. Edson also received the Medal of Honor following the battle. The Japanese would attack with an even larger force on October 23-26 with the 17th Army under Lieutenant General Harukichi Hyakutake, but they were once again destroyed. The Japanese conceded defeat at Guadalcanal and withdrew the rest of their forces from the island the first week of February 1943.

Woman Marine

THERESA KARAS YIANILOS

Women have been part of the Marine Corps since 1918 when it was authorized to enlist women for clerical duties to free up battle-ready marines to go overseas into action. This tradition continued in the Second World War when Commandant General Thomas Holcolm authorized the Marine Corps Women's Reserve in November 1942. One of the young women who volunteered was Theresa Karas Yianilos from Tonawanda, New York. In January 1944 Theresa and her training class were sent to Camp Lejune, North Carolina, for basic training. In the following chapter, she describes the day that marks a right of passage for all marines as they came face to face with their drill instructor for the first time.

> MARCH OF THE WOMEN MARINES
> Marines!
> We are the women members
> Of our fighting Corps
> Marines!
> The name is known
> From burning sands to ice bound shores
> Marines!
> We serve that men
> May fight on land and air and sea
> Marines!
> The Eagle, Globe and Anchor carry on
> To make men free

★　★　★　★　★

Our next instructor was another male Marine and rather young, somewhere in his middle twenties. His hat was of World War I vintage with four dents in it. He stood there calmly and surveyed our fumbling efforts with a menacing stare. We had been brought before the infamous drill instructor.

We assembled four abreast and with outstretched arms reached for each other's shoulders to judge our distance while this short stocky male Marine sergeant watched us carefully. His whole body conveyed his utter disgust and boredom with each and every one of us. We could see in his eyes that his judgment of us was not very high.

We had been prepared for this meeting with the D.I. the night before by our platoon sergeant. She had peppered her lectures with warnings that foreshadowed the trials that awaited us.

"After the D.I. gets through with you, you'll appreciate how soft I am on you *Goons*. He is straight from P.I." she said.

P.I. Parris Island!—the notorious Boot Camp for Marines, three hundred and twenty miles away—where they went in as boys and came out as men. I guess they were going to try to do the same to us.

Our platoon sergeant moved back with respect and reverence. The drill instructor replaced her at the head of the platoon.

He stared at us, measuring each of us, in what seemed to be an inordinately long time.

The suspense was uncomfortable.

He then lifted his red face with the sunburned nose towards the magnificent blue North Carolina sky and moaned loudly in great pain, "Holy Mother! First the dogs! Then the niggers! Now the women!"

Then he jutted his chin toward us and from the bottom of his throat came the voice of thunder, "*Knock It Off!*"

All the giggling and friendly chattering stopped as suddenly as if someone had clicked off a radio.

"Some of you *People* are chewing gum! Get rid of it. Don't throw it on the deck. It's yours!"

The wads of Wrigley's spearmint slid down in one gulp.

So this was the Marine Corps' secret weapon. The D.I., the one man responsible for turning out the finest sea soldier in the world. The two-hash marks on his sleeve proclaimed his eight years of service and the dulled insignia on his collar and hat had turned green from the salt spray and his sea duty.

He must have joined when he was seventeen. The Sharpshooter's Cross hung over his left pocket and dangling next to it were three bars and a wreath for pistol, machine gun, bayonet and automatic rifle marksmanship.

I eyed his insignia. Mine were so shining new, proclaiming that I was a Boot. I wish I had his salty antique ones.

"*Atten-Hut!*" His command vibrated across the field.

"Line up forty inches back to breast! In even rows. Square your rows!"

That was not so easy especially with all the big busted women in our row. Bertha came from robust Norwegian stock from Decorah, Iowa, and had a bust measurement of forty-three inches, most of them fore rather than aft. And several of the Boots were tall. Lining up shoulder to shoulder was difficult.

He began his cadence count. "Fo'wd harch! Won Up Ah Reep! Reep foah youh laft!"

I didn't understand a word he said. I only felt the rhythm—one, two, three-four—the left. One, two, left, right, three, four. It was a dance. Not fast like the Jitterbug or the Boogie Woogie but more of a Lambeth Walk.

He began a chant in time with the steps:

> *Yoh hot a good home and youh laft!*
> *Yoh had a good home and youh laft!*
> *Yoh laft!*
> *Laft reet laft!*

"All right! Platoon! Count cadence count!" his voice bellowed.

At first our chanting was timid, our soprano voices week, as we chorused, synchronizing the words with the beat of our footsteps.

> *We had a good home*
> *And we laft!*
> *We had a good home*
> *And we laft!*
> *One two three four*
> *One! Two!*
> *Three, Four!*

"I can't hear you!" He bellowed.

He must have been hard of hearing because we were shouting our heads off. That was not easy for some of us who had been taught since childhood that a lady never raised her voice. Nevertheless the chant grew louder and louder until the hypnotic rhythm and rhyme made it impossible to be on the wrong foot.

We marched on that asphalt pavement back and forth. Each time as we came perilous close to the river, he always commanded a "*to the reeh harch"* which meant "to the rear march." That called for placing one foot behind the other and twisting around and reversing the direction.

The road disappeared right into the river which had no beach and became deep immediately.

This was the road used by amphibious tractors and vehicles, LCVP for landing craft vehicle personnel, which was a combination boat and car. They could be driven by the Fleet Marine Forces from ships off shore directly from the water onto the land. That is what the Marine Corps was all about; why Marines were called Sea-soldiers. They were amphibious and were trained to fight on land and on the sea. Special vehicles had been developed in order for them to make the assaults and establish beachheads.

Our platoon marched straight towards the river again.

We waited for the order to reverse our direction but the command wasn't given.

We approached closer and closer to the deep river's edge. Several ahead of me fell out of step and so did I in anticipation of the command of *"to the rear harch"* to place the right foot behind the left and swing around the moment it was given.

The tension mounted as the river loomed only a few feet away.

I broke first into a fit of giggles. Tension does that to me sometimes.

Glints of iridescent colors on the water made an image inside my head come alive that struck me so funny I could no longer hold in my laughter. My mind's eye saw twenty-eight hats floating on the water, as twenty eight-women, me included, were *one up-a-reeped* to our doom, obedient to the end, while the waters went glub-glub over our heads, drowning us all. It would solve the drill instructor's problem of how he'd like to see us disappear, along with the dogs and niggers, of course.

"Platoon! Halt! Right Face!"

We stopped dead in our tracks inches away from the water's edge. I was right. He had been testing for obedience. Not a muscle moved.

The D.I. glowered. We stood at attention staring straight ahead and I tried to look through him but it was impossible.

He stood three inches away. He was in my face, in my space.

You! Boot! Two steps forward!"

I did as I was commanded, a little frightened but unable to turn off that silly image in my head, which left a wide grin on my face as I tried to control the giggling.

"Put your hands akimbo on your waist!"

I did so with the whole platoon watching, as puzzled as I. I didn't know what was coming next and neither did they.

"Wave them back and forth!"

I flapped my elbows.

"Now tell me! What kind of bird are you?"

I searched his eyes and red face for a clue. A long moment passed by. Bird? Was I supposed to answer? A bluebird of happiness? Another giggle hit me. A parrot? Polly want a cracker? Of course! The American eagle! The bird in the Marine Corps emblem!

"A wise bird! That's what you are! A wise bird!"

"Oh, no, Sir!" I said most sincerely.

He stared unsmiling. I returned his gaze the smile no longer on my lips.

"I wasn't laughing at you—" I started to explain.

"Who gave you permission to speak, Boot?" He was shouting but that didn't frighten me as much as the women officers who could dispense orders and discipline without raising their voices.

He stared right into my face and forced me to look right back.

I suppose this kind of approach might be effective with the male recruits, but any female who hadn't learned how to stare down a boy by the fifth grade had better plan on being a spinster. I remembered that the only way I could get a boy's attention in the third row, fifth seat, across the room, was to simply have a staring contest. It worked every time and soon he was carrying the books home from school, his and mine. But this was a different kind of staring contest and it was uncomfortable. With great relief, this game broke up after a long interminable minute.

I hastily obeyed his command to "Step back into ranks!"

I did a smart neat turn about-face and did exactly as I was told.

The D.I. made our platoon repeat the same marching drill over and over, but he never took us that close to the river's edge again. His dented field hat that gave him a quaint World War One look sat square on his head and bounced up and down.

I caught his stern look watching me more than once. I would have liked to take his hand and tell him I would curb my silly imagination and not to worry about me but of course, that was impossible; the military discipline said no fraternizing.

The D.I. rode us hard. We saw him every day for one-hour drilling on the parade ground. He was intense about his mission and assignment. He had volunteered to transform civilian women into Marines in forty-two days of Boot Camp. When he finished with all of us, we would have the military bearing of Marines.

After the first week, we could see how far we had come. Not that we had been given any kind of praise. It was something we had guessed at by ourselves just watching each other.

He always greeted us as if he had inherited Job's Lot when we came into his life. His uniform was always immaculate yet there was always a rumpled exhausted aura about him even before he spent the twenty minutes teaching us the intricate steps of *Close order drill.*

His day must have been very full teaching the many other groups as well as ours. He was one of several male D.I.'s teaching the Women Marines.

Close Order Drill was a ballet of graceful movements to the beat of *One-two. Three-four. Left foot. Right foot.*

Steps had to be in precision: everyone on the same foot at the same time. Sometimes fast as in a tap dance.

"*Double time*"—one hundred eighty steps a minute.

"*Quick time*"—one hundred twenty steps a minute.

We responded instantaneously to his commands—or tried to.

"*Left flank! Harch!*" This command was one of the most difficult but most graceful drill step.

Our flanking oblique movements pivoting to the guide at the end of our row opened like a hand painted fan to reveal a beautiful picture for a few moments then it closed. Timing was crucial and it took many days to do it right.

Our platoon had it perfect until one day a momentary confusion sent me in the wrong direction and gave the D.I. another cause for a display of apoplexy. I bumped into Jenny Mae who was the guide and confused her into thinking she had made the mistake and was on the wrong foot. She shuffled her feet. Our row did the same. The row behind us shuffled their feet and everyone fell out of step. The beautiful flanking movement disintegrated before his eyes.

Now we stood before the platoon, and once again he singled me out as he vented his frustration.

"You! Boot! You have gotten on the wrong foot with me from the beginning! You! Right guide! Don't you know your left foot from your right?"

My poor Bunkie! Shy sweet Jenny Mae had been chosen guide because she was so tall. She died every time she had to stand there by herself.

There was one thing about my Alabama buddy that we understood: she was very sensitive to her short-comings and wanted to please everyone. Her eyes filled with tears and she hiccupped a few sobs and then some heart-rendering ones.

The D.I. hurriedly ordered us back into the ranks.

Jenny Mae dissolving into tears because she had displeased him had thrown him into confusion.

I just knew the male Marine Boots did not react this way. Nor did the rest of us, generally speaking.

We practiced the same steps over and over day after day, but it was the drill command "*To the rear harch!*" that turned our formation into a Laurel and Hardy comedy routine just when we had it down pat.

Fenton got caught that time; Fenton who was bucking for officer's training, who was always perfect in obeying commands. She couldn't help it either.

The command called for putting the right toe behind the left heel and pivoting in the opposite direction without losing the beat and to continue marching in the opposite direction.

Six of these commands, given in rapid staccato in the middle of a march, had some of us going East, some squinting against the afternoon sun in the West, bumping into each other in a giant patty-cake baker's man routine.

Fenton couldn't restrain her guffaws. Seeing her lose control and break down, of all people, the one who was determined to follow each command with religious exactitude; who always asked questions at all lectures displaying intense interest, even at the impromptu informal talks held in the corner of our squadroom at night; who always sounded off in the correct manner, name first then asking for permission to speak; it was too much. I tried to hide my laughter but my shoulders gave me away and this triggered off the whole platoon. The laughter rolled like waves on the Pacific shores, spreading from one to another as we milled about.

So now Fenton and I stood in front of the platoon with the smiles wiped off our faces. Fenton was mortified and contrite.

Our platoon sergeant continued the lecture that the D.I. had given all the way to the barracks. Her Navy language was nastier and her tongue was sharper than that of the D.I. who usually glowered without saying a word.

"*Stupid! Dope Heads! Snafus! Sad Sacks! Knuckle Heads! Eight Balls!*
The Navy jargon was cute. No one minded hearing her call us those names.

It wasn't real swearing as the men received from the badgering of their D.I.'s who lived with them and watched over them twenty-four hours a day.

Day after day, the D.I. found something wrong with one of us.

I got more than my share of attention.

He didn't like anyone to smile at him, and I learned "*to wipe that smile off my face*," but his disposition remained stern and sour all the same.

"He just doesn't like Women Marines," I said. "I am just a symbol. I refuse to take it personally."

"One of us should bell the cat," said Fenton, the grade school teacher.

"I'd say his trouble is just the opposite," said Laramie. "When a bull is put out to pasture and can't get at the heifers, he gets ornery."

"You all know he can't talk to us. He's assigned to teach us military bearing and discipline through *close order drill* and nothing else."

"Teaching Women Marines is a volunteer assignment. They have to draw straws for it."

"You mean they put us in the same category as going on combat patrol?"

"I can see their CO now," said Brooklyn. "See here, Marines! I need volunteers! Who is going to teach the women which foot is their *loft! Their loft! Reep for your loft!*" She went into a burlesque of peg-legging it across the room.

A song that was very popular, especially with the men, came on the radio and I joined in with my alto:

A woman is two faced . . . A worrisome thing to let you to sing
The blues in the night

Joan said, "Terry, be serious. You're part of the trouble. He's got his eye on you."

"I don't care for his type," I scoffed. "I want someone like *Walking John*. So far I haven't seen any Marine like him. Well, maybe, a couple of those guys at Eighth and Eye in Washington. They were what I expected Marines to be."

"*Walking John?*" asked Pittsburgh as she pinned up her wet hair. It was a chore she had to do every night since the short hair-cut I had promised her hadn't turned it into a natural feather curl as mine had.

"He's that tall handsome Marine in dress blues on the recruiting rosters who is forever marching! I even have a crush on the sketch of the marching Marine in leggings that was done for World War I."

"C'mon Terry. Leave the tall ones for us big gals," said Texas who was sitting on her bunk playing solitaire across from Sherry who was always writing letters to her husband in the submarine service.

"I can't help it. I don't get little mice unless they have a certain look. Strong, determined, handsome, big. I can't describe him exactly. I'll just know when he happens to me!"

"Little mice? What are those?" Brooklyn asked.

"That feeling you get up and down inside when you kiss someone special—makes colors appear inside your head and feels like an elevator button got pushed."

"You'd be surprised how big some of these little guys are," grinned Brooklyn with one of her double entendre comments.

"Size doesn't matter where it counts the most."

Pittsburgh said, "I think the D.I. is cute."

"That's settles it. The D.I. belongs to Pittsburgh," said Laramie in a spirit of generosity.

"As soon as radio silence is lifted and restriction is over, and we can talk to the men around here, I'll try to make time with the D.I. I wonder if he's Catholic with the same Pope as mine?" Pittsburgh asked.

"He certainly seems to be. He's always saying "Jesus Christ" when we foul up."

"My Dad thinks if the Catholics keep having such big families they will take over the country and we'll have a Catholic president some day."

"That will never happen no matter how many kids the Catholics have. There are too many Protestants."

"The Mormons beat the Catholics any day or the Protestants on that score. My great-grandfather had seven wives, and thirty eight children," said Shauna. "He lived to be ninety-four. Everyone of his wives dies before him and his last wife was only seventeen when he married her."

"What kind of men do you have out west?"

"It's the air around Salt Lake City. It is very pure and clear. Mormons don't drink alcohol. They don't smoke and they don't drink coffee either. That has got a lot to do with keeping a body fit."

"What do you do for recreation in Salt Lake City?"

"We dance a lot. Always having dances."

"That'll work it off every time," said Brooklyn.

We packed all our civilian clothes and shipped them back home in our suitcases. We were given duffel bags to hold our gear and spent the evening stenciling our last names on the green canvas bags.

Gone were the awkward mismatched gangling rainbow-clad saddle-shoed individualists.

We had metamorphosed into chic uniformed Marines, brisk and smart, professional from the highly polished cordovan brown oxfords, brown leather gloves to the brim of our red-corded hats and our *Victory Red* lips.

No longer could we be called dames, tomatoes, broads, chicks or any of the other terms of familiarity!

Like butterflies emerging from their cocoons, suddenly we were neat, trim, beautiful American Marines. One look at us told the story. We were a good looking, outstanding group of women. We were definitely not *BAMS*.

A constant stream of women passed before the large full-length mirror, which was a fixture of every Marine barracks, It was nailed on the wall at the exit and entrance of each squadroom. Each Marine had to check his appearance before going before the public. It was an order.

The order for the uniform of the day called for winter greens. It said so on the bulletin board, but that was one notice no one had to read. The excitement of putting on our uniforms for the first time vibrated throughout the barracks.

The first morning of the wearing of the uniform was almost a disaster for the platoon sergeant.

She called, "Muster! Fall out in formation! In five minutes!" Formation in front of the barracks was the first drill each and every morning.

Her platoon didn't make a move towards the exit. A silly problem had come up, which no one had foreseen.

Five minutes later she yelled, "Move it! Move it! Why are you Boots standing around?"

The women had piled up at the mirror in the hall and had squeezed into the *head* in front of all the other mirrors. Our whole squadroom of one hundred and twenty-four women were immobilized in the barracks for the dumbest reason.

Only one or two girls knew how to tie a four-in-hand tie. They were trying their best to teach those who had forgotten the instructions from the night before.

We women knew how to pin a diaper three ways, do needlepoint, embroider, crochet, knit, crewel, and bake cookies from scratch, but none of us knew how to tie a man's four-in-hand tie that was to be worn with our khaki shirts.

"Who knows how to tie a tie?" The wail echoed through the barracks. We were all thumbs and the girls piled up trying to help each other.

"Not that way! You make the loop first. Keep your thumb in place."

"How come the men can do it so easily?"

We put our new khaki green trench coats on and folded the red wool field muffler over the knotted ties and marched out in rhythm to the cadence count. We were impressed with ourselves and wanted to impress the world. The only male who would see us that day was the drill instructor.

"*Won Up A Reep—Reep Fo Yoh Laft!*"

Heads high, shoulders back and arms lightly at the sides, we strutted proudly, the thrill of achievement and glory in ourselves visible in the briskness of our step.

"Marines! You are ready for battalion review. Now put that laft foot down!"

No one missed the inflection on the first word that the D.I. called out. He gave every one of us a shot of pride that had an instant effect. The joy of being called Marines, no longer *Goon* or *Boot* was overwhelming. A warm wave of love flowed invisibly but tangibly from all of us to our D.I., the man who had brought us to this point.

Our backs straightened up more. You could hear every one of the left feet stamping down hard as the heels of our oxfords punched ridges into the squishy asphalt made soft by the sun. Half of us got stuck and it spoiled the look of the formation.

"*Jesus Christ and Holy Mother of Mary!*" cried the D.I. who wasn't allowed to really curse as he could with the men.

"One good thing about taking the Virgin's name in vain, it proves he's Catholic," Pittsburgh said with great satisfaction at the discovery.

The daily marching and exercises in the North Carolina sun began to show on all of us. I never felt healthier, stronger, nor prettier, nor happier. I liked what I saw in the mirror, my new figure, my windburn complexion and firmer muscles. I no longer slouched.

"Look! I have Betty Grable legs," I boasted.

"Mine are Flat Foot Floogies!"

"It's these sitting up exercises every morning, rain or shine, that is reshaping me," lamented Joan. She pressed her fingers together in front of her in a mocking of the NCO physical instructor. "This is going to put me into a B cup. I'll be ruined in the rag business."

"That particular exercise is supposed to make the upper arms strong enough to carry the M-1 rifle in one hand above the water when you're storming the beaches," said Fenton.

"That's fine for the men. What do you think it's doing to the women?"

Joan brought out a tape measure immediately. Groans and squeals of delight alternated with each measurement that was announced. Not every girl was happy. Big breasts spoiled the lines of the Marine Corps uniform just as big hips did.

Laramie sat on the wooden deck and walked five paces forward and backward on her buttocks. "This one is great for your butt. It firms the rear and thighs so you can climb off the debarkation ropes off the sides of LCVPs. Of course, we're not going to have to do that."

""Well, you won't spread into a *BAM* with that exercise."

"How about this one, where you crawl on your belly and have to keep your fanny close to the ground so you won't get it shot off?" I knelt on all fours to demonstrate.

"If you do it properly, it will strength your pelvis for labor pains and to relieve menstrual cramps. If you kick your leg out like this, it will strengthen your uterus." Someone fell to the deck to demonstrate.

Brooklyn flipped over on her stomach to show how to improve the inner thighs while getting shot at.

Other girls from the squadroom fell to the deck. With all the huffing and puffing and laughter, no one heard the sergeant call "Atten-hut!"

Our lieutenant stood next to her, smiling at our gyration.

"At ease," said the lieutenant. "What's that you are doing?"

"Sexercises, Man!" I said forgetting to sound off my name first, trying to salute on my stomach and jump up to attention.

"That is the Marine Corps spirit," said our pretty senior officer. "We must be strong enough to meet all challenges."

Every day we mustered with enthusiasm and high spirits on the parade ground for the Marine Corps exercises under the warm North Carolina sky, so unexpectedly blue and sunny for the winter month of January. Some of the other earlier platoons wore peanut suits, which were made out of tan cotton fabric that wrinkled easily and had old fashioned bloomer shorts with elastic around the bottom. But, we were the 24th Training Battalion and we missed out when the supply ran short. We still were a motley group in our various white shorts and blouses.

Being called a *BAM*, a *broad ass Marine*, wasn't as bad as being one. We took the exercises seriously.

To be strong enough to carry on the traditions of the Marine Corps was the aim of every woman Marine. The trick was to look as if we weren't able to "take over," otherwise the men would panic further. Since womankind had been playing the game of acting the weaker set for centuries, the instructions to follow the male lead were more of the same.

It was going to be difficult to hide our strength and brains in the same old ways once we were called upon to prove our capabilities at the same time. The training companies that had preceded ours who were assigned to duty were showing the Corps what we women were made of, and already they were doing jobs that had always been the bailiwick of the male Marine.

Women had taken over the bus system on Camp Lejeune and Cherry Point. They drove those six by six military trucks for Motor Transport and had the responsibility of dispatching, as well as the maintenance and repairs, of the largest of those green dinosaur trucks that transported the men into bivouac areas in the deepest roughest boondocks. Yet their trim neat figures belied the work they did as bus and truck drivers.

We Women Marines had to tread softly and carry a big stick no matter what our duty was.

Captain Towle, our CO, made a special lecture on this very subject, and pointed out the pioneer terrain we were about to traverse. She was a hard-charger and G.I., as military as the new Commandant of the Marine Corps, Major General Alexander Vandegrift. But, she also was the prime example of the Woman Marine who hid her steel under a pretty face and a non-threatening soft voice.

"Our position requires diplomacy," she said. "We not only have to relieve the men for combat, we must demonstrate we are capable of doing whatever is required, cheerfully with a willing spirit. We must provide that the high standards of the Marine Corps shall be safe in our hands and prove to each Marine that women are necessary to help win this war."

The message came through loud and clear.

We women had to prove our worth but still know our place. We were equal, but some Marines were more equal than others. The Corps could make it very hard if we asked for too much. We had to learn the written rules of the chain of command, but, the unwritten rules, the ones that were custom and tradition, had to be understood by intuition.

Men had the right of way. It wasn't much different in civilian life.

The Marine Corps was more restrictive than the Army or Navy towards the distaff side of its inductees.

"Women Marines will not be sent overseas, into combat areas nor will they serve aboard ships."

The WAACs, Navy nurses, and Red Cross women were in London and in other parts of the world where they had gone once the Allies and Americans had secured the areas. The WAFs ferried planes from one place to another. But, the Women Marines were going to stay in the United States.

★   ★   ★   ★   ★

On June 12, 1948, Congress passed the Women's Armed Services Integration Act authorizing the acceptance of women into the regular component of the Marine Corps. Today, women comprise over six percent of the Corps serving in 93 percent of all occupational fields.

Navajo Weapon

SALLY McCLAIN

One of the most enduring legends to come from the Marine Corps during World War II was the use of Navajo Indians as code talkers. The idea for use of the Navajo language as a code came from Philip Johnston, a World War I veteran who was raised on a reservation as the son of a missionary. He was one of the few people outside the Navajo who could speak the language fluently and understood its complexities. He also knew that Native American languages—notably Choctaw—had been used in World War I to encode messages. In early 1942 Johnston staged tests for Major General Clayton B. Vogel, the commanding general of Amphibious Corps, Pacific Fleet, and his staff to convince them of the Navajo language's value as code. In simulated combat conditions, the Navajo proved they could encode, transmit, and decode a three-line English sentence in twenty seconds, a feat that machines of the time took thirty minutes to accomplish. Vogel recommended to the Commandant of the Marine Corps that the Marines recruit 200 Navajos. By May that year, groups of Navajo were being trained to perform the special duty. Sally McClain documented the history of the Navajo code talkers in her book, *Navajo Weapon: The Navajo Code Talkers*. The following chapter describes their deployment and contributions to the Solomons campaign.

> Were it not for the Navajos, the Marines would never have taken Iwo Jima.
> —Major Howard Connor, 5th Marine Division

★   ★   ★   ★   ★

Cape Gloucester, New Britain—Operation Dexterity

New Britain a crescent-shaped island 370 miles long and 40-50 miles wide, belongs to a group of islands in the Bismarck Archipelago. This part of the Pacific Ocean, lying between New Britain and the Solomon Islands, was known as "the Slot." The purpose of Operation Dexterity was to capture and secure the airfield located on Cape Gloucester at the tip of New Britain.

The north shore of Cape Gloucester was the designated landing area for the 1st Marine Division under the command of General William H. Rupertus. This would be the first action in which the division participated since Guadalcanal. A two-pronged attack on Borgen Bay at Silimati Point and Tauali was set for December 26, 1943.

The Japanese defenders consisted of 9,500 men of the 65th Brigade under the command of Major General Iwao Matsuda, the commander of the forces that had fought on Guadalcanal. A large number of Matsuda's men were already on half-rations and suffering from malaria, dysentery, and numerous fungal infections. Monsoon rains had destroyed their primitive shelters and their health. Matsuda's troops, as physically depleted as they were, would put up a desperate fight to the death to keep the United States from taking another Japanese-held island. The main defense on Aogiri Ridge was laced with 37 bunkers that were mutually supported with interconnecting tunnels.

Colonel Julian N. Frisbie's 7th Regiment landed on Yellow 2 Beach at Tauali, wheeled left, and made their way toward the edge of the airfield. Colonel William J. Whaling's 3rd Battalion landed on Yellow 1 Beach and headed toward Target Hill. By noon of D-Day, the 450-foot Target Hill had been secured without opposition, and by nightfall the marines had established a 1,000-yard defense perimeter.

Matsuda's troops counterattacked with Major Shinchi Takabe's infantry against the center of the perimeter held by the 2nd Battalion/7th Regiment. Amid a torrential rain, Lieutenant Colonel Odell Conoly's company managed to hold off the attack until reinforced by the men of Battery D.

During this attack, Alex Williams was running a message to the 2nd Battalion because its radio was out. On the return trip he became lost and barely escaped being shot by a fellow marine who mistook him for a Japanese defender. "It was raining and the first order of the day was, 'No lights.' Not even a match for a cigarette. I was lost, crawling around trying to feel my way back when I ran into this marine. He asked me for the 'password,' and I thought it was lame duck, so I said it. He asked me to say it again. 'Lame duck.' I guess I didn't say it too well because he said, 'You son of a bitch!' and stuck a bayonet in my back ready to kill me when I tumbled backwards into a foxhole. That foxhole just happened to have Sergeant Curtis in it. He asked, 'What the hell is going on?" I told him that this marine thinks I am a Jap and wants to kill me. Curtis cleared up the matter, and I stayed in his foxhole the rest of the night. Our jobs didn't always involve the radio or telephone. If an urgent message needed to be delivered, right or wrong, we delivered it. We risked being questioned and shot at by our own men, but we got those messages through."

The next day the 2nd Battalion began its forward advance from Tauali to Mount Talawe. It met with fierce opposition that lasted five days. James Nahkai, a code talker in the H&S Battalion, relayed artillery strikes in support of the 2nd Battalion's advance. "Whatever the Colonel wanted to relay to the battalions we sent in code," Nahkai recalled. "If they wanted a certain sector hit we relayed the coordinates and strike time in code to each battalion. We directed the fire of the 105 mm weapons and we never sent a wrong coordinate during the entire operation."

Aogiri Ridge

On December 28 Brigadier General Lemuel Shepherd was ordered to clear the area from Borgen Bay to Aogiri Ridge. The ridge served as the Japanese supply route, and to keep it open they would defend it to the last man. At the base of Aogiri Ridge, the second code talker of the war was killed. William McCabe witnessed Ralph Morgan's death.

"It was funny [strange] the way he got killed. The men were in a foxhole under a tree when a shell landed but didn't explode; it just fell apart and a large piece of schrapnel hit him right on the chin and split his head clean off. He never knew what hit him. We just stood there and looked at him, we didn't know what to do. It didn't seem real."

General Rupertus began planning assaults on three targets that surrounded the Japanese defenses around Borgen Bay: Target Hill, Hill 660, and Aogiri Ridge. On December 29 the Japanese launched their strongest attack near the Cape Gloucester airstrip. Captain Buckley's company fought and attained control of Hill 660, which enabled them to direct artillery barrages against the entrenched enemy and aid the 2nd Battalion/7th Regiment in securing the airfield.

The advance of Shepherd's units toward Aogiri Ridge crossed through swamps that led to a stream 300 yards inland. The forward scouts crossed first. Nothing untoward happened. Then the first platoon began to cross.

"Suicide Creek," as it came to be known, was a swift, shallow, twisting waterway that ran between steep banks 10-20 feet high. The marines did not know that the Japanese had created a moat-like stronghold laced with pillboxes and machine gun nests that were fortified with dirt and coconut logs and could easily sweep both banks.

When the Japanese opened fire on the exposed marines, utter chaos erupted. Men were pinned down with no room to withdraw. Scouts eventually managed to creep across undetected and locate the entrenched Japanese. After the positions were relayed to headquarters via Navajos assigned to Shepherd's communication post, bulldozers were ordered to move into position to begin cutting down the banks, thereby making a path for tanks. It took the bulldozers two days of working around the clock before the tanks could advance and begin the task of demolishing the Japanese strongholds. this action effectively ended the marines' futile attempt to cross Suicide Creek.

As the Japanese were desperately fighting to keep the marines from taking further ground, a replacement commander was giving Jimmy King Sr. a difficult time. "When a replacement battalion commander came in that didn't know all of the forward echelon personnel, they question what we were doing," King recalled. "They would ask us, 'What is the message, what are you saying?'" I told him not to bother me or talk to me because our orders were clear. No one with less than two stars had any business asking us about messages or what we were doing. I would say, 'Well, Mr. So and So, I hate to tell you this but I'm not authorized to tell you what this message is about or what that man is saying over the air. May I have your name, Lieutenant, or Captain, or Major So and So?' I answered directly to the message center Chief and to those with two stars and up, those below two stars didn't interfere with us."

Last Gasp

January 9 and 10 marked the last of the Japanese efforts to keep the supply route along Aogiri Ridge from being severed by the marines. Captain Buckley's weapons company massed a huge Navajo-directed artillery barrage that broke the Japanese defenses surrounding the base of Hill 660. Five days later Cape Gloucester was declared secure.

The successful campaigns on Bougainville and Cape Gloucester gave Allied forces important territory with which to strike at the heart of the Japanese Defense Command at Rabaul. The Navajo code was beginning to make its mark in combat situations, and Headquarters were duly notified. John Kinsel, Kee Etsicitty, Bill Toledo, James Nahkai, William McCabe,

Jimmy King, and others proved that they could send vital information without making a mistake or being deciphered. The Japanese made every effort to disrupt and distract the Navajo transmissions. They would scream, swear, bang pots, and yell, but they never succeeded.

When the code talkers returned with their units to their training areas on Hawaii, they spent long hours learning new terms that had been added to the code as well as long hours doing field exercises. It was hard work, but they knew firsthand the true value of the contribution they were making toward winning the war in the South Pacific.

The success of the code generated a request from Commander Air, South Pacific (ComAirSoPac) Lieutenant Commander L. R. Hird to transfer 10 Navajo code talkers to his command or six to eight weeks of temporary duty. The Air Corps was having an extremely difficult time getting pilots safely through the Slot. A Radio Counter Measures report stated: "Japanese land-based, fire-control and search-light-control radars, admittedly four years behind Allied developments, were instrumental in permitting the Japanese to shoot down our aircraft under unseen conditions. As such, they constituted a serious Air Force problem."

The ability of the Japanese radar to detect and decipher Air Corps flights and transmissions led to Hird's request. Paragraph 3 of his letter, dated January 7, 1944, stated:

> 3. These talkers are to be used on a voice air operational radio circuit at various Solomon Island air bases. While giving valuable assistance to ComAirSoPac they will be obtaining valuable experience on actual operating circuits during a period of time when this Corps does not require them for operational use. It is planned to send other groups to relieve this initial group at approximately six week intervals until they are required for Corps operations.

The staffing of the ComAirSoPac circuits with Navajo code talkers reduced the pilot fatality rate from 53 percent to less than 7 percent in a very short period of time. If the Japanese intelligence command in the field was feeling thwarted by the unidentifiable language traveling through radio and telephone circuits, personnel at Intelligence Headquarters in Nagasaki were feeling hopeful. During the last month of the winter of 1944, the Japanese could positively identify who was sending the messages they could not decipher. They were the Navajos, and the Japanese had one.

Joe Kieyoomia, POW

Joe Kieyoomia joined the Army in March 1941 with the idea that he would serve his two years and then return home. One week after he had been stationed in the Philippines, Pearl Harbor was attacked. The morning the Japanese raids began on the Bataan Peninsula, he knew that his hitch would probably be more than just the standard two years.

He survived the Bataan Death March only to be moved from camp to camp, finally ending up in Japan itself. The day he was removed from Camp O'Donnel, Philippines, his family was notified that he was "missing, presumed dead." He spent 1,240 days as a POW, moving from the Philippines to Hatashi, Matishima, and Nagasaki, Japan.

Kieyoomia believed one of the reasons he was moved to Japan was because the Japanese thought he was of Japanese ancestry. The pronunciation of his name, Key-oh-me, convinced them they could make him see the "light" and return to his true people. They would find out later just how wrong they were.

"One evening," Kieyoomia stated, "I was brought to the commander's quarters for questioning, and they asked me again, for the hundredth time, if I was an American. I told them I was an American Indian, but that only made them angry. 'You are American Japanese! Why are you fighting against your own people?' the commander shouted. The interpreter, a guy named Goon, understood that I was American Indian, but the interrogator didn't. When I refused to confess that I was Japanese, the interrogator hit me with a club, broke my ribs and then my wrist. When I refused to confess again, they dragged me back to the barracks and threw me in a cell.

"We had a British doctor named Whitfield who examined me," continued Kieyoomia, "but all he could do was bind my ribs and give me aspirin. Later that night the pain was so intense they took me to the infirmary. It wasn't much better there. They laid me flat on the floor with only a thin straw mat under me and checked me every four hours.

"Sometime later that month, Goon must have figured out that the talkers on the radio who couldn't be identified must be Indians," Kieyoomia said. "They were having a tough time deciphering the code, and they finally figured that I might be able to help them. When they first made me listen to the broadcasts, I couldn't believe what I was hearing. It sounded like Navajo, just not anything that made sense to me. I understood my language, but I could not figure out the code they were using. That made the interrogators very angry!

"They stripped off all my clothes and threw me out on the parade ground to coax me into cooperating. It was very cold out there, and my feet began to freeze to the ground. They left me out there about half an hour, then clubbed me back into the radio room. My feet were bleeding from being torn from the ground, but I still couldn't help them. They were trying to keep me alive to get something out of me. I liked hearing the Navajo language: it gave me hope. It told me that American forces were getting close, and I felt like I would be liberated the next day. If it hadn't been for the code talkers, I would have been put before a firing squad."[7]

The torture and daily beatings Kieyoomia endured showed the value the Japanese placed on breaking the mysterious transmissions. They became obsessed with trying to force him into giving them something he could not, and he endured these sessions with the same quiet strength that had enabled him to survive the Bataan Death March. As the days and months dragged on, a decision was reached to relocate him to a different POW camp.

"I was transferred to Matishima," Kieyoomia continued, "60 miles south of Nagasaki. This happened the day before America dropped the atomic bomb. When Japan surrendered, Red Cross officials thought I was from Singapore. I told them I was an American Indian. They asked me from what state, and I said, Arizona."

Joe Kieyoomia's official service record simply stated, "Prisoner of War, 9 April 1942 to 4 September 1945." After Red Cross officials matched Kieyoomia to Army records, they placed him on a hospital ship bound for Hawaii. The next four years Kieyoomia spent in a variety of veterans' facilities recovering from malnutrition, dysentery, and multiple operations to mend his damaged arm. He finally made his way home to Shiprock, New Mexico, in 1949.

What would Marine Corps Headquarters have done if it had known the Japanese had a Navajo who spoke and understood the language? The code talkers believed that because theirs was a code within a code, Kieyoomia would have needed firsthand knowledge of the code to decipher it. To effect any advantage from the network, Japanese field command would have needed an entire complement of cooperative Navajo code talkers able to translate on the spot. This was not even a remote possibility. The code talkers agreed that if trying to force Kieyoomia to break the code helped keep him alive, then the code was a blessing. The code, after all, was designed to save lives.

★   ★   ★   ★   ★

The Navajo code talkers took part in every assault the U.S. Marines conducted in the Pacific from 1942 to 1945. They served in all six Marine divisions, Marine Raider battalions, and Marine parachute units, transmitting
messages by telephone and radio in their native language—a code that the
Japanese never broke. By 1945, about 540 Navajos served as Marines. From
375 to 420 of those were trained as code talkers.

Tarawa—The First Day

Tarawa Atoll is part of the Gilbert Islands in the central Pacific. Betio is a small island on the western edge of the atoll, measuring only 300 acres in size, just large enough for a small airfield. During World War II, Tarawa was the eastern most outpost of the Japanese defensive line. Any future operations against the Marshall Islands to the northwest would require an assault against Betio to secure lines of communication. The Japanese, realizing Tarawa's importance, fortified the island and deployed the elite 7th Sasebo Special Naval Landing Force to defend it. Under the able command of Rear Admiral Kenji Shibasaki, Betio and its 4,500-man garrison was yard-for-yard the most heavily defended target the Marines ever assaulted. On November 20, 1943 the Second Marine Division landed on Betio and engage the enemy in a savage three-day, close quarters fight. With the second wave of Marines that morning was *Time* war correspondent Robert Sherrod. He describes that fateful day in this selection from his classic narrative, *Tarawa, The Story of a Battle*.

> It was a time of utmost savagery. I still don't know
> how they took the place.
>
> —Kerr Eby

★   ★   ★   ★   ★

We jumped out of bed at midnight, swimming in sweat. We donned our dungarees and headed for the wardroom. Nobody took more than fifteen minutes to eat his steak, eggs, and fried potatoes and drink his two cups of coffee, but everybody was soaking before he had finished. This was the hottest night of all. Before we filed out, gasping, there was an oversupply of the rumors that attend every battle: one of our cruisers had sunk a Jap surface craft (though not until seventy-seven six-inch shells had been fired, and an accompanying destroyer had let go two torpedoes); one of our ships had been attacked by a Japanese bomber during the night; a searchlight off Betio had already tried to spot our force.

After making last-minute adjustments of my gear, I went up on the flying bridge when General Quarters was buzzed at 0215. There was a half-moon dodging in and out of the clouds forty-five degrees to portside. It was cool up there, with a brisk breeze on the rise. It was possible to make notes when the moon was out. A calm voice came over the loudspeaker: "Target at 112 true, 26,800 yards ahead." "*Blackfish* 870 yards." "*Blackfish* 1000 yards." "*Blackfish* 900 yards." The *Blackfish* was the lead transport, and the *Blue Fox* was next. The faint red signal light of the lead ship slowly flashed on and off as we followed her to Tarawa.

Lieutenant Vanderpoel, the ship's gunnery officer, was talking to me and Lieutenant Commander Fabian, who was to be beach-master on Tarawa. Vanderpoel was indignant. He had seen a lot of this war, at Guadalcanal, Tulagi, Attu, Kiska. And they had never allowed him to fire his guns on the transport. True, they were not heavy guns such as battleships carry, but they might help. If he could just turn them on the shore, as the warships would turn theirs. "Just once I want to shoot," he said, "but this time they said again 'Transports will not fire.' We sit on these damn transports and we don't get to see anything of the war, and the Marines have to go in and do it all. Damn."

By 0330 the Marines had begun loading the outboard boats for the first wave. The sergeants were calling the roll: "Vernon, Simms, Gresholm...." They needed no light to call the well-remembered roll, and they didn't have to send a runner to find any absentees. The Marines were all there. One of the sergeants was giving his men last-minute instructions: "Be sure to correct your elevation and windage. Adjust your sights."

At 0400 I went below. I stood outside the wardroom as the first and second waves walked through and out to their boats. Most of the men were soaked; their green-and-brown-spotted jungle dungarees had turned a darker green when the sweat from their bodies soaked through. They jested with one another. Only a few even whistled to keep up their courage.

"How many you going to kill, Bunky?" one of them shouted at a bespectacled Marine. "All I can get," said Bunky, without smiling, as he wiped his beloved rifle barrel.

"Oh, boy," said a kid well under twenty, "I just want to spit in a dead Jap's face. Just open his mouth and let him have it."

Said another, "I should have joined the Boy Scouts. I knew it."

They were a grimy, unshaven lot. The order had gone out: they must put on clean clothing just before going ashore, in order to diminish the chances of infection from wounds, but now they looked dirty. Under the weight, light though it was, of their combat packs, lifebelts, guns, ammunition, helmets, canvas leggings, bayonets, they were sweating in great profusion. Nobody had shaved for two or three days.

Outside I saw Dr. Edwin J. Welte, a crop-haired, young Minnesotan who had finished medical school only about five years ago. "Well," he said, "nobody is trying to get out of fighting this battle. Out of the whole battalion only eleven are being left in the ship's sick bay. Five are recurring malaria cases, one busted his knee on maneuvers, one is a post-operative appendectomy, one is a chronic knee that somebody palmed off on the regiment, and the rest are minor shipboard accidents. All the malaria cases will be able to go ashore in two days."

Who else was being left behind? "Nobody that I know of, except one pfc. who got obstreperous and they had to throw him in the brig. Only one man in the brig the whole trip, and he's always been a bad character."

We walked back to the junior staff officers' bunkroom, which was full of young Marines indulging in what might have been a college bull session. Outside we could hear the dynamo-hum of the cables letting the boats down into the water. Everybody had on his pack and his helmet, for all these men were going on the assault waves which would start leaving for Betio in ten or fifteen minutes. Young, mustachioed Captain Ben Owens, the Oklahoma boy who was battalion operations officer, looked up as we entered, and said, "Doc, I'm going to get shot in the tail today."

Dr. Welte: "Oh, you want a Purple Heart, huh?"

Owens: "Hell, no, I want a stateside ticket."

Colonel Amey, the battalion boss, came in, stretched mightily, and ho-hummed. I asked him how many Japs we were going to find on Betio. "Not many, apparently," he said. "They've got five-inch guns. They'd have been shooting at us by now."

Owens looked at the deck a minute and said, "That's right. We're only eleven thousand yards offshore now. They've got some eight-inch guns, too. But just wait. You'll hear one whistle over in a minute. When he does, those battlewagons will open up on that son-of-a-bitch and rock that island—"

Owens continued, "Maybe the battlewagons and the bombs will knock out the big guns, but I'm not saying they'll kill all the Japs. I still think we'll get shot at when we go in, and I'm still looking for that stateside ticket, Doc."

Jay Odell, a slender young junior-grade lieutenant who learned how to be a naval air-liaison officer after leaving his Philadelphia newspaper job, had been standing in a corner without saying anything. Now he spoke up, "Everybody is putting too much faith in the statistics about the number of tons that's going to be dropped."

Now, at 0505, we heard a great thud in the southwest. We knew what that meant. The first battleship had fired the first shot. We all rushed out on deck. The show had begun. The show for which thousands of men had spent months of training, scores of ships had sailed thousands of miles, for which Chaplains Kelly and MacQueen had offered their prayers. The curtain was up in the theatre of death.

We were watching when the battleship's second shell left the muzzle of its great gun, headed for Betio. There was a brilliant flash in the darkness of the half-moonlit night. Then a flaming torch arched high into the air and sailed far away, slowly, very slowly, like an easily lobbed tennis ball. The red cinder was nearly halfway to its mark before we heard the thud, a dull roar as if some mythological giant had struck a drum as big as Mount Olympus. There was no sign of an explosion on the unseen island—the second shot had apparently fallen into the water, like the first.

Within three minutes the sky was filled again with the orange-red flash of the big gun, and Olympus boomed again. The red ball of fire that was the high-explosive shell was again dropping toward the horizon. But this time there was a tremendous burst on the land that was Betio. A wall of flame shot five hundred feet into the air, and there was another terrifying explosion as the shell found its mark. Hundreds of the awestruck Marines on the deck of the *Blue Fox* cheered in uncontrollable joy. Our guns had found the enemy. Probably the enemy's big eight-inch guns and their powder magazine on the southwest corner of the island.

Now that we had the range the battleship sought no longer. The next flash was four times as great, and the sky turned a brighter, redder orange, greater than any flash of lightning the Marines had ever seen. Now four shells, weighing more than a ton each, peppered the island. Now Betio began to glow brightly from the fires the bombardment pattern had started.

That was only the beginning. Another battleship took up the firing—four mighty shells poured from its big guns onto another part of the island. Then another battleship breathed its brilliant breath of death. Now a heavy cruiser let go with its eight-inch guns, and several light cruisers opened with their fast-firing six-inch guns. They were followed by the destroyers, many destroyers with many five-inch guns on each, firing almost as fast as machine guns. The sky at times was brighter than noontime on the equator. The arching, glowing cinders that were high-explosive shells sailed through the air as though buckshot were being fired out of many shotguns from all sides of the island. The Marines aboard the *Blue Fox* exulted with each blast on the island. Fire and smoke and sand obscured the island of Betio. Now the Jap, the miserable, little brown man who had started this horrible war against a peace-loving people, was beginning to suffer the consequences. He had asked for this, and he should have known it before he flew into Pearl Harbor that placid Sunday morning. As the warships edged in closer, coming into shore from many thousands of yards until they were only a few thousand yards away from their target, the whole island of Betio seemed to erupt with bright fires that were burning everywhere. They blazed even through the thick wall of smoke that curtained the island.

The first streaks of dawn crept through the sky. The warships continued to fire. All of a sudden they stopped. But here came the planes—not just a few planes: a dozen, a score, a hundred. The first torpedo bombers raced across the smoking conflagration and loosed their big bombs on an island that must have been dead a half hour ago! They were followed by the dive bombers, the old workhorse SBDs and the new Helldivers, the fast SB2Cs that had been more than two years a-borning. The dive bombers lined up, many of thousands of feet over Betio, then they pointed their noses down and dived singly, or in pairs or in threes. Near the end of their dives they hatched the bombs from beneath their bellies; they pulled out gracefully and sailed back to their carriers to get more bombs. Now came the fighter planes, the fast, new Grumman Hellcats, the best planes ever to squat on a carrier. They made their runs just above the awful, gushing pall of smoke, their machine guns spitting hundreds of fifty-caliber bullets a minute.

Surely, we all thought, no mortal men could live through such destroying power.

Surely, I thought, if there were actually any Japs left on the island (which I doubted strongly), they would all be dead by now.

It was a half hour after dawn that I got a first rude shock. A shell splashed into the water not thirty feet from an LST which waited near the

Blue Fox. Our destroyers, which by this time were firing again as the planes finished their bombing and strafing runs, were firing very wide, I surmised. A shell hit not more than fifty yards from our stern, sending a vertical stream of water high in to the air, like a picture of a geyser erupting.

I turned to Major Howard Rice and said, "My God, what wide shooting! Those boys need some practice."

Major Rice looked at me quizzically. Said he, "You don't think that's our own guns doing *that* shooting, do you?"

Then, for the first time, I realized that there were some Japs on Betio. Like a man who has swallowed a piece of steak without chewing it, I said, "Oh."

By this time our first three waves of boats were already in the water, and the fourth and fifth were getting ready to load. But the sudden appearance of the enemy upset our plans. These valuable transports, with their thousands of troops, could not stand idly by and take a chance on being sunk. By now we were within four or five miles of the target. We had no definite knowledge that all the Japs' big guns on Betio were not still working. Captain John McGovern, commodore of the assault transport division, gave the order. The transports heeled around quickly and set out to sea, whence we had come only two hours ago.

The transports streaked out of the danger zone, with the Japs firing vainly at them as they went. The first three waves, including hundreds of boats from many transports, had no choice but to turn around and streak after the mother ships. As they turned and ran, our warships opened up again. By firing his gun the Jap had given away its location. Now the fury of the warships, big and small, mounted into a crescendo of unprecedented fire and thunder. They pounded the Jap with everything in the gunnery officer's book. If there had been an unearthly flash of lightening before daylight, now, at close range, there was a nether world of pandemonium. Hundreds of shells crashed with hundreds of ear-rocking thuds as they poured toward the Jap big-gun position. Soon there was no more firing. The last Jap big gun had been silenced. Now the transports could finish loading their assault waves into the boats, and Betio would soon feel the tread of the U. S. Marines' boondockers.

The fifth wave climbed down the rope nets at 0635, into the landing boats which bobbed drunkenly on the rough sea and smacked into the transport. Within five minutes after we pushed off, a half barrel of water was splashing over the high bow of the Higgins boat every minute. Every one of the thirty-odd men was soaked before we had chugged a half mile. While a Marine held his poncho over our heads I tried to put my fine watch into a small, heavy waterproof envelope. It seemed a pity to lose such a watch, especially since Sergeant Neil Shober, a craftsman with a jeep or with a strip of metal, had made a handsome wristband for the watch out of a piece of Jap Zero wing he had brought from Guadalcanal. Into another envelope I dropped my newly filled cigarette lighter and some valuable pictures; into another a pack of cigarettes.

The sun had hardly leaped above the horizon and we shivered as the cool seawater drenched us, it seemed, beyond the saturation point. I remembered the nip of brandy the doctor had given me. I pulled the little bottle out of my pocket and shared it with the Marine standing next to me. If there was ever an occasion for taking a drink at seven o'clock in the morning this was it.

Later that day I was to tremble all over from fear alone, but not yet. We shook and shivered because we were cold. My only memory of the first hour and a half of the ride toward the beachhead is sheer discomfort, alternating with exaltation. Our warships and planes were now pounding the little island of Betio as no other island had been pounded in the history of warfare. By standing on the gunwale of the boat I could crane my neck around the ramp-bow and see the smoke and dust and flames of Betio. When the attack paused a moment I could see the palm trees outlined against the sea and sky on the other side.

Once I tried to count the number of salvos—not shells, salvos—the battleships, cruisers, and destroyers were pouring on the island. A Marine who had a waterproof watch offered to count off the seconds up to one minute. Long before the minute had ended I had counted over one hundred, but then a dozen more ships opened up and I abandoned the project. I did count the number of planes in sight at one time. It was ninety-two. These ships and these planes were dealing out an unmerciful beating on the Japs, and it was good, good to watch. As we came within two miles of the island we could get a better view of what was happening. There were fires up and down the length of the island. Most of them would be the barracks, the power plant, the kitchens, and other above-ground installations we had studied time and again in the photographs. Once in a while a solid mass of flame would reach for the sky and the roar of an explosion could be heard easily from our position in the water. That would be an oil tank or an ammunition dump. The feeling was good.

It was nearly nine o'clock when the fifth wave arrived at the boat rendezvous and began circling to wait for our turn to go in. I looked around the ramp to see what was on the beach. For the first time I felt that something was wrong. The first waves were not hitting the beach as they should. There were very few boats on the beach, and these were all amphibious tractors which the first wave used. There were no Higgins boats on the beach, as there should have been by now.

Almost before we could guess at what bad news was being foretold, the command boat came alongside. The naval officer shouted, "You'll have to go in right away, as soon as I can get an amphtrack for you. The shelf around the island is too shallow to take the Higgins boats." This was indeed chilling news. It meant something that had been dimly foreseen but hardly expected: the only way the Marines were going to land was in the amphtracks ("alligators") which could crawl over the shallow reef that surrounds Betio. It meant that the landings would be slow, because there were not enough amphtracks for everybody, and we would have to use the emergency shuttle system that had been worked out as a last resort. And suppose the amphtracks were knocked out before they could get enough men ashore to hold what the first wave had taken? And suppose the Marines already ashore were killed faster than they could be replaced under this slow shuttle system?

I felt very dull—a brain fed on the almost positive belief that the Japs had fled Betio would naturally be slower than a six-year-old writing a letter. I could not quite comprehend what was happening.

An amphtrack bobbed alongside our Higgins boat. Said the Marine amphtrack boss, "Quick! Half you men get in here. They need help bad on the beach. A lot of Marines have already been killed and wounded." While the amphtrack was alongside, Jap shells from an automatic weapon began peppering the water around us. "Probably a 40-mm.," said one of the calmer Marine officers.

But the Marines did not hesitate. Hadn't they been told that other Marines "needed help bad"? Major Rice and seventeen others scampered into the amphtrack and headed for the beach. I did not see them again until three days later, when the battle was over.

The half-empty Higgins boat milled around for another ten minutes, getting its share of near misses and air bursts. One Marine picked a half dozen pieces of shrapnel off his lap and swallowed hard. Two amphtracks came by. One of our Marines stood up and waved at them, told them that we were ready and waiting to go to the beach. But both had already been disabled by direct hits. Both had wounded and dead men in them, the drivers said. We milled around another couple of minutes, looking for a chance at what appeared to be a one-way ride, but always remembering that "they need help bad" on the beach.

The next amphtrack crew said they would take us in part of the way, to where we could wade the rest of the way, but amphtracks were getting so scarce he couldn't take us all the way. We jumped into the little tractor boat and quickly settled on the deck. "Oh, God. I'm scared," said the little Marine, a telephone operator, who sat next to me forward in the boat. I gritted my teeth and tried to force a smile that would not come and tried to stop quivering all over (now I was shaking from fear). I said, in an effort to be reassuring. "I'm scared, too." I never made a more truthful statement in all my life. I was not petrified yet, but my joints seemed to be stiffening.

Now, I realized, this is the payoff. Now I knew, positively, that there were Japs, and evidently plenty of them on the island. They were not dead. The bursts of shellfire all around us evidenced the fact that there was plenty of life in them. "This is not going to be a new kind of beachhead landing," I said to myself. "This is going to be traditional—what you have always been told is the toughest of all military operations: a landing, if possible, in the face of the enemy machine guns that can mow men down by the hundreds." This was not even going to be the fifth wave. After the first wave there apparently had not been any organized waves, those organized waves which hit the beach so beautifully in the last rehearsal. There had been only an occasional amphtrack which hit the beach, then turned around (if it wasn't knocked out) and went back for more men. There we were: a single boat, a little wavelet of our own, and we were already getting the hell shot out of us, with a thousand yards to go. I peered over the side of the amphtrack and saw another amphtrack three hundred yards to the left get a direct hit from what looked like a mortar shell.

"It's hell in there," said the amphtrack boss, who was pretty wild-eyed himself. "They've already knocked out a lot of amphtracks and there are a lot of wounded men lying on the beach. See that old hulk of a Jap freighter over there? I'll let you out about there, then go back to get some more men. You can wade in from there." I looked. The rusty old ship was about two hundred yards beyond the pier. That meant some seven hundred yards of wading through the fire of machine guns whose bullets already were whistling over our heads.

The fifteen of us—I think it was fifteen—scurried over the side of the amphtrack into the water that was neck-deep. We started wading.

No sooner had we hit the water than the Jap machine guns really opened up on us. There must have been five or six of these machine guns concentrating their fire on us—there was no nearer target in the water at the time—which meant several hundred bullets per man. I don't believe there was one of the fifteen who wouldn't have sold his chances for an additional twenty-five dollars added to his life-insurance policy. It was painfully slow, wading in such deep water. And we had seven hundred yards to walk slowly into that machine-gun fire, looming into larger targets as we rose onto higher ground. I was scared, as I had never been scared before. But my head was clear. I was extremely alert, as though my brain were dictating that I live these last minutes for all they were worth. I recalled that psychologists say fear in battle is a good thing; it stimulates the adrenalin glands and heavily loads the blood supply with oxygen.

I do not know when it was that I realized I wasn't frightened any longer. I suppose it was when I looked around and saw the amphtrack scooting back for more Marines. Perhaps it was when I noticed that bullets were hitting six inches to the left or six inches to the right. I could have sworn that I could have reached out and touched a hundred bullets. I remember chuckling inside and saying aloud, "You bastards, you certainly are lousy shots." That, as I told Colonel Carlson next day, was what I later described as my hysteria period. Colonel Carlson, who has been shot at in a number of wars, said he understood.

After wading through several centuries and some two hundred yards of shallowing water and deepening machine-gun fire, I looked to the left and saw that we had passed the end of the pier. I didn't know whether any Jap snipers were still under the pier or not, but I knew we couldn't do any worse. I waved to the Marines on my immediate right and shouted, "Let's head for the pier!" Seven of them came. The other seven Marines were far to the right. They followed a naval ensign straight into the beach—there was no Marine officer in our amphtrack. The ensign said later that he thought three of the seven had been killed in the water.

The first three of us lay on the rocks panting, waiting for the other five to join us. They were laboring heavily to make it, and bullets from the machine guns on the beach were still splashing around them like raindrops in a water barrel. By this time we three were safely hidden from the beach by the thick, upright, coconut-log stanchions of the pier. I watched these five men and wondered how on heaven or earth they managed to come so close to death, yet live. Once I thought the last man, a short Marine, would not get under the pier. Twenty yards away, he fell and went under. But he was not hit. In a moment he was up again, struggling through the water, almost exhausted beyond further movement, but still carrying his heavy roll of telephone wire,. When he had gone under I had asked myself whether I had the breath or the courage to go after him. I was relieved when the necessity of answering the question was obviated by his arrival.

We were still four hundred yards from the beach. But now we could crawl in most of the way under the protection of the pier, where we made difficult, if not altogether invisible, targets. After a few minutes of breath-catching we started crawling. A hundred yards from the beach, the pier rested on big coral rocks on the ground, so we had to take to the water again. It was only a little more than knee-deep now.

I looked on both sides of the pier. Our battalion had been supposed to land on the right side, but there was no sign of life anywhere on the right. But on the left there seemed to be three or four hundred people milling around the beach and they were wearing, not Jap uniforms, but the spotted brown-and-green jungle dungarees of the United States Marines. The eight of us decided to go to the left.

We ducked low, creeping along the edge of the pier. We were not even shot at. We came upon a stalled bulldozer. This, I reflected, was the American way to fight a war—to try to get a bulldozer ashore, even before many men had preceded it. Later I learned that a bulldozer is a fine weapon; it can shovel up sand over a low slit in a pillbox, causing the enemy inside to smother. Two Marines tinkered with the bulldozer, but it had sunk too deep in the water that covered an unseen shellhole. A third Marine lay behind the bulldozer seat. He already had a bullet through his thigh. Then the Jap machine gun chattered, rattling its fire against the frontal blade of the bulldozer. We ducked low behind the machine.

"How goes it?" I asked the Marines.

"Pretty tough," one of them said, matter-of-factly. "It's hell if you climb over that seawall. Those bastards have got a lot of machine guns and snipers back there."

After a few minutes the Jap gave up trying to shoot at the four of us behind the bulldozer. I dashed back to the pier, which was only fifteen feet to the left. During the dash I stepped into a shellhole seven feet deep. Then I swam the rest of the way to the pier.

With each movement of the surf a thousand fish washed against the pier—fish six inches to three feet long. Regardless of their effectiveness against Jap emplacements, shellfire and bombing misses could kill a lot of fish by concussion.

I passed a stalled medium tank, which had floundered when it sank into one of the shellholes. A hundred yards farther to the left there was a stalled light tank. To my surprise I saw a nearly naked figure appear from under the water, swim the last few feet to this tank, then jump in through the top of it. At first I thought it was a Marine who had gone to repair the tank. But why would he take all his clothes off, and why swim under water? Perhaps it was a Jap, but why? I reported the incident when I got ashore, but the officer, with his hands already full, paid little attention to the report. We were to hear later from this stalled tank and from many another disabled tank and amphtrack and boat.

Upon reaching the end of the pier I ducked into a foxhole in the sand which was already crowded with three Marines. I took my first close look at bird-shaped Betio. At this point on the bird's belly, behind the pier that stuck out like a leg, there was a gap. This gap was heaped three or four feet high with sand, but the rest of the island's north rim seemed to be a four-foot seawall built of coconut logs which had been driven into the ground. From the water's edge to the seawall there was twenty feet of sand and brown and green coral. These twenty feet were our beachhead. The Japs controlled the rest of the island, excepting this pocket—twenty feet deep and perhaps a hundred yards wide—which had been established by the Second Battalion of the Eighth Marine Regiment, the farthest left of our three assault battalions, plus two other pockets which had been established as fragilely by the other two battalions. The beginning at Betio did not look bright. But several hundred Marines had gone over that seawall to try to kill the Japs who were killing our men as they waded ashore. They went over—though they knew very well that their chances of becoming a casualty within an hour were something like fifty percent.

I stooped low and ran the hundred feet from the end of the pier to a stalled amphtrack which was jammed against the seawall. Beside the amphtrack a dead Marine lay on the sand. He was the first of many dead Americans I saw on Betio. There was a wide streak of blood on the amphtrack, indicating that the dying man had bled a lot.

A big, red-mustached Marine walked over. "Who is he?" he asked.

"An assistant amphtrack driver, sir," another Marine said. "Name was Cowart. He was twenty years old. He married a girl in Wellington."

"Well, cover him up. Will the amphtrack run?"

"No, sir. We've tried to start it, but I guess the starter was knocked out when this man was killed."

I walked over and introduced myself to the red-mustached Marine. His name was Henry Pierson ("Jim") Crowe and he had been an old-time enlisted man. Now he was a major, commanding the assault battalion that had landed at this point.

"Have you seen any other war correspondents, Major?" I asked. The major said he had not. Poor Frank Filan and Dick Johnston, I thought. They were the A.P. photographer and U.P. reporter who were supposed to land with Crowe's battalion.

The major had other business. Many of his Marines had already gone over the seawall to kill Japs. Now telephone wires were being strung between their forward shellhole posts and his command post behind the stalled amphtrack. I saw a chaplain nearby. I asked him if many men from his battalion had been killed. "I just got here," he said. "I haven't seen but two dead except this man by the amphtrack."

I sat down and leaned against the amphtrack, next to the seawall. Now and then bullets would rattle against the amphtrack, but the seawall made a fairly safe place to sit. With several Marines who were there, wiremen, corpsmen, and battalion staff headquarters men, I felt quite luxurious. If I stayed there, in the dip under the wall, I would be quite safe from any of the Japanese bullets which sang overhead in their high soprano. The Jap mortars, like their guns, were being concentrated on our boats as they approached the shore.

Six hundred yards out, near the end of the pier, I watched a Jap shell hit directly on an LCV that was bringing many Marines ashore. The explosion was terrific and parts of the boat flew in all directions. Then there were many Marines swimming in the water.

Two pairs of corpsmen brought two more dead men and placed them beside the dead boy who had been married to the girl from Wellington. Even now the men had been ashore less than an hour. Yet already the smell of death under the equator's sun could be detected faintly.

Our destroyers were only a thousand yards or so offshore by now, and they had begun firing on the tail end of the island, where there were no Americans. The battleships opened up from the other side of the island. Their shells made a great roaring sound when they smacked the land behind where we were sitting. Then we could hear the whish of the shells through the air, then the report from the muzzles of the guns. It seemed odd. It was as though the shells were giving an answer before the question were asked.

I took out my soaked notebooks and opened them up to dry on the hub of the amphtrack. Then I fished the waterproof envelopes out of my wet dungarees. My fine watch was ruined—there was an accumulation of green scum under the crystal. The cigarette lighter in another envelope was also soaked and ruined and already rusted, but the pack of cigarettes were still dry, and they seemed more valuable at the time than either of the other items.

A young Marine walked in front of us, about fifteen feet from where we were sitting, and about five feet from the water's edge. A rifle cracked loudly from behind us. The Marine flinched, grabbed at his head, then ducked to the sand. I thought he had been hit, but, miraculously, he had escaped. He picked up his helmet. There were two inch-wide holes in the top of it, one on each side. The Jap bullet which tore through his helmet had missed his head, but not by more than an eighth of an inch. The Marine's only wound was a scratch on his face, where the helmet had scraped as it was torn savagely off his head.

"All right, god dame it," shouted Major Crowe, "you walk along out there standing up and you're sure as hell going to get shot. Those bastards have got snipers every ten feet back there."

Not fifteen minutes later, in the same spot, I saw the most gruesome sight I had seen in this war. Another young Marine walked briskly along the beach. He grinned at a pal who was sitting next to me. Again there was a shot. The Marine spun all the way around and fell to the ground, dead. From where he lay, a few feet away, he looked up at us. Because he had been shot squarely through the temple his eyes bulged out wide, as in horrific surprise at what had happened to him, though it was impossible that he could ever have known what hit him.

"Somebody go get the son-of-a-bitch," yelled Major Crowe. "He's right back of us here, just waiting for somebody to pass by." That Jap sniper, we knew from the crack of his rifle, was very close.

A Marine jumped over the seawall and began throwing blocks of fused TNT into a coconut-log pillbox about fifteen feet back of the seawall against which we sat. Two more Marines scaled the seawall, one of them carrying a twin-cylindered tank trapped to his shoulders, the other holding the nozzle of the flamethrower. As another charge of TNT boomed inside the pillbox, causing smoke and dust to billow out, a khaki-clad figure ran out the side entrance. The flame thrower, waiting for him, caught him in its withering stream of intense fire. As soon as it touched him, the Jap flared up like a piece of celluloid. He was dead instantly but the bullets in his cartridge belt exploded for a full sixty seconds after he had been charred almost to nothingness. It was the first Jap I saw killed on Betio—the first of four thousand. Zing, zing, zing, the cartridge-belt bullets sang. We all ducked low. Nobody wanted to be killed by a dead Jap.

That incident demonstrated something of the characteristics of the Jap sniper. The Jap who killed the grinning Marine had been waiting all morning in the pillbox, not thirty feet from the beach, for just such a shot.

Jap snipers are poor marksmen, compared to Marine Corps experts. But at thirty feet not even a poor marksman can miss twice.

I stayed around Major Crowe's battalion headquarters most of that first afternoon, watching the drama of life and death that was being enacted around me. Men were being killed and wounded every minute. The casualties passed along the beach on stretchers, borne by the Navy medical corpsmen who took high losses themselves—out of one group of twenty-nine corpsmen, I heard later, twenty-six were killed or wounded before the battle had ended. But these corpsmen casually, almost slowly, bore their poncho-covered cargo in streams along the beach. The faces of the dead were covered; those of the wounded were not. Once in a while it was possible to load an amphtrack with these wounded and send them back out to the ships which had hospital facilities. Almost any man will go through greater danger to save a friend's life than he will endure in killing the enemy who is the cause of that danger.

The number of dead lined up beside the stalled headquarters amphtrack grew steadily. But the procession of the wounded seemed many times greater. There went a stretcher with a Marine whose leg had been nearly torn off; another had been hit in the buttocks by a 13-mm. bullet or 20-mm. shell—a man's fist could have been thrust into the jagged hole; another was pale as death from the loss of much blood—his face seemed to be all bones and yellowish-white skin and he was in great pain.

From a bomb crater about forty feet over the seawall a strong voice called out during a lull in the big-gun firing, "Major, send somebody to help me! The son-of-a-bitch got me!" Without waiting for orders two corpsmen crawled over the seawall in the face of machine-gun fire which opened up as they appeared. They returned quickly, half dragging, half carrying a husky Marine who had been shot through the bone above his knee. The wounded man, groaning, was set beside me. "I think he is in that coconut palm," he said, waving his hand in the direction from which he had come. Then he lay down on the sand and inadvertently groaned some more.

A corpsman bandaged the wounded man's leg and jabbed a morphine syrette into his arm. By this time I had been on the island nearly three hours and my notebooks were dried, if wrinkled. I felt that I should do some reporting. I asked the Marine what his name was. It was a very difficult name, and I know I didn't get it right, even after he had spelled it for me twice, but in my notebook it appears as Pfc. N. Laverntine, Jr.

Another Marine who looked no more than nineteen strolled over the seawall. He sat beside the wounded man, smiled, and said, "Bastard got me in the leg, too. I thought I'd stepped on a god-damn mine. It felt like an electric shock." Then he pulled up his trouser leg, showing a neat bullet hole through the fleshy part of his leg. He—his name was Wilson, which I could spell—was very deprecating about his wound, which wasn't even bleeding.

Seventy-five yards down the beach, near the end of the pier where I had first landed, the Marines had set up an 81-mm. mortar, which they were firing every minute or so. One of them got up to a kneeling position to adjust his instrument. We saw him tumble over the edge of the hole the mortar was set in. Then his companion jumped up to help him. He fell back into the hole. There evidently was another Jap sniper very close to them. I learned later that the first man had been shot through the back; the second who tried to help him had got a bullet through the heart. The men with the TNT and the flamethrower went after a pillbox only a few feet from where the two Marines had been hit. This time the charge of TNT must have been very powerful, because the explosion was as loud as a 75-mm. gun and smoke and dirt flew fifty feet into the air. The sand around the coconut logs was evidently jarred loose, because the flamethrower was sprayed onto the logs, and, although nothing will burn tough, fibrous coconut logs, the flame must have got inside the pillbox. We could hear dozens of bullets popping inside. Later, four dead, charred Japs were found inside the pillbox.

The two wounded men sitting beside me questioned each passerby. "Did ——— get killed?" "Have you seen ——— or ———?" "You old dope, I thought you were dead." "How's ———? Anybody see him?" A new arrival sat down beside us and said, "I got more lead in my tail than ever now—that bastard raised up and grinned and threw his grenade. I got sprinkled, but Joe got him."

The three of them carried on a conversation for the rest of the time I stayed there, about an hour. Between rumblings of five-inch destroyer shells that were exploding within a hundred yards, causing the earth to tremble beneath us, I picked up snatches of their talk. They were not afraid, as men might be expected to be who had been shot. They talked quite calmly about what they had seen and speculated on the fate of their comrades. "I know we've already got over twenty-five percent casualties in my company," one said.

Said the latest arrival, a red-head, "Jones was walking by there right after that other fellow got bumped off. A Jap shot off a piece of his thumb. Jones just laughed and kept going."

"That guy has got plenty of guts."

"That Greenwalt has got plenty, too."

"Where's Peterson?"

"I think he's shot."

"T. C. Martin got a leg blown off."

"Very few people ain't got hit."

I do not know what happened to those three wounded Marines. The plan was to evacuate them back to the ships after dark. I hoped they made it all right. I knew such unperturbable men would be needed for other battles.

By four o'clock the naval gunfire and the planes were really raising hell back of us. The destroyer salvos sounded like thunderclaps: the explosion of the hits right back of us, then the whistling of the shell, then the sound of the rumbling of the guns which reached our ears later. The strafing planes—Grumman Hellcats—were coming over now in great numbers, four, six, and eight at a time. First we could see the two wisps of smoke—a gray-blue wisp from the guns on either wing. Then we could hear the popping of the bullets, which sounded like hot grease in a frying pan. They were tearing into the palm trees and the shellholes scattered inland back of us. Then the dive bombers would appear in the sky above us; two or three at a time would dive screamingly toward the earth and let go their bombs. A moment later we would hear the explosions of the bombs—*ka-whump, ka-whump, ka-whump*. And the earth would shudder and more sand would run into our shoes. Then eight more fighters would appear on a line, roaring in at one or two thousand feet overhead, and the sixteen wisps of smoke would trail behind the eight planes, and the grease-popping sounded like a monumental fish-fry. During all these weird, indescribably great noises, a Jap machine gun usually chattered incessantly—*poppoppoppop*—as if to show us that all the noise had affected it not at all.

Before I left Major Crowe I noticed a young lieutenant who came into the headquarters area. He walked around completely nonchalant, giving orders to the men with him, while the Jap snipers fired at him steadily. He did not even wear a helmet. I knew that no officer could afford to let his men know he was afraid, but I thought this was carrying it a little too far, this walking around, getting shot at bareheaded. I noted the lieutenant's name—Aubrey Edmonds—because I did not see how he could possibly survive the battle. Later I checked up and found that he had been wounded the second day—shot, not through the head, but in the back.

My friend Lieutenant Hawkins of the Scout and Sniper platoon appeared. "Get down, Hawk, or you'll get shot," somebody yelled at him. The Hawk, who had come back for more ammunition, snarled, "Aw, those bastards can't shoot. They can't hit anything." Then he and the men with him leapt over the seawall again. "Hawk's platoon has been out there all day," an officer told me. "They have knocked out a hell of a lot of machine guns."

I got up about 4:30 to look for my own battalion. Someone had told me that its headquarters were in a shellhole about two hundred yards to the west, on the other side of the pier. When I left Major Crowe's battalion I figured it was getting along pretty well. Casualties were high, but the Marines were whittling away at a lot of machine guns and snipers. The firing from in back of us seemed much less terrific now than it had been three or four hours earlier, though we had stopped trying to land more troops until nightfall because the Japs were knocking out too many of our boats in the water. From Crowe's headquarters I could count more than fifty disabled tanks, amphtracks, and boats in the water on both sides of the pier. Major Crowe's battalion had a very tough assignment—the Japs drifted up from the tail of the island to the center all through the battle, we learned later, and the supply seemed inexhaustible—but the assignment was not impossible, it seemed.

I stooped low, trying to get down far enough so that the Japs wouldn't be able to see me over the seawall and walked briskly back along the beach toward the pier. I felt a little ashamed to stoop down, when most of the Marines by now were disdaining the Japs to the extent of walking upright. But I had been shot at and missed so many times during the day that I felt that I didn't want to tempt my luck. By next day I was walking upright, too. I believe that man can get used to anything after a while, even bullets.

The dash across the forty-foot-wide area at the end of the pier, an area which was openly exposed, was dangerous, and almost everyone who tried it was shot at. But I was curious to know what had happened to my own battalion. So I ran across the forty feet, heard, three or four bullets sing by, then dropped behind a big coral rock. There was a deep indentation in the coastline at this point. I could walk around the rim, as some reckless Marines were doing, or I could wade through the waist-deep water of the indentation. I chose to wade. When I had reached the beach again I asked a Marine where Second Battalion headquarters was. He pointed to a shellhole under the seawall about a hundred feet ahead. I ran behind the seawall and dropped into the hole.

There I was greeted by three officers I knew: Lieutenant Colonel Irvine Jordan, an observer from another Marine division; "Swede" Norvik; Lieutenant Odell, the naval aviation liaison man; and Bill Hipple, the A.P. reporter. On Betio everyone was glad to see anyone he knew, because the chances of not seeing him were so heavy. During the six hours since I had landed, for instance, I had become convinced that I was the only correspondent still alive, and I was very glad to see Bill Hipple.

Colonel Jordan was giving a message to a Marine who wrote it down in his yellow book, tore out a sheet, and handed it to a runner who ran up the beach with it. Then he turned to me, "This is really hell. Colonel Amey was killed; his body is lying out there in the water. I was ordered to take over the battalion."

"Where is Major Rice and his staff? Did they make it?" I asked. Ordinarily Major Rice would have taken over the battalion on Colonel Amey's death.

"Haven't heard a word from them. I'm afraid none of them made it. This is all the staff we've got. Odell here has got a bullet through his shoulder, but he's helping."

Said Bill Hipple, "Colonel Amey was right beside me when he was shot. We were within fifty feet of the shore."

Norvik said, "Doc Welte got it, too. He was in our boat."

There were half a dozen Marines in the shellhole headquarters—runners, corpsmen, and communicators. But dozens of others would gather around us, behind the seawall.

"You men, get on up front," Colonel Jordan would say. "They need you out there." A few of the Marines would pick up their guns and head over the seawall, singly, and in twos and threes, but many of them were reluctant to move. Colonel Jordan turned to me, "They don't know me, you see. They haven't got the confidence men should have in their officers."

The firing over the seawall was even heavier than it had been at Major Crowe's headquarters—not so much heavy gunfire and bombing near here, because our own men were scattered through the coconut trees at this point—but every coconut tree seemed to have a Jap sniper in it.

I don't think E Company has got ten men left," said Norvik, his blue eyes opened wide. This was an exaggeration, of course, as battlefield reports often become exaggerated, but it indicates the extent of the casualties the Second Battalion believed it was taking.*

There were two wounded men in a small, Jap-covered coconut-log emplacement on top of the seawall. One of them was in considerable pain

---

* Actually, E Company's casualties were very high. Five of its six officers were killed: Capt. E. G. Walker, Lebanon, Tenn., Lieutenants Maurice F. Reichel, Blytheville, Ark., Louis B. Beck, Cincinnati, Ohio, William C. Culp, West Palm Beach, Fla., and Donald R. Dahlgren, Rector, Mich.

and he had a high fever. The other was not hurt badly. He kept a lookout from the rear opening of the emplacement, in case the Japs tried to overwhelm us. On the rim of the shellhole, on the side nearest the water, there were three or four dead Marines. There had not been time to cover them. The dead and the living were so inextricably mixed that it was sometimes difficult to tell one from another.

"How do you feel, Odell?" said Colonel Jordan. "Don't you want to go back to a ship tonight?" Lieutenant Odell grinned and said, "I'm all right. I'll stick it out here. You need all the help you can get."

It was growing dark. It was easy to see that the attack on Betio had not succeeded as we had hoped it would. Our beachhead at Second Battalion headquarters was, like Major Crowe's, only twenty feet wide. Fifty yards to the westward up the beach, and some fifteen yards inland, Colonel Shoup had set up regimental headquarters behind a big Japanese pillbox—the beachhead at that point amounted to perhaps sixty-five or seventy feet.

"All right, men," shouted Norvik, "dig your foxholes. We'll probably get bombed tonight. I want two men to stay on guard for every one who goes to sleep." To others he said, "I want men in foxholes on top of the seawall and as far inland as you can go. If the Japs rush us tonight, we've got to be ready for them." A Jap sniper took a shot at Norvik, the shrill *pi-i-ing* whistling by his ears. He ducked down and continued ordering the defenses of the battalion—or what was left of it.

As darkness began to settle over Tarawa, we could see more Americans heading for shore through the dimming light. "Couple of companies of reinforcements," said an officer. These men were being unloaded at the end of the pier. They could not yet walk along the pier, but they could crawl beneath it and alongside it. The Japs kept trying to pepper them with machine guns and rifles, but their aim generally was not good. Some men would land at the end of the five-hundred-yard pier, and try to walk down it, but the Japs would increase their fire until the Americans usually had to jump into the water or get hit. Even the artillery which was being brought in, 37-mm. anti-tank guns and 75-mm. pack howitzers, were pushed and pulled through the water—they could have been rolled down the pier in one-tenth the time, if it had been possible.

Bill Hipple and I borrowed a shovel—correspondents rarely carry shovels—walked up the beach about twenty yards, and began looking for a spot to dig a foxhole. We stopped at a coconut-log pillbox and cautiously mounted the seawall to look in it. Inside were four Japs lying beside their machine gun. They were dead.

We jumped off the seawall, back onto the sand. This seemed as good a place as any to dig a foxhole, even if it were only ten feet from four dead Japs who were already beginning to smell. We dug the foxhole wide enough for the two of us, and deep enough so that we would be below the surface of the ground when the Jap bombers came over. We agreed that one would try to sleep while the other stood watch. I knew I was not going to sleep, though I hadn't slept the night before aboard ship—how long ago that seemed, aboard ship! And Bill knew he wasn't going to sleep. For one thing, the Japs would fire their mortars and rifles all night, if only to keep the Marines awake.

I was quite certain that this was my last night on earth. We had twenty feet along perhaps one-sixteenth of one-half of one side of the island, plus a few men in shellholes on either side of the airstrip. The Japs had nearly all the rest. Although we had landed a lot of troops—perhaps three thousand—by this time, most were crowded into such a small space that we did not have room for foxholes to hold them all. And if the Japs counterattacked, what could we do except shoot at them from behind our seawall until they finally overwhelmed us?

For the first time since morning, I was really scared—this was worse than wading into the machine-gun fire, because the unknown was going to happen under cover of darkness. I tried to joke about it. "Well, Bill," I said, "it hasn't been such a bad life." "Yeah," he said, "but I'm so damned young to die."

My knees shook. My whole body trembled like jelly. I peered into the darkness over the seawall, seeing nothing, hearing nothing except an occasional shot from a Jap sniper's rifle. But, I reasoned, it hasn't been a bad life at that. Suppose I don't live until morning? I have already lived fully and quite satisfactorily. Why should I be afraid to die? My family will be well provided for, with my own insurance and the insurance my company carries on its war correspondents. It will be tough on my children, growing up without a father, but at least they will have a very capable mother and the satisfaction of knowing that their father died in the line of duty. And why should any war correspondent assume that he can claim exemption from the death that had already come to Colonel Amey and Doc Welte? If I were not here as a war correspondent I would be here as a Marine, anyway. These people made me sick who were always saying, "Oh, what dangers you war correspondents must go through!" I say: war is dangerous, period. And what right has any American to feel that he should not be in it as fully as any other American? This is, I reflected, the United States; war, not the sailors' war or the Marines' war or the soldiers' war. What the hell?

These thoughts were snapped off like a light when a thousand orange-red flashes lit up the sea a couple of miles out. The sky filled with the outpouring of dozens of ships' guns, red balls of fire followed by deafening roars from over the water. "Look, Bill," I cried, "it's a naval battle! All the guns are firing on the surface of the water!" Of course, it was not a naval battle at all. Some low-flying Jap planes had started for the ships in the harbor, and the ships' anti-aircraft guns had opened up on them. They were frightened away and the firing stopped as suddenly as it had started.

Not long afterward a dozen Jap machine guns started chattering at the men on and off the pier, their pink tracer bullets curving out of the palm trees until they were doused in the water. But—of all things, some of this fire was coming from our own disabled boats in the water, and some of it was not the pink of the Jap tracers, but the orange-red stream of our own guns! Our guns, being turned against our own men. It took some time for this to sink in. Then I realized: the Japs had swum out in the darkness to our disabled boats and amphtracks. There they had manned the machine guns we had left in those boats, and now they were shooting at us. Clever, courageous little bastards! They knew it was suicide, but they knew they might kill some Americans before they themselves were killed.

During the night word was passed down the line: the Japs have broken through to the end of the pier. Now we were cut off, even from Major Crowe's battalion. I had not yet heard any word from the other assault battalion which had landed up on the western tip of Betio.

About an hour before dawn we heard the unmistakable purring of a Jap flying-boat's engines. "Old Washing Machine Charley," commented one of the Marines in a nearby foxhole. "I haven't seen him since we were at Guadalcanal. He doesn't do much harm but he keeps you awake." The bomber circled back and forth across the island, evidently trying to find out what was going on down there. Jap machine guns began chattering back of us and pink streams poured toward the beach; the Nips apparently were trying to direct Washing Machine Charley to us with their effeminate-looking tracers. Charley dropped a couple of bombs, then he flew around a few minutes longer and dropped the rest. They all fell harmlessly into the water. Then he flew away.

During the night I did not see a single Marine fire his rifle. Such firing might have given away our positions. Whatever else, I decided, these Marines were not trigger-happy. They were not forever firing at some figment of their imagination.

★ ★ ★ ★ ★

Tarawa, despite its small size, was of crucial importance to the Marine Corps and the success of the central Pacific campaign. It was a proving ground for the untested doctrines of large-scale amphibious assault against fortified positions. Lessons learned at Tarawa would save countless American lives at Saipan and Iwo Jima. It also hardened the American public to the reality of what the Allies faced in the Pacific War against Japan. The price for the U.S. Marine Corps was 1,001 killed and a further 2,296 wounded. Only one Japanese officer and sixteen enlisted men were taken prisoner, a grim warning of what lay ahead. Robert Sherrod passed away in 1993.

Peleliu—The Bloody Ridges

RUSSELL DAVIS

Of the entire Pacific War island battles, Peleliu may have been the most bitterly fought engagement for the Marines in World War II. Lying at the southern end of the Palau Islands near the equator, the daily temperature could reach 115 degrees Fahrenheit. Measuring only five square miles in size, the island features a series of high ridgelines running parallel along the interior of the northern half of the island. The volcanic structure of the geography riddled the terrain with natural caves and tunnels. It was the perfect defensive position.

When the First Marine Division landed on Peleliu, military intelligence estimated the defenders numbered no more than a few thousand, requiring three days of fighting. What the Marines encountered were over 10,000 enemy soldiers, expertly deployed to make full use of the island's natural defenses. Two months of close combat ensued, costing the 1st Marine Division and the U.S. Army 81st Infantry Division a total of 9,615 casualties with 1,656 killed. Russell Davis was a Marine scout with Second Battalion, First Marines during the fighting on Peleliu. The following chapter is taken from his acclaimed *Marine at War* about the fighting to seize the coral ridgelines of the "Umurbrogol."

> My only answer as to why the Marines get the toughest jobs is
> because the average Leatherneck is a much better fighter. He
> has far more guts, courage, and better officers . . . These boys
> out here have a pride in the Marine Corps and will fight to the
> end no matter what the cost.
> —2nd Lt. Richard C. Kennard

★　★　★　★　★

Old Marines talk of Bloody Nose Ridge as though it were one, but I remember it as a series of crags, ripped bare of all standing vegetation, peeled down to the rotted coral, rolling in smoke, crackling with heat and stinking of wounds and death. In my memory it was always dark up there, even though it must have blazed under the afternoon sun, because the temperature went up over 115°, and men cracked wide open from the heat. It must have been the color of the ridge that made me remember it as always dark—the coral was stained and black, like bad teeth. Or perhaps it was because there was almost always smoke and dust and flying coral in the air. I spent four days and nights up on the ridges, and it is difficult to untangle that time and to remember when specific things happened.

We went against the first ridge on the morning after John was killed. I went up with the assault company, across a clearing littered with stumps and coral and the scrap of war, up and down low hillocks and through a draw, and then onto the foot of the ridge. We got part way up the ride and then the hills opened and fire poured down on our heads. Two riflemen and I were plastered down into a hole and there we lay while the world heaved up all around us. We could do nothing but huddle together in terror. We couldn't go ahead, and nobody told us to do so. We couldn't go back. We were witless and helpless, with nothing to do but lie and take it. We couldn't run and we couldn't fight. Not one of the three of us bothered to fire a shot while we lay there through the morning.

We lay in it. Artillery shrieked. Men shrieked. And small arms whined. Mortars, defective in flight, whimpered overhead, and men whimpered. Every living thing on that hill cried out for something.

"Help, for God's sake, help us!"

"Corpsman! Here! *Corpsman*! Doc, I'm hurt bad."

"Plasma."

"Water."

"Artillery! Get it onto them. Stop them from hitting us like this."

"Air! Air strike! Come over with the air strike."

"Support!"

"Help!"

"*God!*"

In the afternoon Buck and I went out with Lieutenant Mac. He had specifically requested Buck because he enjoyed irritating him. We managed to get almost to the top of the ridge without coming under too much fire. There, Mac spread his map, dry-washed his hands, called his radioman to him, and said: "My message is this: At J—that's Jane—and at five o'clock on Jane Space, we will try one round on for size."

The radioman began to chant:

"*Hello, Dancer Charlie Peter, Hello, Dancer Charlie Peter.*"

"*This is Falcon Oboe Peter. This is Falcon Oboe Peter.*"

"*Come in, Dancer Charlie Peter. Come in, Dancer Charlie Peter.*"

"*Over.*"

The radioman was silent as he received the answering call. Then he said:

"*Dancer Charlie Peter.*

Dancer Charlie Peter.

I hear you five by five.

I hear you five by five.

How do you hear me?

How do you hear me?

Over."

The radioman listened and then said:

"*Dancer, here's a target.*

Dancer, here's a target.

Jane at five o'clock.

Jane at five o'clock.

Fire one. Fire one.

Over."

Mac and I edged up to the ridge line and waited for the first great bird to come howling over. The radioman yelled up to us: "On the way!"

The shell came shrieking over and made a vast flame against a distant hill, beyond a deep draw.

"Lovely," Mac breathed. "Lovely." He called down to his radioman: "Pour it onto Janie."

Shells swished by in a steady stream and the hillside flamed and writhed under the barrage. Mac searched for new targets. "Is that a gun that just stuck its tongue out at Item Three? I do believe it is. We'll get to you, my friend, in due course." He called down the new target and then rubbed his hands together with satisfaction. "Oh, the beauty of high ground! I will never run out of targets."

We ducked down as mortar fire came in over the lip of the ridge.

"Insolence will get you nowhere," Mac chortled. "The Flacon will strike again."

We went on spotting targets and Buck was very good at it. The war went on around us, but we scarcely noticed it. On that hill we were the big guns and the other action was beneath our notice.

We spotted targets all through the afternoon. All around us the riflemen stayed low in their holes, but there was something about calling down the thunder of sixteen-inch guns that made us contemptuous of return fire. We felt no fear and we did not bother to get down when the puny return fire of mortars came in.

The heat was terrible. One big, redheaded man, horribly burned and cracked around the face and lips, suddenly reared out of his hole like a wild horse. "I can't go the heat," he bellowed. "I can take the war but not the heat!"

He shook his fist up at the blazing sun above. Two of his mates pounced on him and rode him down to earth, but he was big and strong and he thrashed away from them. There was something bad for everybody on that hillside.

Mac kept spotting targets until it got too dark to see and then he tried to talk Buck into staying out on the line that night. "I want to be here bright and early," Mac said. "Nothing like a few hot sixteen-inch shells right on the breakfast table. Starts the day right for them."

Buck agreed to stay if we would move down to the foot of the ridge behind the Company Command Post. Mac hated to be that far away from the action but he agreed and we dug in just behind the Company Command Post. We had scooped our holes in the coral, spread our ponchos and arranged our weapons for the night when the Japanese counterattacked over the hill. We had to go back to the ridges with Mac.

The first night on the ridges was a night of terror. Mac pulled fire right in on top of us. He even fired behind us. To control the fire of ships miles away and to fire into the dark on the word of an observer who couldn't see the man in the next hole was a job which required complete confidence and courage. Mac had both. There would be a whispered word from the nervous radioman: "Under way, sir."

"All rightee," Mac would say. "Let's see where this one lands."

Buck and I, our knees pressing together and our hands on our heads, would wait, while the big bird came screeching up out of the darkness behind us. Orange flamed out in a star with a hundred points and the smash of the hit was like a blow from a dark fist, as all the round shook. There was a terrible silence while we waited for the cry for corpsmen to come from our riflemen. But no cry came. Instead a flare popped overhead. In the ghastly light Mac grinned at us. He seemed some terrible Irish "ha'nt" as he said: "Sure, the man who had my job before, poor lad, tried this blessed same thing one night. For the life of me I can't remember what he did wrong exactly. Well, we need not worry at all. It will come to me."

Buck had little sense of humor at best, and no sense of humor at night. He muttered, loud enough for Mac to hear: "That miserable, crazy Mick will kill us all."

Insults, even from enlisted men, never bothered Mac. "Now, now, Sergeant," he cautioned Buck. "I've been on this job almost three days and I've never lost an observer team." To the radioman, he said: "Let's bring that fire in a bit. Where are we?"

Late that night we went back to our holes and Buck was close to collapse. He lay down behind his shallow barricade of splintered wood and coral, got his body down as far as he could get it into the shallow depression we had made in the coral, muttered a few curses on Mac, began to mutter his prayers, and fell dead asleep. It was the first time, that I knew of, that Buck had slept since the landing.

The fourth day got lost in a blaze of heat. Men let the camouflage covers of their helmets down to shade their necks from the sun and to protect them from the sting of the rock dust that was everywhere. The riflemen looked like desert soldiers. Dark men grew darker, and light-complexioned men suffered the tortures of broiled faces, cracked lips, and almost sightless eyes. Many men threw away their helmets and wore only the old, soft, floppy fatigue caps of the Army. The round hat was a favorite in the First Division. It could be bent into any shape and serve against the rain or the sun.

There seemed to be no morning to that fourth day. While the sun blazed, we swung to the right of the first ridge, crossed a road that led nowhere, and came up against a sheer cliff. Down from this cliff, steep and studded with caves and holes, came Japanese fire. Only by hugging the base of it could we move. Machine-gunners were set up across the road, and the riflemen were assembled at the base of the cliff. The orders were to take the cliff. It was a stupid order.

While the riflemen were being assembled, the fire landed on E Company machine guns, and their screams came to our ears and wracked our nerves. Buck, who had been hugging the cliff in terror, reacted as he usually did when there was something to be done. He walked out across the road and stood up on a rock while mortars poured down around him. Buck and a sergeant from E Company organized a team of riflemen snipers and they began to pick off the mortar observers who were up on the forward slope of the ridge. They also got a bazooka man to fire into a nest of mortars. Then they called in the company and battalion mortars and the Japanese fire dried up and died. When it did, Buck ambled back to the protection of the ridge, and, once he was there, he showed fear again. Our companies started up the cliff.

We had lost heavily, ever since the beach, but I had not realized how bad the losses were until our companies moved out on the cliff. Clawing and crawling up the cliff went platoons that were no more than squads, and companies that were no more than large platoons. I counted one platoon. It mustered eighteen men on that push. But they went up.

From the base of the cliff, we could pick out each man and follow him until he got hit, went to ground, or climbed to the top. Not many made the top. As they toiled, caves and gulleys and holes opened up and Japanese dashed out to roll grenades down on them, and sometimes to lock, body to body, in desperate wrestling matches. Knives and bayonets flashed on the hillside. I saw one man bend, straighten, and club and kick at something that attacked his legs like a mad dog. He reached and heaved, and a Japanese soldier came end-over-end down the hill. The machine-gunners yelled encouragement.

As the riflemen climbed higher they grew fewer, until only a handful of men still climbed in the lead squads. These were the pick of the bunch—the few men who would go forward, no matter what was ahead. There were only a few. Of the thousands who land with a division and the hundreds who go up with a company of the line, there are only a few who manage to live and have enough courage to go through anything. They are the bone structure of a fighting outfit. All the rest is so much weight and sometimes merely flab. There aren't more than a few dozen in every thousand men, even in the Marines. They clawed and clubbed and stabbed their way up. The rest of us watched.

Watching them go up, Buck, the old rifleman, said: "Take a look at that sight and remember it. Those are riflemen, boy, and there ain't many like them. I was one once."

I looked up the cliff, but everything had changed. There was no longer anyone in sight. Our men who had gone up were either in holes near the top, dead, or lying out wounded and cooking in the sun. Another wave of riflemen got ready to go up, but before they could move out, heavy fire fell again, tearing apart the command posts and scattering machine-gunners and even dropping in behind the low ridge beyond the road, on the company mortar men. Once more, Buck moved out in it and called targets. This time I went with him, out of shame.

We could see Japanese observers, scurrying around near the top of the ridge line. We put everything we had in on them and Buck even yelled: "I wish that crazy officer was here with his big guns."

Before I could answer, a mortar *whooshed* in and blasted us both from the rock on which we stood. I landed on my feet and ran head-down for the base of the ridge. There, safe under an overhanging ledge, I sat, sobbing with an effort to get my breath. I saw Buck pick himself up, dust himself off, and climb back onto the rock. I sat for ten minutes, and then, ashamed of myself, I went out and relieved Buck. If he knew that I had run, he said nothing about it.

In the afternoon we went out on a long patrol, swinging around the nose of the cliff in a sweep to our right. We still had a few men up on the cliff, but we had learned something. Beyond that cliff was a deep gorge. After fighting up to it, we found ourselves isolated, with no chance to go ahead. So we went around. I went out with Larry and a platoon leader and a dozen men and, we got a long way out until we were pinned into a blockhouse by heavy fire from the hills ahead. The lieutenant decided that somebody had to go back and report, and the job fell to Larry and me.

We moved to the steps of the dugout and stood there while the fire thundered down overhead. It was a very tough blockhouse. The roof creaked and mortar and sand sifted down on us, but it didn't breach. We took off out of the blockhouse, running. On the way in, everything happened. We hit a Japanese patrol and were pinned down and chased. Then we were spotted from the ridge and pinned down with mortars. Then our own naval guns made a wall of fire which blocked us off. Probably, Mac was calling those shots. When we hit the naval guns, Larry said: "We best run for it. Good luck to you!"

We ran for it. I got in but I don't remember arriving or reporting. I remember Buck dumping pineapple juice into my mouth from his canteen cup. The fruit juice had been sent in from the ships of the line, and never was there a more welcome gift. Men were dropping from dehydration and sun. Larry and I drew two cans each, and I drank myself sick, but after the sun went down I could walk again. I even helped Buck prepare our position for the night.

The next morning I got up and joined the line, which was already moving off to our right along the route we had taken the day before. We got all the way to the bunker before we were stopped by fire from ridges which lay beyond a road and a causeway. The colonel took over the bunker as the Battalion Command Post. Later, the Regimental Command Post moved in. It was the best cover in the area. For me, it was like home. When I ran in from the causeway or the swamps, which were off to our right, the bunker was a welcome sight. Once inside, no matter what was coming in overhead, I felt secure. I knew every chink and crack in that foul and damp tomb, but it was home. It was a domed-roof pillbox, two steps down into the ground, concrete on top, steel reinforced, and concrete inside. It took direct hits until the mortar was all shaken out of the chinks between the blocks. But it held.

We were moved over toward a narrow causeway that ran through the swamp toward the road and the ridges. "Hold here," the lieutenant said.

Up on the causeway a memorable thing happened. A Marine came dashing out along it, moving toward the ridge. He was hit and knocked flat. I remember his muddy fingers stretched toward where we lay. He was clenching and unclenching his hand, either from pain or through some death reflex beyond his control. A second man, unable to stand the pitiful sight of that hand, clambered up onto the causeway and drove toward the wounded man. The second man was shot to a skidding stop. He lay on his back, without a twitch. A corpsman, who had seen it, said, "Shove this, I'm gonna get those guys." He rolled up onto the bank, got to his knees and never did stand up. The sniper shot him as he still knelt.

A fourth man, a squat and burly ape of a man with extra long arms, reached up over the edge of the causeway and began to pull the men in. He exposed no more than his long, thick arm, and he must have had phenomenal strength to drag the weight he pulled with one arm. I could see him straining and sweating as he began to tug the first of the wounded men over the edge of the bank. The sniper poured fire in at that thick, hairy arm that seemed to reach up out of the swamp like the tentacle of some hidden monster. Mortars harrumped and clopped into the mud; but the man pulled all three wounded men to safety.

Late in the afternoon, they began to patch the line companies with every able-bodied man they could send up from the rear. In came men from the war-dog platoons, the military police, the Division band, the Division laundry platoon, regimental headquarters men, and battalion clerks. I was assigned to take these men, each of them carrying a load of ammunition, out through the swamp and into the lines. Most of them were quiet and good men who were scared but not too scared to do what they were told. But a few of them had never visited the front lines and had no intention of going out there. They felt that the riflemen were a special breed, created to do all the suffering and dying for the Division.

A fat clerk complained to me: "I haven't been trained for this. What good will I do?"

I had neither pity nor sympathy for him. "You'll do fine, Fatty," I told him. "You will probably stop two bullets and save two good men."

That fat clerk hated me long before we got into the swamp. Twice I caught him lagging back and looking for a chance to duck. Both times he had dumped his ammunition so he could run better. He finally did bolt when we got into the high grass, and I never saw him again.

At the time I was watching another man who was trying to duck out. He had a good reason, too. He was a heavy winner in the Division poker game. He said his pack was stuffed with thousands of dollars in winnings, and he offered me a small piece of his money to let him run to the rear. He wasn't worried about himself as much as he was about the money.

"What if I got hit?" he asked. "Some grave-robbing thief would clean my pack."

"I'll see that they bury it right with you," I promised. "Get those belts of machine gun ammo around your neck and move out."

"I'm a sergeant," he told me.

"That's fine, Sergeant," I said. "I'm a private. Let's go."

We had easy going until we were in the high grass. There it was rough. The men with the belts of machine-gun ammunition couldn't run and they couldn't get down. The men carrying rifle ammunition in ponchos had it worse. Nobody panicked until the first carrier was shot and killed instantly. His partner, carrying the other corner of the poncho, put down his load and howled like a dog, and that noise unnerved everyone in the party. Of the twenty, I got nine men to the lines. Probably, no more than one other man had been hit. The rest either ran back or scattered to hide in holes in the grass. I had no time to flush them out of their cover.

After we got the ammunition out to the line, we couldn't find anybody to take it. Once more the companies were milling around, some men retreating and some attacking, but most of them were just lying there, hoping to get out alive. I dumped my ammunition in a Company Command Post and went back to the bunker. It was like coming home to a house in the suburbs after a hot and hard day in the city.

I spent that last night on the line almost entirely out of the bunker. At dusk, as we were boiling coffee water at the entrance steps, a tremendous fall of artillery came down, and two old machine-gunners—who had transferred into the quartermaster section for safety—were hit and blown down the steps of the bunker. We never did make that coffee. We dragged the wounded men down into the darkened tomb and held matches while a corpsman tried to stop the bleeding. The floor of the bunker was soaked with blood. The salty smell of it was everywhere. When Mac came by looking for an escort out to the line, I was glad to go, and we went out of the Company Command Post.

The remnants of our Second Battalion spent a terrible night up there. But, for the few men up on the higher ridge—mostly from C Company, First Battalion—it was far worse. All through the night we could hear them screaming for illumination or for corpsmen, as the Japs came at them from caves which were all around them on the hillside. Men were hit up there and we could hear them crying and pleading for help, but nobody could help them. The remains of the First and Second Battalion and the Division scout section had been thrown in together, and most of the men were strangers to each other. Two or three men were killed by their own mates that night. Grenades slammed and the stinging sound of the shrapnel came down the hill. The cries of Americans and Japanese were all mixed together. It unstrung even Mac.

"I think we ought to get up there," he told the company commander.

"Stay put," the company commander snarled. "Those are some of my kids catching hell up there. How do you think I feel?" He listened to the whimpering calls from the hills, and his head was down between his knees and he cursed monotonously. But he was right. We would have done them no good. "This will be a long, long night," he said.

"A long night," Mac echoed. "I think I'll say a prayer for those kids. Naval gunfire can't help them, God knows."

Of the sixth and last day on Peleliu, I have no connected memory. Short sequences like bad dreams are all that I can recall.

There was a squat, black-bearded rifleman who spoke with a New Orleans accent. He carried nothing but a rifle and a bandolier of ammunition. His shirt was black with sweat and plastered to him, skin tight, and he looked like a pirate. The colonel was talking to him as he got ready to lead his squad up the hill.

The rifleman said: "Colonel, we can go up there. We been up there before. And we'll go on up again until there's nobody left. But we can't hold that ridge, Colonel. We can't hold it unless there's more of us, sir. We can't hold it at all, sir. I mean—"

The colonel turned away without answering. He was on the verge of exhaustion himself.

I remember, too, an old sergeant with an ugly, Irish face. Perhaps he was only thirty or so but he looked like a hundred-year-old dwarf, red-faced, red beard, undershot jaw, bandy-legged—a wee and ugly gnome. The advance had been signaled, and the sergeant stood up on his twisted legs and waved the men forward toward the hill. A few men stumbled out of their holes. Some could not move. At least, they didn't. They leaned on their weapons and looked sick with dread. The sergeant looked at the men. He turned away and his face twisted with sudden grief and tears came down his bearded cheeks. He waved his hand and rubbed his dirty face with his sleeve.

"Let's get killed up on that high ground there," he said. "It ain't no good to get it down here." As the men stumbled out for him, he said, "That's the good lads."

There were few platoon leaders and few sergeants. The young officers had been hit and the sergeants had been hit or they had folded, and the "duty" fell on those who would take it. Rank meant nothing. Privates, who had something left, led sergeants who didn't have it any more, but who would follow, even if they wouldn't order other men to. One big Italian man moved forward, dragging his blanket, unwilling to part with it, even though it tangled in his legs. Another man had his head covered with a poncho, so that only his eyes showed. The eyes were like those of a small burrowing animal driven to ground and cornered. A small Jewish man, who carried a company radio, moved around in a circle. He was determined to move, but he was too damaged by shock and fatigue to get his bearings. A scout, who walked near him, pointed him toward the hill and the two of them staggered out.

The whole motley lot—a fighting outfit only in the minds of a few officers in the First Regiment and in the First Division—started up the hill. I have never understood why. Not one of them refused. They were the hard core—the men who couldn't or wouldn't quit. They would go up a thousand blazing hills and through a hundred blasted valleys, as long as their legs would carry them. They were Marine riflemen.

A machine-gunner, a Lithuanian, sat calmly at his gun, alone and beyond the causeway. Fire threw rock dust and powder and shrapnel all around him, but he did not move and he did not even flinch. He made no effort to protect himself. His gun was neatly set and laid in to cover the break in the ridge through which any counterattack would come.

He said to me: "I can't go up that hill again. I got no legs now. But no Japs will come through that hole while I'm here." He was sharp-faced and clean, even in the middle of the barrage. I remember that.

In a swamp, an old sergeant crouched in his hole. He had been away from his outfit for two days and his were the motions of a hunted animal. "I got nothing more inside," he said. "Nothing. I don't even know anybody who is still alive. They're all gone, boy. Done, the whole lash-up."

I never found out what we were doing, tactically, on the sixth day. At first, I did what they told me to do, but no more. I ran around to the jumbled messes that were called companies, and I tried to help our colonel keep some control of the scattered survivors of many outfits that made the last push up the ridges. Things started bad and got worse and, finally, hopeless. I quit.

I picked up the rifle of a dead Marine and I went up the hill. I remember no more than a few yards of scarred hillside, blasted white with shellfire and hot to touch. I didn't worry about death any more. I had resigned from the human race. I only wanted to be as far forward as any man when my turn came. My fingers were smashed and burned, but I felt no pain. I crawled and scrambled forward and lay still, without any feeling toward any human thing. In the next hole was a rifleman. He peered at me through red and painful eyes. Then we both looked away. I didn't care about him. He didn't care about me. I thought he was a fool and he probably thought I was the same. We had both resigned from the human club. As a fighting outfit, the First Marine Regiment was finished. We were no longer even human beings. I fired at anything that moved in front of me. Friends or foe. I had no friends. I just wanted to kill.

The history of the First Division says that we were relieved late in the afternoon of the sixth day. I don't remember coming down the hill, but I remember sitting by a roadside, in tears. I don't know why. I hadn't cried at all up on the hill. I suppose I was becoming a human again, after some time away from being one. When you come off the hard places, you crawl on your stomach and then move on your hands and knees and then go forward crouching and, at last, you walk erect, and then you feel like a man and it feels awful. Ever since Peleliu I have wondered if animals in danger feel things keenly. I didn't, the one time I turned into an animal. I didn't even feel the pain in my hands until after I was off the line.

The Division History says that by nightfall on the seventh day the First Marine Regiment reported their casualties—1,749 men. That was out of 3,500. It seemed as though there were more. The line companies were decimated.

We camped back near the first ridge and ate hot food and read our accumulated mail. Then we moved across the island near Purple Beach and camped in a swamp, and the first night I was on guard a Japanese infiltrater got close in on me, and I stood up just as he threw a hand grenade. We saw each other at the same time and I was quicker, or scareder. He knocked me down with the concussion of the grenade, but not before I knocked him flat with the direct burst of a Tommy gun. I took one small piece in the lower part of my back. I would have used it to get off the island, but we were going anyway.

On a dark and rainy day, eighteen days after we landed, we went out through heavy, oil swells and under lowering skies to load onto LSTs and eventually a hospital transport, the *Tryon*. We had had a few days' rest, but some of us had trouble getting up the cargo nets and over the rail with what equipment we still carried. My fingers bothered me still. The back was nothing. I remember the big, thick wrists of the sailor who helped me over the rail, who had looked into our faces and seen what was plainly there. He wanted to be comforting. He said: "You gave it to 'em real good, boys. Good on ya.'"

★   ★   ★   ★   ★

An F Company rifleman heaved himself over onto the deck and, for a moment, he lay there helpless like an overturned bug or turtle. Then he got his legs under himself and stood up and pain showed in his face. He said to the sailor: "No—no, we didn't give it to 'em good. We didn't give it to 'em at all. We got beat." He looked back toward the low-lying island and shook his head, as though he still couldn't believe what had happened there.

"We won before. We'll win the next one. But this time we got beat, swabbie.

"And that's the truth of it."

The Old Breed and the Costs of War

EUGENE B. SLEDGE

Eugene B. Sledge became part of the Marine Corps' 1st Marine Division, 3d Battalion, 5th Marines after volunteering for service in December of 1942. His first taste of combat came at Peleliu, one of the most bitterly fought engagements of the Pacific War, in September of 1944. He would see action again at Okinawa the following year. His memoir of his experiences as a Marine was written at the urging of his family, only later to be published in the unforgettable *With the Old Breed: At Peleliu and Okinawa*. The historian John Keegan credits Sledge's memoir as a "one of the most arresting documents in war literature." E. B. Sledge would recount and elaborate on his experiences in a lecture for the Mises Institute in Atlanta, 1994, entitled "The Old Breed and the Costs of War."

> Rifles were high and holy things to them, and they knew five-inch broadside guns. They talked patronizingly of the war, and were concerned about rations. They were the Leathernecks, the Old Timers. . . . They were the old breed of American regular, regarding the service as home and war as an occupation; and they transmitted their temper and character and viewpoints to the high-hearted volunteer mass which filled the ranks of the Marine Brigade . . .
>
> —John W. Thomason, Jr.

★   ★   ★   ★   ★

The first day of boot camp, 1943. (I had been in college for one year, and then joined the Marine Corps.) The drill instructor set the tone for the next several weeks: "You people are stupid." We hadn't taken any sort of test, or

136

had any type of evaluation, but he said to us, "You people are stupid, and if any of you think you can tell me what to do, step outside and I will whip you ass right now." None of us stepped outside. That was the reality of the Marine Corps I entered, a reality which descended upon you quickly and mercilessly.

One day, early on in boot camp, I got out of step. I usually managed to keep the cadence, but I was just a little off that day. The drill instructor walked up beside me, and in a very quiet menacing voice said, "Boy, you pick up the cadence, or they're gonna have to take us both to sick bay, because it's going to take a major operation to get my foot out of your rear end." You know, I never lost the cadence after that.

I graduated from boot camp on Christmas Eve, 1943. On Christmas Day, most of us in my platoon were assigned to infantry school, Camp Elliott, near Los Angeles. After several weeks of intensive, rigorous infantry training, we boarded the U.S.S. *President Polk*, an old luxury liner converted into a troopship. After 28 days at sea, packed on the *Polk* like thousands of sardines, we landed in New Caledonia. While there, we trained hard with every infantry weapon from the 7-inch-blade Kabar knife to the bayonet, from the flamethrower to the 37mm antitank cannon. We also became thoroughly familiar with all Japanese weapons. Running up and down high, rugged mountains conditioned us to be as physically tough as possible. Twenty-five mile forced marches and amphibious landings along the coast were frequent. All the instructors were combat veterans who knew what lay ahead of us—and who knew that our survival chances were slim.

In June, we shipped out to an island near the Solomon Islands, where we joined the veteran, elite First Marine Division, nicknamed "The Old Breed." I was assigned to a rifle, or line company (meaning the front line), K Company, 3rd Battalion, 5th marine (Regiment), First Marine Division. K Company became my "home," and the veterans treated us replacements like brothers with the understanding we had to prove ourselves in combat. They were the best teachers in the world in how to kill Japs because simply said, that is the infantryman's job, to *kill* the enemy. No euphemisms were needed. We were told frankly that we were expected to uphold the high standards of the 5th Marines. It was decorated at Belleau Wood in World War I, in the Banana Wars, and recently on Guadalcanal. The Company was made up of young men of very high caliber. I was 20 years old; many others were teenagers, some were veterans, some were college men—all were volunteers. They were the finest, bravest men I ever knew. At Peleliu, K Company suffered 64 percent casualties—we actually lost more men than we started with.

Julius Caesar said, "Terror robs men of their power of reason and judgment and impairs their physical capacity." On the battlefield, the primary emotion is sheer, absolute terror. Even the veterans, like my gunnery sergeant, who didn't seem to have a nerve in his body, told me at the first postwar reunion of the First Marine Division I attended, "Sledgehammer, I was scared as you were, but I just couldn't show it." And he said, "You remember that patrol we went on in that swamp on Peleliu—the 40 of us, who were to hold the advance of 1,500 Japs? They were supposed to be on the other side of the swamp, and we were supposed to hold them up long enough to get help." He then said, "That was a *suicide* patrol. I didn't tell anybody that." Well, 40-odd years later, when he told me that, I fell into the nearest chair.

It has been said that the combat veteran has to *live through* the experience and then, if he survives, he has to *live with* it the rest of his life. How you handle yourself and what you make of yourself depends a great deal on your upbringing, your discipline, and things of this sort.

I want to make some remarks about the people we fought, the Japanese soldiers. To us they were "Japs." The Japanese soldier was dedicated to his cause; he fought to the death because that was the way he had been trained. He was loyal to the Emperor, unbelievably physically tough, and well disciplined. When he was inducted into the Japanese army he was brutalized by his superiors. Brutality was institutionalized in the Japanese army. There are documented cases of the cruelty imposed on Japanese troops in training—the barbarism lasted through the first year. If the soldier even looked at his sergeant without the proper respect (what might be called silent contempt), he was in trouble. I picked up many a rotten coconut on working details when I was in base camp because of silent contempt, i.e. the way I looked at somebody in authority. But a Japanese lieutenant would have his troops stand at attention and then take a hobnail shoe and beat his men in the face until their faces bled. With such cruel treatment from their superior officers, they were conditioned to treat their enemies with utter barbarity. Compassion was something that was totally foreign to them. That is why they could rampage through China and commit rape and murder. The soldier was told that the rape of enemy women was macho. Take Nanking for instance, where thousands of Chinese were murdered and raped over a period of about three to four weeks. The best kept secret of World War II is the truth about Japanese atrocities. But business is good with Japan, so do not embarrass her people, as our liberal news media does the Germans with almost monthly programs about the holocaust. There is not much even written about the Japanese conduct; do not even worry about embarrassing a young Japanese by bringing it up, because the only thing they are taught about World War II is that the U.S. bombed Japan.

In regard to the bombing of Nagasaki and Hiroshima, as Paul Fussell says, "Anybody who thinks it was a bad idea says so because his life wasn't saved by it." But ours were. We were scheduled to invade Japan, and we literally would have had to kill every man, woman, and child. The Japanese had a strong song that said "100,000,000 souls will die for the Emperor." Despite revisionist claims, if we had invaded Japan, we would have suffered enormous casualties, and the fighting would have lasted for *years*.

War to the infantryman meant killing. If you had any qualms about killing the enemy, you had better get over it in a hurry, because when you made an attack, or they made an attack, it was kill or be killed. I must admit, the first Japs I saw close by, I did not pull the trigger. Three ran out of a pillbox and Snafu Shelton, my foxhole buddy, said, "What the hell's the matter with you, do you want them in the foxhole here with us?" I said, "No." Then seven more ran out of that pillbox with their bayonets fixed, and I was firing at them before he was. Typical of the Japanese, and rarely described, they ran out of the pillbox each holding his bayoneted rifle in the right hand, and un-buttoned britches held up with the left hand. When they got killed, they dropped their britches. There was something in their religion, or the military Code of Bushido, that designated the lower abdomen as the place of man-hood, instead of the chest as it is in Western culture. We saw thousands of them killed on Okinawa lying about, practically in their birthday clothes. With their last ounce of strength, they had pulled their trousers down. At this pillbox, a Jap stood up at an opening in the side and tried to throw a grenade at us. I shot him in the chest and the grenade exploded as he fell. I felt no regret.

The front line is a place of passion, terror, and hatred. We hated the Japs with a passion, so I felt no regret when killing them. It has been said by some revisionists that we hated them because we were racist; this is non-sense. The Japanese were hated because they fought with savagery beyond necessity according to the Code of Bushido. This meant you had to kill every last one of them before you could get off an island.

Jap brutality extended to our wounded. We all acted as stretcher-bearers, as needed, and had to get to the wounded man on the stretcher and were apt to get shot. If they could, the Japs shot the wounded man on the stretcher, and then tried to shoot down the stretcher team. I had a good friend, "Doc," who was a medical corpsman. During an attack up a long slop-ing ridge on Okinawa, he was working on a wounded Marine. Doc almost had this boy fixed up and a sniper shot Doc in the left leg up in the hip region. I ran up there with two stretcher teams to get them down. We got Doc up on the stretcher, and that sniper, son of a bitch, shot Doc in the other hip just as we got him on the stretcher. Now, why didn't he shoot to kill him? Well, he shot him in two places to immobilize him, so that we would have to carry Doc, then he could shoot at us. Well, we out-ran all the Olympic runners getting Doc and the other wounded man down that ridge so all of us could get out of his way. Fortunately, he didn't hit any of the rest of us.

Wild excitement existed on the front line. When you are so close to a Jap you can throw a hand grenade at him, but you know you had better not throw it because he will throw it back at you before it explodes, you have a decision to make!

During an attack, either ours or theirs, the artillery and mortar bombardment was so loud it was thunderous. You couldn't even talk to the Marine next to you, and the ground swayed and shook from concussion as shells erupted all around and steel fragments tore through the air and through men's bodies. On Okinawa, some of the Japanese artillery barrages went on for four and five days. When the shells finally stopped we were all shaking. You couldn't hold your rifle steady. Your nerves had been so knocked about by all that terrific concussion. All the while we were carrying wounded and dead out. We moved them to the rear if we could, but sometimes shells fell so thickly we couldn't move the dead. The violence was inconceivable.

To the infantryman, artillery is one of the worst things you have to put up with—right up there with machine guns, snipers, mortars, hand grenades, and tanks. As for enemy artillery, we were especially unlucky at Okinawa. The Japanese started with a full complement of artillery there. They had *additional* artillery shipped to the Philippines, but before the ships got to the Philippines, they were rerouted to Okinawa, because the Philippines were going to fall. So that meant those of us who landed on Okinawa got a double dose of shelling. Those terrible shellings shattered the nerves of many front-line Marines.

We got new second lieutenants with each set of replacements. Many were full of bravado and swagger they had learned at Quantico in officer training. One good shelling knocked it out of them, whether they got hit or not. Poor souls, they usually didn't last but a few days before death or wounding.

At Peleliu we had to attack several hundred yards across the open airfield through heavy Jap fire from every type of weapon they had. Machine gun fire was something you could get away from if you could hunker down in a foxhole, but if it caught you out in the open, it was terrifying. When I ran across the airfield at Peleliu, I could see bluish-white Jap tracers coming by me just like the railings on a porch, the bullets making a "snapping" sound close by. The big shells were erupting and thundering to such an extent you couldn't even yell to the Marine next to you. The ground swayed back and forth. To be shelled out in the open, on your feet, was nerve shattering terror. After the war was over, a friend of mine said, "Sledgehammer, did you know that Billy 'cracked up' back there on the airfield, and they had to actually drag him across here under cover?" And I said "No, I didn't know that, what happened to him?" My buddy looked sick, and said, "Well, you remember Joe, we all went through boot camp together? Joe got hit in the head and it splattered his brains all over Billy's face." I gasped in horror. It was that kind of thing that was apt to happen at any time in infantry combat.

You developed a "close personal" relationship with a sniper, because you could only cringe in your foxhole with your buddy, and my buddy was Snafu Shelton, who was from the swamps of Louisiana. Snafu could cuss a blue streak, and conversation under fire resulted in a very fascinating juxtaposition of emotions—The Lord's Prayer and Twenty-third Psalm on my part, and "God damn you son-of-a-bitch," on Snafu's part.

We knew that sniper was after us personally, so we should curse him personally. Japanese snipers were crack shots. There were actual records of them hitting Marines on Peleliu at 600 yards. The volume of fire that came at us when the Japanese made an attack was tremendous. When you think of the amount of steel and fragments and bullets that came at a man, it is amazing any of us survived. My company suffered 64 percent casualties at Peleliu; it lasted thirty days and thirty nights, because the Japs fought us all night.

I recently received a letter from an Air Force man who had been stationed on Okinawa, and he said he read my book, *With the Old Breed: At Peleliu and Okinawa.* He said he examined the ground on a particular ridge we defended during a Japanese major attack. It was no suicide Banzai charge, not the stupid kind that allowed John Wayne to mow them down by the thousands. This had been a well-planned counterattack at Okinawa. This airman was just curious as to the volume of fire to which we had been subjected. He measured off a square foot of ground and then dug just below the surface. He wrote me that he found thirty pieces of shrapnel or bullets in that single square foot. In combat, I thought I was going to catch all thirty every time I took a step. Every man thought that he was the object of the whole, entire Japanese barrage.

The nights were sheer terror in the Pacific. Savage hand-to-hand combat was often the rule rather than the exception. It was terrifying, dirty, sickening, and vile. About an hour after darkness fell on the battlefield (anywhere in the Pacific), single or small groups of Japs began creeping toward our foxholes. No Marine moved out of his foxhole after dark. If he had to identify himself he whispered the password. My buddy and I took turns trying to catch a "cat nap" and keeping our eyes and ears concentrated on even the least suspicious sound. Star shells and mortar flare shells were used periodically (each flare had a small parachute) and brightly illuminated our area. Between these periods of blessed light we crouched in our hole, Kabar knife in one hand and a grenade, rifle, or Thompson submachine gun in the other. We strained our eyes and ears in the inky blackness to catch the first warning of a Jap creeping close. The tension was awful. The Japs crept in by ones and twos. If we, or some other Marine, saw them first, the eerie silence in our area exploded with the firing of our weapons—the bang of our firearm and the pop of grenade detonator caps followed by the loud "BANG!" of our grenades. If the Japs came in undetected, there was the pop of a Japanese grenade detonator followed by the bang of their grenades, as they tried to throw them into Marine positions. This was followed by wild, incoherent Japs screaming as they rushed us swinging Samurai saber, bayonet, or rifle butt. Marine curses and warnings to neighboring foxholes sounded. Amid the sound of the thud of body blows as men yelled, screamed, cursed, and choked back groans of pain, men fought hand-to-hand with the savagery probably typical of Neanderthal man. There were yells for flares, and the hoarse shouts "corpsman" when the Marines were wounded. This went on almost every night after the heavy fighting of the day. We were exhausted after each close encounter. We usually lost Marines, killed or wounded, but we always killed the Japs. Strict discipline, complete reliance on other Marines, and cool heads prevented total panic on our part in these terrifying fights. It was war at its most elemental, brutal level as men slashed, stabbed, shot, or brained their enemies. Snafu and I never let a Jap get into our foxhole because of our alertness, but it happened many times in neighboring foxholes, and we lost some fine buddies this way. All night, bursts of firing along the lines indicated where these desperate struggles took place, while shells screamed and whistled back and forth overhead.

At night, the Japanese tried to "infiltrate" the lines. At Peleliu, they had a whole battalion to raid the lines in small groups. They would slip up as close as they could to us, throw a grenade into our foxholes, and then come in screaming with a saber or bayonet. Now, the idea of a saber in modern war might sound ridiculous, but I had a buddy whose right arm was amputated by a Jap officer who slipped up close and then jumped in his position. I had another buddy who lost two fingers while he was holding onto his rifle parrying a saber thrust. The Jap swung his saber and cut the Marine's hand, and then my buddy hit the Jap just like you hit a baseball, with the butt of his rifle; that ended the fight. The Japs usually got killed in those night attacks but we always had casualties, too.

The typical German soldier was a superb soldier from everything anybody writes about them. He wanted to fight as honorably as he could and then get home to his family. The typical Japanese soldier wanted to fight honorably, but instead of wanting to go home, the Japanese soldier wanted to die for the Emperor, so that meant you had to kill him before you could get it over with. Of course, he made that difficult because he wanted to make sure that when he died, he took you with him. If you advanced to a new position and the enemy wounded were lying around there, somebody routinely went around and shot them in the head. Some of the outfits called these men "the 'possum squad." The Japs would resort to any kind of ruse to trick us, such as slipping behind the lines at night and calling for a corpsman and begging for assistance. Often, they would play dead in order to lure us closer until they could kill us with a bayonet or knife. Fortunately, I went into a veteran outfit as a replacement, so I learned many of these tricks from men who had combat experience. Also, you could distinguish the intention of the Jap voice and you could recognize them.

The fatigue a combat infantryman is exposed to is absolutely beyond description. Nothing like it in civilian life even approaches the intensity of physical and nervous exhaustion caused by close combat. Sometimes on the news you will see exhausted football players, or exhausted basketball players. But any combat veteran can tell you what real fatigue does to a man. When one goes for two weeks or for thirty days, we were literally shuffling around like zombies. I had weighed about 145 pounds when I went into the Okinawa campaign, and when it was over and we got up North and built a tent camp, I weighted about 120 pounds.

The front-line companies suffered staggering casualties during fierce combat. K company had invaded Peleliu with 325 Marines; only 85 survived death or wounds. Replacements were added to bring the company up to normal strength of 235 Marines to invade Okinawa. During this battle, the company absorbed 250 replacements to make up for the continuous losses. Only fifty Marines remained at the end. Of these, only twenty-six had made the landing, and only ten were never wounded.

Everybody lost weight because of the sheer stress and extreme physical exhaustion. You can't imagine the hard labor just bringing up ammunition through the mud. The 30-caliber ball, which was the standard ammunition for the M-1 rifle, was in a wooden box which weighed over 100 pounds. The "genius" who designed the box placed the little finger groove in each end. You were supposed to put the tips of your fingers in there to lift up a box that weighted over 100 pounds. In the rains, and with mud smeared all over the box, this, of course, just brought forth more creative cursing on the part of the troops. To move each box across rough terrain, often under fire, in driving rain, and through deep mud, required two Marines. Each man firmly gripped the bottom corners of one end—usually slippery with mud. Heavy boxes of grenades fortunately had two rope handles. Machine gun ammo boxes had well-designed folding metal handles.

It has been shown that the longer combat went on, the worse the stress became, and the more exhausted the troops became because the "Fight or Flight Syndrome" physiologically took over. We were all keyed up, the adrenaline was pumping, and when that goes on for almost three months, one doesn't have much reserve left. When buddies were killed or wounded many of us just simply cried, because we were very closely knit. Even replacements became absorbed into the "brotherhood" of unit cohesion. We had a great deal of respect for each other, because in the Marine Corps you were taught loyalty. The greatest sin you could commit was to let a buddy down, so we knew we could depend on any man that had a Marine uniform, whether we knew his name or not.

We generally could not move forward without tanks, because the Japs would simply mow us all down the way infantry was massacred in World War I. By following tanks, the infantry could have some protection, and the tank could be firing its 75mm gun at the same time. On Okinawa, we went through a period of about ten days of torrential rain; this meant the tanks could not move. We were right in front of Shuri, the main Japanese defense bastion. The outfit that had tried to take Half Moon Hill before my battalion moved up had very heavy casualties. They could not remove their dead because of the thousands of Jap shells unleashed on the area. The day we moved onto Half Moon Hill, torrential rains began and did not slacken for ten days. Tanks bogged down and all our attacks had to stop, so we occupied the Hill amid death and heavy shell fire. Almost every shell hole in the area had a dead Marine in it, and they were all infested with maggots. The rain washed the maggots off the dead over the top of the soil into our foxholes. In the foxhole that Snafu and I had dug, we had to put boards in the bottom and then dig a sump hole in one end. We frequently bailed it out with an old helmet that a casualty had left. If we hadn't bailed, the foxhole would have flooded. It was just like a colander immersed in water. Water came over the edges of the hole, and water came through the soil of the sides. It looked like sprouts—just like turning on the spigot, it was raining so hard. We stayed soaked, cold, and muddy. It must have been fifty degrees Fahrenheit at night, our teeth chattering as we shivered on the wet, cold battlefield.

The Japs were attacking every night, and we were killing them in our lines every night. In the Pacific, decay was rapid. We threw mud on the dead bodies with our entrenching tools to hold down the swarms of big flies and maggots. The next day, or the next few days, shells came in and blew the corpses apart. There were body parts lying all over the place; we called it "Maggot Ridge." If we went down the ridge and slipped and fell, we slid all the way down to the bottom. Then, when we came up to our feet, the maggots were falling out of our dungaree pockets, our cartridge belts and everything else. Many men nauseated and threw up. The stench was awful; beyond description. Also, the personal filth that the infantryman had to endure was inconceivable. There was one period of three months during which we existed without a bath, just living in the slimy mud. My mouth felt like it was full of mud, but we had no way to brush our teeth. Still, we had to stay alert. We had to be attuned to every sound at night, even amidst the rush of shells and rattle of machine guns. On Half Moon, as elsewhere, the Japs slipped around at night, and they were experts at it. Of course, you can imagine the odor of the dead. The only way we could eat anything (our stomachs were tied in knots) was to use a little tripod-like device we could put a sterno tablet on and heat a can of rations beans or coffee—always before dark, because any light after dark would draw sniper fire. Once heated, we had to eat the beans quickly or the torrential rain filled the ration can with cold water.

We had tremendous loyalty to our units and this was mainly the cement that kept us together. When we were out there and "the stuff hit the fan," it was a matter of life and death. Sure, we were all fighting for the Constitution, but basically, each man was fighting for his buddy, and he was fighting for you, because that was war at the elemental level. There wasn't anything between us and the Japs except space. Sometimes at night, that space was not more than a few feet. If they got in your foxhole, it was a hell of a lot closer than that.

The aftermath of all this was that there were widows and there were orphans. Many of our men were very young and had not married;

others were married, and some had children. The one curse that we were all left with from combat, whether we were married or single, was the nightmares. I had them for twenty-five years. I would wake up in a cold sweat and screaming—having gone through something in a dream that was just as realistic as what I had survived. Some nights I was afraid to go to sleep, so I would stay up late reading, and hoping the nightmares wouldn't come. But all the survivors hear the memories, like a curse, for the rest of their lives.

The dead we mourn. If he was a buddy, you wept over him. History remembers the wounded men as numbers—often as just statistics. But for some of the wounded, the physical pain has been with them every day since the war. I have a buddy nabbed John Huber who lives in Virginia. He is one of the finest men I ever knew. Now, fifty years later, he had to have another of numerous surgical operations because his hip had to be replaced. The wound threw his spine out of line. Then, after years of suffering, it threw his right ankle out of line. He has never complained; he is alive. To Huber, to complain would be ridiculous.

Another friend, Jim Kronaizl, whose family lived in the Dakotas on a big wheat farm, had his post-war life altered by his wound. It was his ambition, his dream, to get back and work that wheat farm after the war. He loved the independence of farming and the outdoors. One day, on Okinawa, I was standing on the front edge of a little ridge. A deep standing foxhole was right in front of me. I was watching the front line through binoculars because we had been pulled off the line. We had had an attack the day before and lost heavily in my company, so the Battalion C.O. pulled us off the line for a few days rest. I had seen mortar shells coming toward us, so I got the binoculars and was watching our front. Six or eight buddies were behind me playing cards around an ammo box. I said, "You guys better look out, that Jap gunner is walking those shells right down this little valley." Well, I got what a Marine usually got in a case like that, "Oh hell, Sledgehammer, you're just nervous in the service." So I said, "Okay I'm telling you, you'd better look out." At that moment, there was a terrific crash as a shell exploded right down in front of me down at ground level. The concussion knocked me off my feet and down into my foxhole—amazingly, I was still standing upright. How in God's name I didn't get my head blown off I'll never know, but poor Kronaizl received a bad wound in the head and was carried to the nearby aid station. After the war, he had a bad seizure and he fell off his tractor. He told me, "When I fell, I luckily kicked the tractor gear lever in neutral, otherwise the tractor would have run over me. I went to my doctor and he said, 'Son, you are going to have these seizures all the rest of your life because of that head wound. Get off that farm.'" So, Jim said, "Sledgehammer, I had to give up the farm, and if you can believe it, loving the outdoors like I do, I am now in a damn insurance office."

Another buddy, Jim Day from California, had a horse farm. His dream, when he returned home, was to make it into a horse ranch. At Peleliu, a Japanese machine gun shattered one of Jim's legs. It was a heavy machine gun, and the Jap was so close to us he just moved the gun a little bit and poor Jim just toppled over. There was his leg, shattered, a bloody pulp as he was lying on the ground, blood spurting out of the stump. Later, when Jim came to the First Marine Division reunions (maybe some of you can't conceive of this), we would have to help him go to the bathroom. His wife had to do that at home. The poor man couldn't handle it by himself, because of that stump of a leg cut off at the hip. He died a premature death after years of pain and back trouble.

I had a wonderful friend named Marion Vermeer, who had been a lumberjack from Washington State before enlisting in the Marines. He wanted to be a lumberjack when he went back home. One day on Half Moon Hill on Okinawa, the Japs put some pressure on the Army unit on our left, and the Army line moved to the rear a little distance. That meant there was a bend in our line to the left. The Japs got close with a seventy-millimeter mountain gun and sighted it along our line from the left flank. This artillery piece was on small wheels so they could move it around quickly. But a seventy-millimeter is a rather large shell and was a high velocity shell. The Japs fired the first shell, and it went right behind our lines and exploded to our rear where some of our knocked-out tanks were. Somebody said, "What the hell was that?" One of the NCOs said, "That was a mountain gun." The next shell came screaming along our front line, no more than a foot over my head, I am not exaggerating. It passed the foxhole next to me with two young Marines who were replacements and exploded in Marion's foxhole. Marion was dug in with Bill Leyden and another Marine. Bill was blown up into the air and Vermeer just fell over. The two boys in the hole next to me were hit. One of them jumped up and was flailing the air with his arms and fell dead. The other was yelling, "Oh, Jesus Christ, it hurts so bad, make me die, I can't stand it for Christ's sake, Jesus do something." And then he just toppled over onto the mud dead. I started over to their foxhole and the sergeant said, "Sledgehammer, get back on that mortar." The mortar was right at the base of the ridge, and I had more experience than the gunner that was on the mortar at the time. He said, "If they locate that mountain gun, I'm gonna need to get on the mortar and shell that Jap gun crew." So, I must admit I was glad to get down below the crest of the ridge. Fortunately, the Jap gun didn't fire anymore. A little later though, they brought Vermeer by me on a stretcher, his right leg below the knee was just a bloody bandage. Thrown onto the stretcher was his field shoe with his bloody ankle sticking out of it. He said, "Sledgehammer, you think I'll ever be able to be a lumberjack again?" and I said, "Sure old buddy you'll make it, you'll be back in all those beautiful trees doing what you want to do." I felt as though I had been stabbed in the heart. They carried him twenty yards, and then put the stretcher down; he was dead. All of the Marines who were dug near me, and the four on the stretcher team, all had tears streaming down our muddy, bearded faces. Bill Leyden was seriously wounded, and lost part of his right hand. Since the war, he has been bothered by seizures caused by the concussion that blew him into the air. Both Leyden and Vermeer had been wounded on Peleliu.

Those are some of the tragedies that are called "The Costs of War" to those who actually fight on the front lines. The following applies to every Marine and Soldier who fought up-front:

> And when he goes to Heaven
> To St. Peter he'll tell
> Another Marine reporting, Sir,
> I've served my time in Hell.

To the Summit with the Flag

RICHARD WHEELER

Richard Wheeler was a member of 3rd Platoon, Company E, 2nd Battalion, 28th Marines, 5th Marine Division that landed at Iwo Jima on February 19, 1945. Their mission was to cut across the narrowest stretch of the island cutting off the Japanese defenders of Mount Suribachi, the dominant land feature on the southern tip of the island, from reinforcement. Once this was accomplished, the 166-meter-high Suribachi had to be taken to deny the enemy its use to call accurate fire on the American-held beaches. Richard Wheeler documented the five-day struggle in *The Bloody Battle for Suribachi,* first published in 1965. In the following chapter he describes the heroism of the forty-man patrol that first placed the American flag on Suribachi, later immortalized by Joe Rosenthal's photograph of the Marines raising a larger, replacement flag a short time later. The photo would become the most famous of the war, and an icon of American victory.

> The raising of that flag on Suribachi means a
> Marine Corps for the next 500 years.
> —James Forrestal

★ ★ ★ ★ ★

Up to this time our regiment had been taking more punishment than it had been dealing, but now it began to strike back with a vengeance. Its three battalions hammered fiercely at the semicircle of defenses, destroying the enemy in growing numbers and pressing ever closer to the volcano's base.

Our rifle companies had plenty of help. Constantly busy with demolitions were elements of the 5th Engineer Battalion. These men sometimes forgot they belonged to a support unit and took on bunkers, pillboxes and caves that lay out ahead of the front liens. Also continuing their vigorous aid were the regiment's tanks, howitzers, halftracks and 37-millimeter guns. Assisting from the air were alert observation planes, and lying close offshore were ships that fired when notified of targets. Supply lines to the front were maintained by amphibian vehicles and men on foot.

The two-day assault on the fortifications was accompanied by a sustained din. Only our flamethrowers wrought their slaughter quietly. They went into action with a metallic click and a long whoosh. But these were no doubt the most terrifying sounds the Japanese heard.

Hand-to-hand fighting sometimes resulted when enemy soldiers would suddenly dart from cover to attack or to make a break for the safety of more remote defenses. There were a number of bayonetings and knife killings. One Marine, attacked by a saber-swinging Japanese officer, caught the blade with his bare hands, wrested it from the man and hacked him to death with it. I saw this Marine later when he was brought aboard the hospital ship I occupied a mile or two offshore. He stopped by my bunk and told me his story. Both his hands were badly gashed and were swathed in bandages—but he still had the Japanese sword.

Several organized counterattacks were launched, but each was soon broken up. It isn't likely that the Japanese expected to accomplish much with these measures, but charging the advancing Marines was a way of death that many doubtless preferred to being exterminated in their failing defenses.

At one time during the bloody activities a Marine officer who could speak Japanese took a loud-speaker into the front lines and called upon Suribachi's surviving defenders to lay down their arms and surrender. But the appeal was ignored.

Attacking on the extreme left, the 3rd Platoon and the other units of Easy Company reached the volcano's base on the afternoon of the first day. They next sliced around its left flank. Once they had reached the area where the defenses thinned, they were ordered by Colonel Johnson to dig in and hold.

A similar attack was made by the 1st Battalion on the right. But in the center, where the 3rd Battalion was operating, going was tougher. An extra day was required for these units to batter their way to the base.

By the end of D-plus-3 the fight was largely won. There were still substantial numbers of the enemy in caves and other places of concealment, but hundreds had been slain and the pernicious power of the fortress had been broken.

It was time for the regiment to start climbing. But the craggy 550-foot dome was so steep that a cooperative move could not be made. It was discovered that the only route to the crater lay in the 2nd Battalion zone, so the job of planning the climb fell to Colonel Johnson. And he soon decided to send one of his rifle platoons up as an assault patrol.

The twenty-five men of the 3rd Platoon were by this time very dirty and very tired. They no longer looked nor felt like crack combat troops. Although they'd just had a relatively free day their rest had been marred by a chilling rain. They hardly yearned for the distinction of being the first Marines to tackle the volcano. But the colonel didn't bother to ask them how they felt about it.

By this time our unit had more than proved its combat capability. It almost seemed as though our high-spirited lieutenant had been granted the fifty men he'd wished for in training—the fifty who weren't afraid to die and could take any position.

About 8:00 o'clock on the morning of D-plus-4 Lieutenant Harold Schrier, our company executive officer, assembled the platoon. After its thin ranks had been bolstered by replacements from other Easy Company units, he led it back around the volcano to 2nd Battalion headquarters near the northeast base.

The men found our dynamic battalion commander standing outside an improvised pup tent sipping from a cup of steaming coffee. He was wearing his fatigue cap with its visor bent upward, and this gave him a jaunty appearance that belied his stern nature. He was smiling this morning, however, so he must have been pleased with the way things were going.

While Johnson and Harold Schrier consulted, the men were issued an abundant replenishment of cartridges, hand grenades, demolitions and flamethrower fuel. They were also provided large water cans from which they filled their canteens. During these preparations they were joined by a radioman, two teams of stretcher bearers and a photographer, Staff Sergeant Louis R. Lowery of *Leatherneck* magazine.

As the forty-man patrol loaded up to move out, the colonel handed Schrier a folded American flag that had been brought ashore by our battalion adjutant, 1st Lieutenant George G. Wells. He had been carrying it in his map case. The flag had been obtained from the *Missoula*, the transport that had borne our battalion to Saipan, our staging area.

Johnson's orders were simple. The patrol was to climb to the summit, secure the crater and raise the flag. Though our men hoped fervently that their mission would prove as uncomplicated as the colonel made it sound, most had serious misgivings.

Harold Keller said later: "When I looked at the two stretchers that were being sent along, I thought to myself, 'We'll probably need a hell of a lot more than that.'"

However, Johnson had earlier sent two small patrols up the dome on reconnoitering missions, and both had reached the rim of the crater and had then withdrawn without running into any trouble.

Falling into an irregular column, our men headed directly for the volcano's base. They moved briskly at first, soon passing a Marine howitzer that had taken a direct hit from an enemy gun in the north. There were two dead men lying by the weapon. A little farther on they passed several enemy corpses, one of which was wearing bright orange shoes.

When the route turned steep and going became difficult, the lieutenant sent out flankers to guard the vulnerable column against surprise attack. Heavily laden with weapons and ammunition, the men climbed slowly and were forced to stop from time to time to catch their breath. Some areas were so steep they had to be negotiated on hands and knees. Though several cave entrances were sighted, no resistance developed.

Far below, the Marines located about the northeast base watched the patrol's laborious ascent. Also observing, some through binoculars, were many men of the fleet.

Within a half hour after leaving battalion headquarters the patrol reached the crater's rim. Schrier called a halt here while he took stock of the situation. He could see two or three battered gun emplacements and some cave entrances, but there were no Japanese in evidence. So he gave the signal for the men to start filing over.

My bold friend Howard Snyder went over first. Had I remained unwounded I probably would have been second—whether I wanted to be or not. As it was, Harold Keller occupied this spot. Chick Robeson was third. Then came Harold Schrier, his radioman and Leo Rozek. Robert Leader was seventh, and, fully expecting to be fired at, he hoped that number seven was really the lucky number it was supposed to be.

As the men entered the crater they fanned out and took up positions just inside the rim. They were tensed for action, but the rim caves and the yawning reaches below them remained silent. Finally one of the men stood up and urinated down the crater's slope. But even this insulting gesture didn't bring the Japanese to life.

While half the patrol stayed at the rim, the other half now began to press into the crater to probe for resistance and to look for something that could be used as a flagpole.

Harold Keller, moving in the lead, made the first contact with the enemy. He says of this: "The Jap started to climb out of a deep hole, his back toward me. I fired three times from the hip, and he dropped out of sight."

Several caves now began to disgorge hand grenades. The Marines in the hot spots took cover and replied with grenades of their own. Some of these came flying back out of the dark entrances before exploding.

Even while this action waxed, Robert Leader and Lou Rozek discovered a long piece of pipe, seemingly a remnant of a raincatching system, and passed it to the summit. Waiting with the flag were Harold Schrier, Ernest Thomas, Hank Hansen and Chuck Lindberg. They promptly began fixing it to the pole.

It was about 10:30 a.m. when the pole was planted and the Stars and stripes, seized by the wind, began to whip proudly over the volcano. The date February 23, 1945, had suddenly become historically significant. Mount Suribachi was the first piece of Japanese-owned territory—not counting mandates like Saipan—to be captured by American forces during World War II.

The Marines watching from below raised the cry, "There goes the flag!" And the electrifying word quickly spread to all the units about the volcano's base and to the regiments fighting the main battle to the north. Our combat-weary troops felt a great swell of pride and exultation. They felt a certain relief too. A part of the "impregnable" island had fallen. Victory seemed a little nearer now. Some men cheered, and some wiped at brimming eyes.

The cry was also taken up by the fleet. Ship whistles tooted a spirited salute. Aboard my hospital ship I thrilled to the news as it came over the public address system—though I wasn't aware at the time that it was my own platoon that had raised the flag.

Word of the achievement would also soon be heartening the people at home, who had been following the progress of the battle anxiously, dismayed by the reports of our mounting casualties.

Photographer Lou Lowery snapped the flag raising from a hole where he crouched with BAR man Chick Robeson. Chick had been urged to join the flag-raising group for the picture but had refused, insisting that he was no "Hollywood Marine." In addition to the four flag raisers—Schrier, Thomas, Hansen and Lindberg—also identifiable on the photo is Pfc. James R. Michels, the man on guard in the foreground.

Though most of our men were aware of the significance of their accomplishment, no one at first did much thinking in terms of pride and glory.

All were concerned about the effect the sight of the colors would have on the enemy. They were in danger of getting resistance not only from the Japanese close at hand but from artillery units in the north. The forty men had raised the flag, but they were by no means certain they would be able to defend it successfully.

Shells from the north wouldn't come until later, but the flag was promptly challenged by the Japanese on the summit. First a rifleman stepped out of a cave and fired at the photographer and Chick Robeson. The Japanese missed, but Robeson didn't. He swung his BAR up for a long burst, and the man dropped heavily.

"You got him!" Harold Schrier said.

The body was quickly seized by the feet and dragged part way back into the cave. But now an officer stepped out. Grimacing bitterly, he charged toward the flag-raising group brandishing a sword that had only half a blade. He had probably broken the weapon on purpose so it would have no value as a souvenir.

Howard Snyder advanced to meet this attack with the .45 pistol I had given him. He took deliberate aim as the frenzied man bore down. But when he pressed the trigger there was only a metallic snap. The weapon misfired.

Snyder had to scramble out of the way, but a dozen Marines were now alerted to the cave threat. A volley of rifle fire, led off by Pfc. Clarence H. Garrett, turned the one-man charge into a headlong tumble.

Our men now moved against the resisting area, and they were met by a flurry of hand grenades. The cave turned out to be a large one with several entrances.

Flanking the openings, the Marines once more countered with grenades of their own. Then the entrances were hosed with flamethrowers and blown shut with demolitions.

Photographer Lowery, covering the action at considerable risk, soon had another close shave. A Japanese lobbed a grenade at him, and he was forced to leap down the side of the volcano. Tumbling for fifty feet before he was able to catch hold of a bush, he broke his camera.

This cave was a far greater threat to the flag raisers than was realized at the time. Howard Snyder and Chick Robeson would make the discovery a few days later, when they dug the cave open to look for souvenirs.

Robeson says of the venture: "The stench that met us was so foul that we had to put on gas masks. We went in with a small flashlight, and we found it to be a large cave in two parts. Dead Japs lay all about, so thick that we had to tread on some. I believe there were at least 150. Many had held hand grenades to their stomachs, I suppose after we had sealed them in. We found souvenirs galore. And also some maps and papers that we turned over to Schrier. But we really caught hell for being so stupid, and the cave was blown shut a second time—so completely that no darned fools could try such a trick again."

Why these Japanese hadn't tried to bolt from the cave and over-whelm the flag-raising patrol is a mystery. They had our men outnumbered four-to-one. What makes the situation even more unaccountable is that there were other occupied caves on the summit. The number of Japanese who could have hurled themselves against the patrol will never be known, but there were surely enough to have killed every man in it.

Other platoons soon joined the patrol at the summit and began to help with the crater mop-up. Similar operations were still going on at the volcano's base and had also been started on its outer slopes.

It was about three hours after the flag was planted that Colonel Johnson made the decision that it be replaced. The 3rd Platoon's flag measured only fifty-four by twenty-eight inches, and it was lost to distant view. Since the sight of the colors was important to the morale of our troops, who still had a lot of fighting to do before Iwo was secured, Johnson felt that a larger set was needed. So a flag that was eight feet by four-feet-eight-inches was obtained from LST 779, a vessel beached near Suribachi's eastern base.

As the new flag was being carried up the volcano, Joe Rosenthal, a civilian photographer who was covering the Iwo operation for the Associated Press, learned of the move and decided to follow. And this decision resulted in the now-famous photograph—the photograph that pushed the 3rd Platoon's heroic story into the background and rendered our flag raisers name-less. Although about half the platoon was present at the second raising, only one of our men, Corpsman John Bradley, is on Rosenthal's picture.

So much has been written about the second event that it needn't be discussed here. But this much ought to be said: the photograph deserves to be popular; it depicts an authentic combat scene, even though the circumstances were less impromptu and dangerous than those of the earlier raising.

There is an interesting footnote to the Suribachi story. When Lieu-tenant Wells learned, aboard his hospital ship, that it was his platoon that had raised the flag over the volcano, he refused to remain a casualty. He talked a doctor into supplying him with a first aid kit full of morphine and sulfa, and he hitched a ride ashore in a press boat. Limping painfully to Suribachi, he was met at its base by Chuck Lindberg and Bob Goode, who carried him to the summit. There he enjoyed a warm reunion with his men. And in spite of a fuming telephone protest from Colonel Johnson, he reassumed command of the platoon and directed the rest of its mop-up operations.

By the time Mount Suribachi was finally declared secured, the 28th Marines had lost about nine hundred men. But the grimmest part of the tale is that our regiment's ordeal was only beginning. The unit was alerted for its move to the northern front on D-plus-9.

Lieutenant Wells tried to go along north with the 3rd Platoon, but he didn't get very far.

Chick Robeson says of this: "Colonel Johnson caught him and really gave him hell. I'll always remember the way we marched off in a double column with Wells standing between us and grabbing each of us emotionally, almost in tears because he had to stay behind. He was truly a great Marine."

In spite of his wounds, Wells managed to remain on the island until it was secured. Thus he became technically a veteran of the entire battle.

During its twenty-five days in the north, the 28th contributed much to the battle's success. But the numberless northern defenses proved every bit as tough as Suribachi's, and our valiant combat team was cut to pieces. Among the many officers killed was Colonel Johnson, who advanced into a shellburst that literally blew him apart.

As for the 3rd Platoon, it was virtually wiped out. Nineteen more of our men were killed or wounded, and two suffered combat fatigue. Our casualty rate for the whole operation was a staggering 91 percent.

The four men who made it through the battle were Harold Keller, James Michels (who took a minor wound that he disregarded), Graydon Dyce and Private Philip L. Ward. Pfc. Manuel Panizo came close to making it; he was wounded on the last day.

Our young platoon sergeant, Ernest Thomas, Navy Cross winner and flag raiser, was fatally shot while trying to summon tank aid to get our men out of a tight spot. His death seemed particularly sad because he was a brilliant, personable youth who appeared destined for high achievement.

Among the slain were also: flag raiser Hank Hansen, the man Donald Ruhl had sacrificed himself to save; Katie Midkiff, who had fretted wryly in training about being one of our lieutenant's fifty men who weren't afraid to die; and my good friend and fearless example, Howard Snyder, who had looked forward to the landing—and to returning safely to his pretty bride. His death ended a friendship we had both counted on continuing after the war.

Chuck Lindberg, flag raiser and Silver Star winner, finally had to lay down his devastating flamethrower when he caught a bullet in the forearm.

He withdrew from the field shaking the fist of his good arm at the concealed sniper.

BAR man Chick Robeson was shot in the hand while exposing himself to cover Corpsman Bradley and a man he was treating under fire. The bullet shattered two of Chick's fingers.

Our Massachusetts art student, Robert Leader, was shot through the middle while advancing on a bunker with a hand grenade. Harold Keller managed to drag him to safety, and he survived the critical wound to become a well-known liturgical artist and head of the art department at the University of Notre Dame.

Ex-raider Keller, the only one of our noncoms to get through unhurt, had to be especially lucky to make it, since he was repeatedly in the fore of the action. But he says casually of his escape: "After I got hit on Bougainville, I guess there were just no more Jap bullets with my name on them."

This, then, is the way it was with the 3rd Platoon of Company E, 2nd Battalion, 28th Marines. It is my earnest hope that these pages will win my former comrades some of the attention they deserve. Not only were they Iwo Jima's real flag-raising heroes, but they probably showed as much spirit in battle as any comparable group in American history. I am very proud to have served with them.

★   ★   ★   ★   ★

Men like these—men with fighting hearts and boundless courage—are still one of our country's greatest assets. Let us hope there will always be enough of their kind to rally to the flag when its glory is threatened.

Men from Mars

ERNIE PYLE

Ernie Pyle was America's most beloved war correspondent during World War II. In an age of heavy censorship and before television, Pyle's writings from the battlefronts of Europe became the eyes and ears of a nation yearning to know of their loved ones at war.

Generals and strategy were not the subjects of his writing, but he never failed to mention where a man was from or the everyday hardships of life at the front. By 1944 Pyle had established himself as one of the world's outstanding reporters and *Time* hailed him as "America's most widely read war correspondent." His work would earn him a Pulitzer Prize for journalism in 1945 before he sailed to the Pacific to cover the invasion of Iwo Jima and Okinawa. There he would write about the Marines for the first time, men he described as "the friendliest bunch I have ever been with." The following chapter is taken from Pyle's final collection of wartime writings, *The Last Chapter*, about the first days on Okinawa with Easy Company, 7th Marines.

> Marine Corps blitzes have all been so bitter and the Marines have performed so magnificently that I had conjured up a mental picture of a Marine that bore a close resemblance to a man from Mars.
>
> —Ernie Pyle

★ ★ ★ ★ ★

After a short time with the headquarters of the marine regiment, I moved to a company and lived and marched with them for several days. The company was a part of the First Marine Division. I introduced myself to the company commander who took me on a half hour's walking trip around the company area before leaving me with the men. They had turned in for the night and put out perimeter defenses so that no infiltrating Japs could get through and also so that any big attack could be dealt with. The company was on a hill about 300 yards long and 100 yards wide. The men were dug in down the sides of the hill and there was a mortar platoon at the foot, all set up to throw mortars in any direction.

Our part of the island had not then been declared "secured," and we had received warning of possible attacks from sea that night. Nobody was taking any chances. "This is the most perfect defensive position we've ever had in our lives," the company commander said. "One company could hold off a whole battalion for days. If the Japs had defended these hills they could have kept us fighting for a week."

The company commander was Captain Julian Dusenbury from Claussen, South Carolina, a young man with a soft southern voice. His black hair was almost shaved and he was a little yellow from taking atabrine. He was easygoing with is men and you could tell they liked him. It happened that his twenty-fourth birthday was on April 1—the Easter Sunday we landed on Okinawa. His mother had written that she hoped he'd have a happy birthday. "That was the happiest birthday present I ever had," he said, "going through Love-day without a single casualty in the company."

Captain Dusenbury said I could have my choice of two places to spend the first night with his company. One was with him in his command post, a big, round Japanese gun emplacement made of sandbags. The Japs had never occupied it, but they had stuck a log out of it, pointing it toward the sea so that to aerial reconnaissance it looked like a gun. Captain Dusenbury and a couple of his officers had spread ponchos on the ground inside the emplacement, had hung their telephone on a nearby tree and were ready for business. There was no roof on the emplacement. It was right on top of a hill and cold and very windy.

My other choice was with a couple of enlisted men who had room for me in a little gypsylike hide-out they'd made. It was a tiny, level place about halfway down the hillside and away from the sea. They'd made a roof for it by tying ponchos to trees, and in a farmhouse they had found some Japanese straw mats which they'd spread on the ground. I chose the second of these two places, partly because it was warmer, and also because I wanted to be with the enlisted men.

My two "roommates" were Corporal Martin Clayton, Jr., of 3400 Princeton Street, Dallas, Texas, and Pfc. William Gross of 322 North Foster

Street, Lansing, Michigan. Clayton was nicknamed "Bird Dog" and nobody ever called him anything else. He was tall, thin, and dark, almost Latin looking. He sported a puny little mustache he'd been trying to grow for weeks, and he made fun of it. Gross was simply called Gross. He was very quiet, and thoughtful of little things, and both of them looked after me for several days. The two of them had become very close friends, and after the war they intended to go to UCLA together to finished their education.

The boys said we could all three sleep side by side in the same "bed." So I got out my contribution to the night's beauty rest, and very much appreciated it was, too. Those marines had been sleeping every night on the ground with no cover, except for their cold, rubberized ponchos, and they had almost frozen to death. Their packs were so heavy they hadn't been able to bring blankets ashore with them. But I had carried a blanket as well as a poncho.

Our next-door neighbors, about three feet away, had a similar level spot on the hillside, and they had also roofed it with ponchos. These two men were Sergeant Neil Anderson of Coronado, California, and Sergeant George Valido of Tampa, Florida. So we chummed up and the five of us made a fire and cooked supper under a tree just in front of our "house."

Other little groups of marines had fires going all over the hillside. As we were eating, another marine came past and presented Bird Dog with a big piece of fresh roasted pig they had just cooked. Bird Dog gave me some and it sure was good after days of K rations. Several of the boys found their K rations moldy, and mine were too. They were the old-fashioned kind and we finally decided they were the 1942 rations which had been stored, probably in Australia, all this time.

Suddenly, from a few yards downhill, we heard somebody yelling and cussing, and then there was a lot of laughter. One marine had heated a ration can and, because it was pressure packed, it blew up when he pried it open and sprayed hot egg yolks over him. Usually the boys opened a can a little before heating to release the pressure so that it couldn't explode.

After supper we burned our ration boxes on the fire, brushed our teeth with water from our canteens, and then just sat talking on the ground around the fire. Other marines drifted along and after a while there were more than a dozen sitting around. We smoked cigarettes and talked of a hundred things. The first topic was, as in all groups, about our surprise at no opposition to our landing. Then they got to asking me what I thought about things over here and how it compared with Europe. And when did I think the war would end? Of course, I didn't know any of the answers but it made conversation. The boys told jokes, they cussed a lot, they dragged out stories

of their past blitzes, and they spoke gravely about war and what would happen to them when they finally got home.

We talked like that for about an hour, and then it grew dark and a
shouted order came along the hillside to put out the fires. It was passed on
and on, and the boys drifted away to their own foxholes or hillside dugouts,
and Bird Dog, Gross, and I went to bed. There was nothing else to do after
dark in blackout country.

That was one of the most miserable damn nights out of hundreds
of miserable nights I ever spent in this war. It was too early to go to sleep,
so we just lay there in the dark and talked some more. You could hear voices
faintly all over the hillside. We didn't take off our clothes, of course; nobody
does in the field. I did take off my boots but Bird Dog and Gross left theirs
on since they had to stand watch on the field telephones from 1 till 2 a.m.
The three of us lay jammed up against each other, with Bird Dog in the
middle. We smoked one cigarette after another. We didn't have to hide them
under the blanket since we were in a protected position where a cigarette
couldn't be seen very far.

The mosquitoes started buzzing around our heads. Okinawa mosquitoes sound like flamethrowers; they can't be driven off or brushed away.
I got a little bottle of mosquito lotion out of my pocket and doused my face
and neck, though I knew it would do no good. The other boys didn't even
bother. After a while the hillside grew silent. The hours went past. By an occasional slap at the mosquitoes each of us knew the others weren't asleep.

Suddenly Bird Dog sat up and pulled down his socks and started
scratching. The fleas in the grass were after him. For some strange reason I
am immune to fleas. Though half the boys had red welds from hundreds of
itchy little flea bites, I have never had one. But I'm the world's choicest
morsel for mosquitoes. Every morning I woke up with at least one eye
swollen shut.

That was the way it was all night—me with a double dose of mosquitoes and the rest with a mixture of mosquitoes and fleas. You could hear
marines softly cursing all night long around the hillside. Suddenly there was
a terrific outburst just downhill from us and a marine came jumping out into
the moonlight, swearing and jerking at his clothes. "I can't stand these god-
dam things any longer," he cried, "I've got to take my clothes off."

We all laughed under our ponchos while he stood there in the
moonlight and stripped off every stitch, even though it was very chilly. He
shook and brushed his clothes, doused them with insect powder, and then
put them back on. This unfortunate soul was Corporal Leland Taylor of 101

Francis Court, Jackson, Michigan. He was thirty-three years old and his nickname was Pop. Pop was a "character." He had a black beard and even in the front lines he wore a khaki overseas dress cap, both of which made him conspicuous. After Pop went back to bed everything was quiet for several hours, but hardly anybody was asleep. The next morning the boys on guard said that Pop must have smoked three packs of cigarettes that night. It was the same way with Bird Dog, Gross, and me.

One of the boys on guard came to wake my bedmates at a quarter to one, but they weren't asleep. I thought I might get to sleep while they were away, but I didn't. The mosquitoes were really crucifying me. The boys came back about two o'clock, took off their shoes and lay down. With my blanket over the three of us we were as warm as toast; at least we had that.

All night, without even raising our heads, we could see flashes of the big guns of our fleet across the island. They were shelling the southern part and shooting flares to light up the front lines there. Sometimes we could actually see red-hot shells, traveling horizontally the whole length of their flight, ten miles away from us, and then we saw them explode. Every so often throughout the night our own company's mortars were called upon to shoot a flare over the beach behind us, just to make sure nothing was coming in.

Once there was a distinct rustling of the bushes in front of us. Of course the first thing I thought of was a Jap, but immediately I figured a Jap wouldn't make that much noise, and I decided it was one of the horses the mortar boys had commandeered, crashing through the bushes. And that's what it turned out to be.

Pop Taylor also had the Jap idea, at first. The next morning "Brady" Bradshaw, who was sleeping with Pop, said Pop shook him violently during the night to wake him up and borrow a .45, just in case. Brady laughed and laughed about it, for lying on the ground between them all the time was an arsenal of two carbines, two shotguns, and Pop's own .45.

Along about 4:30 I guess we did sleep a little from sheer exhaustion. That gave the mosquitoes a clear field. When we woke up at dawn and crawled stiffly out into the daylight my right eye was swollen shut, as usual.

All of which isn't a very war-like night to describe, but there are lots of things besides bullets that make war hell.

We started moving right after breakfast. We were to march about a mile and a half, then dig in and stay in one place for several days, patrolling and routing out the few hidden Japs in that area. We were in no danger on the march—at least we thought we weren't, and not all the marines wore steel helmets. Some wore green twill caps, some baseball caps, some even wore civilian felt hats they had found in Japanese homes. For some reason soldiers the world over like to put on odd local headgear. I've seen soldiers in Italy wearing black silk opera hats, and over here I've seen marines in combat uniform wearing panama hats. I've always enjoyed going along with an infantry company on the move, even some of the horrible moves we had to make in Italy and France. But that morning it was a really pleasant one. It was early and the air was good. The temperature was perfect and the country was pretty. We all felt that sense of ease that comes of knowing nothing too bad is ahead of you. Some of the boys were even smoking cigars.

There were always funny sights in a moving column of soldiers. Our mortar platoon had commandeered a dozen local horses to carry heavy pieces. One of the marines had tied the pack onto his horse with a Japanese obi—one of those rams of sash Japanese women wear on their backs. There he was, dirty and unshaved, leading a sorrel horse with a big bowtie of black and while silk, three feet wide, tied across its chest, and another one tied under its belly, the ends standing out on both sides.

Troops carry the oddest things when they move. One marine had a Jap photo album in his hand. One had a wicker basket. Another had a lacquered serving tray. They even had a Columbia phonograph with Jap records, strapped onto a horse. Many of them wore Japanese insignia or pieces of uniform. Later an order came out that any marine caught wearing Jap clothing would be put on burial detail. Maybe that was to keep marines from shooting each other by mistake.

There were frequent holdups ahead of us and we would stop and sit down every hundred yards or so. One marine, commenting on the slow progress, said:"Sometimes we take off like a ruptured duck, and other times we just creep along." The word was passed down the line, "Keep your eyes open for planes." About every sixth man turned his head to repeat it, and the word was sent back along the column like a wave. Toward the rear it came out: "Keep your eyes open for planes—keep your eyes open for cabbages—keep your eyes open for geisha girls."

We were walking almost on each other's heels, a solid double line of marines. Bird Dog was behind me. He said, "A column like this would be a Jap pilot's delight."

Another said, "If a Jap pilot came over the hill, we'd all go down like bowling pins." But no Japs came.

At one of our halts the word came back that we could sit down, but we were not to take off our packs. From down the line came music, a French harp and ukelele playing "You Are My Sunshine." When it was finished the marines called back request numbers. The little concert went on for five or ten minutes out there in the Okinawa fields. The harmonicist was Pfc. William Gabriel, a bazookaman from a farm on Rural Route 13, about ten miles out of Houston, Texas. He was only nineteen, but a veteran who had sustained one wound. He was a redhead and the shyest soldier I'd ever met, so bashful he could hardly talk. But he surely could make a harmonica talk. Playing with him on a sort of ukelele common to Okinawa was an officer, Lieutenant "Bones" Carsters of 6023 Miramar Boulevard, Los Angeles. It was an instrument with three strings, its head made of tightly stretched snakeskin. It gave me the willies just to look at one.

When we started ahead again, the way was clear and that time we went like the well-known ruptured duck and after about a mile we arrived, all panting.

When I saw my first Jap soldiers it was midforenoon and we had just reached our new bivouac area. The boys threw off their packs, sat down on the ground, and took off their helmets to mop their perspiring foreheads. We were in a small grassy spot at the foot of a hill. Most of the hillsides had caves in which household stuff was hidden. They were a rich field for souvenir hunters, and all marines are souvenir hunters. So immediately two of our boys, instead of resting, started up through the brush, looking for caves and souvenirs. They had gone about fifty yards when one of them yelled, "There's a Jap soldier under this bush."

We didn't get too excited, since most of us figured he meant a dead Jap. But three or four of the boys got up and went up the hill. A few moments later somebody else yelled, "Hey, here's another one. They're alive and they've got rifles."

The boys went at them in earnest. The Japs were lying under two bushes, with their hands up over their ears and pretending to be asleep. The marines surrounded the bushes and, with guns pointing, ordered the Japs out. But the Japs were too scared to move. They just lay there, blinking.

The average Jap soldier would have come out shooting, but, thank goodness, these were of a different stripe. They were so terrified the marines had to go into the bushes, lift them by the shoulders and throw them out in the open. My contribution to the capture consisted of standing at one side and looking as mean as I could.

One Jap was small, about thirty years old. The other was just a boy of sixteen or seventeen, but good-sized and well built. He had the rank of superior private and the other was a corporal. They were Japanese from Japan, and not the Okinawan home guard. They were both trembling all over. The muscles in the corporal's jaw were twitching. The kid's face was a sickly white and he was so paralyzed he couldn't even understand sign language.

We never knew why those two Japs didn't fight. They had good rifles and potato-masher hand grenades. They could have stood behind their bushes and heaved grenades into our tightly packed group and got themselves two dozen casualties, easily. The marines took their arms. One marine tried to direct the corporal in handbook Japanese, but the fellow couldn't understand. The scared kid just stood there, sweating like an ox. I guess he thought he was dead. Finally we sent them back to the regiment.

The two marines who flushed the Japs were Corporal Jack Ossege of Silver Grove, Kentucky, across the river from Cincinnati, and Pfc. Lawrence Bennett of Port Huron, Michigan. Okinawa was the first blitz for Bennett and these were the first Jap soldiers he'd ever seen. He was thirty years old, married, and had a baby girl. Back home he was a freight dispatcher.

The Jap corporal had a metal photo holder like a cigarette case in which were photos that we took to be of three Japanese movie stars. They were pretty, and everybody had to have a look.

Ossege had been through one Pacific blitz, but this was the first time he had ever taken Japs alive. He was an old hand at souvenir hunting and he made sure of getting a Jap rifle. That rifle was the envy of everybody; later, when we were sitting around discussing the capture, the other boys tried to buy or trade him out of it. Pop Taylor offered him $100 for it, and the answer was no. Then Taylor offered four quarts of whisky. The answer still was no. Then he offered eight quarts. Ossege weakened a little. He said, "Where would you get eight quarts of whisky?" Pop said he had no idea. So Ossege kept the rifle.

It's wonderful to see a bunch of American troops go about making themselves at home wherever they get a chance to settle down for a few days. My company dug in at the edge of a bomb-shattered village. The village was quaint and not without charm. I was astonished at its similarity to the villages of Sicily and Italy, for it didn't really seem Oriental. The houses were wooden one-story buildings, surrounded by little vegetable gardens. Instead of fences, each lot was divided by rows of shrubs or trees. The cobblestoned streets, winding and walled head-high on both sides, were just wide enough for a jeep.

A large part of the town lay shattered. Scores of the houses had been burned, and only ashes and red roofing tile were left. Wandering around, I counted the bodies of four Okinawans still in the street. Otherwise the town was deserted. The people had fled to their caves in the hillsides, taking most of their personal belongings with them. There is almost no furniture in Japanese houses, so they didn't have to worry about that.

After a few days the grapevine carried the news to them that we were treating them well, and they began to come out in droves to give themselves up. I heard one story about a hundred Okinawa civilians who had a Jap soldier among them; when they realized the atrocity stories he had told them about the Americans were untrue, our MPs had to step in to keep them from beating him.

Our company commander picked out a nice little house on a rise at the edge of town for his command post. The house was very light, fairly clean, and the floors were covered with woven straw mats. A couple of officers and a dozen men moved in and slept on the floor, and we cooked our rations over an open stone cookstove in the rear.

Then the word went around for the men of the company to plan to stay for several days. Two platoons were assigned to dig in along the outer sides of the nearby hills for perimeter defense. The boys were told they could keep the horses they had commandeered, that they could carry wooden panels out of the houses to make little doghouses for themselves, but not to take anything else. And they could have fires, except during air alerts.

They weren't to start their daily mop-up patrols in the brush until the next day, so they had the afternoon off to clean themselves up and fix up their little houses. Different men did different things. Some built elaborate homes about the size of chicken houses, with floor mats and chairs and kerosene lanterns hanging from the roof. One Mexican boy dug a hole, covered it with boards, and then camouflaged it so perfectly with brush you couldn't really see it. Some spent the afternoon taking baths and washing clothes in the river. Others rode bicycles around town, or rode their horses up and down. Some foraged around town through the deserted houses. Some went looking for chickens to cook. Some sat in groups and talked. Some just slept.

An order eventually went out against wearing Jap clothing or eating any of the local vegetables, pork, goat, beef, or fowl. But before the order came, some marines had dug up lots of Japanese kimonos out of the smashed houses and put them on while washing their single set of clothes. It was a funny sight—those few dozen dirty and unshaved marines walking around in women's pink and blue kimonos. A typical example was Private Raymond Adams of Fleason, Tennessee. He had fixed himself a dugout right on the edge of a bluff above the river, with a grand view and a nice little grassy front yard. There he had driven stakes and built a fire, over which he hung his helmet like a kettle, and he was stewing a chicken. He had taken off his clothes and put on a beautiful pink-and-white kimono.

Later a friend came along with a Jap bicycle minus one pedal, and Adams tried without much success to ride it up and down a nearby lane. If there ever is a war play about marines I hope they include one tough-looking private in a pink-and-white kimono, stewing chicken, and trying to ride a one-pedaled bicycle through a shattered Japanese village. Private Adams was married and had an eight-month-old son he had never seen. If the baby could have seen his father that day he would probably have got the colic from laughing.

When I was aboard ship somebody walked off with my fatigue and combat jackets, so I was given one of those Navy jackets lined with fleece. It was much warmer and nicer than what I'd had. On the back it had stenciled in big white letters: U.S. Navy. I wore it when I first walked through the company's defense area and later that evening, when we were sitting on the ground around a little fire warming our supper of K rations. By that time I'd got acquainted with a good many of the boys and we felt at home with one another.

We had some real coffee which we poured into our canteen cups, and we sat around drinking it before dark. Then one of the boys started laughing and said to me, "You know, when you first showed up, we saw that big Navy stencil on your back and after you passed, I said to the others: 'That guy's an admiral. Look at the old gray-haired bastard. He's been in the Navy all his life. He'll get a medal out of this, sure as hell.'"

The originator of this bright idea was Pfc. Albert Schwab of 1743 East 14th Street, Tulsa, Oklahoma. He was a flame thrower, and flame throwers have to be rugged guys, for the apparatus they carry weighs about seventy-five pounds and also they are very apt to be shot at by the enemy. But to see Albert sitting there telling that joke on himself and me, you'd never have known he was a rugged boy at all. I'm not an admiral and I won't get any medal, but you do get a lot of laughs out of this war business when things aren't going too badly.

One morning after breakfast about a dozen of us were sitting on the mat-covered floor talking things over while sipping our coffee. Several days' accumulation of grime covered everybody. Suddenly Bones stood up and said, "I cleaned my fingernails this morning and it sure does feel good."

And then my friend Bird Dog held his own begrimed hands out in front of him, looked at them a long time, and said, "If I was to go to dinner in Dallas and lay them things up on a white tablecloth I wonder what would happen."

A good many of the Okinawan civilians wandering along the roadside bowed low to every American they met. Whether this was from fear or native courtesy I do not know, but anyhow they did it. And the Americans, being Americans, usually bowed right back.

One of my marine friends got mixed up in one of those little bowing incidents. He was Pfc. Roy Sellers, a machine gunner from Amelia, Ohio. Roy was married and had a little girl two years old. He used to be a machinist at the Cincinnati Milling Machine Company and he played semi-pro ball too. When Roy had a beard he looked just like a tramp in a stage play. He was only twenty-seven, but looked much older; in fact he went by the nickname "Old Man."

On this occasion Old Man was trying to ride a Japanese bicycle along the bank of a little river where we camped. The ground was rough and the bicycle had only one pedal and Roy was having a struggle to keep it upright. Just then an old Okinawan, bareheaded and dressed in a black kimono and carrying a dirty sack, walked through our little camp. He wasn't supposed to be at large but it was none of our business and we didn't molest him. He was bowing to everyone, right and left, as he passed. Then he met Machine Gunner Sellers on his one-pedaled bicycle. Roy was already having his troubles, but as he came abreast of the Okinawan, he bowed deeply over the handle bars, hit a rut, lost his balance, and over he went. The Okinawan, with Oriental inscrutability, returned the bow and never looked back.

We all laughed our heads off. "Who's bowing to whom around here," we asked. Roy denied he had bowed first, but we knew better. He decided to give his old bicycle away to somebody less polite than himself.

As our company was moving forward one day I looked down the line of closely packed marines and I thought for a moment I was back in Italy. There for sure was Bill Mauldin's cartoon character of GI Joe—the solemn, bearded, dirty, drooping, weary old man of the infantry. This character was Pfc. Urban Vachon of French-Canadian extraction, who came from Laconia, New Hampshire. He had a brother, William, fighting in Germany. Urban was such a perfect ringer for Mauldin's soldier that I asked the regimental photographer to take a picture of him to send back to the States. If you've seen it, you can prove to any disbelievers that soldiers do look the way Mauldin made them look.

We camped one night on a little hillside that led up to a bluff overlooking a small river. The bluff dropped straight down for a long way, and up there on top it was just like a little park, terraced, although it wasn't farmed, and the grass was soft and green, with small, straight-limbed pine trees dotted all over it. Looking down from the bluff, the river made a turn. Across it was an old stone bridge at the end of which was a village—or what had been a village. Now it was just a jumble of ashes and sagging thatched roofs. In every direction little valleys led away from the turn in the river—as pretty and gentle a sight as you every saw. It has the softness of antiquity about it and the miniature charm and daintiness typical of Japanese prints. And the sad, uncanny silence that follows the bedlam of war.

A bright sun made the morning hot, and a refreshing little breeze sang through the pine trees. There wasn't a shot or a warlike sound within hearing. I sat on the bluff for a long time, just looking. I noticed a lot of the marines sitting and just looking too.

You could come from a dozen different parts of America and still find scenery on Okinawa that looked like your country at home. Southern boys said the reddish clay and the pine trees reminded them of Georgia. Westerners saw California in the green rolling hills, partly wooded, partly patchworked with little green fields. And the farmed plains looked like our Midwest.

Okinawa is one of the few places I've been in this war where our troops didn't gripe about what an awful place it was. In fact, most of the boys said they would like Okinawa if it weren't at war with us and if the people weren't so dirty. The countryside is neat and the little farms are well kept. At the time the climate was superb and the views undeniably pretty. The worst crosses to bear were the mosquitoes, the fleas, and the sight of the pathetic people.

Most of the roads on Okinawa were narrow dirt trails for small horse-drawn carts, but there were several wider gravel roads. One man aptly described it as "an excellent network of poor roads." Our heavy traffic, of course, played hob with the roads; already they were tire-deep in dust and traveling troops had masklike faces, caked with dust. Bulldozers and scrapers were constantly at work.

I've mentioned before our fear of snakes before we got to Okinawa. All the booklets given us ahead of time dwelt at length on snakes, telling us that there were three kinds of adders, all of them fatally poisonous. We were warned not to wander off the main roads, not to stop under the trees lest snakes drop on us. (As if you could fight a war without getting off the roads!) Some of the troop briefings had the marines more scared of snakes than of Japs.

I kept a close watch and made a lot of inquiries, and found that in the central part of Okinawa where we were there are practically no snakes at all. Our troops walked, poked, sprawled, and slept on nearly every square yard of the ground. And in my regiment, for one, only two snakes were seen. One was found dead; the other was killed by a battalion surgeon who coiled it into a gallon glass jar and sent it to the regimental command post as a souvenir. It was a vicious rattler, a type called *habu*.

Those were the only snakes I heard of. There was a rumor that in one battalion they caught and made pets of a couple of snakes, but I didn't believe it. The local people said the island was full of snakes up until the middle thirties when some mongooses were imported which killed most of them. But we didn't see any mongooses, so we didn't know whether the story was true or not. Correspondent John Lardner said his only explanation was that St. Patrick came through here once as a tourist and took all the snakes with him.

Leland Taylor, the marine corporal known as "Pop," found four pairs of the most beautiful Japanese pajamas you ever saw in a wicker basket hidden in a cave. They were apparently brand-new, had never even been worn. They were thrilling to look at and soft to the touch. Pop carried the basket around on his arm from place to place until he could get a chance to ship them home to his wife.

One morning I wandered down to our mortar platoon and ran into a young fellow with whom I had a great deal in common. We were both from Albuquerque and we both had mosquito trouble. He was Pfc. Dick Trauth of 508 West Santa Fe Street. Both his eyes were swollen almost shut from mosquito bites, and at least one of mine was swollen shut every morning. We both looked very funny. Dick still was just a boy. He'd been nineteen months in the marines and a year overseas—a veteran of combat and still only seventeen years old. Dick wrote letters to movie stars and Shirley Temple had sent him a picture, autographed to his company just as he asked her to do. Dick was very shy and quiet and I had a feeling he must be terribly lonesome, but the other boys said he wasn't and that he got along fine.

One of the marines who drove me around in a jeep whenever I had to go anywhere was Pfc. Buzz Vitere of 2403 Hoffman Street, Bronx, New York. Buzz had other accomplishments besides jeep driving; he was known as the Bing Crosby of the Marine Corps. If you shut your eyes and didn't listen very hard you could hardly tell the difference. I first met Buzz on the transport coming up to Okinawa. He and a friend gave an impromptu concert on deck every afternoon. They would sit on a hatch in the warm tropical sun and pretty soon there would be scores of marines and sailors packed around then, listening in appreciative silence. It made the trip to war almost like a Caribbean luxury cruise.

Buzz's partner was Pfc. Johnny Marturello of 225 Livingston Street, Des Moines, Iowa. Johnny played the accordion. He was an Italian, of course, and had the Italian flair for the accordion. He sang too, but he said as a singer his name was "Frank No-so-hotra." Johnny played one piece he composed himself—a lovely thing. He sent it to the GI Publishing Co., or whatever it was in the States, and I feel positive if it could be widely played it would become a hit. The piece is a sentimental song called "Why Do I Have to Be Here Alone?" Johnny wrote it for his girl back home, but he grinned and admitted they were "on the outs."

Johnny went ashore on Love-day and his accordion followed two days after. In his spare moments he sat at the side of the road and played for bunches of Okinawans whom the marines had rounded up. They seemed to like it. Johnny had a lot of trouble with his accordion down south in the tropical climates. Parts would warp and stick and mildew, and he continually had to take the thing apart and dry and clean it, but it was worth the trouble. It kept Johnny from getting too homesick. He knew the accordion would probably be ruined by the climate, but he didn't care. He brought it along with him from America just for his own morale. "I can always get a new accordion," Johnny said, "but I can't get a new ME."

Nearly two years back when I was with Oklahoma's Forty-fifth Division in Sicily and later in Italy, I learned they had a number of Navajo Indians in communications. When secret orders had to be given over the phone these boys gave them to one another in Navajo. Practically nobody in the world understands Navajo except another Navajo. My regiment here had the same thing. There were about eight Indians who did this special work. They were good marines and very proud of it.

There were two brothers among them, both named Joe. Their last names were different; I guess that's a Navajo custom, though I never knew it before. One brother, Pfc. Joe Gatewood, went to the Indian school in Albuquerque. In fact, our house is on the very same street, and Joe said it sure was good to see somebody from home. Joe had been out in the Pacific for three years; he had been wounded and been awarded the Purple Heart. He was thirty-four and had five children back home he wanted to see.

Joe's brother was Joe Kellwood who had also been in the Pacific three years. A couple of the others were Pfc. Alex Williams of Winslow, Arizona, and Private Oscar Carroll of Fort Defiance, Arizona, which is the capital of the Navajo reservation. Most of the boys were from around Fort Defiance and used to work for the Indian Bureau.

The Indian boys knew before we got to Okinawa that the invasion landing wasn't going to be very tough. They were the only ones in the convoy who did know it. For one thing they saw signs, and for another they used their own influence.

Before the convoy left the far south tropical island where the Navajos had been training since the last campaign, the boys put on a ceremonial dance. The Red Cross furnished some colored cloth and paint to stain their faces and they made up the rest of their Indian costumes from chicken feathers, sea shells, coconuts, empty ration cans, and rifle cartridges. Then they did their own native ceremonial chants and dances out there under the tropical palm trees with several thousand marines as a grave audience. In their chant they asked the great gods in the sky to sap the Japanese of their strength for this blitz. They put the finger of weakness on the Japs, and they ended their ceremonial chant by singing the Marine Corps song in Navajo.

I asked Joe Gatewood if they really felt their dance had something to do with the ease of our landing, and he said the boys did believe so and were very serious about it, himself included. "I knew nothing was going to happen to us," Joe said, "for on the way up here there was a rainbow over the convoy and I knew then everything would be all right."

One day I was walking through the edge of a rubbled Okinawa village where marine telephone linemen were stringing wire to the tops of the native telephone poles. As I passed, one of the two linemen at the top called down rather nervously that he was afraid the wobbly pole was going to break under the weight; to which one of the men on the ground, apparently their sergeant, called back reassuringly, "You've got nothing to worry about. That's imperial Japanese stuff. It can't break."

There are very few cattle on Okinawa, but there are many goats and horses. The horses are small like western ponies and mostly bay or sorrel. Most of them are skinny, but if they are well fed they are good-looking horses. They are all well broken and tame. The marines acquired them by the hundreds; our company alone had more than twenty. The boys put their heavier packs on them; more than that, they just seemed to enjoy riding them up and down the country roads. They rigged up rope halters and one marine made a bridle using a piece of bamboo for a bit. They dug up old pads and even some goatskins to use as saddle blankets. But it was surprising how many men in a company of marines didn't really know how to ride a horse.

There was one very small marine who was as nice as he could be, always smiling and making some crack. The boys said that in battle he didn't give a damn for anything. The first afternoon I joined his company he didn't know who I was and as we passed, he said very respectfully, "Good evening, colonel." I had to chuckle to myself. Later he mentioned it and we laughed about it and then he started calling me Ernie.

He was Corporal Charles Bradshaw of 526 South Holmes Avenue, Indianapolis. Though only nineteen he was on his third campaign in the Pacific. He had had three pieces of shrapnel in him and from time to time they would try to work out through the skin. One was just about to come out of his finger.

In the Marines, Corporal Bradshaw was called "Brady" for short. Before joining up he worked on a section gang for the Pennsylvania Railroad. He usually wore one of those wide-brimmed green cloth hats instead of the regulation marine cap and he always carried a .45. It had a slightly curved 25-cent piece embedded in the handle—as he said, "to make it worth something."

In a cave Brady found two huge photograph albums full of snapshots of Japanese girls, Chinese girls, young Japs in uniform, and family poses. He treasured it as though it were full of people he knew. He studied it for hours and hoped to take it home with him. "Anything for a souvenir" could be the motto of the Marine Corps.

Another Indianapolis marine I met on Okinawa was Pfc. Dallas Rhude of 1437 East Raymond Street, who used to be a newspaperman. He worked on the Indianapolis *Times*; he started carrying it as a newsboy when he was eight, then got into the editorial room as a copy boy and kept that job till he joined the Marine Corps. He was a replacement; in other words, he was in the pool from which the gaps made by casualties are filled. But since there had been very few casualties he hadn't replaced anybody yet. Dallas spent twenty-two months in Panama, was home for a little while, and now had been in the Pacific for four months. He said that the Okinawa climate sure beat Panama.

Marines may be killers, but they're also just as sentimental as anybody else. I had talked with one pleasant boy in our company but there was no little incident to write about him, so I hadn't put his name down. The morning I left the company and was saying goodby all around, I could sense that he wanted to tell me something, so I hung around until it came out. It was about his daughter, born about six weeks back. This marine was Corporal Robert Kingan of 2430 Talbot Avenue, Cuyahoga Falls, Ohio. He had been a marine for thirteen months and in the Pacific seven months. Naturally he had never seen his daughter, but he had a letter from her!

It was a V letter written in a childish scrawl and said: "Hello, daddy. I am Karen Louise. I was born February twenty-fifth at four minutes after nine. I weigh five pounds and eight ounces. Your Daughter, Karen."

And then there was a P.S. on the bottom:"Postmaster—Please rush. My daddy doesn't know I am here."

Bob didn't know whether it was his wife or his mother-in-law who wrote the letter. He thought maybe it was his mother-in-law—Mrs. A. H. Morgan—since it had her return address on it. So I put that down and then asked Bob what his mother-in-law's first name was. He looked off into space for a moment, and then started laughing."I don't know what her first name is," he said. "I just always called her Mrs. Morgan!"

The major part of the battle was being fought by the Army—my old friends, the doughfoots. This time the marines had it easy.

Marines Corps blitzes in the Pacific had all been so bitter and the men had fought so magnificently that I had conjured up a mental picture of a marine as someone who bore a close resemblance to a man from Mars. I was almost afraid of them. I did find them confident, but neither cocky nor smart-alecky. They had fears, and qualms, and hatred for war the same as anybody else. They wanted to go home just as badly as any soldiers I've ever met. They are proud to be marines and they wouldn't be in any other branch of the service, yet they are not arrogant about it. And I found they have a healthy respect for the infantry.

One day we were sitting on a hillside talking about the infantry. One marine spoke of a certain division—a division they had fought beside—and was singing it praises."It's as good as any marine division," he said.

"What was that you said?" a listener cut in.

The marine repeated it and emphasized it a little. Another marine stood up and called out, loudly, "Did you hear what he said? This guy says there's an army division as good as any marine division. He must be crazy. Haw, haw, haw!"

And yet other boys chimed in, arguing very soberly, and sided with the one who had praised the army division.

Before I came into the field, several marine officers asked me to try to sense just what the marine spirit is, what is its source, and what keeps it alive. In peacetime when the Marine Corps was a small outfit, with its campaigns highlighted, everybody was a volunteer and you could understand why they felt so superior. But with the war the Marine Corps had grown by hundreds of thousands of men. It became an outfit of ordinary people—some big, some little, some even draftees. It had changed, in fact, until marines looked to me exactly like a company of soldiers in Europe. Yet that Marine Corps spirit still remained. I never did find out what perpetuated it. The men were not necessarily better trained, nor were they any better equipped; often they were not so well supplied as other troops. But a marine still considered himself a better soldier than anybody else, even though nine-tenths of them didn't want to be soldiers at all.

They were very much aware of the terrible casualties they'd had in this Pacific war. They were even proud of that too, in a way. Any argument about superiority among units was settled by citing the greatest number of casualties. Many of them even envisioned the end of the Marine Corps at Okinawa. If the marine divisions had been beaten as they were on Iwo Jima, the boys felt it would have been difficult to find enough men of Marine Corps caliber to reconstitute all the divisions. They even had a sadly sardonic song about their approach to Okinawa, the theme of which was "Goodby, Marines!"

The boys of my regiment were continuously apologizing to me because the Okinawa campaign started out so mildly. They felt I might think less of them because they didn't show me a blood bath. Nothing could have been further from the truth. I was probably the happiest American there about the way it turned out for us. I told them that kind of campaign suited me, and without exception they came back with the answer that it suited them too. I heard it said so many times that it almost became a chant: "If they could all be like this, we wouldn't mind war so much."

No, marines don't thirst for battles. I've read and heard enough about them to have no doubts whatever about the things they can do when they have to. They are o.k. for my money, in battle or out.

★   ★   ★   ★   ★

April 18, 1945, Ernie Pyle accompanied a routine patrol on the nearby island of Ie Shima where he was killed by enemy fire. Saddened by their loss, the soldiers paid tribute to their fallen friend with a simple plaque reading: AT THIS SPOT, THE 77TH INFANTRY DIVISION LOST A BUDDY, ERNIE PYLE, 18 APRIL 1945. President Truman declared, "No man in this war has so well told the story of the American fighting man as American fighting men wanted it told. He deserves the gratitude of all his countrymen."

Frozen Chosin

MARTIN RUSS

One of the finest chronicles of combat to appear in recent years was Martin Russ's *Breakout*, published in 1999. *Breakout* is the detailed story of the Marines fighting their way back to the coast after being surrounded and cut off by six Chinese divisions (60,000 men) in the Chosin Reservoir area in late 1950. During their "breakout," the Marines killed over 25,000 Chinese while wounding about 12,500 between October 15 and December 15. Marine casualties were 700 dead, 200 missing, 2,500 wounded, and 6,200 frostbite cases.

When the action was called a "retreat," a "Retreat Hell!" remark came into legend. The phrase has been attributed to various officers over the years, but finally Martin Russ has chased it to earth. The phrase originally came during World War I when Marine Corps Lloyd Williams answered a messenger from the French commander as the U.S. troops were arriving at Belleau Wood in 1918. "Retreat, hell. We just got here!"

In the Chosin Reservoir action, the closest phrases to the remark came from comments by Marine Major General Oliver P. Smith speaking to a British reporter at Hagaru, North Korea. "There can be no retreat when there's no rear. You can't retreat, or even withdraw, when you're surrounded. The only thing you can do is to break out, and in order to do that you have to attack, and that is what we're about to do. Heck, all we're doing is attacking in a different direction."

One last comment about the "retreat" question. Here is Lieutenant Joseph Owen, reported by Martin Russ: "We kicked the shit out of the Chinese the first time we met them, which was at Sudong, and we were still kicking the shit out of them when we crossed the Tredway Bridge. They were surrendering to us, not the other way around. Retreat, you say?" — Lamar Underwood

All right, they're on our left, they're on our right, they're in
front of us, they're behind us . . . they can't get away this time.
                                        — Lewis B. "Chesty" Puller

★   ★   ★   ★   ★

Back in September there had been some resentment in Easy Company over
the sudden influx of Reservists, and when the veterans of the First Platoon
learned that their new officer was a "weekend warrior," they expected the
worst. Lt. Yancey, getting wind of this, gathered his thirty-five men on the grass
of a soccer field outside Uijongbu and delivered a short address. "I know what's
on your mind, you Regulars. Yes, I'm a Reserve officer, but I earned this commission the hard way, and I'm not going to stand for any foolishness about
Regulars versus Reservists. When the fighting begins you won't be able to
tell one from the other. We're all United States Marines."

Yancey let them find out for themselves that he had won a battlefield
commission by leading a squad against a crowd of Japanese, accounting for
thirty dead himself, including the commanding officer "who attempted with
great vigor to decapitate me with a samurai sword." Yancey had joined the
Reserves after the war, got married, and opened a business called Yancey's
Liquors in Little Rock.

Corpsman James Claypool: "Yancey and I were wondering how
Private Stanley Robinson was doing back at Regiment as Litzenberg's
bodyguard. I was worried that outside the umbrella of Yancey's supervi-
sion this youngster might be unable to restrain the wild streak in him.
This was the kid who was considered such a badass he had to be brought
aboard ship under guard. . . . Well, guess who came toiling up the hill late
that afternoon? We were glad to see him and his BAR; but I noticed he
was limping and got him to sit down and take off his boots even before
he reported to Mr. Yancey.

"I was always fanatical about foot care. During the march to Yu-
damni, whenever we took a break I was all over those kids: 'I want those
shoe-pacs off and I want those felt liners out and I want those socks
changed.' I made them dry their feet and rub them. I made them keep their
wet socks inside their clothing to dry out. I wouldn't let anybody keep their
shoe-pacs on when they crawled into their bags. I wouldn't let them wear
dirty socks because the dirt in the cloth was like fine sandpaper and led to

abrasions. As soon as we occupied 1282 I went right to work on their feet, making them clean them with snow, applying boric-acid ointment after they were dry.

"Robinson of course tried to give me a hard time. I looked him in the eye and said, 'Are you going to argue with me?' He thought it over and finally unlaced his boot. I was shocked by what I saw. The skin between his toes was raw, and the skin on his ankles too. There was infection. He had the equivalent of second- and third-degree burns. He was virtually crippled with frostbite. 'You're going back down the hill,' I told him.

" 'The hell I am.'

" 'Robinson . . .'

" 'Don't fuck with me, swabbie.'

"In the end I had to go tell Yancey; it was like a teacher reporting a defiant student to the principal. I told Yancey that Robinson's feet were beyond my resources to treat, that he would probably have to be evacuated. He didn't ask to look at Robinson's feet; he just accepted my word for it. 'Robbie, I'm glad to see you,' he told him, 'but you're going to have to go back down the hill and turn yourself in to Battalion Aid.' Robinson was so angry he didn't even say good-bye. We watched him limp down the back trail. We were *all* disappointed.

"After Robinson departed, Yancey got into a tense discussion with PFC James Gallagher. Gallagher was a blatant racist from Philadelphia. You might think the jarheads of that day were racist in general, so many of them hailing from the poor white South, but that wasn't the case; a fellow like Gallagher really stood out. His Irish father and Italian mother lived in a neighborhood that black folks were beginning to move into and Gallagher didn't like it. Yancey, though a Southerner, wouldn't tolerate racism in is platoon.

"He was a daring young man, that Gallagher. Short, powerful, tough. Face like an Italian leprechaun. At Sudong he was as much a hero as Robinson, running half a mile up 698 with a machine gun and two boxes of ammo to keep Robinson's company on the crest. Frankly, I didn't like the kid much, but I was glad he was on our side. Anyway, Yancey was trying to set him straight when someone on watch interrupted to call our attention to a man in white on the skyline a few hundred yards to the left front. He had a pair of binoculars trained on us. We let him look. We didn't have anything to hide."

Captain Walter Phillips had placed Yancey's and 1st Lt. Leonard Clements's platoons in a semicircle on the crest. The usual fifty percent watch was in effect. Phillips and Captain Milton Hull on Hill 1240 had arranged to send out a patrol from each company every half hour, to meet halfway along the saddle connecting the two hills. The night's password: *Lua lua lei*. The countersign: *Hawaii*. Shortly before dusk, Yancey sent Corporal Lee Phillips and his squad about three hundred yards out and told him to dig in. This was to be Easy Company's listening post for the night. Phillips had barely reached the spot when two F4U Corsairs came roaring in over 1282; both cut loose with a burst that plowed long furrows in the snow, barely missing Phillips and his men. 1st Lt. Neal E. Heffernan, the forward air controller, got on the radio and called them off: "Secure the mission, Blueberry!"

Yancey: "I brought Phillips in after that because I didn't trust those airdales."

("When the Chosin Few get together at these reunions, you know," says Yancey, "they always pay tribute to the Corsair pilots and their close air support; but some of us recall the times when the pilots were too eager or got their signals crossed and instead of threatening the shambos they threatened the marines. That's the reality of it.")

The moon came up over the southern skyline at a little past six. Yancey: "It rose behind us, and that worried me, because we were silhouetted on the skyline. In front of us was this desolate landscape with the lake off to the right, with open spaces of black ice where wind had blown away the snow."

Some of the Marines thought they heard music in the distance; when the wind changed, they realized it was the sound of Chinese bugles, faint and eerie.

At 9:45 p.m. Easy Company's radio operator picked up an odd warning from Dog Company on 1240: "Heads up, over there! One of our guys just got bayoneted in his bag." While the radio operator was trying to confirm this, word was quietly passed along the crest of 1282 that "Mr. Yancey wants to see bayonets on the end of those rifles and carbines."

Corporal Earl Pickens, machine gunner: "Sergeant Cruz was the first to detect movement out front. As he was reaching for the sound-power phone, a Chinese soldier jumped up about ten feet in front of us and charged. I saw Cruz thrust out his .45 and shoot him in the face before I realized what was going on. When Gallagher opened up with the machine gun, it was music to my ears, because I had been worried about the gun freezing up. Because of their white uniforms, all you could see were their shadows and the muzzle blasts of their burp guns. There were only a handful of them, though. It was another probe, aimed at drawing our fire so they could tell where our automatic weapons were."

After the Chinese were driven off, Captains Phillips and Hull, conferring by radio, decided to cancel the hourly patrols along the connecting saddle. It remained quiet on 1282 and 120 for two hours.

"Something you gotta see, Lieutenant."

"Later, I'm busy."

But Gallagher persisted and Yancey went over. Yancey: "You get to see some strange sights in war. Here's Gallagher with this grin on his face, and what he's grinning about is this string of bodies stretching right up to the gun, with the elbow of the last one actually touching the forward leg of the tripod. 'Pretty good, huh, Lieutenant?' I told him to drag in two or three of the bodies and use them like sandbags in front of his position. He thought that was a great idea."

Yancey went back to making his rounds. Some of the young Marines needed calming down. "Sure, they'll be back," he told them, "but we're ready for them, understand? Just do what I tell you."

A shot rang out at long range and the spent bullet grazed Yancey's right cheek and lodged in his nose. Calmly he removed one glove and plucked it out. Yancey: "Blood was oozing down my cheek into my mouth, but then it froze up, I didn't say anything about this to anyone."

Knots of Chinese had now slipped across the saddle between the two hills and were beginning to fire directly down on the 5th Marines headquarters in the valley below.

2nd Lt. Thomas Gibson, a 4.2-inch mortar officer on phone watch, began getting inquiries about green tracers flying across the sky. The roar of the Coleman lantern masked the start of the battle; Gibson hadn't heard any gunfire at all. After the third inquiry he stepped outside for a look, and there they were. Gibson: "Americans don't use green tracers. I went back inside and woke up the operations officer and told him about it. He wasn't impressed; he went back to sleep. After making the appropriate notations in the logbook, I started checking around by phone. I couldn't find anyone who was stirred up about it. When the tempo of the firing began to pick up, I shook the ops officer awake again. Squinting one eye open, he cocked an ear and was just telling me there was nothing to worry about when a long burst of automatic fire came ripping through the tent, rattling the tin spark-arrestor on top. I think the ops officer was shod and armed and outside before the burst ended."

Everybody was flying out of their tents now, taking up defensive positions in the roadside ditch. Lt. Col. Raymond Murray: "We had been subjected to night attacks throughout our operations in Korea, so at first I considered this just another local action. But all of a sudden the command post came under fire and that's when I began to pay attention. I turned to my exec and said, 'We better get our asses out of here.' I recalled a mound of earth next to the road and thought that if we could get a phone line put in over there we could operate with a bit of cover. I was able to stay in touch with all three battalions without any of them knowing I had opened shop in the middle of an empty field. When I called Taplett and asked what was happening in his neighborhood, he said the enemy was attacking his command post at that very moment and could he call me back later. We heard lots of gunfire over in his sector and a good deal of shouting. At first I assumed it was the Chinese doing the shouting and thought he was being overrun. I was on the point of bringing Jack Steven's battalion [1/5] into counterattacking position, but then Tap called back to say that two of his platoons were counterattacking and I realized it was our guys who were doing all the yelling."

Murray, on learning that Roise's flanks were in the air, decided it was time to pull 25 back and have Roise tie in with William Harris's 3/7 on the left and Taplett's 3/5 on the right.

At 5:45 a.m. on the twenty-eighth the regimental commander alerted Roise to the probability that his battalion would be retracted. Rearward was not a direction Marines liked to go; Roise's immediate reaction, when he found the coordinates Murray had given him on the map, was that there had been a map-reading error at regiment. He asked for confirmation of the coordinates and was surprised when they were confirmed.

Thus Lt. Col. Harold Roise learned that the forward momentum of the 1st Marine Division had been brought to a half, perhaps permanently as far as this particular campaign was concerned. Years later he told an interviewer, "I had a hard time accepting it. When an entire battalion is geared up for a sustained attack, it's hard to cancel out. I felt frustrated, frankly. I think we all did."

Yancey: "It had been quiet for an hour or two, then we began hearing these odd noises down at the bottom of the slope, like hundreds of feet walking slowly across a big carpet of cornflakes." Yancey cranked the handle on the field phone. The response was a whisper from the company exec, 1st Lt. Raymond Ball.

"That you, Ray?"

"Go ahead, John."

""They're coming up the hill."

"You sure?"

"I can hear the fuckers crunching through the snow. How about some illumination?"

"Hold on."

1st Lt. William Schreier, mortar officer: "The cold weather affected the burning rate of the fuses. The first rounds hit the ground before they flashed. We increased the charges to maximum and finally got them to illuminate overhead. We only had about thirty rounds of illum and less than a hundred of high explosive. This wasn't nearly enough, as we were soon to discover."

By then the crunching noise had stopped and the Marines of the First Platoon heard the shrill voice of an officer shouting in English: "Thank God nobody lives forever!"

Yancey: "I don't need to tell you that's not the kind of thing you expect to hear on an Asian battlefield; but it's what the man said and we all heard it. I had a violent reaction: I decided he must have learned his English at a Christian missionary school. The son of a bitch had been fed and sheltered and given a good education by Americans—and here he was leading Red troops against us. That annoyed me."

The first flare popped overhead, and Yancey spotted the officer in front of the first rank of troops, holding a machine-pistol in one hand. The Marines were shocked to see several ranks of Chinese arrayed behind him, spaced ten or fifteen yards apart, the whole formation ascending the slope. The battle of 1282 began in earnest when Yancey yelled, "You're damn right nobody lives forever, you renegade bastard!" and brought him down with a burst from his carbine. The ranks continued to ascend, the soldiers now wailing in a minor key: "Son of a bitch Marine we kill. Son of a bitch Marine you die."

Yancey: "It was altogether most eerie."

Corpsman Claypool: "Gallagher, firing short bursts with his machine gun, was taking incoming in return; but he never flinched. The company mortars were in pits just behind us, and every time they fired there were sparks and fireworks as a round left the tube. I heard someone yelling for a corpsman and that meant I had to leave the protection of my hole. Then a star round burst overhead and everything in that wilderness of snow below us was brilliantly illuminated. I saw men in white writhing on the round while others stepped over or around them. The Marines fired methodically, spanged empty, reloaded, fired again. Sergeant Allen Madden, Yancey's platoon sergeant, saw me and beckoned and pointed to two downed Marines. Together we carried the first one out of the line of fire, and when I came back for the second I had a shelter half to use as a sled; but there were more wounded Marines now and I didn't have time to lay the cloth down and load each man aboard, so I began dragging them backward by their parka hoods."

Captain Walter Phillips, already wounded in the arm and leg, was hobbling about offering encouragement. "You're doing fine," he told his troops.

The Chinese were hurling their grenades in clusters. ("They looked the flights of blackbirds," said Yancey.) Some of the survivors said they saw Chinese carrying *baskets* of grenades. Yancey was moving from hole to hole, passing out bandoliers of M-1 ammunition, when an explosion blew him off his feet, a piece of shrapnel piercing the roof of his mouth. "After that, blood kept trickling down my throat and I kept spitting it out."

Captain Phillips's voice broke through the din again and again: "You're doing well, Marines. . . . Stay loose, Marines. . . . You're doing fine, Marines."

Corporal Earl Pickens: "The Chinese were charging us continually, wave after wave. They wanted that hill."

Staff Sergeant Robert Kennemore, a machine-gun section leader, was making himself useful by crawling among the wounded and dead, collecting ammunition and distributing it to those who needed it. The Chinese were so close that he could hear them tapping the handles of their potato-masher grenades on the frozen ground to arm them. In the gloom below, Kennemore thought he saw a group of Chinese dragging a machine gunner from a foxhole by the legs, clubbing him, bayoneting him. Kennemore maneuvered down the slope, looking for a shooting position,

"Where are you going?" It was Captain Phillips, white-faced and wobbly.

"One of my gunners, sir—"

"Don't go down there, you damn fool." The officer resumed his painful progress along the lines while Kennemore dragged a load of ammo to the other gun in his section, still in action with a crew of three despite the hail of fire. A Chinese grenade plopped in the snow beside the assistant gunner; Kennemore scooped it up and sidearmed it down the slope before it exploded. Another landed nearby and there was only time for Kennemore to put his foot on it, driving it into the snow, as a third grenade landed beside it. Kennemore, willing to die to save his fellow Marines, dropped his knee on it and absorbed the force of both explosions. The three crewmen were temporarily deafened but otherwise unhurt.

Yancey: "Sometime during the night I caught a glimpse of Ray Ball firing his carbine from a sitting position. The Chinese were coming over the ride on the right flank and he was calmly picking them off, one by one. He continued to do this until a burp gunner blindsided him, catching him in the side with a burst. I thought he was dead but he wasn't."

Easy Company's machine gun platoon leader, a second lieutenant, had been sent down the reverse slope earlier to report to the battalion command post, where he was to link up with ammo-bearers and reinforcements and guide them back to 1282. Yancey: "I heard Ray Ball talking with him on the radio, telling him to get his ass back to 1282. The lieutenant said he would try, and Ray said, 'Try? That's not good enough.'" The lieutenant, for reasons of his own, could not bring himself to return to that hilltop scene of concentrated, deadly chaos, where it seemed a company of United States Marines was in the process of being wiped out.

Private Stanley Robinson lay disgruntled and foot-sore on a stretcher in the battalion aid station, listening to the sound of distant firefights, wondering how Easy Company was doing. An ambulance jeep pulled up outside; litter-bearers brought in a stretcher and put a wounded man down beside him.

"What outfit you with?"

"Easy Company, 7th."

"They got hit pretty good?"

"Clobbered. The captain and Mr. Ball are down. Mr. Yancey's been hit but he's still going."

Robinson sat up. In the darkness of the tent he began to pull on his boots, grunting with pain as he stuffed his swollen feet into the stiff shoe-pacs. It took several minutes to do the job. At last he stood up, pulled on his dirty parka, and went stumbling through the tent flaps. Outside he snatched up a rifle and cartridge belt from the pile of discards. A corpsman appeared. "Where do you think you're going, Robinson?"

"What does it look like, Doc?"

"Go back inside."

"Get the fuck outta my way."

The scrawny youngster slung the rifle and tottered toward the big hill like a crippled old man. An hour later, having been forced to crawl up the steeper portions of the path, he was asking directions to the First Platoon.

"Top of the hill, straight over."

"Seen Mr. Yancey?"

"He's been hit twice, but he's still at it."

Yancey was hunched beside a machine gunner, directing his fire, when he felt a sharp slap on the bottom of his boot. "I looked down and there he was, with his off-kilter grin, looking sloppier and dirtier than ever. 'What the hell are *you* doing here?"

" 'I heard you candyassed pogues needed help.'

" 'I'll be damned.'

" 'So,' said Robinson, 'you got any work for a BAR man?'

"I pointed over the right. 'See those kids over there? Go over and get 'em squared away. They need a little encouragement.' Robbie was younger than any of them, but I knew he would get results."

Claypool: "Robinson had returned to his true home."

Yancey's platoon was running out of men. He went over to talk to 1st Lt. Leonard Clements about it. "'Clem, can you spare a squad? I got to get these shambos off my flank.' As we were talking, a bullet caught him dead center in the forehead and down he went. He had just called the squad leader over. 'The lieutenant's dead.' I told him. 'Get your kids in hand and follow me.' I scooped up some other Marines and ended up with about twenty altogether, including Robbie and his four or five."

PFC Wilmer Swett: "He shouted, 'Here we go,' and him and Robinson took off, but when he looked back there was nobody following him. This pissed him off royally. 'Gung ho, you miserable cowardly bastards! I said *Follow me.*' He stood there waiting, and one by one the rest of us moved up, and pretty soon we had something like a skirmish line in motion."

Yancey: "Once we got going, two or three of the kids actually moved ahead of me. I recognize how hard it is to get your ass in gear in a situation like that, where chances are you're going to get killed or at least hurt pretty bad; but that's what Marines are supposed to do. Marines don't get any slack."

The battle atop 1282 began tapering off around 2 a.m., as the Chinese, responding to the signal from a bugle, began to pull back down the slope. Soon it was quiet except for the moans of the wounded and dying.

The next assault began around 3 a.m. Yancey turned to his runner, PFC Marshall McCann. "I don't need you right now, McCann. Get up there in the hole with Rick, and make every shot count." Soon after the attack began, Yancey heard a Marine yell, "I'm hit."

"Where're you hit?"

"In the balls."

Yancey crawled across open ground and took a look. "You ain't shot in the balls, you're grazed in the hams. Pick up that rifle and earn your pay!"

Corpsman Claypool: "When you get hit, your first thought is that you're dying. This one Marine was knocked down by a burst from a burp gun, but I found that his skin wasn't even broken. His parka and field jacket and wool sweater and vest and wool shirt and utility jacket and long johns had saved him. He was convinced he was dying of multiple wounds.

" 'I tell ya, I'm on the way out, Doc.'

" 'Uh-huh.'

" 'Doc, listen to me—I been hit all over!'

" 'Son, you're not even wounded.'

"That really offended him. He called me an old bastard."

(Dr. Henry Litvin: "Somewhere in your book I hope you'll tell the reader about the role of the Navy corpsman. He was the guy who stopped the bleeding and made it possible for a wounded Marine either to stay in action or at least stay alive until he could be sent back to the surgical team. The up-front Navy corpsman was the most important link in the whole chain of evacuation.")

Claypool: "Whenever a Marine would die on me I would just move over to the next man. At the start of the battle I would write 'KIA' [killed in action] on each tag along with the approximate time of death and attach it to the top button of his jacket. But soon we had so many casualties I didn't have time to tag them. Several times that night the thought crossed my mind that I wasn't going to get off that hill alive. With so many dead and dying Marines around me, it was obvious my chances were slender. There were so many grenades going off that I stopped paying attention to them. I spent a lot of time bent over, and sometimes when I stood up, the tail of my parka wouldn't drop down because it was pinned against my pants by slivers of shrapnel; every so often I'd reach back and yank the tail down and pull the slivers out of the cloth."

Claypool kept seeing Yancey stalk back and forth, yelling and spitting blood, shouting through a blood-clogged throat. "Gung ho, Marines!" By the light of the flares he made a perfect target.

"Gung ho," said Gallagher.

"Gung ho," said Robinson.

Yancey: "It was as close to Custer's Last Stand as you can get outside of the movies. I kept asking myself, 'Where did all these shambos come from?' "

Claypool: "A couple of times I tried to stop him and treat his wounds but he was too busy moving 'the kids' to the best spots to keep the Chinese from overwhelming us. No one wanted to argue with Yancey, and none of us wanted to stay on that damn hill without him being there too."

The Marine line was faltering, about to break. Captain Phillips appeared behind them holding an M-1 rifle tipped with a bayonet. Turning it upside down, he rammed it into the hard earth with all his diminishing strength. "This is Easy Company," he shouted hoarsely, "and this is where we stand!"

Shortly afterward, a burst of fire cut him down. Lt. Ball, nearly immobilized with multiple wounds, took command, yelling instructions and occasionally firing his carbine from a sitting position.

Claypool: "The other company corpsman was a guy named George Fisher. He was a good-natured fellow much younger than me—I was twenty-six at the time—and much smaller. George was sort of insignificant looking, peering out at the world through a pair of government-issue glasses. We worked pretty well together. Because I was so much bigger, I was the one who dragged the wounded Marines off the line if they couldn't negotiate under their own power, while George stayed busy at the aid tent."

Yancey: "Yes, I remember George Fisher very well—for two reasons. First of all, he cried a lot. The suffering of the Marines really tore him up, and he couldn't hide it. Second, he had no aptitude for the work at all: he was not only physically clumsy, he was sort of delicate, and he seemed to have to force himself to keep going. But he did his duty. Marines have a lot of respect for their Navy corpsmen, as you know."

Claypool: "We put as many of the wounded as we could in sleeping bags to keep them warm so that shock wouldn't kill them. We tried to save our morphine for Marines hit in the chest or gut. (You had to hold the syrettes in your mouth to keep them thawed out.) Often we had to inject a wounded man on the little-finger side of the wrist. Not a very sterile situation: everyone's wrist was black with dirt and soot from the campfires. We had too little morphine, too few bandages, too little time, and we had to make decisions that were extremely unpleasant. On the spot we had to decide which Marines were worth working on and which to ignore since they were going to die shortly, and sometimes you didn't even have time to stop and hold a kid's hand. Most of them asked for their mother. I was accustomed to all that from World War Two. George wasn't."

A Chinese soldier about twenty yards away fired a burst in Yancey's direction, and one of the rounds hit him under the right eye, jarring the eyeball loose from its socket and knocking him over. With his left eye Yancey saw the soldier crouch down and jam another magazine into his weapon. Yancey groped around for the carbine and, not finding it, took the .45 from under his armpit and pumped two rounds into the soldier. Then, as carefully as he could, Yancey removed his gloves and pushed the eye back where it belonged. "It was like pushing a hard-boiled egg into a knothole, but it went in and stayed there."

It was clear by now that unless the companies on 1282 and 1240 were reinforced, the northern defense line was going to fold. Phillips's Easy Company was barely handing on; Hull's Dog Company had been shoved off 1240 but was presently fighting its way back to the top. During the lull after midnight, Phillips called Lt. Col. Davis and, in the understated Marine style of the day, asked for assistance. "We've taken too many casualties. We're holding, but we can use some help."

With the luckless Randolph Lockwood stuck in Hagaru, Raymond Davis, as we have seen, was burdened with five rifle companies, at least two of which were now in serious trouble. After Davis discussed the situation with Murray at the combined regimental headquarters, reinforcements from First Battalion, 5th Marines, were placed on full alert. A platoon of Captain Jack Jones's Charlie Company/5 was assigned to support Hull's counterattack on 1240; the other two were sent to rescue Phillips's remnant on 1282.

Lt. Col. John W. Stevens, 1/5's commanding officer, recalls that the confusion of the moment was compounded by a frantic call from the C.O. of the Third Battalion, 7th, Lt. Col. William Harris, begging Stevens to send his entire battalion to extricate him from entrapment. "I more or less put him on hold—told him I'd call back. After that I went out to brief the troops [elements of Jones's and Heater's companies] who were about to climb the back of the two northern hills in the dark. The briefing didn't have a great deal of substance. All I could tell them was that when they got to the top of their respective hills they could expect a terrific fight."

Captain Jack Jones recalls the resentment he felt at having his company split up; it was against doctrine. On the other hand, he recognized it was an emergency and what was needed on the hilltop were warm bodies, armed.

PFC Ray Walker, Able Company, 5th: "We were bedded down close to the village and feeling pretty secure. I had just stretched out on a pile of straw and saw a stream of green tracers come scooting over the crest of a hill north of us. It was quite a show: The tracers raced like comets, bouncing off slopes, zooming straight up toward the stars—and every once in awhile you could see the yellowish light from Chinese flares. My enjoyment of the show was interrupted by the appearance of Gunnery Sergeant Stanley Millar.

" 'All right, drop your cocks and grab your socks! We're going up that hill.'

" 'What's going on, Gunny?'

" 'The 7th Marines need help, as usual. Saddle up!'

"Right away we started bitching about the pitiful Reservists who couldn't handle a few stragglers and were now whining for the Regulars to come get them out of a fix." About half of the 7th Regiment was made up of Reservists.

2nd Lt. Nicholas Trapnell, Able/5, recalls that things got quiet when the reinforcements began climbing the slope, and that the point man kept calling out: "Easy Company ...Where you at, Easy Company? ...Hey, Easy Company!"

Lt. John Yancey: "We didn't know reinforcements were on the way, because our phone lines were cut and the radio had been smashed in the fight. During this second lull, one of the things we found time for was wrapping the dead Marines in ponchos and carrying them to the top of the back trail so the ammo carriers could drag them off the hill."

When the moon went down behind the mountain, Yancey had a reaction to the sudden darkness: he thought he saw "all sorts of boogymen." The Chinese corpses down below came to life; wriggling, rolling over, crawling, sitting up, getting to their feet—turning into nightmare monsters.

Corpsman Claypool: "There were bodies everywhere, especially in front of Gallagher's and Robinson's positions. I watched Robinson search through a dead soldier's pack and pockets. He found a lump of rice mixed with some other grain cooked into a ball about the size of a grapefruit, wrapped in a brown handkerchief. He showed it to me: 'Look at this, Doc!'"

Lt. Robert Bey and his men were watching the Chinese on the crest as Staff Sergeant Daniel Murphy approached him. Bey: "The only thing I could hear up there was the Chinese language being spoken. There was no question they had the top of the hill."

"If you let me counterattack," said Murphy, "I think we can push them back from the command post."

Bey turned his Third Squad over to Murphy. Corpsman Claypool volunteered to go along. He was warmly welcomed. Claypool: " 'Volunteer' might not be the right word. I was coming down from Yancey's command post when I spotted several Chinese soldiers. They didn't see me, and I hugged the ground until they passed by. When Sergeant Murphy was getting his group together, I figured that maybe being with them was the safest place on the hill, so I tagged along. In terms of numbers we didn't amount to much: Murphy and Sergeant Keith's squad plus five stragglers from Lieutenant Clements's platoon; but we clawed our way upslope and chased the Chinese off the crest. I saw a Chinese officer up close: he was wearing a dark sweater under his coat and the coat was open. What I remember best about him, though, is that he didn't shoot me with the revolver he was carrying."

As he started tending to the wounded, Claypool could hear Murphy asking questions, "Where's everybody?"

"The Skipper's dead. Mr. Ball's dying."

"How about Lieutenant Clements?"

"Dead."

A voice sounded out of the darkness. "The hell I am!" Lt. Leonard Clements had been struck in the forehead by a burp gun bullet and lived to tell about it. Clements: "It felt like someone had hauled off with a sledgehammer. I didn't dare touch the spot with my hand because I was afraid part of my head was gone. When I asked after Lieutenant Yancey, someone said he had been shot several times and had bled to death. Funny, John thought I was dead and I thought John was dead."

Clements then spotted what he later called "this squared-away gent" climbing toward him, followed by a column of fresh-looking Marines. "I'm Jack Jones," said the squared-away gent. "I've got part of a company with me."

"Let me show you where my people are," said Clements.

By the light of a flare, the dying Lt. Ball greeted Captain Jones with a smile and a feeble wave.

Lt. William Schreier: "We were all wounded." Schreier himself was having difficulty walking, surprised that a simple wound in the wrist could affect him so strongly. What he didn't know was that a piece of shrapnel was lodged in his chest, that one of his lungs had collapsed and the other was filling with fluid. Try as he might, he couldn't function, and he was soon headed downhill on a stretcher. Schreier: "I felt bad because there was lots of fighting left to be done and I wanted to do my share. But I just couldn't hack it."

The lull in the battle came to an end with a bugle call, followed by "the most amazing pyrotechnical display I've ever seen," according to Lieutenant Trapnell. "Roman candles, Vesuvius fountains, pinwheels, skyrockets, and an infinite number of firecrackers. When that was over, the enemy started to climb toward us once again. The slopes of the saddle were quite steep, and the enemy got close before the shooting started up again. We smelled them before we saw them. Some folks are skeptical about this business of the garlic. It wasn't only garlic on the breath, it was in the clothing too. When you eat garlic over a period of time, it exudes from your pores and, believe me, it carries.

"Soon we were engaged across our entire front and hard pressed to keep them from spilling over into the draw behind us. When it got light enough, you could see that the whole top of the hill had been ground to pumice by grenades, mortars, and artillery shells."

PFC Ray Walker's BAR had stopped working; he couldn't get the bolt to slide forward. A group of enemy soldiers went by on his left; they saw the young Marine but didn't do anything about it. Walker was busy dismantling his weapon: he removed the trigger group, threw it one way, took out the firing pin, threw that another way. There were weapons all around, and he picked up an M-1 and fired one round with it before it malfunctioned too. Down the hill he saw a Chinese soldier walk up behind a Marine gunner ("very casually, as if he were a barber about to give a customer a haircut"), put a pistol to his head, pull the trigger, and walk on down the slope. Walker: "By this time I was frantically trying to find a weapon that worked and feeling nakeder and nakeder. Then a small Marine with curly black hair appeared and said, 'I know where we can get some grenades.' We dragged a whole case back to the spot, opened it with a K-Bar, and began tossing grenades down the slope. There was so much lead flying that there was no sense trying to find a safe place to throw from. By this time it looked like the whole hill was crawling with big white worms."

Walker never understood how it happened, but when he reached for the next grenade it was already sputtering, the spoon gone. He threw up his right arm and was backing away when it went off. Shrapnel from the explosion broke his right ulna, penetrated his left chest, and cut his lip, forehead, and fingers. A corpsman named Parker took an ampule of morphine out of his mouth and gave Walker a shot. A few minutes later, just at daybreak, he was heading down the backside of the hill with a group of wounded Marines that included John Yancey.

Corpsman Claypool was stepping around some brush and rocks looking for wounded Marines when he saw a Chinese soldier sitting with his body facing the corpsman but with his head twisted around and his weapon aimed toward a line of wounded descending the reverse slope. When Claypool shot him—from about ten yards away—his head hit his knees and the quilted hat with earflaps flew off. "He didn't know what hit him, didn't have time to experience the dread of death."

It was light enough now for air strikes, and the first one of the day was so close that the Marines on 1282 saw the upended wing of a Corsair flash by on the other side of the ridge, going from left to right—so close it seemed as though the pilot was scraping off his payload only a few yards in front of them.

Lt. Yancey's jaw was dislocated—he was never sure how it happened—and he had bound it up with a strip of blanket. Spotting Captain Jones, he went up to him and tried to give him an informal briefing on the situation on 1282. His face was crusted blood, one eye was closed, and he was groggy from all the concussion grenades. Captain Jones took one look and told him to join the walking wounded being escorted down the hill.

Yancey:"A sergeant yelled at me, 'This way down!' and reached toward me with a long stick. I grabbed hold of it and he led me down the trail. By the time we got to Battalion Aid, I was bleeding again, so one of the corpsmen tied me sitting up to a tent pole to keep me from choking in my own blood."

Claypool: "None of us would have survived the night if Yancey hadn't been there. No one else could have bullied his troops into standing and facing almost certain death the way he did. Sometimes I wonder if maybe Yancey single-handedly saved the Marines at Yudam-ni, not just the Marines on 1282; because if the Chinese had taken 1282, they would have poured through the breach and overrun the 5th and 7th Marines command posts. All I know for sure is that the Chinese would have overrun 1282 if Yancey hadn't been there.

"I have one more thing to say about him. If a son or grandson of mine had to serve in combat, I wouldn't want him to serve in John Yancey's platoon. His troops took twice as much ground and killed twice as many Chinese, but he also lost twice as many men. Then again, that's the way Marines do business. . . . But not with *my* kids."

The official history sums up the action on 1282 as follows: "[It was] basically the story of the suicide of the 1st Battalion, 235th CCF [Chinese Communist Forces] Regiment." There is no official tally of Chinese dead in the battle for 1282, but there were hundreds of corpses piled up on the forward slope and on the crest. As for the Marines, Easy/7 suffered 120 dead and wounded, out of the original 176. (Stanley Robinson and James Gallagher walked off the hill unscathed.) Jones's Charles/5 had ten dead, thirty wounded. Heater's Able/5: five dead, thirty-seven wounded.

The second lieutenant who was sent down the hill for ammunition never did return. Such military cowards are in a peculiar way immortalized along with the heroes; they are often mentioned in discussions, the veterans still shaking their heads over a former comrade's moment of weakness on the field of battle. His privacy is always protected; the name is never mentioned in the presence of outsiders. Contempt or disgust are hardly ever expressed toward him. If any emotion is manifest it is likely to be pity, for everyone understands that the coward has to live with his shame for the rest of his life. In the case of this particular officer, his transgression was major: he could not bring himself to return at a moment when his unit desperately needed the ammunition and reinforcements he had been sent for.

Ignoring his own wounds, PFC Ray Walker spent part of that morning helping men who couldn't stand up to urinate into cans, "so they wouldn't wet themselves." He came across his assistant BAR man, PFC Middlekauf, on a stretcher; Middlekauf's jaw was badly swollen from a shrapnel wound. "I made some hot cocoa and helped him sit up and drink it." (Thirty-four years later, a portly, bald gentlemen introduced himself at a Chosin Few reunion and thanked Walker for the companionship and comfort he had provided at a lonely moment.)

A Marine he didn't recognize came through the tent flaps.

"Hey, Walker—aren't you a friend of Reuben Fields? I got him outside in the truck."

"What's wrong with him?"

"He's had the course."

"You mean he's dead?"

"Not quite."

Walker: "Reuben Fields was a moonshiner's boy from Harlan County Kentucky. I helped carry him in, busted ulna notwithstanding. He was unconscious and moaning. The doctors wouldn't treat him. I was indignant, then outraged—until someone explained that he was brain-injured and beyond help. We carried him back outside and put him down on some hay. He died in my arms. I cried. At least he wasn't alone."

Claypool: "Later that morning I found Mr. Ball down in the battalion aid station. He was just conscious enough to recognize me. 'What about the company?' he asked."

'Still holding on, sir.'

"He was gray from lack of blood. What plasma we had was frozen and unusable. The sun hadn't hit the valley floor yet and it was awfully cold in the tent. I took the sleeping bags off two dead Marines—not an easy job, when with rigor mortis—and put them around the lieutenant, stuffing the edge under the stretcher, tucking him in for the long journey. I was holding his hand when he passed. It was around 0830.

"I was going to miss Lieutenant Ball, and Captain Phillips too. They were close friends, by the way, and they complemented each other. Lieutenant Ball was quiet and studious and thorough. Captain Phillips was outgoing and dashing, a natural troop commander. Both of them had dedicated their adult lives to the Marine Corps, and they made being a Marine something special. I admired them. But then I admired the whole damn outfit. Easy Company, 7th Marines—they were the most exceptional group of people I've ever encountered."

A Rumor of War

PHILIP CAPUTO

Philip Caputo was a young Marine platoon leader assigned to the first combat unit sent to Vietnam in March 1965. Sixteen months later he returned to the United States, his youthful bravado and belief in the righteousness of the war shattered by his experiences. He would return to Vietnam again in 1975 to cover the fall of Saigon as a Pulitzer Prize winning journalist for the *Chicago Tribune*. In 1977 he published a highly acclaimed memoir of his wartime experiences, *A Rumor of War*. His candid and emotionally charged writing transcends time, inviting the reader to stand in his shoes and face the same life or death decisions. In the following chapter Caputo describes a patrol he led that sights enemy soldiers in a small village across a narrow river. It is a story that encapsulates at least part of the Vietnam infantryman's war—the merciless heat, the fear of the unknown, the sudden exhilaration of combat, and the terrible wounds inflicted by unseen enemies. The book remains a testament to the courage of men under fire, the effects of combat on the hearts and minds of those in harm's way, and to the true nature of war.

> The worn white soldiers in Khaki dress,
> Who tramped through the jungle and camped in the byre,
> Who died in the swamp and were tombed in the mire.
> —Rudyard Kipling
> "The Ballad of Boh Da Thone"

★   ★   ★   ★   ★

Creeping through the stunted grass, I seemed to be making as much racket as a man stumbling through piles of dry leaves. Please don't let them hear me or see me, I prayed silently. Please let everything go right. Let me get them,

195

all of them. Guilt washed over me because I was asking God to help me kill. I felt guilty, but I prayed anyway. Let me get them, all of them. I want all of them. The edge of the clearing was less than ten yards away, but it seemed I would never get there. It kept receding, like a mirage. My heartbeat sounded like a kettle-drum pounding in a tunnel. I was certain the Viet Cong could hear it or the sound of my breathing.

The rifle shot was deafening compared to the dead silence that had preceded it. The bullet kicked up dust a few yards from my face, and I whirled around on my stomach like a crab. Crowe and Allen were down and rolling over—the round had passed right between them—rolling over to fire while Lonehill, on one knee, sent a long, ecstatic burst into the hedgerows across the river. One of the Viet Cong threw up his arms and seemed to rise several inches off the ground before he fell heavily on his back, his rifle twirling through the air like a majorette's baton. It was as if an invisible giant had picked him up, then slammed him to the earth. I could not see the VC's body; one of his comrades must have pulled him into the underbrush as I was getting to my feet. The third Viet Cong had taken cover behind the shrine. I hadn't seen him, but instinct told me he was there. Lonehill was firing into the hedgerows, Crowe blasting away with his twelve-gauge, although the shot-pattern was too wide to be lethal at that range. I began running toward them, realized I still had to get the rest of the platoon, pivoted to run back into the woods, and went down when a line of bullets chewed the earth beside me. Staggering to my feet, I went down again as the VC behind the shrine fired a second time with his BAR or machine gun—I couldn't tell which. Lying in a shallow dip in the ground, I made love to the earth. The Viet Cong around the river bend had opened up, so that, on the peninsula of land formed by the horseshoe bend, the four of us were caught in a cross fire. I tried once more to make it to the edge of the clearing but was struck in the face by spraying dust as soon as I lifted my head to run. The experience of being under heavy fire is like suffocating; air suddenly becomes as lethal as a poison gas, its very molecules seem to be composed of pieces of lead flying at two thousand miles an hour. The bullets hissed and cracked over my head, and I yelled—no, screamed—"Allen. I'm pinned down. Pour it on 'em, goddamnit. Your right front, around the bend. Pour It On 'Em Goddamnit." The three marines managed to sound like a small army, with Crowe's shotgun roaring loudly. Then came the flat, dull blasts of 40-millimeters as Allen laid down a barrage with his grenade launcher.

An eerie sense of calm came over me. My mind was working with a speed and clarity I would have found remarkable if I had had the time to reflect upon it. I knew what I was going to do. The platoon could not assault across the deep, fast river, but it could pour a withering fire into the Viet Cong. If that did not kill all of them, it would at least kill some and drive the rest out of the village. But first, I had to bring up a machine gun to suppress the fire coming from around the river bend, and a rocket launcher to knock out the enemy automatic weapon in place behind the cement-walled shrine. That had to be done before the platoon could be deployed safely. They would bunch up in the small clearing and a lot of them would be hit if the enemy fire wasn't suppressed first. And it had to be done quickly, before the Viet Cong recovered from their surprise and started to fire more accurately. The whole plan of attack flashed through my mind in a matter of seconds. At the same time, my body was tensing itself to spring. Quite separate from my thoughts or will, it was concentrating itself to make a rush for the tree line. And that intense concentration of physical energy was born of fear. I could not remain in the hollow for longer than a few more seconds. After that, the Viet Cong would range in on me, a stationery target in an exposed position. I had to move, to face and overcome the danger. I understood then why a cornered animal is so dangerous; he is terrified and every instinct in him focuses on a single end: destroying the thing that frightens him.

Without a command from my conscious mind, I lunged into the woods and crashed down the trail, calling for a machine gun and a 3.5-inch rocket team. They came up, stumbling beneath their heavy weapons, and sprinted across the clearing to where Allen's men were still firing. The three-five's backblast made an ear-splitting crack an instant before its armor-piercing shell slammed into the shrine and bits of concrete and tile spiraled up out of the smoke. The machine gun sprayed the hedgerows, the casings of the long, slim 7.62-mm bullets clanging as they flew rapidly out of the gun's ejection port. Elated, I emptied my carbine in to the hole the rocket launcher had made in the shrine's wall. Then a second three-five shell went off and there was no more firing from the enemy gun.

"First and third squads up!" I shouted, running back toward the woods. "First and third up, on line. Second watch our rear."

Led by big Sergeant Wehr, the platoon guide, the marines broke out of the jungle at a run. Wehr, who had just arrived in Vietnam, seemed a little bewildered by the invisible things crackling in the air.

"On line, I said! On line here. First on the left, third squad on the right. On line and start putting rapid fire into the ville."

Bent low beneath the enemy fire, the marines quickly shoot themselves into a skirmish line, wheeling like skaters playing crack-the-whip, extending their front along one leg of the river bend. Then the line surged across the clearing, the men firing short, spasmodic bursts from the hip and the whole line going down when it reached the riverbank, going down and opening up with an unrestrained rapid fire. I could not hear any individual shots, just a loud, continuous tearing noise. The hedgerows fifty yards away shook as if struck by a violent wind, and a hut flew apart when it was hit by a three-five shell. Pieces of bamboo and thatch were tossed up by the blast and then tumbled down, the thatch flaming as it fell.

I scrambled along the line on my hands and knees, shouting myself hoarse to control the platoon's fire. The marines were in a frenzy, pouring volley after volley into the village, some yelling unintelligibly, some screaming obscenities. Allen ran up to me. His blue eyes looked crazed. He said he had seen some of the Viet Cong pulling out and one of them falling, hit by machine-gun fire. A bullet smacked into the earth between us and we went rolling over and came rolling back up again, me laughing hysterically, Allen looking even more crazed as he pumped 40-millimeters into the village. A few moments later, Miller called on the radio and confirmed that we had driven the VC out of Hoi-Vuc; a sniper in his company had seen a squad of them fleeing down a trail, and had killed two.

There was still some enemy fire coming at us, but it was ragged and badly aimed. I passed the word that the Viet Cong were on the run and that D Company had killed two more. The platoon became as excited as a predator that sees the back of its fleeing prey; a few marines slid down the bank and started shooting from the water's edge. I could feel the whole line wanting to charge across the river. The platoon was one thing, one being poised to spring and smash the life out of whatever stood in its way. I could feel it, and, feeling it, sent Lance Corporal Labiak's fireteam downstream, to look for a ford. If we could get across the river, we could finish the job. I wanted to get across the river in the worst way. I wanted to level the village and kill the rest of the Viet Cong in close combat. I wanted us to tear their guts out with bayonets.

We took some sniper fire and silenced it with M-79 grenades. Labiak came back, soaked up to his chest. The river could not be crossed, he said. The bottom dropped off sharply and the current had almost swept him off his feet. Well, all right, there would be no pursuit, no final, climactic bayonet charge. Still, I felt a drunken elation. Not only the sudden release from danger made me feel it, but the thrill of having seen the platoon perform perfectly under heavy fire and under my command. I had never experienced anything like it before. When the line wheeled and charged across the clearing, the enemy bullets whining past them, wheeled and charged almost with drill-field precision, an ache as profound as the ache of orgasm passed through me. And perhaps that is why some officers make careers of the infantry, why they endure the petty regulations, the discomforts and degradations, the dull years of peacetime duty in dreary posts: just to experience a single moment when a group of soldiers under your command and in the extreme stress of combat do exactly what you want them to do, as if they are extensions of yourself.

I could not come down from the high produced by the action. The fire-fight was over, except for a few desultory exchanges, but I did not want it to be over. So, when a sniper opened up from a tree line beyond the village, I did something slightly mad. Ordering the platoon to train their rifles on the tree line, I walked up and down the clearing, trying to draw the sniper's fire.

"When he opens up, every man put five rounds rapid into the tree line," I said, walking back and forth and feeling as invulnerable as an Indian wearing his ghost shirt.

Nothing happened.

I stopped walking and, facing the tree line, waved my arms. "C'mon, Charlie, hit me, you son of a bitch," I yelled at the top of my lungs. "Ho Chi Minh Sucks, Fuck Communism, Hit Me, Charlie."

Some of the marines started laughing, and when I heard one of them mutter, "That stocky little fucker's crazy," I started laughing too. I was crazy. I was soaring high, very high in a delirium of violence.

"C'mon and hit me, Charlie," I yelled again, firing a burst into the tree line with my carbine. "You Son Of A Bitch, Try And Hit Me. Fuck Uncle Ho. Hanoi By Christmas."

I was John Wayne in *Sands of Iwo Jima*. I was Aldo Ray in *Battle Cry*. I was a young, somewhat immature officer flying on an overdose of adrenalin because I had just won a close-quarters fight without suffering a single casualty.

The sniper declined my offer, and I gradually calmed down. A call from Captain Miller brought me back to the real world. The platoon had done a fine job, he said. It was a diversionary force, and by God, it had certainly provided the VC with plenty of diversion. He ordered us to remain in position for the night. I did not particularly like that idea; the enemy knew where we were and would probably mortar us. On the other hand, that's what we were supposed to do, divert the enemy's attention away from Miller's company.

The platoon formed a perimeter and started to dig in. Knowing we would probably be shelled, we dug the holes deep, or as deeply as we could in the gummy, resistant soil. When Jones and I finished, we stuck our entrenching tools in the parapet and slid into the hole for a cigarette. A cigarette had never tasted quite so good. I was still elevated. Smoking, I cleaned my carbine, running the rag lovingly over the varnished stock, the barrel, and the long, curved banana clip, enjoying the feel and the sound of the bolt mechanism as I worked it back and forth. I had not killed anyone with it, but I had caused a few deaths, and a part of me had enjoyed that, too, enjoyed watching the first Viet Cong die.

The reprieve from the monsoons ended that night. Our foxholes were turned into miniature swimming pools. Sniper fire cracked over us most of the night. Although it had only a slim chance of hitting its mark, it kept us on edge. Every fifteen or twenty minutes there was a *crack-crack-crack* and nothing visible but a swirling blackness and the white mists rising over the river. In the early hours before dawn, it stopped raining. With neither rain nor wind to keep them down, swarms of mosquitoes rose from the damp earth to feed on us. The leeches had a banquet too.

Lying in a half-sleep in six inches of water, I heard a shrill wailing and someone yelling "Innncommiiing!" and then a sound as of lightning striking a tree, a splitting sound. The earth shuddered.

"Jesus Christ, what was that?" asked Jones, next to me on radio watch.

"Whatever it was, it wasn't a sixty or an eighty-two. Get D Company. It might be our own stuff."

Reaching back over his shoulder, Jones unhooked the handset of the PRC-10 and intoned, "Delta Six, this is Charley Two, over . . . Delta Six, Delta Six, this is Charley Two. Charley Two, do you read me, over . . . This is Bound Charley Two calling Bound Delta Six, do you read me, Six, over . . ."

There was another high-pitched whistling, growing louder. The ground shook again as the shell smashed into the riverbank less than fifty yards away. A shower of earth, twigs, and hot shrapnel struck the river with a hiss.

"Delta Six, this is Charley Two," Jones said, lying with one arm over the back of his neck. "Do you read me Delta Six, over." He turned to me. I rolled onto my side and felt the cold shock of water pouring down my shirt and into the crotch of my trousers. "Sire, I can't reach D Company. The batteries must've gotten wet."

"Goddamn radios. Goddamn junk shit they send us. Well keep trying. If that's our own stuff, we can get them to cease firing."

"What if it ain't our own stuff?"

"Then maybe we'll get our asses blown away. Keep trying."

"Delta Six, Delta Six, this is Bound Charley Two calling Bound Delta Six, over."

A faint voice, broken by static, crackled in the receiver.

"... two ... position ... over."

"Delta Six. You're breaking up. Say again."

"This is Delta Six ... your position ... over."

I grabbed the handset and gave our map coordinates, hoping the voice on the other end was not one of the VC, who sometimes monitored our radio traffic. "Listen, Delta Six, we have impacting rounds less than five-zero meters from this position. Could be Victor Charlie one-twenties or rockets. Interrogatory: is our own arty firing now? If our arty firing now, tell them to cease fire."

"Two, read you ... say again all over ..."

"Say again Delta Six." Another shell came in. "Delta Six, say again."

"... say again all after impacting, Charley Two, over."

"I say again, impacting rounds ..." A fourth shell crashed into the riverbank and I thought of Lance Corporal Smith's fire-team, who were on a listening post near there. "Delta Six, you probably could hear that last one. Could be Victor Charlie one-twenty mike-mike mortars. Interrogatory: is our own arty firing a mission near this position? Over."

"Reading you weak and garbled, Two. Say again all after mortars."

"Aw, Jesus fucking Christ. . . ." I started to repeat the message, then rolled over, burying my head in my hands, holding it up just far enough to keep my mouth out of the water. It had become academic as to whether the shells were our own or the enemy's. For the full concentration was coming in with a crazed howling and someone was again yelling "Innncommii-ing!" The shells seemed to take forever to fall. For what seemed a long time, we heard the lunatic chorus wailing in the sky, our bodies braced for the coming shock, hearts constricted, all thoughts suspended.

Then the storm struck. The shells, impacting about twenty-five yards from the perimeter, exploded one right after another, creating one enormous blast that went on for five minutes. Shrapnel flew overhead with a sound like that of taut steel wires snapping. Jones and I, huddled beside each other like two frightened children, pressed ourselves against the earth. I tried to become part of the quaking earth and wished we had dug the foxhole deeper than three feet. I wanted God to shut that roaring out of my ears. Make it stop. Please God, *make it stop.* One shell struck very close. I could not tell exactly where. It seemed to explode just outside the platoon's small perimeter, and I though we were going to be blown out of the hole, out and up into that lethal space where the shrapnel scythed the air. The ground slammed against my chest, bouncing me up an inch or so, and a part of me kept going up. I felt myself floating up out of myself, up to the tops of the trees. Hovering there, I felt an ineffable calm. I could see the flashing shells, but they no longer frightened me, because I was a spirit. I saw myself lying face down in the foxhole, my arms wrapped around the back of my neck. I felt no fear, just a great calm and a genial contempt for the puny creature cringing in the foxhole below me. I wondered if I was dying. Well, if I am, I thought, it is not so bad. Dying is actually pleasant. It is painless. Death is an end to pain. Rich the treasure, sweet the pleasure, sweet is pleasure after pain. Death is a pleasure. The Big D is the world's most powerful narcotic, the ultimate anesthetic.

Then the shelling stopped, and my spirit, reluctantly leaving the peace of its elevated plane, slipped back into my body. I was whole again. I was a whole man. The Jesuits at college had stressed that: the purpose of a Jesuit education is to create a whole man. And I was a whole man again in my foxhole; a whole in a hole.

I crawled out to the edge of the perimeter and called to Smith's fire-team.

"Yes, sir," Smith said in a whisper.

"You guys all right?"

"Outside of being cold, wet, miserable, hungry, and scared shitless, we're just fine, sir."

"No casualties?"

"No sir. Because I'm black, the shells couldn't see me."

I laughed to myself, thinking. They're all right, the best you could ask for. They've been through a fire-fight and a shelling and they're making jokes about it.

The platoon survived the shelling. There was a brief period of total quiet, then the sniping started again. *Crack-crack-crack.* In the wet dawn, we brewed tins of C-ration coffee and shivered ourselves warm while Jones worked on the radio. I sat sipping the coffee on the parapet of the foxhole. Sergeant Pryor walked over and slumped down next to me, a sweat-yellowed cigarette hanging from his lips. He looked like the others, his sunken eyes rimmed with the blackness of fatigue, his face and hands lumpy masses of insect bites.

"Well, sir, I don't mind saying that yesterday and today were the longest day and night of my life. Especially last night. That was the longest night of my life."

"How long've you got to go?" I asked, as one convict to another.

"Seven, eight months. Seven, eight more months of this shit. I'm so goddamned tired. Is the radio working yet, sir?"

"No. We're still out of contact."

"Shit."

"Without that radio, we might as well be on the dark side of the moon."

Pryor laughed mirthlessly. "Might as well be?" He field-stripped his cigarette, scattering the paper and tobacco as an old man might scatter bird-seed in a park. "Might as well be? Where do you think we are, lieutenant?"

After trying for half an hour, Jones reached D Company. Miller ordered the platoon to move northward to Hill 92, in the foothills, and set up a patrol base.

It took us six or seven hours to get there. The column wound through a labyrinth of draws and ravines, through the knee-deep muck of the marshes, and over narrow jungle tracks. We walked always in the rain and were constantly harassed by snipers. Halfway to the hill, the platoon was held up by a brush and log barricade the Viet Cong had thrown across the trail. The barricade was in a gully where the trail was hemmed by two steep hills, both covered with jungle so thick we could not have gone through it with a bulldozer. Unable to go around the barricade, we would have to blast through it with grenades. Walking up to it with Lance Corporal Crowe, I saw a strand of spider's silk glistening in the mass of brush and leaves. Only a few inches of it showed, and it was straight and taut and did not move in the wind blowing through the gully. Fear shot through me like a jet of liquefied gas.

"Crowe," I said, "move real careful around that barricade. It's booby-trapped. I can see part of the trip wire."

"Yes, sir."

I did some quick, basic arithmetic: the hand grenades would go off four to five seconds after we released the spoons. There was a culver thirty, perhaps forty, feet behind us, where the trail started to curve around one of the hills. We would have to pull the pins, place the grenades where they would have the most effect, being careful not to put the slightest pressure on the trip wire, then run and take cover in the culvert. I spelled it out to Crowe and asked him if he thought we could make it.

"We'll have five seconds max."

"I think we can do it, sir. If we don't, they'll mail us home in envelopes."

Each of us took out a fragmentation grenade. Smooth-surfaced, egg-shaped, and about the size of pears, they did not look capable of blowing a man in half.

"Crowe, we're going to do it by the numbers. When I say pull the pin, we'll pull the pins, keep the spoons down, and then set the grenades down. You set yours under that log on the left. I'll put mine on the right. Don't touch a thing. Set it down real easy. Then you take off first, so we don't bump into each other. Got it?"

"Yes, sir."

I wiped the slick film of sweat off my palm and straightened the pin so it could be pulled quickly. (No, you do not pull grenade pins with your teeth, the way it's done in the movies. If you did, the only thing to come out would be your teeth.)

"Pull the pin."

We pulled them and, keeping the spoons depressed in the web of our hands, set the grenades down. I tried not to look at the thin, shining strand of spider's silk. Crowe took off running, with me behind him. We dove into the culvert, covering our heads with our hands. I counted: "Thousand-one, thousand-two, thousand-three . . ." Silence. ". . . Thousand-four, thousand-five, thousand-six."

"Son of a goddamned bitch, they're both duds. Nothing works, Crowe. Radios, grenades, nothing. Goddamnit."

"We'll have to do it over, sir." It was more a question than a statement.

"Yes, we will."

Walking back up the trail, my legs felt semiparalyzed, the way they feel in nightmares of pursuit and helpless flight. There was no guarantee that the grenades would not blow up in our faces. Perhaps they had defective, slow-burning fuses. My legs kept getting heavier and heavier, and then I felt the worst fear of all: the fear of fear. For I seemed very near the point of total paralysis, and that terrified me more than anything. *Hey, didja hear about Lieutenant Caputo? He froze out on that patrol. Dude just froze up because of a booby trap. Sheee-hit, fuckin' worthless officers.* I talked myself into covering the last twenty feet to the barricade, as a father might talk to a toddler taking his first steps. First the right foot. Now the left. Now the right again. That's it. Almost there, little fella.

"Pull the pin, Crowe."

We set the grenades down. The four of them looked like a nest of olive-green eggs.

"Okay, take off!"

We pounded down the trail and made swan dives into the culvert. The grenades and the booby trap went off with a shattering boom. Debris sifted down on us. Crowe smiled victoriously.

The platoon reached Hill 92 in the midafternoon. The men were worn out by that time, their shoulders aching from the weight of rifles, packs, and flak jackets. They had been under one kind of fire or another for twenty-four hours and were dazed with fatigue. Rigging shelters against the drumming rain, they lay down to rest. Some did not bother to build shelters. They had ceased to care even for themselves. I walked around, checking their feet. A few had serious cases of immersion foot, their shriveled skin covered with red pustules and blisters. It amazed me that they could walk at all. We ate lunch. Our rations were the same as the Viet Cong's: cooked rice rolled into a ball and stuffed with raisins. The riceballs were easier to carry than the heavy C-ration tins and alleviated the diarrhea from which we all suffered. Eating the rice on that desolate hill, it occurred to me that we were becoming more and more like our enemy. We ate what they ate. We could now move through the jungle as stealthily as they. We endured common miseries. In fact, we had more in common with the Viet Cong than we did with that army of clerks and staff officers in the rear.

I was putting on dry socks when Captain Neal called on the radio. A Christmas cease-fire had gone into effect. The operation had been secured. My platoon was to return to friendly lines as quickly as possible. Why not lift us out with helicopters? I asked. No, Neal said, that was out of the question. I passed the word and the troops cheered. "Hey-hey. We're gonna get some slack. Merry fuckin' Christmas."

"No, no. I want to stay out here," said PFC Baum. "I just love it out here in the mud and the rain and the shit."

Shouldering our packs, we tramped down to Purple Heart Trail, the quickest route back. The trail forked near Dieu Phoung, a hamlet several hundred yards west of Charley Hill. The right fork led along the river, the left over the foothills toward the outpost. We took the latter because it was shorter and less likely to be mined or ambushed.

Outside the hamlet was a flooded rice paddy with a steep embankment at its far end. A barbed wire fence, anchored at one end to a dead tree, ran along the length of the embankment. The trail climbed through a hole in the fence near the tree. The lead squad, Sergeant Pryor's, Jones, and I crossed the rice paddy. The water was cold and chest-deep in places, and the rain dimpled the water in a way that reminded me of an evening rise on a trout stream. That was how the Ontonogan River looked in the evenings, in the place where it made a slow, wide bend around a wooded bluff upstream from the rock, white-water narrows at the Burned Dam. There, the river had been deep and smooth where it curved, and the big trout rising made rings in the copper-colored water. Bill, my fishing buddy, and I used to cast for browns in the deep pool at sunset. We never caught many, but we had a fine time, casting and talking about the things we were going to do when we left school, about all that awaited us in the great outside world, which seemed so full of promise. We were boys and thought everything was possible. The memory sent a momentary pang through me; not so much a feeling of homesickness as one of separation—a distancing from the hopeful boy I had been, a longing to be like that again.

Pryor's squad climbed the embankment, the men slipping on the muddy trail, slipping and falling into each other until they were bunched in a knot. The rest of the platoon waded through the rice paddy behind us, holding their rifles in the air. A snake made a series of Ss in the black water as it slithered between two men in the column. On dry ground again, Pryor's marines picked up their interval and hiked up the ridgeline that rose above the embankment. The Cordillera loomed in the distance, high and indomitable. The last two squads started to struggle up the bank, bunching up as one man after another slipped and slid into the man behind him.

Standing up by the dead tree, I helped pull a few marines up the trail. "Pass it back not to bunch up," I said. To my left, a stream whispered through a brushy ravine. "Don't bunch up," a marine said. "Pass it back." On the other side of the paddy, the rear of the column was filing past a hut at the edge of the hamlet. Smoke started to roll from the hut and a woman ran out yelling.

"Bittner," I called to the platoon sergeant, who was bringing up the rear, "what the hell's going on?"

"Can't hear you, sir."

"The hut. Who the hell set fire to the hut?"

"Somebody said you passed the word to burn the hut, sir."

"What?"

"The word came back to burn the hut, sir."

"Jesus Christ. I said, 'Don't bunch up." Don't Bunch Up. Put that fire out."

"Yes, sir."

I stood by the leafless tree, watching the marines douse the fire with helmets full of water. Fortunately, the thatch had been wet to begin with and did not burn quickly. Turning to walk back toward the point squad, I saw Allen stumbling on the trial.

"Allen, how're you doing?" I asked, extending my arm. Taking hold of it, he hauled himself over the lip of the embankment.

"Hackin' it, lieutenant. I'm hackin' it okay," Allen said, walking beside me. Ahead, I could see Pryor's squad trudging up the ridge and the point man briefly silhouetted on the ridgeline before he went down the other side. "But this here cease-fire's come along at the right time," Allen was saying. "Could use a little slack. This here cease-fire's the first slack . . ."

There was a roaring and a hot, hard slap of wind and a needle pricking my thigh and something clubbed me in the small of the back. I fell face down into the mud, my ears ringing. Lying on my belly, I heard an automatic carbine rattle for a few seconds, then someone calling "Corpsman! Corpsman!" Because of the ringing in my ears, the shots and voice sounded far away. "Corpsman! Corpsman!" Someone else yelled "Incoming!" I got to my hands and knees, wondering what fool had yelled "incoming." That had not been a shell, but a mine, a big mine. Who the hell had yelled "incoming"? You did, you idiot. It was your voice. Why did you say that? The fence. The barbed wire fence was the last thing you saw as you fell. You had fallen toward the fence, and it was like that time when you were six and walking in the woods with your friend Stanley. Stanley was nine, and he had been frightening you with stories about bears in the woods. Then you had heard a roaring, growling sound in the distance and, thinking it was a bear, you had run to the highway, tried to climb the barbed wire fence at the roadside, and caught your trousers on the barbs. Hanging there, you had cried, "Stanley, it's a bear! A bear, Stanley!" And Stan had come up laughing because the growling noise you had heard was a road-grader coming up the highway. It had not been a bear, but a machine. And this roaring had not been a shell, but a mine.

I stood, trying to clear my head. I was a little wobbly, but unmarked except for a sliver of shrapnel stuck in one of my trouser legs. I pulled it out. It was still hot, but it had not even broken my skin. Allen was next to me on all fours, mumbling, "What happened? I don't believe it. My God, oh my God." Some thirty to forty feet behind us, there was a patch of scorched, cratered earth, a drifting pall of smoke, and the dead tree, its trunk charred and cracked. Sergeant Wehr was lying near the crater. He rose to his feet, then fell when one leg collapsed beneath him. Wehr stood up again and the leg crumpled again, and, squatting on his good leg, holding the wounded one straight out in front of him, he spun around like a man doing a Cossack dance, then fell onto his back, waving one arm back and forth across his chest. "Boom. Boom," he said, the arm flopping back and forth. "Mah fust patrol, an' boom."

Allen got to his feet, his eyes glassy and a dazed grin on his face. He staggered toward me. "What happened, sir?" he asked, toppling against me and sliding down my chest, his hands clutching at my shirt. Before I could get a grip on him, he fell again to all fours, then collapsed onto his stomach. "My God what happened?" he said. "I don't believe it. My head hurts." Then I saw the blood oozing from the wound in the back of his head and neck. "Dear God my head hurts. Oh it hurts. I don't believe it."

Still slightly stunned, I had only a vague idea of what had happened. A mine, yes. It must have been an ambush-detonated mine. All of Pryor's squad had passed by that spot before the mine exploded. I had been standing on that very spot, near the tree, not ten seconds before the blast. If it had been a booby trap or a pressure mine, it would have gone off then. And then the carbine fire. Yes, an electrically detonated mine set off from ambush, a routine occurrence for the rear-echelon boys who looked at the "overall picture," a personal cataclysm for those who experienced it.

Kneeling beside Allen, I reached behind for my first-aid kit and went numb when I felt the big shredded hole in the back of my flak jacket. I pulled out a couple of pieces of shrapnel. They were cylindrical and about the size of double-0 buckshot. A Claymore, probably homemade, judging from the black smoke. They had used black powder. The rotten-egg stink of it was in the air. Well, that shrapnel would have done a fine job on my spine if it had not been for the flak jacket. *My spine.* Oh God—if I had remained on that spot another ten seconds, they would have been picking pieces of me out of the trees. Chance. Pure chance. Allen, right beside me, had been wounded in the head. I had not been hurt. Chance. The one true god of modern war is blind chance.

Taking out a compress, I tried to staunch Allen's bleeding. "My God, it hurts," he said. "My head hurts."

"Listen, Allen. You'll be okay. I don't think it broke any bones. You'll be all right." My hands reeked from his blood. "You're going to get plenty of slack now. Lotsa slack in division med. We'll have you evacked in no time."

"My God it hurts. I don't believe it. It hurts."

"I know, Bill. It hurts. It's good that you can feel it," I said, remembering the sharp sting of that tiny sliver in my thigh. And it had done nothing more than raise a bump the size of a beesting. Oh yes, I'll bet your wounds hurt, Lance Corporal Bill Allen.

My head had cleared, and the ringing in my ears quieted to a faint buzz. I told Pryor and Aiker to form their squads into a perimeter around the paddy field. Casualty parties started to carry the wounded out of the paddy and up to the level stretch of ground between the embankment and the base of the ridgeline. It was a small space, but it would have to do as a landing zone.

A rifleman and I picked up Sergeant Wehr, each of us taking one of the big man's arms. "Boom, Boom" he said, hobbling with his arms around our necks. "Mah fust patrol, lieutenant, an' boom, ah got hit. Gawd-damn." A corpsman cut Wehr's trouser leg open with a knife and started to dress his wounds. There was a lot of blood. Two marines dragged Sanchez up from the paddy. His face had been so peppered with shrapnel that I hardly recognized him. Except for his eyes. The fragments had somehow missed his eyes. He was unconscious and his eyes were half closed; two white slits in a mass of raspberry red. Sanchez looked as if he had been clawed by some invisible beast. The marines fanned him with their hands.

"He keeps going out, sir," said one of the riflemen. "If he don't get evacked pretty quick, we're afraid he'll go out for good."

"Okay, okay, as soon as we get the others up."

"Rodella, sir. Get Rodella up. Think he's got a fucking chest wound."

I slid down the embankment and splashed over to where the corpsman, Doc Kaiser, was working to save Corporal Rodella. There were gauze and compresses all over his chest and abdomen. One dressing, covering the hole the shrapnel had torn in one of his lungs, was soaked in blood. With each breath he took, pink bubbles of blood formed and burst around the hole. He made a wheezing sound. I tried talking to him, but he could not say anything because his windpipe would fill with blood. Rodella, who had been twice wounded before, was now in danger of drowning in his own blood. It was his eyes that troubled me most. They were the hurt, dumb eyes of a child who has been severely beaten and does not know why. It was his eyes and his silence and the foamy blood and the gurgling, wheezing sound in his chest that aroused in me a sorrow so deep and a rage so strong that I could not distinguish the one emotion from the other.

I helped the corpsman carry Rodella to the landing zone. His comrades were around him, but he was alone. We could see the look of separation in his eyes. He was alone in the world of the badly wounded, isolated by a pain none could share with him and by the terror of the darkness that was threatening to envelop him.

Then we got the last one, Corporal Greeley, a machine-gunner whose left arm was hanging by a few strands of muscle; all the rest was a scarlet mush. Greeley was conscious and angry. "Fuck it," he said over and over. "Fuck it. Fuck it. Fuck the cease-fire. Ain't no fuckin' cease-fire, but they can't kill me. Ain't no fuckin' booby trap gonna kill me." Carrying him, I felt my own anger, a very cold, very deep anger that had no specific object. It was just an icy, abiding fury; a hatred for everything in existence except those men. Yes, except those men of mine, any one of whom was better than all the men who had sent them to war.

I radioed for a medevac. The usual complications followed. How many wounded were there? Nine; four walking wounded, five needing evacuation. *Nine?* Nine casualties from a single mine? What kind of mine was it? Electrically detonated, black-power, a homemade Claymore probably. But what happened? Goddamnit, I'll tell you later. Get me a medevac. I've got at least one, maybe two who'll be DOW if we don't get them out of here. How big was the mine? Four to five pounds of explosive, plenty of shrapnel. It was placed on an embankment and the platoon was down in a rice paddy below it. Most of the shrapnel went over their heads. Otherwise, I'd have several KIAs. Okay? Now get me those birds. "Boom. Boom," said Sergeant Wehr. "Mah fust patrol en' boom, ah get hit." Charley Two, I need the first letter of the last names and the serial numbers of the WIAs needing evac. Now? Yes, now. Rodella and Sanchez had lapsed into unconsciousness. The corpsmen and some marines were fanning them. Doc Kaiser looked at me pleadingly.

"Hang loose, doc," I said. "The birds'll be here, but the assholes in the puzzle-palace have to do their paperwork first. Bittner! Sergeant Bittner, get me the dog tags of the evacs, and hustle."

"Yes, sir," said Bittner, who was one of the walking wounded. A green battle dressing was wrapped around his forehead. One of the walking wounded. We were all walking wounded.

Bittner gave me the dog tags. I tore off the green masking tape that kept the tags from rattling and gave Captain Neal the required information. Then the radio broke down. Jones changed batteries and started giving long test-counts: "Ten-niner-eight-seven . . ." I heard Neal's voice again. Did I have any serious casualties? For Christ's sake, yes, why do you think I'm asking for a medevac?

"Charley Two," said Neal, "you must have not been supervising your men properly. They must have been awfully bunched up to take nine casualties from one mine."

"Charley Six," I said, my voice cracking with rage. "You get me those birds now. If one of these kids dies because of this petty bullshit I'm going to raise some-kinda hell. I want those birds."

There was a long pause. At last the word came: "Birds on the way."

The helicopters swooped in out of the somber sky, landing in the green smoke billowing from the smoke grenade I had thrown to mark the LZ. The crew chiefs pushed stretchers out of the hatches. We laid the casualties on the stretchers and lifted them into the Hueys, the rain falling on us all the time. The aircraft took off, and watching the wounded soaring out of that miserable patch of jungle, we almost envied them.

Just before the platoon resumed its march, someone found a length of electrical detonating cord lying in the grass near the village. The village would have been as likely an ambush site as any: the VC only had to press the detonator and then blend in with the civilians, if indeed there were any true civilians in the village. Or they could have hidden in one of the tunnels under the houses. All right, I though, tit for tat. No cease-fire for us, none for you, either. I ordered both rocket launcher teams to fire white-phosphorus shells into the hamlet. They fired four altogether. The shells, flashing orange, burst into pure white clouds, the chunks of flaming phosphorus arcing over the trees. About half the village went up in flames. I could hear people yelling, and I saw several figures running through the white smoke. I did not feel a sense of vengeance, any more than I felt remorse or regret. I did not even feel angry. Listening to the shouts and watching the people running out of their burning homes, I did not feel anything at all.

★   ★   ★   ★   ★

And ye shall hear of wars and rumors of wars. See that ye be
not troubled, for all these things must come to pass, but the end
is not yet . . . . for nation shall rise against nation and kingdom
against kingdom . . . then shall they deliver you up to be af-
flicted and shall put you to death . . . but he that shall endure
unto the end, he shall be saved.

—Matthew 24:6-13

The Khe Sanh

RON STEINMAN

The Marine Corps base at Khe Sanh was one of the most remote outposts in Vietnam, astride the volatile border regions with Laos and North Vietnam. In January 1968, as part of the communist Tet offensive, North Vietnamese General Vo Nguyen Giap deployed an estimated three divisions against the base effectively placing the Marines under siege, raining down thousands of heavy artillery shells, rockets and mortar fire on the Marines. In 1954 General Giap had defeated the French in a similar position at Dien Bien Phu bringing an end to French occupation of Vietnam. President Lyndon Johnson refused to allow the same fate to the Marines at Khe Sanh, and every resource was committed to the battle. Ron Steinman was NBC's bureau chief in Saigon from 1966 to 1968 and covered the Tet offensive. In 2000 he published an anthology of Vietnam veterans' narratives as a companion to the ABC television series, *Vietnam: The Soldiers' Story.* The following selections from Marines who took part in the Khe Sanh battles provide a glimpse of the heroics and sacrifices of the men who fought there.

> Through it all, the troops did their duty. They stood their
> watches, flew their aircraft or serviced helicopter zones,
> manned outposts, engaged the enemy and raised the flag as
> zealously at the end as at the beginning. They were never asked
> to stand back-to-back against the flagpole with fixed bayonets,
> but rather to endure. By enduring, they triumphed. They were
> magnificent!
>
> — Capt. William H. Dabney

★ ★ ★ ★ ★

Captain Rocky Darger—Helicopter Pilot U.S.M.C.

The zones that we went into consistently—Hill 861, 881 North, 881 South—those were the three primary zones we seemed to work the most. The weather was an absolute nightmare. We would single-handedly go in there because all the LZs were so small, you couldn't get in with more than one aircraft. But after a while it seemed to be kind of a safer bet to go in with a lot of helicopters. Usually the number seemed to be eight and then we would coordinate our timing to be in the LZ maybe thirty seconds apart, so you get all eight helicopters in there and out of there maybe in four or five minutes at the very most. We'd carry external loads when were just doing resupply that would be hanging underneath the helicopter and we would actually go in, do a quick hover, release the load in the zone and then get out of there.

Occasionally, though, you'd be going in and you'd be dropping off troops or you might be picking troops up, and then you would have to land. And when you did, the co-pilot's responsibility when you touched down to the ground was to push the stopwatch on the panel and at twenty seconds he'd start lifting the power and we'd have to be out of there because within thirty seconds there'd be mortar rounds in the zone.

One day I remember sitting in the zone and looking down at a couple of marines. They were in a trench right down below me as we were sitting in the LZ and they were sticking their M-16s up over the edge of the trench and shooting over the top of their heads because they didn't want to get their heads over the trench in view because all eyes were on us when these helicopters were in those LZs.

The one grunt on the ground I would have really liked to have met was the radioman that directed us into the LZ on Hill 861. Sometimes when we'd be coming there, knowing we were going to start taking fire and stuff right away, he would be standing on top of the command bunker to get a better view to help get us into the LZ. He didn't use normal radio chatter. It was more a real down-to-earth way of talking and he was very comforting and very helpful. He actually got in trouble with some of the officers in his company because of the way he was talking to the pilots. We frankly got word out there and said, "Leave the guy alone. He's tremendous." I don't know his name. I'd sure love to find out.

When you're taking rounds you can hear the clicking when they're hitting the fuselage of the plane or you can see the instruments jump out in your lap because .30 caliber rounds come through the front of the helicopter.

But you wouldn't hear anything other than when it finally hit the plane. You didn't know the mortar was there till it hit you. There really wasn't any warning on that at all. You might fly into 881 four days in a row and take no fire at all and the next day, just get the living hell shot out of you. So you never knew. It was a big surprise, the biggest surprise. I remember someone describing being a helicopter crewman as hours and hours of boredom punctuated by moments of stark terror, and I think that's a pretty apt description because you might fly for three or four weeks and nothing would happen and then in a period of one day, you'd be changing helicopters because the other ones were too shot up. And that's the way it went. Khe Sanh was like that.

Early on it was pretty intense. It was a major changing point in my life, going up there. You have to keep doing what your job is and you just get along. I don't know how else to describe it. There was a period in the hooch that I was in, we had ten pilots in there, where we lost four or five pilots like in three days, not counting the crewmen that were on board, and you, you just go on.

The weather at Khe Sanh seemed to be a constant overcast. Sometimes, to resupply the hills leading to Khe Sanh, we would actually slide over the side of the mountain and just start sliding up through the fog, trying to get up to the top of the mountain to the outposts to resupply them and then, in turn, pick up medevacs and slide back down the side of the mountain till we had visual flight again. That could get a little harrowing. The difficulty in dealing with grunts is they may be in dire need of ammunition or food, water, and because they were all socked in, they couldn't understand why we couldn't come in and just hover down through the clouds and land in their zone. Once you can't see outside, you don't know if you're flying backwards, forwards, sideways, or what. It was very frustrating sometimes when we wouldn't fly into their LZ that was completely zero-zero weather. That is to say, no visibility forward. You couldn't see anything. It was solid overcast. Solid fog.

I remember sitting in an LZ while we were trying to load on a forced recon team of about five or six marines, three of which were trying to carry two dead fellow marines and all their equipment. We are trying to get them on board the helicopter. And they were under heavy fire from a large number of NVA. We sat in the zone for over a minute and a half. I knew we weren't going to get out of there because we were taking all of this fire and we had no suppressing fire and I accepted the fact that we were going to die there. I looked at Captain Weigand and the only thing I could think to say was, "This is it," and he just nodded his head because we weren't going to leave until all those marines were on board. At the same time, fifty to one hundred yards away, you could see these flashing lights all in the tree line shooting at us and lots of flashing lights. And it amazed me that anyone carrying a rifle could have just killed us because we were sitting there in this little glass cockpit and crewmen are in the back with little pieces of thin aluminum between them and death. We got everyone out of there and no one was injured. I still don't understand it to this day. I had accepted the inevitability that I was going to get killed. And once I did that, my sanity . . . I just didn't worry about it anymore, and that was real early on. And thereafter, I had a different attitude about what I was doing. I have a different attitude about death today because of that.

The camaraderie that you have with people in that type situation can't ever by duplicated. Things you do for the grunt on the ground you've never met, it's hard to imagine. You're willing to sacrifice your life, and if you're the decision-maker, the aircraft commander, you may sacrifice the lives of four other people on the aircraft for one person. The one thing more than anything else I got out of the entire experience was it seemed like everyone wouldn't trade places with the other guy. The grunts would always look at the helicopter crewmen and say, "God, I wouldn't do that for anything. At least I can hide in my hole." I think on the other hand, when we were able to fly out of an LZ and fly back to the security of a larger base, we wouldn't have crawled into that foxhole for anything.

Captain Earle G. Breeding, Echo Company, 2nd Battalion, 26th Marines

Earle G. Breeding first arrives at the Khe Sanh Combat Base in June 1967. In the spring there had been serious combat in the mountains and jungles surrounding the isolated base. Through the remainder of the summer, the fall, and into the early winter, there is only sporadic action in the area. All the marine hill positions are important first lines of defense against possible ground attacks by the North Vietnamese. On January 26, 1968, he and his men climb Hill 861 Alpha outside the base. Breeding stays on Hill 861 A through the middle of April, when General William Westmoreland sends in the U.S. Army's Seventh Cavalry, effectively ending the siege.

We continued on and we got to the top of Hill 861 Alpha around midnight. The troops were just exhausted because we had to climb up a wash to get there. And I've looked at the map many times and I don't see the rough terrain that we went up, but we went up. Fortunately we encountered nothing on the way up or when we got up there. The weather, thank heavens, the weather was good, on one hand. See, we had no water. We went three days up there without food or water. And we were fogged in. The fog worked for us; it worked against us. At night you could gather a little bit of moisture on ponchos. I would really liked to have had a little rain up there, so we could have had water to drink. But if we had had very much rain, then we would have had an awful problem with what trenches we had dug and what have you. Probably at night, best of my recollection now, we were wearing, like, field jackets and what not. So it probably got down into the upper forties, lower fifties at night. Daytime, break in the clouds, it would warm up.

And it was on the 5th of February that they hit us bad.

We were mortared so much up there until we finally figured out how to live without taking casualties. At best, it's terrifying. You get used to it after a while, though. You really do. A case of survival of the fittest. You could pitch a pup tent in the middle of one of New York's busiest streets and after a while, you'd learn how to survive out there—given the opportunity. It got to the point when we were being mortared that we didn't ask did anybody get hit. It was who got hit. And once you can get yourself dug in enough and get some cover, then we figured out how they were doing it and when they were doing it. You can beat the system. We beat the system well, once we became acclimated to what was going on.

They diverted B-52s, with some rather large bombs, flying up there at about fifty thousand feet. Not quite in on us. As I understand it, they ran closer than they had ever intentionally run in on friendly troops, and they're dropping these huge bombs with pinpoint accuracy. To go back a little, with all the firing that we were doing and all the support fires I had coming in, there's no way I could tell friendly fire from unfriendly fire. And then all of a sudden, this whole hill started shaking like an earthquake, and I thought, Oh, my Lord, they've tunneled underneath us, which I was worried about and they were trying to set off charges to blow the whole hill up, which turned out later not to be the case. That was a B-52 strike. It just rattled that hill. It was unbelievable. As the plane are flying, you don't hear the planes. They're too high. Then all of a sudden, you see these bombs starting to explode, an effect like an arc as they go off in succession. It's an awesome thing to see them.

We were fogged in an awful lot. It's very difficult to bring a helicopter in, in dense fog. I brought one in myself one night to get a wounded man out. And in total darkness, absolute total darkness. And he had no lights. I did it by talking to him on the radio. I could hear him coming. Eventually I said, "You're right on top of me. Don't go forward and don't go sideways. Come on down." And I walked around with my hand in the air and I finally felt a tire. I talked to him. I said, "You're five feet off the ground, four, three, two. You're one foot off the ground." Then we got the wounded man on there, and I climbed upside the helicopter and talked to the pilot. I told him, I said, "When you take off, make sure you go straight up and not forward 'cause you got a tree ten feet in front of you." But all he had to do was to rise up and break off to the left. At that time I thought that was just real simple. Since then I found out from helicopter pilots that when you don't have a horizon reference it's difficult to know whether you're moving forward a few feet or not. But he did. He got out of there.

There are an awful lot of parents out there of Vietnam veterans who have returned who entrusted the lives of their sons and husbands to the teenager, to the American teenager. When you take an eighteen-, nineteen-, twenty-year-old young lad and entrust him with lives of men, and I mean really entrust them with their lives, he has more responsibility than any bank president ever thought about having. Friendships formed the camaraderie. The faith you learn in your fellow man. When you stop to think that your sheer existence is in the hands of some teenagers that you hardly know, you develop one type of faith. Another type of faith is that the Marine Corps won't let you down. They were held together primarily by esprit de corps. They were given lectures before they went over there that they were going to stop the flow of communism, and God, mother, country, apple pie, Chevrolets, and all the rest of it. It doesn't take very long once you're over there to realize that that's a bunch of hogwash. What he gets is a strong feeling of ethnocentricity. The "we" feeling. "We" as a unit. "We" as a small unit. He starts fighting because of the guy next to him. We had very high morale. Oh, there was an awful lot of complaining about everything. But morale was good. Morale was very good.

Sergeant Glenn Prentice, Forward Observer, Radio Operator, India Company, 3rd Battalion 26th Marines

In the beginning just before the siege we knew there was something happening. We had a lot of air strikes and artillery strikes really close to the base. We had to wear our flak jackets and helmets days before. I was walking to the mess hall real early in the morning of January 21, and I noticed some streaks of light coming in. They started impacting on the road. One hit the mess hall.

Another rocket hit the ammunition dump. I can remember running from the ammunition dump and being knocked down by the concussion explosion. It was very intense. We had the ammunition dump blowing up and those incoming North Vietnamese rounds. We had a lot of incoming rounds. Some days, like thirteen hundred rounds impacting on the area, twelve hundred rounds, a thousand rounds hitting different areas of the base. It was mainly survival. The NVA gunners would pick certain areas of the base, and Charlie Company was hit quite frequently. It was an artillery battery firing against the NVA batteries and positions. When we were on Hill 881, I and the other marines would sit outside of the area near the landing zone and watch the rounds coming in and actually be real close to the incoming rounds to warn the helicopter pilot and also warn the marines that the next round would be impacting in their area. It was very interesting and intense. Very risky to do that.

They had different mortar rounds positioned on us. And rockets. Each of those have a distinct sound. Based on the sound, we had between fifteen seconds and twenty seconds to find cover. The other rounds we had was a recoilless rifle. We called those two seconds. And when we heard that sound, we knew we only had two seconds to hit the ground and we'd drop down immediately where we were. Some of the mortar rounds close to the battery area had a thumping sound, and we only had about another ten seconds before those rounds impacted. So depending on the sounds we heard, we looked around to see the best cover. Either the bunkers or the trench lines or just dropping down right where you were. And if you didn't develop that hearing, you didn't last very long.

The first part of the siege, the way we used to combat the rats was just leave the light on. That didn't work, so we left music on. That kind of scared away the rats. Then towards the end of the siege, the rates were so big and brazen, we'd actually have to have somebody standing watch on the rats with a big cane and hit the rats off your stomach or head where it landed so it wouldn't bite you in the nose or fingers. The rats were scary. We'd poison them. Take peanut butter and heat tablets, and we'd mix them together and then they'd eat and it would kill them. Sometimes it worked, sometimes it didn't. Sometimes it just made them mad.

A bunker was an engineering feat, I guess. With all the marines, it was how do you build something to withstand a rocket round or an artillery round or a mortar round. And that was like building a fort when you were a little kid. So we stole matting from the runway and we stole different things from the Seabees and we'd kind of put it together. We used wooden ammunition carts for building blocks and filled them with dirt. We had a whole series of supports and sand bags and hollow areas to basically protect against the rocket rounds and artillery rounds and the mortar rounds. We had one experience where we didn't quite meet the specifications. The delayed round went through the bunker and it actually hit the floor inside but then failed to go off. Everybody was in the bunker. We had eight people in the bunker and it went through the roof and landed halfway through the door and floor and it didn't go off.

The air force would come in sometimes and land. And we would try to buy booze from them. Because there was no beer or whiskey or anything. We knew the ARVNs had rice brandy. They were at the battalion right in front of us. So we went out there to buy some rice brandy. We had to sneak through the lines and buy two bottles of rice brandy. We got into a firefight on the way in, and on the way back we ran into our battery commander and he chastised us for buying the rice brandy and poured it out in front of us. It was kind of funny, but it was risking your life to have some rice brandy. Kind of interesting.

Day to day, every day was different. It was basically survival. You had to listen to the incoming rounds. We had to repair phone lines. We had to stand radio watches. We had to be on working parties to repair the bunkers from incoming rounds. It was very dangerous. People were killed going to the head or to the outhouses. People were killed repairing sandbags. People were killed just getting water. You didn't know when the incoming rounds would come. During fire missions it was very intense. We had to go out and stand up. Normally when we had incoming rounds, the infantry could go into the bunkers and trench lines. In the batteries we had to fire the guns and stand up. We were in harm's way. It was very emotional just seeing the gunners firing back.

One of the scariest parts for me was when we had a big artillery hit. I'm deathly afraid of fire. I got caught in the open and I jumped under a supply rack. One of the rounds hit the fuel tank. There were fires in the battery area, and I was pretty afraid of getting caught on fire. I jumped back to the bunker full speed and dove into the bunker headfirst and really ripped off my clothes. It was kind of funny. They saw me all naked. I'd rather be naked than burned. And that was pretty intense for me that day.

Being radio operators, we were a prime target for the snipers and the NVA infantry. We had to kind of disguise ourselves especially when we knew we were going into a hot area. They didn't teach us this in boot camp. It was passed down from radio operator to radio operator who'd been in major firefights. We had three-foot antennas above our head. We had handsets that looked like phones. So we had to disguise these. We cut holes in our sleeves and put the antenna down our sleeves. We put our handsets in our jackets and we put haversacks or coverings over our radios just so they couldn't tell who we were. We also never looked through the binoculars during the time because that denoted we were forward observers. We got rid of our .45s and took M-16s so they couldn't tell we were radio operators. We did all that to survive. People who didn't do that tended to be killed or wounded a lot faster and more critically.

Being so close to death many times, death was measured in inches and moments. You help one another. When you got wounded you were there for your friend. Your friends saved your life. It happened countless times. A friend would walk up to you and say, "Let's get something to eat," and you'd go someplace else, and the next moment, the place you were standing in wouldn't exist anymore.

Corporal Kevin MacCauley, Radio Operator, Bravo Company, 3rd Reconnaissance Battalion, U.S.M.C.

When MacCauley went to Vietnam, like many kids from New York City, he had never before seen the jungle, let alone anything more wild than a cat, dog, or pigeon. Add to that the weight he carried, and he was suddenly in world he never imagined.

In addition to what was called a PRC 25 radio, which weighed about twenty-five, thirty pounds, I carried a spare battery. Then I carried food for the duration of the patrol, six to eight days. I would carry water in quart canteens. All our pack and our cartridge belt and all the armaments and ammo that we carried with us was about seventy to eighty pounds for the regular grunt soldiers and with the radio, mine was close to one hundred pounds. The area that we were in, Khe Sanh, was a very hilly, mountainous area. You went from triple canopy jungle to what they called elephant grass. The insects, the flora and fauna, was something that was totally alien to anything that I had experienced. The elephant grass has such sharp edges that you would be cut to shreds just walking through it. The animals out there were just absolutely amazing. One patrol, we were waiting for the helicopters to pick us up and an eight-and-half-foot-long Bengal tiger came out in front of us, not more than six feet away. I had a rifle ready to shoot it in case it jumped at us and I was aiming all over the sky, I was so nervous. Another occasion we had elephants in the area. We had apes.

When monsoon season hit us, I don't think I've been colder in my entire life. Khe Sanh was socked in by clouds, and you'd have a mist, twenty-three out of twenty-four hours a day. I'm wrapped in a sleeping bag, wearing a field jacket because it was so cold. And the temperature dropped from daytime to nighttime, a good thirty to forty degrees. It really was cold up there at night. Out in the bush you were just totally exposed to the elements. We didn't carry ponchos because when the rain hit the ponchos, it made too much noise. So we just laid out there. If it rained, we got wet. It was hot, we baked. It was cold, we shivered.

There are stories of being separated from my team and running around like a chicken with my head cut off till one of the other guys found me and brought me back down to the landing zone. I thought they were going to leave me out there, but it was my own stupid fault for doing stuff like that. Watching a monkey jump out of a tree onto a patrol leader's face and having him smack at it, trying to get it off himself in the middle of the night, and we're all sitting there is total hostile territory laughing our heads off, watching this fool trying to protect himself from a monkey.

And turning around and looking at the faces of the guys who came in off a patrol where they had to stop at Graves Registration to drop off a friend's body. That will always be with me.

We took a lot of casualties in January and February. It seemed as though the guys who would kill were killed. We took nineteen guys killed during that period of time, and we just took wounded day after day after day. I sent people out on working parties, and they wouldn't come back. Some guy would go out and get something, and he wouldn't come back. And you never saw the wounded, so that added to a certain degree of demoralization.

The bunker that got hit was a bad experience. It's not nice ripping a bunker apart and finding only pieces left of people you had been talking to fifteen minutes earlier. As we got the top off, I found one guy who was just picked up by the blast and pushed up against the ceiling of the bunker, which was basically runway matting. And I never saw a person bleed as much as what this poor guy did. He survived but he was terribly wounded. And the four guys who were killed were horribly mangled. You're never really prepared for your first view of a dead person. And you got close with guys such that you would make plans for one another. And unfortunately, a lot of the plans were totally destroyed by what happened to us. So there are a number of experiences that I went through that still cause nightmares and still cause a lot of heartache.

Morale, at times, was very, very high, and morale, at times, was very, very low. We thought we were invincible. We didn't like the idea of being held on the base because everybody said that, you know, the marines are hard chargers. We should be out there in the bush, going after the North Vietnamese. But on the other side of the coin, we would sit there and say, all right. Come on. Come on at us. Come at us. We'll take as many of you with us before we go than what they could afford. So our morale was high as far as that's concerned. But it never came about. There never was the actual big ground battle at Khe Sanh.

Basically it was hell. There was no place that was safe. One day we took over seventeen hundred rounds of mixed artillery and rocket fire. Another day we took in the neighborhood of six hundred rounds over the space of a four-hour period. And you're sitting in a bunker supposedly safe, ten feet below the ground. The safety just wasn't there. The 24th of January we had one of our bunkers hit. Had twenty-two guys in it. Eighteen were wounded and four were killed. And we thought we were safe inside and we weren't. Day after day we would constantly fill sandbags. You got so tired that you did sleep some. But the rats running around inside the bunker and on top in and around the sandbags, it really didn't make for much sleeping. You figure a room, not even a room, a space of about maybe ten feet wide by about six foot high by maybe thirty feet long and you'd have eighteen, nineteen, twenty guys inside that space. You'd be lying next to, on top of, underneath the guys in your platoon or squad, however many people could fit in the bunker. That's where we existed. It wasn't a pleasant situation, but it was the only situation that we had. It was the only way we could keep ourselves safe from the small pieces of shrapnel that were flying around, it seemed like all the time.

I went from November until probably the end of March without taking a shower. We had rain barrels that we used in the event there was a fire. And every once in a while you'd go down there and use the pretty much stagnant water to try and clean yourself up. Really never had the opportunity the better part of five months to wash your clothes. It would rot off on you, and you'd get a resupply. The water we did have was specifically for drinking. You really didn't use it for washing cloths or taking showers. There was a whole bunch of us who looked really strange with little tufts of hair growing out of our adolescent faces that we thought looked like the most macho beards and mustaches but we looked ridiculous, to say the least.

Well, we went through an awful lot of Tabasco sauce and ketchup and any other condiments we could get our hands on trying to make

C-rations a little more palatable. Ham and eggs really wasn't one of our fa-vorite foods, but the odds of the draw you would get ham and eggs. The worst thing that you'd get out of C-rations was what they called ham and lima beans and we had other terms—we called it ham and mothers. I'll use that half a word, anyway. They were the most God-awful tasting stuff in the world.

You know, this is something totally alien for an eighteen-, nineteen-year-old kid. I mean, when we were at home, we were either members of the 4-H Club or we were altar boys or we were captains of the football team. Now all of a sudden we were placed into a war. And I guess it was our baptism of fire, so to speak.

If you asked us in the beginning of January whether or not we were going to go home to Mom and Dad and see our girlfriends, a lot of us would have said might not be there, might not be there. I left Khe Sanh in April. I flew in there prior to the siege, right after the hill fights, and the country-side was absolutely gorgeous. We flew out in a CH-53 helicopter. As we lifted off the runway, we kind of corkscrewed up into the sky to avoid any of the machine guns and anti-aircraft guns that still might be in the area, and the thing that amazed me, the entire surrounding countryside was just totally denuded of trees. Everything was bomb craters. I turned and I looked at that, and I said, "God, look what we've done to this area. We've take a beautiful, beautiful area and we've turned it into the moon." There was noth-ing but craters.

The bad times are still remembered, but you kind of look at the good times, and it brings a twinkle to your eye and a smile to your face when you think of things. We were always kibitzing and joking around. We were the greatest bunch of pranksters. Some of the pranks took a rather bizarre type of turn. One guy would unscrew the fuse on top of an M-26 hand grenade and he would break the fuse off and screw the top back on, pull the pin, let the spoon fly, and throw it at a bunch of guys. And every-body would jump and run away, and he'd stand there and laugh his fool head off. Well, it happened twice and then we beat the hell out of him, told him not to do stuff like that again. But we did anything to break the nervousness and even break the fear that we had.

Semper Fi meant "Always Faithful," but it was always faithful to the guy next to you. You would do anything for the guy next to you. You would lay down your life for the guy next to you. There were never any grandiose thoughts of, you know, we're over here fighting for the American way of life, for apple pie and mother. We were fighting basically for the guy next to us. You would fight because you were afraid of what the guy next to you might think if you didn't fight. I don't ever remember meeting a coward in Vietnam. A lot of guys dealt with things a different way, but you wanted to be part of a team. You wanted to part of a platoon, and the only way that you could do that was being faithful, *Semper Fi*, to the guy next to you. And that was the most important thing for us.

Corporal Kreig Lofton, Helicopter Crew Chief U.S.M.C.

I had been in Vietnam maybe eight months. I was pretty salty. We had arrived at Dong Ha to pick up fresh troops. These guys got on my helicopter, and they were in brand-new uniforms. Brand-new greens. All their equipment was brand-new. And I remember being struck by their rosy cheeks. Just a look of how young these guys were, and I was twenty years old at the time. I suddenly realized right then that I was seeing them through the eyes of an old man. I had somehow become so callous and so uncaring about anybody but my flight crew that I realized that these reinforcements had no idea what they were in for, and it was a very tough moment.

We would launch very early in the morning, sometimes before dawn. As we approached the designated drop point, I was surprised at the small-arms fire that we had received, maybe just a few rounds, maybe some intense heavy weapons. We would insert these guys into a zone. They would start moving immediately and sometimes they would immediately get back on the radio and say, "Come and get us. We're in trouble." Invariably they wouldn't be in the same position. They'd been trying to run for it because we inserted them right in the neighborhood of the NVA battalion or company. So they're running for their lives. They were not able to make it to the top of the mountain. They'd be stuck. They couldn't go up. They couldn't go down. We'd have to hover on the side of the hill and pull them in one at a time. And they'd be carrying wounded with them, their equipment, and sometimes dead marines. We would immediately start taking fire. I'd have to talk them into the zone and try to ensure that the helicopter blades didn't hit our guys or the side of a mountain or a tree. All the time under heavy fire.

We started receiving incoming rounds a little bit after 5:30 in the morning. The ammo dump was hit. Finally there was a massive explosion that leveled everything on the combat base. The concussion traveled through your body and almost knocked the air out of you. Word passed looking for the air crew. We were still receiving sporadic artillery and mortars. We assembled air crew and made a mad dash completely across the combat base which was probably three football fields wide, running from hole to hole, trying to dodge the incoming. We launched and all the hills were calling for medevacs to come in. I remember looking at 861, seeing bodies in the wires, large numbers of NVA dead, marine dead as well. The impact from the NVA artillery and rockets was so great on that one location that the top of the hill was completely obscured by dust and debris. Tracers going everywhere. We circled for what seemed like an eternity until finally it died down and we went in, picked up the wounded and whatever dead they could throw on, and we pulled out of there.

When we were inserting troops into the zones, we had to slow down. We had to fly very low, come in, set them down, and when you're doing that, you're a very big target. A helicopter is the thing that the NVA common soldier wants to shoot down. It's the ultimate trophy. It will get him leave-time with his family. It will give him extra pay. Grunts don't really enjoy that. I didn't enjoy coming out of a low and slow, but that's the frame of reference for a helicopter going into a LZ.

The marines loading wounded men on to our helicopters were very motivated to make sure they made it happen very quickly because they were a target as well. If they weren't killed being loaded onto our helicopter, we would take them to Charlie Med, the primary hospital, where the NVA had the area completely zeroed in. They were timing their incoming rounds to when the helicopters landed to drop off the wounded that the rounds would hit there at the same time. So a guy that was wounded on the hill had three, four chances actually of dying. The initial wounds, the wounds coming off the hill, the wounds dropping him off at Charlie Med, and if he had to be medevacked out again. After we supported the hills, the last thing we would do, we would go in and pick up the dead that were in body bags from Khe Sanh. And we would take many helicopters to do that on some days. It could be forty, fifty, sixty dead marines in bags stacked up waiting for the helicopters. We would load them on and take them to Dong Ha. It was the last thing during the day.

There's typically ten guys in a hooch, and you're living with those ten twenty-four hours a day until the time they go home, you go home. You're flying with a lot of them. You know their families, though you never met them. You know their hopes, their dreams. So you bond tightly because combat has a tendency to remove a lot of the veneer at certain times. You're very vulnerable, more so than you thought you could be. So you share with each other your concerns and your fears, sometimes even though you're supposed to be big bad marines, killing machines. That's not the case. You still are subject to the same emotions that all human beings are.

I left Khe Sanh looking down on it and headed east down the mountain. It was very difficult for me. I saw the suffering that the marines went through. We had suffered through this. All the casualties that had mounted up in seventy-seven days. It was all for nothing. You know, we were totally abandoning it. I was having a hard time understanding that. And I still don't quite understand it.

Lieutenant Ray Stubbe, Chaplain, U.S. Navy

I arrived there in mid-July of '67. At that time it was a nice place. It was actually very beautiful. It was detached from the rear. We didn't get generals too often or people poking around. It was cool, being high in the mountains. It was very colorful. It was full of activity. Most people regarded it as a good place to visit. Our experience on Khe Sanh is just something that, like one of our people says, "Then is always now," or "Now is always then." In July, August '67, life was a matter of digging bunkers, going on patrols. It may seem like really nothing was happening, and yet for those that were there, just the simple fact of going on patrol means going up and down very steep hills, being cut by elephant grass, and forming blisters that never really heal, broken bones, tripping over things, getting thoroughly exhausted. The humidity and the heat in the valleys being so intense, there were dehydration cases, cases of malaria. One fellow even dying from malaria was then taken naked up into a helicopter and coated with water and alcohol to try to cool him down, but he died anyway.

Those months were just heavy work in a beautiful setting. Then the rains came in September, October, November. Rains like you wouldn't believe. Ten, fifteen inches a day, day on, day off, where you would never get dry. Truthfully I can say I was never colder than I was at Khe Sanh because skin gets wrinkled and chapped and it's like immersed in water all the time. It did get quite cool there during the monsoon season. At that time it was a matter of collapsed bunkers, the misery of never being dry, of mail not getting in, the necessity of air drops. The airstrip started to wash away which necessitated tearing up the whole airstrip, putting down crushed rock from a nearby quarry, and then putting the airstrip back down again. So for a period of time in September through November, we were basically isolated. We didn't know quite what was happening. It was a time of uncertainty. It was a miserable time. The beauty vanished quickly.

All at once woof, woof, and bang, and the base was under attack. I was by myself in my bunker at the time and I guess it's human. I didn't want to be alone. But I knew and I had been told that you don't run during an attack because mortars explode upward like a V, unlike a rocket which splatters or artillery. The supplies are all burning, and the oil, the gas, the drums of oil, they're all burning, big billows of smoke. The ammo dump started cooking off. Little flechette darts and CS gas powder covered the base, and the tears were coming down. Later on there was a lull and there were some casualties and a chopper came in, and one of the corpsmen came running back and said, "My casualty, who had a wounded leg, outran me to the chopper."

During the siege most of the time I was hopping around from bunker to bunker, trench to trench, and I did hold my church services, but they were only three minutes long. I gave out Communion. I had a one- or two-sentence sermon. At the time, I think the text that I worked with was Jesus calming the waters. And a short prayer, and then I'd just sort of sit with the guys and see how things were. The men would joke with each other. They'd say, those bad shooters. That one was way off the mark. Or they would talk about their girlfriends or whatever. Then I'd move on to the next place. I did maybe fifteen or twenty of those a day during the siege. Some were underground. They told me never to gather any more than three or four people above ground because we had a ridge line to the north where they had spotters that could see us, and they'd call incoming on us. There were some that were out in the open. I would take off my helmet and have church.

There was a necessity for people to move casualties. Sometimes during the incoming, people would see somebody wounded out there or couldn't move and would dash out during the incoming to rescue them. This happened all the time. People would share their last drops of water with each other. We ran out of water quite a few times. Our water point would be hit. We would go for three or four days without water a lot of times on the base. Longer on the hills, maybe seven or eight days sometimes. We were down to one C-ration a day, and people would share that with each other.

I would say the men stayed pretty constant during the siege. They were still full of energy, ran faster, drove faster, never lost their humanity or concern for one another. Joking. Humor. They were in touch with fears, with laughs, with death, with life. The only people that cracked up, and there were a couple of them, were basically older people that probably had been through Korea or World War II. I have learned since that's probably accumulative, like radiation. You get so much, and that's it. These were people who would curl up in a corner of a bunker. There was one in the recon area who was as tickler for polished boots and close order drill before the siege, and when the rounds starting to come, he was curled up in the corner. His men actually dragged him out of the bunker and slapped him because they were desperate for a leader. So there were some very interesting everyday heroics.

I spent a night as a matter of fact in a bunker on the line near our position. I'm not sure why I did that. I just did. There was an intense nervousness, jitteriness, people moving in and out all the time. We would make a little stove by taking a C-ration opener on our can, putting a bit of C-4 or a heat tab in there and mixing a little envelope of coffee with a can of water. We were drinking that. There was a record player in there. Some men had radios, some had record players, and some had a little 45 record player. It was playing the Creedence Clearwater version of "I Heard It Through the Grapevine," which is a very jumpy version. "Do-do-do, I heard it through grapevine," kind of thing. The music sort of was the way they were. They were just jumpy. It was getting near the end of the day. One of the marines in the trench was reading his prayer book. They were talking about what they wanted to do back home, what their plans were, what kind of car they were going to get, about their girlfriends. They'd joke about them and share their love letters with each other. About two weeks later that very bunker took a direct hit, and everyone was killed in there. I went down there with the Charlie Med people to help bring out the bodies. One fellow was missing his head. There was a neck with the strings of flesh. I carried him out. We were looking for his head. We couldn't find it anywhere. It evidently just exploded or something. They were very young. They were very, very young. These people were basically eighteen. They would do anything to save another person.

Khe Sanh sat on an extinct volcano. The place was born in violence and heat, and that's the legacy that remained. Like steel becomes coated with dust, everything became coated with that reddish-brown dust. Almost impregnated with something you could not blow off. It became gritted, embedded in the paint and in the sandbags that were left, in anything that was standing. It got into our skin. When I left there, I would take a shower. It got into the skin so deeply that three months later you'd be rubbing taking a shower and you'd wipe yourself with a white towel and you get that brownish-red on the towel. It was almost as though the Khe Sanh soil penetrated our soul. It got inside us. It got into us.

They would make what they called roll-outs, which were little cavities in the bottom edge side of the trench that they could roll into and still be safe in case a round did land in the trench. Anyway, this clay when it got wet became as slippery as ice for vehicles or people. When it became saturated, it became pea soup, and anything below ground collapsed. We had built underground, and then the monsoons came and washed it all away. It was in many ways like World War I: gas trenches, fog, wires, same living conditions, dysentery. Just like World War I trench warfare. We would dig this long trench and it would collapse at times. Somebody would be in the roll-out and be buried under ten feet of dirt. Then the others would start clawing the dirt with their hands and their entrenching tools, until they found these men. There were two men who were encased, and they rescued them. They both lived with mouth-to-mouth resuscitation. A first few casualties are just very wrenching. Absolutely shocking, especially if you see a fellow missing his abdominal wall and you just see his intestines, or a man without an arm.

The fog would roll in in the morning. It was cool. It was mysterious. It was paradoxically a sense of relief and fear at the same time. It also gave us a time to relax. Everything is contrasts. We knew we weren't going to get any incoming. We could walk around. We could run around. We could re-supply. We could get our C-rations. We could do our repairs. We could build our bunkers. We could check in on our mail. See how people were. We could do anything. The fog would shroud any possibility of knowing what the enemy was doing as they crept closer. Were they massing? This is what the troops thought. We just knew that they were out there and, perhaps, probably creeping in. And then when the fog lifted, we might suddenly see in Cinemascope-fashion, a wall of people coming in on us. And so the fog created a kind of fear.

At night there's no lights. Before the siege there were no lights. Some people needed lights but for the trooper there were no lights. When the sun went down, that was it. Then if you had to walk around the base with all this internal concertina, with all these unexploded pieces of ordnance, trucks, jeeps, and wrecks of airplanes, walls of sandbags and old tent pegs that were still poking out, you were obviously going to trip somewhere. Then all of a sudden, there's a few rounds of incoming and you don't know where to run for cover. Probably just lay as flat as you can. At night most people were either on watch, on the lines, peering out into the unknown. It wasn't a sense of desperation. There was a sense of isolation. We were very vulnerable. There was that awareness.

I built my own bunker. I had wooden pallets on the deck and a parachute over the tops and the walls. I had a little three-by-three-foot field desk. I happened to have a metal-framed rack, a bed. Casualties were in there, and they were sitting on my bed. Four or five of them. They were laying on these wooden pallets. During the night others came in. There were so many people in there, feet were dangling out. An air force officer was right next to me, sitting on the floor on the deck. And he was looking stunned. We looked at his back and there was a little piece of shrapnel right on the top of his flak jacket. Had it been one more inch higher, he would have gotten it in his spine. A round must have gone off right next to him. And he was in shock. A young fellow that I knew very well was dabbing his head with a roll of toilet paper that I had. It was filled with blood, and he kept crumpling these little pieces of toilet paper on the floor. Eventually, the floor was filled with reddish toilet paper. In the morning everyone left. I was walking around, and I found the fellow who had been dabbing his head. I said, "Well, they didn't evacuate you?" He said, "Oh, no. The blood on my head was the blood of all my buddies that were killed." It wasn't his own wound.

As any marine who has been in combat will tell you, you don't want to leave your buddies. It's like being welded almost, in the heat of the battle. You develop such a closeness that is indescribably close. You don't want to abandon it. You feel alone. People are still sensitive. It's like one casualty after another. Numbness sets in. It's probably a survival technique. I have no doubt the feelings were still there. It's just we were not in touch with them. Perhaps since leaving, those feelings now emerge in dreams, with all the horror and fear. With veterans not just from Vietnam but from World War II and the Civil War, whatever. The people I don't think changed. They remained the same. They still rescued one another. They still did their job. They were unintimidated. They'd go for refuge during incoming but as soon as it would lift, they'd be right out. They weren't cowering in the trenches or bunkers. They were maybe the most marvelous people as I group I've ever been with.

★   ★   ★   ★   ★

In what many consider the most concentrated application of aerial firepower in the history of warfare, the United States Air Force, Marines and

Navy flew over 22,000 air support missions to defend the Khe Sahn. On April 1, Operation *Pegasus* was launched to reestablish overland contact with the base. The Khe Sahn was a tactical victory for the United States. It remains unclear if General Giap intended to try and storm the base or to use the attacks on the Khe Sahn as a diversion to other objectives of the Tet offensive.

Phase Line Green

NICHOLAS WARR

In the early morning hours of January 31, 1968, as part of the massive Tet offensive, a division-sized force of North Vietnamese Army and Viet Cong soldiers launched a well-coordinated attack on the city of Hué. As a former imperial capital, the city was an important symbol of a united Vietnam. The recapture of the city was tasked to three understrength battalions of the First and Fifth Marine Regiments, the South Vietnamese 1st Divison, supported by U.S. Army 7th and 12th Cavalry Regiments. Facing them were 10,000 veteran North Vietnamese regulars and Viet Cong, entrenched throughout a maze of buildings and the historic Citadel and Imperial Palace. Denied the use of heavy artillery, naval and air support in the opening days of the battle, the Marines fought on in the heaviest urban combat since World War II. Nicholas Warr was a young lieutenant leading Charlie Company, First Battalion, Fifth Marines during the fighting at Hué. In 1997 he published a brutally honest and controversial memoir of his experiences *Phase Line Green.*

> Courage is endurance for one moment more…
> —Unknown Marine Second Lieutenant in Vietnam

★　★　★　★　★

13 February 1968

Early on the morning of 13 February 1968, the Marines of 1/5 left the relative safety of the First ARVN Division compound and headed southeast toward our designated line of departure, phase line green. Alpha Company was on point, Charlie Company followed closely behind with Charlie One, as usual, on company point. One platoon from Delta Company provided rear security for the battalion CP group.

Dawn had reluctantly and halfheartedly defeated the dismal darkness of the previous night, but the winter sun could not penetrate a thick, long-hanging, gloomy cloud cover with anything other than a minimum of illumination. The only thing complementary about the weather conditions was that the rain also appeared reluctant to show itself, and we were dry, at least for the time being.

Walking slowly, keeping at least a ten-meter interval between each man, the Marines of 1/5 maintained a staggered column on either side of the street called Dinh Bo Linh after a fifth-century Vietnamese king. Dinh Bo Linh was a two-lane city street parallel to the eastern wall of the Citadel Dinh Bo Linh would eventually deliver us from the First ARVN Division compound to phase line green.

Alpha Company, as 1/5's point element and responsible for coverage of the eastern Citadel wall and the narrow city block adjacent to the wall, would turn left one block before they reached phase line green. Phase line green was, of course, a street, and its actual name was Mai Thuc Loan. Mai Thuc Loan was named in honor of a Vietnamese general who fought against both the Chinese and the French as they encroached on Vietnamese soil during the sixteenth century.

Alpha Company would make the appropriate turn to the east and then deeply parallel to phase line green and move through the houses until they reached the point of departure. Charlie Company would move up behind them, deploy in a similar fashion along the three blocks of our responsibility, cover each other's flanks, and move forward until we reached phase line green. Once we were in position on phase line green, we would be given the word to commence a coordinated frontal assault on the NVA who were waiting for us, according to all the available intelligence reports, somewhere south of phase line green.

Because of the ten-meter interval and the deliberately slow and careful pace established by Alpha Company through the quiet, ancient suburbia of Hué inside the Citadel wall, it was very easy to become distracted by the sights. Spacious old estates were the dominant theme along both sides of Dinh Bo Linh, our present route of approach. Dinh Bo Linh was lined by several mansions, surrounded and separated by a mature and somewhat overgrown landscape of trees, shrubs, and spacious grounds, interspersed with reflecting ponds. The mansions were all surrounded by substantial stone walls, four to six feet high, and occupied large chunks of each city block. As we progressed southward, the larger estates gave way to a more normal suburban setting, consisting of many smaller houses in orderly rows facing the east-west-running streets. The only thing consistent about the larger estates and the smaller houses was the distinctly discomforting lack of noise coming from them. It was as though this section of Hué was utterly void of humanity. Inside the Citadel, Hué was a ghost town.

My attention was abruptly wrenched away from the immediate scenery and back in the direction of Alpha Company by the all-too-familiar "whump" of a mortar or rocket explosion, followed by several more of the same, punctuated by a ragged trickle and then a rushing torrent of small-arms fire. Alpha Company, whose point element was several hundred meters ahead of us and who had made their designated left turn several minutes before, had stepped in the shit, no question about it. A healthy firefight was under way, obviously involving Alpha Company,

Without the necessity of commands, the Marines of Charlie Company took cover as best they could along the walls lining Dinh Bo Linh and waited. Finally, after what seemed like hours but was probably only several minutes, the rear element of Alpha Company started to move again, and they turned the corner. Charlie One's point fire team started to move out after them, following about fifty meters behind Alpha's rear element. In my normal position, following just behind the point fire team, I was one of the first Charlie Company Marines to find out what had happened to Alpha Company.

As I began to make the appropriate left turn, Benny and I stopped cold as we were confronted by a fearful sight. Walking slowly and painfully toward us, 1st Lt. F. P. Wilbourne, Alpha Company's executive officer, was carefully making his way on his own, back toward the battalion rear area. Wilbourne had actually been the company commander of Alpha Company for a short time before 1/5 headed toward Hué, but he had been bumped down the ladder of command just a couple of days before by a Capt. J. J. Bowe, and Wilbourne was now the executive officer.

If we hadn't heard the firefight, if we hadn't seen the blood that covered his entire body from head to toe, we would have been tempted to ask him if he had shit his pants, since he was walking with stiff legs and arms, like someone who had rectally embarrassed himself. But as he approached us it quickly became obvious that Lieutenant Wilbourne had been hit by a shower of shrapnel, and though none of his wounds appeared to be life-threatening, the cumulative effect was that Alpha's XO had become a bloody sieve.

Recognizing me as a Charlie Company platoon commander, Lieutenant Wilbourne stopped his arduous trek momentarily. Although it obviously pained him to do so, he pointed out that several of my men were in an exposed position, still nonchalantly turning the corner of the intersection, and he quietly chewed my butt.

Wilbourne said, "The Alpha CP group just got wasted because we were standing right out in the middle of an intersection, a block *behind* phase line green, clusterfucked around an M-48 tank. The gooks ran out into the street about a block and a half in front of us and fired three RPG rockets, hitting the M-48 directly in the turret with their first shot. Shit, the skipper and the gunny were both blown away, and Alpha has been effectively eliminated on the battalion's left flank. Delta is moving up to take our places, and we'll be falling back to provide rear security. Fuck, the tank commander had his head blown off! Now, you tell your people that if they keep dirty-bopping across the damned streets, they're gonna get themselves blown away, too!"

Having said his piece, he started his painful trek toward the rear of the battalion column once again. As he walked away, he continued to mutter at me that we should get our collective heads out of our asses, get out of the middle of the fucking street, and make goddamned sure to stay alert and keep our heads down.

As I turned away from Wilbourne's unwelcome visage, I noticed that I didn't have to say a damned thing. Most of Charlie One had seen and heard him, and they were taking a distinctly lower stance along the sides of the road and were moving very quickly across the open areas when they had to cross the intersection. Shit, Alpha Company was history before the battle had even begun.

The battalion's assault was delayed for what again seemed like hours as a platoon from Delta Company moved up and relieved Alpha Company, and we got positioned along Tang Bat Ho, another street named for ancient Vietnamese royalty. The street ran parallel to phase line green, one block north of our point of departure. A shallow, muddy ditch ran alongside Tang Bat Ho, and Charlie One hunkered down in the ditch as the rest of Charlie Company got into position and as Delta switched positions with Alpha. As we waited, I resisted letting my attention wander toward the scene of destruction surrounding the now-disabled M-48 tank about fifty meters away and tried to concentrate on other things besides the frantic efforts to save the critically injured and to evacuate the dead members of the Alpha Company CP, but we couldn't avoid knowing exactly what was happening. During the first brief skirmish inside the Citadel, the NVA had struck unexpectedly and viciously, and as a result, several KIAs (killed in action) and many WIAs (wounded in action) had rendered the Alpha CP group totally ineffective as a command unit. Alpha would have to fall back into battalion reserve status and regroup.

As Benny's Prick-25 squawked to life, the orders from Charlie Six tersely broke into my thoughts. "Move out. Maintain contact on both flanks. Move up to the line of departure, and prepare to attack across phase line green."

Charlie One's three squads had lined up three abreast, broken into their fire team units. Slowly and cautiously, we moved into and around each house, taking our time, making sure that we weren't going to accidentally walk past any hidden enemy positions, constantly conscious and fearful of a counterattack from the rear. The houses in this block were much smaller than the estates we had passed on our way; they were very close together and often very difficult to walk around. This was not really a problem, because we had to clear each house anyway, but we still checked the narrow, brushy spaces between the houses to make sure we weren't missing anything.

The shouts of Marines communicating with each other as they practiced for the first time the tactics of house-to-house fighting penetrated the sullen air, muffled by the walls and the damp morning air. These barking commands, obviously made by Americans, reached my ears and gave me some comfort that at least the men of Charlie One were taking this very seriously. They had seen the instant destruction of the Alpha CP group, and they didn't want to be hit unexpectedly.

As was normal when Charlie One was in a frontal assault formation, Benny and I tagged along behind the center squad, Ed Estes's squad, in the middle of the block and kept in touch with the other two squads via their PRC-6 radios, much smaller and much less effective communication devices than the Prick-25. The Prick-6, resembling an overgrown walkie-talkie, quickly proved to be ineffective in penetrating the walls of the houses that the Charlie One Marines were clearing, and it quickly became clear that we would have to rely on runners for a lot of our intraplatoon communications. Each platoon of a Marine company had one Prick-25, for communications with the company CP group and the battalion and support nets for calling in artillery and air support, and we had three or four Prick-6s, which were designed for close-in communications between squads. The Prick-25s worked great; the Prick-6s were completely useless.

Charlie One was organized into three squads, each of roughly thirteen Marines, broken down further into three fire teams and a squad leader. Each squad was further reinforced by a team who lugged and handled the awesome and devastating firepower of the M-60 machine guns. Sometimes they had the added luxury of an M-79 man, who carried the forty-millimeter grenade launcher and somewhere between forty and sixty rounds of accurate and deadly high-explosive firepower. On the morning of 13 February 1968, Charlie One's table of organization was comprised of a total of fifty-one Marines, including the attached M-60 teams, me, Benny Benwaring, and the two Navy corpsmen assigned to travel with us.

The Marine fire team is the basic and fundamental tactical unit of the U.S. Marine Corps, and many hours of every Marine's training after boot camp were focused on the maneuvers of the fire team. The Marines of every fire team were drilled not only on individual movements and covering their buddy's back, but also on the importance of maintaining the integrity of their fire team. Thus it was natural in our current situation that one fire team would be responsible for clearing one house at a time. This tactic worked out very conveniently in the first block, which contained fifteen or sixteen houses, half of them facing north along Tang Bat Ho and half of them facing south along Mai Thuc Loan (phase line green). In this particular block, unlike most other blocks in southeast Hué inside the Citadel, the houses and their respective yards were separated by a narrow alley. The nine fire teams of Charlie One, with Benny and me trailing the center fire team of the center squad, cleared the first seven or eight houses facing Tang Bat Hot. Then, making sure that their flanks were covered on both sides, the men moved slowly and cautiously across the narrow alley, through old, flimsy gates defining the back yards of the houses facing phase line green, and entered the back doors of the eight or so houses along phase line green almost simultaneously.

As Benny and I waited for the fire team ahead of us to clear their assigned house, I checked out the intersecting alley and noticed that although it was very overgrown, it defined a pathway that went all the way to both sides of the block. I could clearly see both of the streets that intersected phase line green and defined Charlie One's left and right flanks. As it was very overgrown, I was not at all disturbed that I couldn't see any Marines across the street on our left flank. An M-48 tank rumbled slowly past the alley on the street to our right and inched toward phase line green. I wondered momentarily how the tank crews were feeling, with their hands tied by not being able to fire their ninety-millimeter cannons and knowing that one of their group had been eliminated from the battle already.

Estes came back out the back door and signaled that this center house was cleared, and Benny and I moved in through the back door. Although these homes were small by American standards, they were very substantial by Vietnamese standards, at least from our limited experience in the paddies and jungles in other parts of I Corps. We stepped up three low steps onto a raised wooden floor and immediately entered a hallway leading from the rear to the front of the house; a stairway led to a second floor. Walking past the stairway into an empty front room, which was lined at the front by multipaned windows framing the front door, we walked through the eerily empty front room. The dim daylight illuminated the front room, and the street, Mai Thuc Loan, phase line green, was dimly visible through the front windows.

As Estes and Benny, just ahead of me, walked through the front room, through the front door, and out into the street, something nagged at me. Something wasn't right here. My feet kept walking. My mind knew that something was terribly wrong, but it couldn't grasp the problem, and my feet kept walking.

As I passed through the front door of that dreary small house out into Mai Thuc Loan and turned my head to the left and then back to the right, I saw my men all standing there along the narrow sidewalk that lined the north side of phase line green. Some of them crouched behind the inadequate trunks of the shade trees lining this side of the street. I couldn't formulate any of the words in my mind. But I knew then, and I will know for the rest of my life, just exactly what was wrong. They had followed my orders to the letter. None of them had *crossed* the street, none of them had *crossed* phase line green, but every damned one of them, every swinging dick of Charlie One, was completely exposed *out in* the street. Charlie One was a collective sitting duck, standing out in the open along the narrow sidewalk in front of the houses. Some of them were crouching behind the trees, but most of them were just standing there, looking at each other, looking at me as I walked out of the front door of the center house.

My mind had no coherent thoughts in that one moment, that one heartbeat that will live forever as a cancer in my soul, I have had uncounted moments since then, during which I've eternally debated what my first words, at that crucial moment, should have been. The raging debate in my soul swings from the extremes of: "Charge!!" to "Shit!!!" to "What the fuck are you idiots doing out in the street? Didn't common sense tell you to stay *inside* the houses until I give you the order to attack?" These debates are all totally useless; they are nothing more than a futile raging, and they will never be anything more than wishful thinking.

Here's what came out of my mouth: "Get The Fuck Outta The Street!!"

I wish that the next few seconds had ticked away at normal speed, but with contemptuous certainly, time instantly changed into the slow motion of frustrating nightmares, of trying to run away from unseen but hideous monsters, only to be hindered by glue-covered feet or concrete shoes. I was only in that street that morning for a few seconds, but trying to escape the inevitable explosion of the well-prepared ambush of the entrenched NVA thirty feet in front of us, those seconds seemed like hours. Part of me will be there, in that street, for those terrible moments, for the rest of my days.

I have no idea why I didn't just turn around and run back inside the house I had just walked out of. That would have been the most obvious and fastest route to safety. I have no idea why I didn't turn left, or charge straight ahead. I have no idea why I turned to the right, screaming those immortal words at the top of my lungs and running as fast as my legs have ever run before or since, yet taking forever to get to wherever it was that I thought that I was going. I turned to the right, and I was following other Marines, my men, as the shit royally hit the fan.

The NVA were dug in and waiting for us on the other side of the street. They occupied the first- and second-floor windows, and many of the NVA were on the roofs. Several automatic weapons raked the street from our left flank, from the tower that protected the eastern entrance to the Citadel. And I ran, and ran, and ran, and I got nowhere fast.

There was no place to hide; I was shit outta luck.

Just before reaching the intersection of Mai Thuc Loan and Dinh Bo Linh, my first nightmare of that fateful day came to a spectacular and horrible conclusion. I was following a man from Charlie One Charlie, the third squad of Charlie One. He was one of its fire team leaders, a lance corporal named Gibson. Running one step in front of me, he was shot through the back by the NVA. The combined force of his running body and the AK-47 round that had slammed into him proved just enough to flatten a corner courtyard gate, which became my escape valve. As Lance Corporal Gibson's bleeding body knocked down the gate, my feet propelled me into the safety of the corner courtyard as I leaped over his crumbling body. I was closely followed by Benny Benwaring, who had gone where his leader had led him, regardless of the insanity of the direction.

The peaceful sanctity of this small corner courtyard had been shattered by our abrupt arrival. The scene was a nightmare, something out of Dante's Inferno, with the severely bleeding lance corporal sprawled on top of the wrecked remnants of the gate and several other shocked Marines huddled in the corner, protected by a substantial six-foot-high masonry wall but unable to return fire effectively. Doc English, one of Charlie One's Navy corpsmen, was one of the men in the courtyard, and he immediately began working on the severe wounds that were threatening to take the life of Lance Corporal Gibson. The ferocity of the enemy small-arms fire had not abated; it sounded like an NVA battalion was just on the other side of the street, shooting at us with everything they had. We had really stepped in the shit this time.

I asked Benny Benwaring to get the other squads on the Prick-6, but after a few frustrating attempts that resulted in a very unsatisfactory and un-helpful squelch of static noise, it was clear that if I wanted to find out what was going on, I would have to communicate by runner. Benny was monitor-ing the company radio net on the Prick-25, and it was very quickly evident that everyone else in the battalions was fully engaged with an entrenched enemy on the other side of phase line green. Charlie Six's instructions were to take care of our casualties, make damned sure of the integrity of our pres-ent positions, return fire, and await further instructions.

The leader of this squad. Charlie One Charlie, had begun to assert his leadership; he had made sure that the other Marines in the courtyard had good cover and were returning fire to the best of their ability. Doc English was doing everything he could for the wounded man, and it was killing me not to know what was going on with the rest of my platoon. I decided to go find out for myself.

Instructing Benny to stay with Doc English in case he needed help evacuating the injured man and to monitor the company net, I took off out the back gate of the corner courtyard into the alley. Turning right into the alley that would allow me to get to the other squads, I started running down the narrow, vine-draped alley. As I ran past a well, I tripped on some-thing and nearly fell on my face, but whatever I had tripped on was a small hindrance, and I kept my feet and continued running. Two more heartbeats went by before the booby-trapped grenade exploded, knocking me for-ward onto my hands and knees, but my feet kept pumping, and I kind of skipped off my hands and knees, bounced back on my feet, and just kept running. The force of the grenade's explosion had hit my legs and lower back, but nothing hurt at the moment. My mind didn't even register that I might be wounded and numb. I just kept running. (I didn't think much about the incident until three weeks later, back in a GP tent in Phu Bai, when I was finally able to take off my utility trousers for the first time, and four small pieces of shrapnel clinked to the floor. I had been running so fast, and the NVA had been so inept at setting up booby traps, that I was out of the effective range of the shrapnel by the time it had exploded. When I saw those pieces of shrapnel fall from my trousers in Phu Bai, I thanked my lucky stars that it had been an NVA who had set up the booby trap, and not a Viet Cong. The latter would have known to remove the time-delay fuse from the detonator of the booby-trapped grenade, creating an instant explosion rather than one that happened a few seconds after the pin had been pulled out by the trip wire.)

Crazily, at that moment, running down the alley, I was taken back to my childhood for a few seconds. Once again I was sitting by my four brothers in the living room of the farmhouse on the Coos River in southwestern Oregon, watching the family's eight-millimeter home movies. We were all laughing like crazy as we made my older brother, Steve, go back and forth, forward and reverse, from the back door of my grandmother's house to her outhouse. My father, who had been a fanatic with the old hand-crank eight-millimeter movie projector and who was also a frustrated actor/director, had on many occasions enlisted us boys to be actors in his crackpot, slapstick productions. On this particular occasion, Dad had thought it would be hilarious if Steve would burst out the back door of Grandma's old house, run down the four back steps, along the fifty-foot boardwalk that connected the back of the house with the outhouse, running as fast as possible, with the obvious theme that Steve was running to save his clean britches. In one of those rare and impromptu moments, Steve had slipped on the rain-soaked, ancient wooden slats of the boardwalk while Dad was filming and had fallen on his butt when his feet flew out from under him. But he had amazingly kept his feet pumping, and without losing any ground speed, Steve had bounced off his butt, regained his feet, and completed his urgent journey. All of this had been captured on film, and with the help of the reverse switch on the ancient eight-millimeter projector, my family spent many hilarious evenings forcing Steve to run back and forth, back and forth, while assaulting him verbally with appropriate comments like, "Hey, Steve, why'd you keep running? You probably did it in your pants when you hit the boardwalk, so the emergency was over." You get the drift.

At that moment, running down that shrouded alleyway, I giggled, just briefly, at the similarity of the events, but I quickly smothered that thought because there was nothing funny about any of this. I needed to know what was going on with the other squads, and fast.

Running to the opposite end of the alley, I ran inside the last building on the east corner of the block and found the squad leader of Charlie One Bravo, the squad who had covered the left side of our frontal assault formation. I quickly discerned that our situation was not good. Staff Sergeant Mullan, who had been traveling with Charlie One Bravo on our left flank, was gone. He had been standing out in the street like the rest of Charlie One and had been shot in the head during the initial burst of fire. The squad leader shakily told me that although Sergeant Mullan had been alive when they took him on a quickly improvised stretcher back toward the battalion rear for medevac, it didn't look like he could possibly survive. The side of his head had been severely wounded, probably by an AK-47, and he was unconscious and just barely breathing when he was carried away. Doc Lowdermilk, who had administered first aid, didn't give him much hope of survival.

The blows of losing Sergeant Mullan, who had truly been the leader of this platoon and my mentor while I was going through on-the-job training, was devastating, but there was no time to mourn or even to consider this loss, because we had a much worse situation on our hands. According to the squad leader, there were at least three dead Marines still out in the street, and he thought that Estes's squad had a wounded man down in the street as well. The wounded man was still alive, but stuck out in the street and exposed to enemy gunfire.

Making sure that Charlie One Bravo kept returning fire at the suspected enemy positions and that they kept their heads down as much as possible, I ran back into the alley and retraced my earlier steps following Estes's squad through the back yard and into the back door of the house that had been my initial entry into phase line green.

Bedlam greeted me. Exposed as they were in the front room, several Marines were returning fire toward the enemy across the street. Estes was hunched down in the hallway and was using the stairway for cover. When I came up behind him, he turned toward me with a look of anger and frustration that immediately spelled out the disastrous situation. There truly were three men down in the street right in front of this house, right where I had stood when I had first walked into phase line green and screamed those immortal words. I realized momentarily that if I had turned around and tried to go back inside this house through the front door, there was a very high likelihood that either Benny or I would have been one of the Marines down in the street.

Estes looked at me with a terrible burning fire in his eyes, and he quickly summed up the most serious problem. "Morgan is still alive, Lieutenant. He's hit bad, but we could hear him yelling at us to come get him just a couple of minutes ago. He's totally exposed, but he's hit bad and he can't move. We gotta get him outta there."

Enemy gunfire continued to rake the front room of the house, having long since shattered the windows, and effectively pinned down the Marines in the front room, making the effectiveness of their return fire questionable. From our position in the hallway, I couldn't see Morgan, but I could see two other green-clad bodies a little further out in the street. "How about those other two guys, Estes?"

"They're definitely wasted, Lieutenant. They were knocked down in the initial burst, and they've taken a lot more hits since. Neither of them have moved, and we haven't heard any sounds from them at all. But Morgan is still alive. What the fuck are we going to do?"

I said, "Let's try to give him some cover with smoke grenades, and then ask for a volunteer to go out and get him." Morgan's fire team leader, hunkering down under the window sill in the front room, immediately volunteered to make the effort. After sending two other Marines via the alley to the adjacent squads to tell them to lay down a heavy volume of fire when they saw the smoke pop in the street, we executed the plan.

Two smoke grenades went out the shattered front window, one on either side of Morgan's position, and the fire team leader, a lance corporal named Hallmark, rushed out into the hellfire. The volume of the small-arms fire, both incoming and outgoing, increased immediately, and after three long seconds, Lance Corporal Hallmark staggered back into the front room, blood gushing like a water faucet from his lower left leg. He collapsed in the hallway, screaming and holding his leg, as Doc Lowdermilk pounced on him and started the first aid necessary to stop the flow of blood and save the young man's life. Although the bone was most likely broken and he was in a great deal of pain, the young man had a hard time keeping a grin off his face, because he knew that this wound would put him on the sidelines and get him the hell out of Hué. But the grin vanished immediately when we asked him about Morgan.

Hallmark looked up at me through his pain and said, "Fuck me, Lieutenant, I couldn't tell if he was dead or alive. The shit is really hitting the fan out there, and I lost my grip on him when I got hit. I couldn't drag him over the curb, he's just too goddamned heavy. He might still be alive, but he's unconscious for sure. I think he got hit a couple more times when I tried to get him."

Estes and I helped Doc Lowdermilk carry the young hero out to the back yard and assigned another Marine to help him limp back to the battalion rear for medevac. As I watched them leave out the back gate, my mind was racing a million miles per hours, but none of my thoughts were at all helpful. Morgan was still down in the street, and we didn't know for sure if he was dead or alive. The Marine Corps has long had a proud tradition of making every effort possible to evacuate the dead and wounded from the battlefield, but the cards were stacked against us. Every time we sent more men into the street to try to recover the wounded or dead, even with the cover of smoke, it looked like we were just going to take more casualties, making a terrible situation even worse.

As I turned back toward the house, my vision fixed on L. Cpl. Ed Estes, who was obviously having the same terrible thoughts, but who was now insanely maddened by one other fact: Morgan was not just another Marine, he was his friend. They had been together for over six months, had survived the daisy-chain command-detonated mine outside Hoi An together, and had shared many night ambush patrols and uncountable daytime hours filled with terror and uncertainty. And now Morgan was down in the street and probably still alive. Estes was his squad leader, and he felt completely responsible.

As these thoughts surged through his mind, they were obvious to me as the emotions played across his angry face. Estes was turning slowly in place, walking in a tight circle, frustrated by Morgan's situation, scared to death like the rest of us about the prospects of making another attempt to go get him. As I watched this horrible internal struggle, Estes made a complete 360-degree pivot, as though his right foot was staked to the ground. Our eyes connected for only a moment, and I instantly knew what Estes was going to do. I froze, unable to move, unable to make a sound. Estes completed his pivot, and when he saw the back door of the house, he screamed in fury, "Morgan!!" Unable to believe that Estes was going to run out into that damnable hell, I could only scream his name, "Estes!!!"

L. Cpl. Edward S. Estes knew what he was running to face, but Ed Estes was unable to stop himself. His friend, PFC Charles R. Morgan, was down in the street, and it was up to Estes to help him. Estes ran into the house, down the hallway, through the front room, and out the front door into a terrible hail of enemy gunfire, which was now concentrated on the front door. The smoke in the street was dissipating, and by the time I got inside the back door, finally able to move, Estes was lost to my view for a moment in the smoke. But just for a moment.

Ed Estes didn't even make it to Morgan. He had hardly stepped outside the doorway when an AK-47 round tore through his neck, entering his

Adam's apple. Knowing then that Morgan was dead and that he was also probably dead, Ed Estes turned around and, still trying to run, stumbled back into the house, back through the front room, and collapsed at my feet in the hallway. He had been grasping his neck, but I had clearly seen the entry bullet hole in his Adam's apple. A thick, steady stream of blood was gushing from the hole, leaking heavily through his fingers.

Doc Lowdermilk was also Ed Estes's friend, and now Ed was dying. Doc Lowdermilk jumped on him and rolled him over on his back and onto my lap. Doc pulled Ed's hand away from his neck so that he could assess the damage and do what he could to save his friend's life.

Doc looked over at me with despair in his eyes and said, "We gotta do an emergency tracheotomy; his windpipe's crushed. I need a tube, something to stick into the opening when I cut into his windpipe."

I was stunned, stupid, unable to think or to move. None of the other Marines was any more help. Estes was dying on my lap, making feeble convulsive motions, and I couldn't move.

"Break down your .45, Lieutenant, goddammit. I can use the barrel as a temporary airway."

Still stunned, I was just barely able to pull my never-used pistol out of my Marine Corps–issue holster and break it down without looking at it as I had done so many times at Quantico and Basic School. I handed Doc Lowdermilk the barrel after he cut Estes's throat, and then he inserted the barrel into the bloody opening. Estes had stopped breathing, and Dock Lowdermilk started to push down on his chest to try to jump-start his breathing, when we noticed the terrible pool of blood forming under Estes and leaking from under his body.

Doc Lowdermilk gently turned Estes over, and we all knew at that moment that Estes was beyond any help that we could give him. The NVA bullet had entered his windpipe, and if it had gone straight back out his neck he might have had a chance for survival. But this particular NVA must have been shooting through a second-story window or from the roof of the house across the street, because the Trajectory had been downward. The bullet had traveled through Estes's heart and out his lower back, probably shattering his spine for good measure.

Ed Estes, Squad Leader for Charlie One Alpha, was dead.

Stunned as we all were in that dim hallway, we were all forced to start living again when another Marine from Estes's squad was shot through the chest. He had been in the front room sitting up against a side wall, and an NVA gunner had moved into a position where he could shoot down into the front room. We dragged him out of the front room, and I yelled at the rest of the Marines in the front room to get out of there and to take up positions upstairs or on the roof. This particular front room had become way too deadly.

We carried Estes's body out of the house into the back yard and laid him out on an old outdoor table. The firing in the street had diminished to a less frantic and more sporadic level, and I stood there for a while, looking at Estes. I was in shock, and I think I would have remained standing there for a long time, but flies started to buzz around Estes's head, and his face started to take on the ugly greenish cast of the newly deceased. I couldn't bear to look at him anymore. I pulled this wasted young man's poncho over his face, picked up his discarded M-16 rifle that had been propped up against the table by one of the other men, and turned my back on Ed Estes forever.

I don't remember too much about the next hour or so, I think time stopped for me. I vaguely remember returning to the house and walking into a back room that the owners had stuffed with the furniture from the front room and sitting down in a rocking chair. I closed my eyes and started rocking.

I remember rocking in that chair and thinking about the small dairy farm where I had grown up in Coos River, Oregon, and my pet cow, Honey, and the peaceful summer afternoons when I would lie on Honey's side and soak up the welcome and infrequent sunshine. Those were the most peaceful and least disturbing moments of my life, and my mind was subconsciously trying to submerge itself in memories of a peaceful moment. I could just not deal with the cruelty and savagery of our situation on phase line green and the death of many good men, in particular the death of Ed Estes. He was a young man who had accepted the responsibility of fighting for his country, of taking care of his men, and who had paid the ultimate penalty for facing up to those responsibilities.

So I sat in that rocking chair, holding Estes's M-16 in my hands between my knees, and rocked away God knows how many minutes. The other Marines from what remained of Estes's squad were reluctant to disturb me, and I probably spent nearly a half hour as a seven-year-old again, finding some peace with a cow named Honey.

Finally, Benny Benwaring brought me back into the present. He had left the corner courtyard and followed my footsteps into that house. Seeing me sitting there, blank-eyed, rocking gently and quietly, he probably figured I had gone off my rocker, so to speak, but he had summoned the courage to shake my arm and force me back into the present.

Benny spoke quietly but insistently: "Lieutenant, the skipper is trying to reach you. We've got orders from battalion to attack across the street."

Part of me came back to life and I somehow reassumed the role and responsibilities of Marine platoon commander, Charlie One Actual. Another part of me stayed in that rocking chair and is still there today, rocking away, thinking about the torn lives and destruction focused on that bloody street. Many of the events I witnessed and participated in on that street that day and the terrible days that followed are so etched in my memory banks that I can hear the sounds, smell the smells, and scream the screams in my mind as though they happened yesterday.

Charlie One was ordered to attack across phase line green three times that day, so the Marines of Charlie One attacked across the deadly avenue three times that day. After the first attack, it quickly became obvious that the main concentration of the NVA's forces were established right across the street from Charlie One, and our battalion commander had now decided that if we could successfully attack and penetrate the enemy's defenses at this point, we could break the back of their resistance and overwhelm them.

Repeated attempts were made to reverse the orders that restricted our heavy support. I pleaded with Scott Nelson to plead with Major Thompson to get us some artillery or air support. At least the major could allow the M-48 tanks to fire their ninety-millimeter cannons into the enemy positions, to soften the positions somewhat, to do something to force our enemy to get his head down, so that we had even a shred of a chance at success in a frontal assault.

My frantic requests for heavy firepower were all turned down flat. At one point, Charlie Six Actual got on the radio with me directly, reminded me of our orders, and told me to pull my men together and to assault the enemy. Running from position to position, Benny Benwaring and I set up the initial attack as best we could, which required one fire team in each squad to attack across the street, while the other fire teams provided covering fire. It didn't work; no one even got halfway across the street. The awful result was several more wounded Marines and another KIA. Now there was yet another dead Marine down in the street.

During the first abortive assault, I noticed that we were taking a high volume of enemy fire from our left flank, from the tower that guarded the east entrance to the Citadel. The NVA apparently occupied the tower in force and had many automatic weapons. From about a block and a half away, a distance of little more than a hundred meters, this firepower was devastating to the Marines who were trying to cross the street in full view of the NVA gunners in their tower positions.

After reporting back to Scott Nelson that we had been unsuccessful in getting a foothold on the other side of the street, he maintained that our orders hadn't changed and that we should get ready to try again. I was getting an awful feeling about the security of our left flank, so Benny and I took off down the alley to its intersection with the street that defined our connection with Delta Company on our left. When I got to the corner of the alley and the street, my heart sank. The M-48 tank that had been the center of the attack on the Alpha Company CP group, having been assigned a new tank commander and put back into action (albeit still under strict orders not to fire its cannon), was now positioned *behind* the intersection of the alley and the street. Furthermore, I couldn't see any Marines from Delta Company in their assigned positions along phase line green.

Benny and I ran across the street and dived behind the tank, as enemy gunners spotted us and started shooting in our direction. I asked for the whereabouts of the Delta Company platoon commander who was responsible for covering our left flank, and I finally found him in a house *behind the alley.* When I confronted him and tried to explain that they were not in position at phase line green, he looked at me like I was crazy and said that his men were in position where they were supposed to be and that they were taking terrible enemy fire from the tower. The Delta Company platoon had stopped their forward movement at the alley, and the platoon commander refused to look closely at his map or even consider that they were a half block in back of their assigned positions.

Leaving him in disgust, I returned to the back of the tank, got on the direct telephone that was designed for the trailing infantry to communicate with the tank commander, and ordered him to move up past the alley to the street corner and at least open up with his machine guns. The tank commander, repeating what the Delta platoon commander said, refused to budge. Charlie One's left flank was totally exposed, and it looked like it was going to stay that way.

Running back across the street into the alley, I called Scott Nelson and reported this news. He said he would check it out with battalion and get back to me, and in the meantime, we were to get ready to attack.

After only a couple of minutes, Nelson called me back, forcefully letting me know that I must be mistaken, because the Delta Company platoon commander had assured battalion that he was in the correct position, right on the north side of phase line green. Another frantic request to provide artillery or air support was immediately rejected by Nelson. We were on our own, and we were to attack again within the next ten minutes.

Our second attack involved selecting one squad—the right-most squad (the furthest from our left flank)—to be the assault force, with the remaining two squads setting up covering fire. As ordered, the Marines from Charlie One Charlie, the right-flank squad, attacked across the street, but they were again forced back by a ferocious concentration of enemy fire. The results were predictable: more wounded and yet another dead Marine down in the street.

Benny and I found ourselves back in the corner courtyard after the second assault, trying to assess the damage. Doc English was still there in the courtyard, working frantically on two more wounded Marines who had been hit in the second assault. Doc told me about the Marine down in the street; he could see him through the knocked-down gate from his position, which provided some security from the enemy fire because of the angles, and he knew that this Marine was dead. There were now, by my best count, five dead Charlie One Marines in the street; two more dead, including Estes, who had been evacuated; and many, many wounded. Our fighting strength had been cut in half, and we hadn't been able to budge the enemy an inch.

At this point, as I pleaded yet again with Scott Nelson that our left flank was exposed and that we needed artillery and air support or at least let the goddamned tanks start firing their cannons. SSgt. Robert H. Odum came running into the small corner courtyard from across the street that separated our platoons. He was the platoon sergeant for Charlie Three, the Charlie Company platoon that was assigned the next block on our right flank and that was taking heavy enemy fire from its immediate front. His platoon, however, had yet to be ordered to attack and had not had any Marines knocked down in an exposed position in the street. He was obviously pissed, and although he handled the situation with respect for my rank and the chain of command drilled into all Marines throughout their careers, he was obviously upset with me, that a Marine platoon commander could allow one of his men to stay out in the street without some attempts being made to recover his body.

"Lieutenant, one of your men is down in the street, right out in front of that tank. Maybe you weren't aware, sir?" Sergeant Odum's voice barely covered the sarcasm that was obviously intended to urge me to action.

I replied, "I am well aware of that, Sergeant Odum, and while I appreciate your efforts at running over here to inform me of this fact, I'd appreciate it if you would go back to your men."

Sergeant Odum said, "Sir, with all due respect, we must try to get that man back out of the street." Sergeant Odum was a very good staff NCO, well liked by his platoon commander and his men alike, and he was going to persist.

Rather testily now, I said, "Sergeant Odum, that man is dead. Doc English saw him get hit. He took at least one in the head, and he's been shot several times since. He's dead. I've lost several other Marines attempting to get their buddies out of the street, and while I appreciate your concern for that Marine and for the Marine Corps' traditions, I will not lose another Marine trying to get dead bodies out of the street. If I had any hope that he was still alive, *which he is not*, I'd be making the effort to get him right now without your help. Now, go back to your platoon."

Sergeant Odum looked me right in the eye, started taking his pack off, and said, "Well, Lieutenant, if you won't make an effort, I will. If it's not too much trouble, sir, have your men give me some covering fire."

No more words were spoken. He was determined, and there was no way that I was going to stop him. The few remaining Marines from Charlie One Charlie didn't have to be told to start shooting at the enemy positions across the street. Sergeant Odum tightened up his helmet's chin strap, made sure his flak jacket was buttoned all the way to the top, set his M–16 aside temporarily, took out his .45-caliber pistol, pulled back the slide, and seated a round in the chamber. His plan was to go back to the alley and crawl behind the M–48 tank sitting just on the other side of the courtyard wall. Then he would crawl between the tank and the wall, until he got to the street. When he finally got into this position, he would leave his position of cover, rush to the downed Marine, and drag him out of the street in between the wall and the tank.

The Marines in the courtyard increased their covering fire, and Sergeant Odum crawled forward.

I couldn't directly see what happened to Sergeant Odum out in the street, but I could watch the events in the street by watching the changing expressions on Doc English's face. Doc English saw, from his barely protected position as he worked frantically on a wounded Marine, everything that happened in graphic detail. He could not avoid watching what happened to Sergeant Odum, and I could see it all very clearly reflected on Doc English's face. When Sergeant Odum made his move, the enemy gunners, no more than fifty feet away from him, saw him immediately and opened up. Doc English's face was already filled with anguish at everything going on all around him—the wounded man in his lap, the dead man in the street, and the heroic and very dangerous effort Sergeant Odum had decided to make to recover the dead Marine. Then the expression on Doc English's face got worse; for a moment his face looked like death itself. I am absolutely positive that this one second in Doc English's life will remain with him forever; the look on his face will remain seared into my brain forever. Sergeant Odum was shot in the face, his lower jaw blown off by an AK-47 round.

I thought from the look on Doc English's face that Sergeant Odum was dead, but he was not. Sergeant Odum did realize then that he would not be able to save the poor dead Marine in the street, though, and he had the presence of mind or enough life-preserving instincts to abandon the dead Marine and crawl back behind the tank and back into the courtyard.

Sergeant Odum couldn't say anything. He tried, looking me right in the eye, but I had no way of knowing if he was saying that I had been right or if he was calling me a cowardly asshole. The AK-47 round had entered his face just below his left eye and had exited his face below his chin. Everything below his upper lip had been blown into mushy strips of flesh and blood. There was no mouth; there were no teeth. There were just shreds of bloody skin.

Sergeant Odum stood up, carefully holstered his pistol, and pulled out a canteen from his utility belt pouch. He calmly poured the contents of his canteen over his shattered lower face, as if he believed that he could simply wash out this nightmare as he would wash out a badly done watercolor portrait and then attempt to paint his lower jaw back in. Doc English quickly finished his bandaging efforts on the other wounded Marine that he had been working on, broke out several more bandages from his medical kit, and crawled across the gate's opening to assist Sergeant Odum. There wasn't much he could do for him except apply the bandages and hope the bleeding would slow down long enough to get him safely medevacced. Without my needing to speak a word, Doc English knew that I wanted him to help Sergeant Odum get to the rear. Sergeant Odum resisted all attempts to have him lie down on a poncho stretcher, however, and the last time I saw him he was walking under his own power, with Doc English and a small entourage of Charlie One Charlie Marines carrying the other wounded men back to the battalion rear for medevac.

That was the last time, with one notable exception, that Charlie Company made any attempts to recover dead marines from an exposed position in a street during the battle for Hué. There were many heroic efforts made to help wounded men while they were still alive, but after Sergeant Odum walked away from phase line green, all recovery efforts for the dead were made after darkness provided at least the illusion of cover. The only other time that an obviously dead Marine was recovered from the street in daylight hours took place several days later, and it was under highly unusual circumstances. But that story will wait.

As harsh as it sounded, and although it was very contrary to Marine Corps tradition, I gave direct orders to the rest of Charlie One that no further attempts would be made to get any dead Marines out of the street. We would do whatever we could to help save wounded men in exposed positions, but we would take no further risks by trying to retrieve dead bodies during daylight hours. After my brief and unhappy debate with Sergeant Odum on the subject, there were no further arguments.

One more attempt was made to assault across phase line green in the waning hours of that miserable afternoon. Scott Nelson and Major Thompson still did not believe that our left flank was exposed, and they resisted all pleas to provide heavy firepower. The powers that be had established the rules of engagement, and we would go forward across phase line green using the limited firepower of our small-arms weapons, or we would die. And so, Charlie One died.

Our third attempt to assault across phase line green resulted in getting two Marines completely across the street, but it also resulted in several more wounded and two more KIAs. The two Marines who made it across the street were immediately pinned down behind two separate, low walls. They had made it across the street, but both of them were totally pinned down, unable to move right or left without dying. One of these men, an E-5 sergeant named Bossert, who had taken over as Charlie One's platoon sergeant after we lost Sergeant Mullan, had a PRC-6 radio with him. Since he was out in the street and we had good line of sight from the roof of the house that Estes had died in, we could talk with him. He didn't want to talk above a whisper, because he could hear the NVA talking very close by, and he was afraid that if they knew he was across the street and still alive, they'd find him and blow him away. He could communicate, by hand signals, with the other Marine who had made it across further down the street. Sergeant Bossert was able to tell him to hold on until after dark and then run back across the street to our side when he thought it was safe.

Benny and I had climbed up on the roof of the two-story house along with a couple more Marines from Charlie One Alpha before the third assault, but we couldn't stay on the roof very long before several NVA gunners spotted us and started pouring small-arms fire in our direction. After we had lobbed some M-79 grenades from the blooper, they had quickly figured out where we were and we had to get back down off the roof posthaste.

Returning to our right flank once again for the umpteenth time that day, I crawled out behind the M-48 tank that had sat on the corner all afternoon long without once firing its cannon and got the tank commander on the phone. In as demented and angry a voice as I could muster, I told him that if he didn't start shooting his cannon at the enemy across the street, I would blow his tank up with a satchel charge. Either I wasn't very convincing, or he just didn't give a shit. He repeated that his orders were not to fire the cannon, but his machine guns did start shooting faster than they had up to that point.

I finally convinced Scott Nelson that there was no way that we could effectively assault as entrenched enemy across that street without heavy support, and that our left flank was exposed to boot. A few minutes later, he showed up in the corner courtyard.

Without speaking, I led him down the alley to our exposed left flank, and pointed out Delta Company positions, half a block behind phase line green. He finally agreed that our left flank was exposed. As we moved back down the alley, we made contact with each squad, and by the time we got back to the corner courtyard, our head count was down to twenty-three Marines still able to fight. Eight Charlie One Marines still able to fight. Eight Charlie One Marines had died that day, 13 February 1968, and twenty more had been seriously wounded and had to be medevacced.

As we huddled in that shattered courtyard, I think Scott Nelson was just starting to believe me, and he started to get just a little pissed off at Major Thompson. He got on his Prick-25, gave a terse report, and after a long wait, he was told to move back away from phase line green after we had recovered the two live Marines who had made it across the street and our dead bodies in the street and to take up defensive positions in the houses on the north side of the alley. The decision had been made to replace Charlie One with Alpha Company (complete with a newly assigned company commander) the next morning, so that they could execute the attack orders that we had not been able to carry out.

Late that night, after we had recovered our lost Marines under the cover of darkness and after I had made sure that both our flanks were secure and our defensive positions were well prepared to repel any counterattack or any attempt to sneak through our lines, I told Benny to wake me for the early morning radio watch. I found a dry bed in a corner of a small house, crawled under the mosquito netting and dropped immediately into the sleep of the damned.

★   ★   ★   ★   ★

By the end of February, the enemy had been driven from Hué at the cost of 142 Marines dead and 857 wounded. Yet the strategic victory ultimately went to the Communists. The scenes of bloody fighting in Hué, Saigon and other cities in Vietnam during the Tet offensive so shocked Americans at home that public opinion turned decisively against continued American involvement in Vietnam.

Stalking the General

CHARLES W. HENDERSON

Arkansas native Carlos N. Hathcock II is one of the great legends of the United States Marine Corps. At the age of seventeen, he enlisted with the Marines in 1959 and quickly established himself as an expert marksman. He would set the Marine Corps record on the "A" Course with a score of 248 points out of a possible 250 and win the coveted Wimbledon Cup at Camp Perry in 1965. The following year he was sent to Vietnam to be part of a newly established sniper program. In his two combat tours of Vietnam he became one of the most successful snipers in American history, so feared by the Viet Cong they placed a bounty of three years pay for any soldier who could kill him. Charles W. Henderson, a twenty-three year veteran of the Marine Corps wrote Hathcock's biography in 1990 entitled, *Marine Sniper*. The following chapter details Hathcock's most dangerous mission behind enemy lines to target a North Vietnamese general.

> There survives one lone wolf of the battlefield. He hunts not
> with the pack. Single-handed, or accompanied by one compan-
> ion, he seeks cover near the fighting. Sometimes he holes-in be-
> hind the tottering walls of a shell-ridden hut, far from the
> shelter of his lines. Again, at dead of night, he rolls out across the
> shell-torn fields, burrowing deep into the sodden ground. . . .
> His game is not to send a hail of rapid fire into a squad or com-
> pany; it is to pick off with one well-directed, rapidly delivered
> shot a single enemy. . .
> —U.S. Marine Corps General George O. Van Orden

★　★　★　★　★

The late afternoon sun shone through the camouflage netting draped over the old plantation house that now served as a North Vietnamese Army division's command center. The yellow light cast spotty shadows through the window and over the old commander who sat behind his table-like desk, scratching out a note.

His division continued to expand and improve. But the old commander was like the great tiger that lived in these mountains and now limped because of a thorn that festered in his paw. This "thorn" was the increasing number of U.S. Marine snipers and especially the one who wore a white feather in his hat—a symbol that enraged the Communist general because he saw it as an insult to the abilities of his best guerillas. News of someone sighting the sniper who wore the white feather spread fear among his troops, as well as among the local peasants. Whenever this man was seen, people died.

He gazed out the window, looking through the blotchy netting as the blood red sun stood at the crest of the mountains that arose from the sanctuary of Laos. The setting sun's highlights sparkled from the gold and silver that ornamented the large, red patches sewn on his collar. He thought of the war and the increasing numbers of American soldiers and weapons that now flooded into South Vietnam. And he thought of the increasing number of heavy bombs dropped daily from the bellies of high-flying B-52s.

As those bombs fell along the Demilitarized Zone and the Laotian border, Hathcock wadded a green-and-white cigarette pack and tossed it into the wooden ammunition box that he had turned into a combination nightstand, stool, and trash container. He lay back on his cot and took a long and deep drag off his last cigarette. The sun now set behind the distant hilltops in the west, and he watched the blazing orange sky turn dark as night fell.

As he lay there, he thought of his conversation with Gunny Wilson earlier that day just after he'd finished writing to Jo; recounting his past six months as a sniper made him realize that many things had permanently changed in his life. The Carlos Hathcock who reported to Maj. George E. Bartlett at 1st Marine Division's military police company nearly one year ago at Chu Lai, and who worked there as a machine gunner and desk sergeant, was a completely changed person from the Carlos Hathcock who spent the last six months on duty as a sniper and assistant chief sniper instructor at Da Nang. When he reported to the "Mustang"* major, himself a competitive

---

*Slang term used to describe Marine officers who were commissioned from the enlisted ranks.

marksman, Carlos had never killed anyone. He had never known the heat of combat or the reality of war. Now, he had eighty kills confirmed to his credit and had trained several hundred snipers, more than one hundred of them personally. When he came to Chu Lai, he equated marksmanship to targets. Now he equated targets to living, breathing human beings.

In a few days, he would pick up the orders that canceled his temporary additional duty as a sniper, and he would return to the Military Police Company, his parent command, that would process him for travel back to the World. He came to Vietnam a green kid, twenty-three years old, still immature and full of ideals and dreams. Now, his face bore wrinkles at twenty-four years, his ideals and dreams were tempered by the lessons of combat. And his boyishness had disappeared, drained from his soul at Elephant Valley, Charlie Ridge, An Hoa, and Da Nang. Now he felt old.

Hathcock looked at the letter that he had written to Jo apologizing for not telling her that he was actually a working sniper, not just an instructor. The idea of her reading about it in the newspaper continued to rouse his anger. "Once I got home, I would have told her," he thought. "I just didn't want her worrying."

"Sergeant Hathcock! You in there?" a voice called in the night.

"Yo!" Hathcock called from his cot and raised himself on his elbows to see outside his hooch. "Yeah, Burke, what's up?"

Burke peered through the screen door. "Gunny needs to see you. I think they want you for one more trip to the bush."

Hathcock sprang to his feet like a fireman hearing the alarm sound. "What do you know? They tell you anything?"

"No. Gunny just said for me to roust you up."

Hathcock slipped on his shirt as he walked toward the sniper headquarters where he could see two figures standing outside.

"Looks like some sort of powwow," Burke said in a low voice as they drew near.

A hulking Marine captain who looked as though he could play on any National Football League team's front line stood next to the gunny. Wrapping his enormous paw around Hathcock's outstretched palm he started shaking it.

"I've heard a lot about you, especially from Major Wight. That's why I made the trip down here to see you. We have a very risky job. And we think you're the only man who can pull it off and survive. I know you're due to go home in a matter of days, so I'm not here to order you. You may accept or reject our proposal. I can only tell you that the need is urgent."

The words "the only man who can pull it off" overshadowed everything else the captain said. No sales pitch was necessary beyond that. Hathcock knew that if they believed that he was the only man who had a chance at surviving this mission, then he must accept. If he rejected the request they'd select a less experienced sniper. A man who had less chance of surviving. He couldn't go home with that on his conscience.

"What's the job, Sir?" he said, folding his arms, ready for some sort of hint at this very dangerous assignment.

"I can't say. You have to accept or reject this request based totally on the prospect that it will be extremely hazardous. The odds of your surviving are slim, so I can only ask you to volunteer.

"If you accept, you will come with me and receive a briefing and a package containing all the information and planning that we've done on this mission. You can then tailor this plan to suit your needs and abilities. You will receive total support."

Hathcock scraped the toe of his book through the dirt and thought of the short-timer stories about Marines who took one more mission with only days remaining in-country and died on it. To take such a mission violated a superstition. Go on patrol when you're a newbee or a short-timer and you're dead. But, he also thought that the odds stood in his favor more than in any other sniper's, despite the short-timer superstition.

He looked at Burke, standing silently in the moonlight. What if they turned to him or to the gunny or the top? Which friend would he allow to go in his place?

He looked at the captain and took a deep breath. "Sir, I'll go, I wouldn't be able to face myself if I didn't."

The captain put his arm over Hathcock's shoulder and patted him. "I've got a map and some recon photos up at operations, we'll talk there."

The two Marines walked away from the sniper hooch, and Burke watched them disappear in the darkness. A feeling of emptiness suddenly pulled at his soul: he would never go hunting with his partner again. The reality of it struck him as he watched his friend leave. He wished he could go too.

"Oh, Carlos, oh, Carlos, you ain't a comin' back alive from this one! You and your big ideas," Carlos Hathcock said aloud. Johnny Burke sat on a wooden crate scrubbing his M-14's bolt-face with a doubled-up pipe cleaner. Carlos sat on another crate. Between his feet a topographical map and several photos lay spread on the dirty plywood floor of the sniper platoon's command hooch.

"How on earth did I ever get myself into this one?" Hathcock said with a sigh.

"You're the best, Sergeant Hathcock. That's why you wear that white feather, isn't it?" Burke said, looking up.

Hathcock glanced at his partner. "Maybe. But, I ain't so sure about this one. Come here and look at these recon photos. I tell you, this one's suicide."

Burke laid his bolt on a towel and walked across the hooch. Hathcock had drawn an orange line on the plastic film that he had laminated to the face of the map to make it weatherproof. The line represented the patch that the patrol, which dropped him off, would take. He was pondering the best route from there to his mission's ultimate destination.

"There ain't a stitch of cover within two thousand yards of that place," Hathcock said, pointing to an aerial photo that corresponded to an area on the map around which he had drawn a red circle. "I've got the tree line for cover up to here," his finger tapped the circle as he spoke. "All I'm ever gonna get at the guy is one shot. I've gotta make it count. Once that round goes, all hell's gonna break loose so the odds for a second shot are zero. I can't gamble on connecting at two thousand yards—it's gotta be eight hundred yards or less. That means I've gotta cover about fifteen hundred yards of open ground without being seen."

Burke knelt on one knee and shook his head. "Sergeant Hathcock, I don't know!"

Hathcock looked at Burke, an unusual expression of worry crossing his face, "I know." He looked back at the map and photos and again leaned his elbows on his knees, clasping his hands together beneath his chin, as if in subconscious prayer, "I've gotta go worm-style across there and hope they don't walk across me."

Burke walked back to his crate and sat down. He picked up his rifle's bolt and began scrubbing its face with a fresh pipe cleaner.

"Sergeant Hathcock, if anybody has the answer, you do. If it can be done, you can do it. But I gotta tell you the honest truth. Goin' into the NVA's headquarters and blowin' away their stud duck takes one hell of a lot more guts than I've got. Too bad you can't tell 'em to forget it."

"Nope," Hathcock replied without looking up. "Ain't my style. Job's gotta be done."

Carlos looked at his watch and softly laid it inside his footlocker with all his other personal items. He would leave everything behind on this stalk.

He took his bush hat with his left hand and gently slipped the wispy white feather from its hatband, dropping it between the pages of his Marine Corps issue New Testament. He placed the cigarette-pack size book in one corner of his footlocker and dropped shut the locker's wooden lid. Snapping the combination lock on the big box's hasp, he tucked on his bush hat, slung his rifle over his shoulder, and walked out to meet fate head-on.

As he walked through Hill 55's complex of deeply dug and heavily sandbagged bunkers, hard-backed tents, and antennae farms, Carlos listened to the new day come alive.

"Goooood morning, Vietnam!" a voice boomed from a nearby radio tuned to AFVN. "It's six-oh-five in the A-M and time to . . . Shout!" Joey Dee and the Star-Lighters' all-time rock and roll favorite, "Shout," echoed through the camp from scattered radios tuned to the Da Nang American Forces Radio station.

A black Marine with a gold-capped front tooth sat on a stack of sandbags next to his rocking and rolling radio. His steel helmet pot, half-filled with milky colored water, sat in the dirt before him. Lather covered his face, and he stretched his neck tight as he shaved under his chin, rolling his eyes downward in order to look in a mirror balanced atop the radio. Hathcock thought about how long it had been since he had stood in front of a bathroom sink and shaved with hot water.

He walked down the hill beyond the bunkers and joined a group of Marines wearing helmets and flack jackets. Each man had two fragmentation grenades and several pouches full of ammunition, balanced by two full canteens hanging on their cartridge belts. Carlos had only his rifle, one canteen hooked to his belt and a KaBar knife. He reached in his pocket and touched the tube of camouflage greasepaint resting there. He was scared.

The walk to the landing zone did not take long, neither did the flight—due west and well into the high mountain that bordered Laos.

The Marine rifle squad moved quickly taking him to the departure point, and by noon Hathcock sat alone, his back against a tree, surrounded by heavy vegetation. He was preparing himself mentally for what he knew lay ahead. The fear that lay like a heavy animal inside his chest would need some calming.

Day One

Carlos had calculated perfectly, as always in the past, and arrived at the tree line's edge just as the sun set. He covered his exposed skin with shades of light and dark green greasepaint from the tub that he carried in his pocket. Every buttonhole and strap on his uniform held various-shaped leaves and grass.

Here, at the edge of the open country, he saw the NVA's heavily guarded buildings with their camouflaging and their fortified gun positions. He had no idea where in Southeast Asia he was at the moment and had not wished to ask. The terrain map he had studied had had no place names. From their flight path and the distance covered, he would not have been surprised if he was in Laos or even North Vietnam.

Under the cover of darkness, Carlos retouched his camouflage paint and exchanged the forest's deep green leaves for the lighter green and straw-colored grass that now surrounded him and covered the vast open land ahead. He drew his canteen and poured a capful of water. He brought the lid to his lips and sipped, his eyes constantly shifting and looking for signs of movement, his nose testing the air for any smell of other men.

For the next hour, he continued preparing himself, drinking sips of water from his canteen lid and relaxing in the tree line's cover.

Finally, his every move fluid and slow like that of a clock's minute hand, he lay on his side and slipped into the open. His Winchester rifle was clutched tightly against his chest.

His body was in constant motion, but the motion was so slow that a man staring at him from ten feet away would in all probability have seen no movement. He traveled inches per minute and yards per hour. From now until he reached his goal, Hathcock would not eat or sleep and he would drink rarely.

He had had no idea that he would have to move this slowly. The dry grass was about a foot above his head as he crawled slowly on. Hathcock noticed the stars in the clear night sky and prayed for rain. If it came he could move quickly, since the enemy's vision would be obscured and the shower's noise would cover his. Dampness would also soften the crackling dry grass and weeds.

The Marine sniper had crawled approximately thirty feet from the tree line when he heard the first enemy patrol approaching his position. His eyes strained to find them in the moonless dark. He knew they were closing in on him by each crunching footstep's increasing loudness. Hathcock held his breath. The patrol was very near. His lungs burned, and his heart pounded. Sweat gushed from every pore on his body. He was worried they would smell him. Absolutely motionless, he stared back at the trail of bent and broken grass that lay behind him.

Hathcock thought, "If they see me, then that's how. They'll see my trail." His lungs could take no more pain—he must have air. He felt like a pearl diver gone too deep, seeing the water's mirrored surface over him. Too much distance lay between him and the sweet air above. He remembered, as a boy, diving deep and swimming up, and how his lungs ached just as he reached the water's surface. Hathcock relaxed his lungs slowly—silently releasing the captive breath. He longed to gulp a replenishing surge of oxygen, but instead filled his lungs silently and very slowly with tiny puffs of air.

Movement near his feet nearly made him scream. A leg flashed by him. Another and another flickered past. The NVA patrol was now between him and the safety of the trees.

He heard one soldier clear his throat. Another whispered something in Vietnamese. Hathcock thought, "These guys are goofing off. They aren't even looking. They're safely in their own backyard and don't suspect a thing."

As the patrol passed, Hathcock watched them traipsing along beside the tree line, oblivious of his presence. "That looseness just might save my life," he thought. "Boy, will they be sorry," he told himself. A smile crossed his face, and his confidence soared. As soon as the enemy was out of earshot, he pushed on through the night.

Day Two

The hour before sunrise has a sleep-inducing effect. Nearly any soldier who has had to remain awake through the night will testify that the worst hour, when fighting sleep poses the greatest challenge, occurs when the night is darkest, coolest, and quietest—an hour or so before dawn.

Hathcock had to rest, but he could not afford risking sleep. In the past months, he had taught himself to nap, yet remain awake, his eyes wide open. He did not know what sort of self-hypnosis made it possible, but he always felt very rested following one of these ten-minute respites.

The flickering light from a small cooking fire caught his attention and brought him out of his catnap. "These dumb hamburgers!" he thought, "Another time and another place, and you would have been mine, Charlie."

An iron pot filled with boiling water and rice hung over the fire. Three NVA soldiers squatted nearby, sleepily waiting for their breakfast to finish cooking. They manned the "Quad-51" machine-gun position on the left flank of the compound. A narrow trail through the grass led from the compound, passed next to the machine-gun nest, made a sharp left turn, and then led arrow-straight to the trees. Lights shone through several windows of the main house. Carlos supposed that it had been a French plantation in years past.

Inside, the short, graying general leaned over a porcelain bowl filled with cold water. A thick white undershirt covered his hairless, sagging chest and wrinkled belly. Baggy white shorts covered his bottom. He wore no shoes but stood on the glossy teak floor in his stocking feet. The old officer's brown uniform rested neatly on hangers hooked to a peg on the door. Gold clusters and braid shone on the uniform's wide, red shoulder-boards and on the broad red patches sewn on his collar.

In an adjoining room that had been made into an office, the general's aide-de-camp huddled over papers shuffling them into order for the old man. They would inspect a battalion today. The day before, the general and his entourage had walked the perimeter, inspecting the security of his headquarters. He had found it satisfactory.

Hathcock had seen him, but the old man was too distant from the Marine sniper's firing point. Now the sun fully lit the new day. In the distance, Hathcock watched a white car pull away from the house, drive up the trail, and disappear into the tree line.

"Old man's gone for a while, I reckon," he told himself. "Good. That means that those guys will really slack off."

By late afternoon, Hathcock had put five hundred yards between himself and the tree line. More than twenty hours had passed since he had left the jungle's cover.

Just before sunset the white sedan drove up to the house and stopped. Carlos watched the indistinguishable figures walk toward the door. "Just keep it up, Homer—you and your hot dogs. I'll get you."

The evening security patrol began its first tour of the perimeter. Ten NVA soldiers fanned into a line and began closing toward Hathcock. He stopped his oozing wormlike slither and waited. He watched as the soldiers approached him in the dimming light. "It could have been worse," Hathcock thought. "They could have come before sunset."

After lying flat in the dirt for twenty-four hours, Carlos had attracted a following of ants. His body ached from hundreds of small lumps left by their bites. He wondered if enough ant bites could eventually kill a man. Sweat poured into his eyes as the enemy patrol came on. They were spread on-line with twenty- to thirty-feet wide gaps between them.

"Here I am, gettin' hell stung out of me," Hathcock thought, "my body crawlin' with critters, layin' here can't move—and here comes Homer and his friends. Hell, I'll probably crawl all the way up, never to be seen, kill this old muckety-muck, and then when I try to leave, I'll die from all these critter bites. The ants will cart off my bones, and I'll wind up MIA forever."

Carlos watched the approaching patrol. He could see only three of the soldiers now, the remaining seven were on his blind, right-hand side. He watched the three NVA riflemen plod closer and closer.

"If the guy on my right don't step on me, I'll get by this one too," he reassured himself. But the soldiers were looking far ahead, toward the tree line, and they were oblivious to the sniper they had just passed.

Day Three

The sun found Carlos Hathcock twelve hundred yards from the compound's headquarters, its doorways and windows now clearly visible to him. He watched as the soldiers relieved and posted the guard. "It's as though they're back at Hanoi," he thought. Over everything hung the calm air of routine.

Throughout the day, he observed couriers filing in and out of the compound, reporting to the man with the red collar. The sniper kept to his steady pace. He could feel adrenalin surging at the thought that tonight he would halt and prepare to fire with dawn's first light.

He thought of how he had succeeded thus far. He also turned his attention to his escape. To the right of where Carlos would eventually lie, a small, almost imperceptible gully ran nearly to the tree line. Once he fired his shot, he planned to slide along the shallow and gently sloping gully and disappear through the trees.

"It's a good thing, Carlos," he told himself. "These hamburgers are so loose here, it'll take them half a day to figure out what happened."

Hathcock squirmed forward a few more inches and then, looking ahead of him, his confidence faded at the same time that his entire body stiffened.

The hunger, which had wrapped his stomach in knots for two days, vanished. The blood drained out of his face and the whole world took a violent spin. He wanted to jump up and run. He wanted to scream. He wanted to do anything rather than continue to lie there and look into the eye of a jade-green bamboo viper that lay coiled in the grass six inches from his face.

Panic ripped through every fiber of self-discipline that Carlos had ever been able to string together. He felt numb as his eyes focused on the deadly snake's emerald head, its ruby-colored eyes evilly slanted above head-sensing pits.

The snake was motionless but the sniper felt his own body shaking. "Gotta get hold here," he breathed slowly. "Oh Jesus! What if he bites me in the face! Control yourself! He ain't bit you yet." He knew this snake was neurotoxic like the cobra. One pop, even a little one, would kill him in minutes. "You've come too far to let a bamboo snake end it all," he told himself as he lay still and watched the viper flick its black, forked tongue from its yellow-rimmed mouth, testing the air.

Almost as though the shaken Marine had never existed, the glossy snake turned its head, whisked silently between broad stems of grass, and disappeared.

After Hathcock's heart slowed to its normal rhythm and the shaking effects of the adrenalin that sent his blood coursing through his temples had subsided, his nagging hunger returned, accompanied by a sudden thirst. "Where's the groceries!" he exclaimed to himself. "Where's the water!"

His hand found the canteen lid, and he began to carefully unscrew it from the flask. Half an hour later, he felt the wet relief of the now warm liquid soaking into his swollen tongue like water on a dry sponge.

Hathcock moved on, wincing with every inch he went. His hip, knee, and arm were covered with blisters from the three days of constant pushing. Shards of pain shot through his side. He had less than two hundred yards left to travel, and compromise began tempting him now.

"You can do it from here," he considered. In all his years of marksmanship competition, his best scores came from the thousand-yard line. "It's been all bull's-eyes and Vs from this distance," Carlos told himself. But in all his years of shooting, never had one shot been so critical.

A second voice told Carlos, "Stick to the plan. Don't change things now. Survival depends on it. Survive." Carlos always listened to that voice. It had kept him alive. "You thought out this plan when you were rested; now you're tired. Gotta stick to the plan—got to."

He pushed on toward where the slight depression came slicing through the grass. It was very much as he had estimated—almost precisely eight hundred yards from the target.

Darkness fell and, as he drew near to his planned firing position, Hathcock's anticipation mounted. He versed himself on everything in these surroundings that might affect his bullets flight. He was constantly aware of humidity, wind speed, and wind direction. The faint sound of men laughing caught his ear. He could imagine the North Vietnamese general and his officers drinking and toasting each other around a dining room table. "That general had better enjoy himself while he still can." Hathcock thought.

The Marine sniper watched as the nightly patrol began another round. "They don't even consider a ground attack," he reflected. "They're more worried about air assaults. Look at the bunkers and holes they've got around here. Everything's covered."

The last guard changed as Carlos Hathcock reached the shallow gully he had spotted on aerial photographs and that he had spent the last three days crawling toward. it was not even six inches deep, but it was wide enough for a man to lie in. The depression, which stretched fifteen hundred yards to the distant tree line, actually began here in the middle of the open field, and at its head there was a slight rise, on the back side of which Hathcock positioned his rifle. He unfolded a handkerchief-size cloth and laid it down beneath the weapon's muzzle so that the gases the rifle expelled from the barrel when he fired it would not raise up dust from the ground and give away his position.

Day Four

When the sun sent its first rays across the wide clearing, the Marine sniper's eyes already blinked through the eight-power scope atop his rifle, searching for his target.

He had estimated the distance correctly—his experienced eyes verified eight hundred yards to the walkway. "I've got to get him standing still with either his face or his back toward me," Carlos told himself. "Don't compromise." He watched for signs of wind—trees rustling, smoke drifting from the cooking fires next to sandbagged gun positions, the waving of the grass and weeds between him and his target. But more important than these, he watched the mirage, how it danced and boiled above the earth and tilted with the wind.

From that he could calculate the wind velocity by dividing the angle of the mirage by four. After determining that, he could multiply the velocity times eight, which represented this particular range in hundreds of yards, and then divide that again by four and have the number of "clicks" or half-minutes of angle he would need for windage.

The sun climbed higher and sweat trickled down the sniper's cheeks. His eyes still fixed to the scope's lens, he felt his neck burn from the overhead sun that baked the ground powder dry and left the grass wilting in its heat.

From somewhere behind the complex of bunkers came the sound of an automobile's engine. The white sedan wheeled around the bunkers and stopped short of the walkway upon which Carlos held the rifle scope's cross hairs. The driver waited with the motor running.

"Here we go," Hathcock told himself. "Get a firm grip. Watch the cross hairs." The general stepped through the doorway, and Hathcock centered the man's profile in his scope. He waited for him to turn face-on. He did, but as the commander turned and walked toward the sniper's sight, the general's aide-de-camp stepped ahead of him. "Dummy! Don't you know that aides always walk to the left of their generals? Get out of the way!"

At every moment since the sun rose Hathcock had refined his attunement to the environment with computerlike detail and speed, judging the light, the humidity, the slight breeze that intermittently blew across his line of fire. He factored in the now-increasing heat and how the rise in temperature would elevate the mark of his bullet by causing the powder to burn more quickly when he fired. The air density and humidity would affect the velocity of his bullet, and the light would change the way his target appeared.

Based on his estimations, he decided to place his scope's reticle on the general's left breast, in case the breeze carried the round eight inches right. The bright sunlight warned the sniper to keep his aim high on the man's chest, but not too high, in case the heat raised the bullet's flight a few inches.

The group of officers walking out with the general departed toward the side of the house. It left only the old man and his youthful aide. Carlos waited. The young officer took his place at the left side of his superior. Hathcock said, "Now stop." Both men did. The sniper's cross hairs lay directly on the general's heart.

Hathcock's mind raced through all his marksmanship principles, "Good firm grip, watch the cross hairs, squeeze the trigger, wait for the recoil. Don't hold your breath too long, breathe and relax, let it come to the natural pause, watch the cross hairs, squeeeeeeeeeze."

Recoil sent a jolt down his shoulder. He blinked and the general lay flat on his back. Blood gushed from the old officer's chest and his lifeless eyes stared into the sun's whiteness.

The general's aide-de-camp dove to the ground and began crawling toward a sandbagged gun position. The other officers, who had only seconds earlier left their commander's side, ran for cover.

The Marine sniper slid into the slight gully and, flat on his belly, began pulling himself stealthily along the ground with both arms. His rate of retreat seemed light-speed compared to his inbound time. Still smooth and deliberate, he traveled many feet of ground per minute. He now covered a distance, approximately equivalent to that which he had crawled across in three days, in four or five hours. The fact that no patrol approached him during his retreat told him that no one had seen his muzzle flash. In daylight, at eight hundred yards, that didn't surprise him. The patrols would be out, but they would be searching hundreds of acres. Once he thought he heard one far to his left.

It was almost nightfall when he reached the jungle's edge. Squirming past the outer layer of greenery, Hathcock lifted himself off his knees for the first time in three days. The pain was an excruciating counterpoint to his inner exhilaration. He hurried through the heavy forest. He was wary of mines and booby traps, but going as quickly as he dared, he covered the three kilometers to his preplanned pickup coordinate in a matter of a few hours.

There Carlos sat in a bush and waited, well aware that patrols might be scouring the jungle for his trail. His heart settled to a resting pulse. The songs of birds and other jungle creatures replaced the sound of heaving breath that had pounded in his ears. And as the hubbub settled to tranquility, he thought of Arkansas and how similar this moment seemed to many childhood days behind his grandmother's house, when he sat in the bushes there—the old Mauser across his lap and his Shetland collie dog panting at his side. He closed his eyes for the first time in four days.

"Sergeant Hathcock," a voice whispered. "I thought you knew better than to doze off like that." The Marine who led the squad that had left Hathcock four days earlier now knelt by the bush where the Marine sniper waited.

Hathcock smiled slowly, not even opening his eyes at first. "I knew you were there," he said. "I heard your squad tromping up the ridge five minutes ago."

"Let's get going. Charlie's crawling over these hills, and we've got a lot of ground to cover between here and the LZ," the squad leader told him. "When we left the Hill, Charlie's lines were burning up. I guess you got that general?"

"Well, he hit the ground mighty hard," Hathcock said, pulling out his canteen and swallowing its last few drops. "Spare any water?"

"Sure," the Marine said, handing Hathcock a canteen and sloshing its contents out the open top. "We better book.* Charlie's mad as hell now. They'd love to get you after today."

Hathcock felt uneasy when the squad leader told him, "Charlie's

---

*Marine jargon meaning to go or to leave. Until early 1970s, Marines were required to sign out on liberty in the duty NCOs log book as they picked up their liberty cards. From that came the term "Book Out," which was shortened to "Book."

mad as hell." During the flight back to Hill 55, he wondered if the assassination of the general would only arouse the North Vietnamese and Viet Cong to fight with greater fury.

He would always have mixed feelings about this day's work. As American casualties rose sharply in the weeks that followed, he began to feel that this was one sniper killing that might have been a mistake.

When Hathcock stepped off the helicopter, home at Hill 55's landing site, a group of smiling and whooping Marines met him. Burke stood among them and said, "White Feather made it."

Hathcock smiled.

The giant of a captain who'd recruited Hathcock for the mission slapped him across the back so hard that Carlos wondered if he had dislocated any bones. The hulking Marine put a pot roast-size hand on Hathcock's shoulder and said, "Son, I'm sure as hell glad to see you back in one piece. Lot of us kept you in our prayers. You did one hell of a job."

Walking up the hill toward his hooch, Hathcock felt the great fatigue from the mission finally take hold. He longed to lie down and sleep for days. But his standards were demanding. And despite the fact that this was his last mission—that he would leave Hill 55 in a few days to return to the MP company and on to the World by way of Okinawa—he remained true to them. He cleaned his rifle and gear before he rested.

★　　★　　★　　★　　★

Carlos Hathcock returned to the United States in 1969 after receiving burns suffered while pulling seven other Marines to safety from their burning amphibian tractor after being hit by a land mine. He would stay in the Marine Corps to help establish a scout and sniper school at the Marine base in Quantico, Virginia. Multiple sclerosis claimed his life in February 1999 at the age of fifty-seven.

Storming Kuwait with
the U.S. Marines

MOLLY MOORE

Molly E. Moore served as the senior military correspondent for the *Washington Post* at the time of the first Gulf War in August 1990. She was the only American reporter to get a sustained close-up view of ground operations throughout the Gulf War attached to the headquarters of Lt. Gen. Walter Boomer, commander of the Marine expeditionary force. Her observations and dispatches became some of the finest war reporting since World War II. In the following chapter, Moore describes the opening hours of the ground campaign as the Marines stormed into Kuwait in February 1991.

> I can't say enough about the two Marine divisions. If I use words
> like brilliant, it would really be an under-description of the ab-
> solutely superb job they did in breaching the so-called impenetra-
> ble barrier . . . Absolutely superb operation, a textbook, and I think
> it'll be studied for many, many years to come as the way to do it.
> —General H. Norman Schwarzkopf

★ ★ ★ ★ ★

6:50 a.m., Monday, February 25, 1991, G-day Plus One, Marine Corps Forward Command Post, Khanjar, Saudi Arabia

Thirty-eight male Marines and I were going to war.

Colonel Bill Steed, chin strap of his helmet dangling and a green bandanna knotted around his throat, leaned into the front seat of my battle wagon, a camouflage-painted Chevrolet Blazer. "Do you want a weapon?"

"Reporters aren't allowed to carry weapons," I replied from the back seat, where I was squeezed between a large radio and a young sergeant toting an assault rifle.

"You sure?" Steed pressed.

I faltered for a few seconds. What if our truck was surrounded by Iraqi troops? What if some Iraqi with a bayonet came charging after me in the desert?

"I'm sure," I said quickly, before I could change my mind.

Steed shook his head and fumbled through his pockets, pulling out a palm-sized notebook. He flipped through several pages and looked up at me. "Who is your next of kin?"

I swallowed hard. Until that moment, I'd viewed my foray into the battlefield with Boomer as a big adventure.

I gave him John's name and telephone number and our home address, spitting the words out before my voice cracked. Steed nodded, snapped the notebook shut, and walked away.

Our chief trail driver, Captain Dave Garza, stood in a circle of men nearby, issuing last-minute instructions: "If we get ambushed, you'll hear 'Ambush left, ambush right!' We'll zoom ahead. We won't zigzag."

Boomer looked more rested than the night before, but he seemed even grimmer. Throughout the night, the U.S. military's electronic eavesdropping aircraft had detected large-scale movements of Iraqi signs that they could be preparing to launch counterattacks against the advancing Marines. The Iraqis had attempted a series of small counterattacks during the night, which the Marines had quickly quashed.

The 1st Marine Division was poised for an offensive on the critical Jaber Airfield, but the last regiment of the 2nd Marine Division was still pushing through the second Iraqi minefield and remained vulnerable to attack. The poor visibility caused by fog, rain, and smoke from the burning wellheads was making movement across the battlefield treacherous. To the west, the Army was struggling through sandstorms and rain, continuing its sweep across Iraq.

Boomer poked his head inside the mobile command post, a bulky armored vehicle that looked like a tank on wheels. Instead of a tank's big gun tube, however, this armored wagon had only a .50 caliber machine gun mounted on the top. Inside, it was crammed with banks of radios. Three black swivel chairs were bolted to the floor in front, a set of giant wooden rosary beads hung from a hook at the rear.

"What kind of ammo are we carrying?" Boomer asked Garza, who ticked off the list of bullets, guns, and grenades. Boomer nodded.

"Load 'em up, men!" Garza shouted as Boomer hoisted himself into the war wagon.

Major Chris Weldon, Boomer's chief gofer and military assistant, climbed into the Blazer's front passenger's seat.

"Anybody listen to the news this morning?" he asked, slamming the door shut.

"No sir," replied the driver, Sergeant Mark Chapin, a tall, thin man with dark hair and a thin black mustache.

I thought it odd that Weldon, Boomer's right-hand man at the headquarters command post, had to listen to the radio to find out what was going on in the war.

At 7:07 a.m., on the second day of the ground war, the eleven-vehicle convoy pulled out of the camp in a roar of smoke and straining engines. Our Blazer was directly behind Boomer. Our radio code name was Two Echo.

Sergeant Paul Blair sat to my left, clutching a strange-looking sawed-off assault rifle.

"What's your job on this trip?" I asked.

"I'm the radioman," Blair replied, adding, "and the general doesn't know it, ma'am, but I'm his bodyguard."

"He doesn't know it?"

"Well, ma'am, when he first came out here, they sent four bodyguards with him. He sent them back to Pendleton. Said he didn't need bodyguards. He may think he doesn't need 'em. Other folks disagree."

Boomer would catch on soon enough. How discreet could you be carrying a weapon that looked like it could blow the torso off a terrorist with a single squeeze of the trigger?

The desert was covered in a green fuzz of tiny grass blades that made it seem slightly less hostile. We drove past deserted revetments, the former homes of tanks now blitzing across Kuwait. Entire Marine tent villages had become ghost towns, canvas flaps snapping in the wind. The desert had an empty, abandoned look. Even the camels and the Bedouins had cleared out for the war.

7:15 a.m., Monday, February 25, 1991, G-day Plus One, Task Force Ripper, the Edge of Jaber Airfield, Kuwait

For Lieutenant Bill Delaney, the dawn of the second day of the ground war never really arrived. The morning was as black as night in central Kuwait, where hundreds of burning oil wells belched black smoke into the sky. Delaney and his tank crews had not moved since setting up camp the night before on the fringes of Jaber Airfield, twenty-four miles inside Kuwait.

For the past three hours, Delaney had listened as loud booms rumbled across the desert. Radio chatter told him that other Marine units had been firing sporadically at Iraqi tanks and other vehicles on three sides of his encampment. His company had not been ordered to engage. The radio reports were steady: a tank column advancing from the north, vehicles on the flank, armor approaching from the rear. Maybe the Iraqis had regrouped overnight and were ready for a real battle, Delaney though anxiously.

He hoped TOW missile gunners, with their thermal sights that could read engine heat through the darkness, could continue to hold off the Iraqi tanks and armor, TOWs were their protectors, their eyes in the night. If his tankers had to enter the fray, it would be like a knife fight in an alley. Neither his tanks, with their minimal night-vision equipment, nor the Iraqis, who had no night-vision gear, would be able to see in this darkness. As he eavesdropped on the radio discussions, the TOW gunners assigned to his battalion were blasting twenty approaching Iraqi vehicles. He noted they could see only a fraction of their normal distance through their thermal sights.

Even when the faint light of day began to push through the oily cloud cover, Delaney could see barely a hundred yards in front of him. Fearing enemy ambushes and large-scale fratricide, the 1st Marine Division ordered Task Force Ripper, Delaney's regiment, to hold their ground; the planned attack on the airfield would be delayed until conditions improved. Delaney was relieved that he wouldn't have to send his men into the alley fight.

7:45 a.m., Monday, February 25, 1991, G-day Plus One, 1st Marine Division Forward Command Post, South of the Burqan Oil Field

Brigadier General Tom Draude scanned the morning intelligence reports that had been transmitted to his 1st Marine Division command post. For the past four hours, electronic-eavesdropping places had been detecting enemy radio communications inside the burning Burqan oil field: Iraqi units were massing at two locations for counterattacks against the American forces. His young intelligence officer had been correct after all, Draude thought.

All but one of the Marine artillery units in this sector were aimed westward toward the expected battle at Jaber Airfield. By the time they turned toward the oil field, the Iraqis could already be on the attack.

"Can we get naval gunfire?" Draude asked the staff. Officers worked the radios and reported back: Negative, the inland oil field was out of the twenty-three-mile range of the battleships offshore in the Persian Gulf.

Draude and his division commander, Major General Mike Myatt, ordered a massive 155 millimeter artillery barrage at the two suspected Iraqi gathering points in the field. The two generals viewed it as a deadly, high-technology version of throwing rocks into a bush to see what you could flush out. For any Iraqi troops within the hailstorm of artillery, it would seem as though the entire desert had exploded.

A few minutes before the artillery barrage was scheduled to begin, Draude received a disturbing radio report from the commanders of Task Force Papa Bear, one of the 1st Marine Division's tank regiments, who had set up a forward command post about six miles southeast of the division field headquarters.

As artillery shells rumbled in the distance, the commanders of Task Force Papa Bear leaned over a wrinkled map on the hood of a humvee, co-ordinating plans for their attack on Jaber Airfield. It was not only suspected of housing Iraqi field headquarters, but was considered strategically important to the Marines, who wanted it as a forward refueling base for helicopters and other aircraft. Papa Bear, along with Task Force Ripper, would provide the heavy armored attack force for the 1st Marine Division.

The task force commanders' war council with their field chiefs had been delayed an hour and a half because most of the men couldn't find the command post in the soupy fog southeast of the Burqan oil field.

In the middle of his briefing, Major John Turner, Papa Bear's operations officer, noticed several Marines locking and loading their M-16s. One Marine dropped to his knees, hoisting an antitank AT-4 rocket launcher to his shoulder. Turner looked up and stared straight into the main gun of a tank barely a hundred yards away.

Why the hell were his Marines sending a tank to the command post? he wondered. He squinted through the smoky fog. That looked like a Chinese armored personnel carrier next to the tank. Damn! That's not one of ours, he suddenly realized. It's an Iraqi!

The smoke was so thick the Iraqis had stumbled unseen through a gap between the command post's sentries. Startled troops scrambled in every direction. Through the haze, Turner could see a second Chinese personnel carrier pull to a stop near the tank. Before he could react, the commander's hatch popped open and an Iraqi major scrambled out, waving a white flag.

"I brought these men to surrender," he shouted in broken English as twenty other soldiers climbed out of their armored coaches. "But the rest of the brigade is coming, and most of them want to fight."

The captured Iraqi's report was radioed immediately to the division headquarters.

At the 1st Marine Division command post, Draude kicked himself again for brushing off the young intelligence officer's analysis the previous night. But the artillery batteries of Task Force King were ready to fire into the Burqan oil field to see what they could flush. At 8:17 a.m., sixty-six howitzer gunners across the desert unleashed 244 rounds into the smoking oil field. Three minutes later, a second barrage of 496 shells from seventy-eight howitzers rained on the desert. Some of the shells spewed eighty armor-piercing bomblets on impact.

Within a few minutes Draude heard the division radios erupt with reports of enemy tanks roaring out of the burning oil field in three separate attacks. The artillery barrages had scattered Iraqi armor like rabbits out of a bush, he thought.

Minutes after the artillery attack on the oil field, the fog shrouding Papa Bear's mobile command post exploded with machine-gun fire and tank rounds. Operations chief Major John Turner dove beneath the humvee as machine-gun tracers whisked past his knees.

About twenty Iraqi tanks and thirty armored personnel carriers charged out of the burning oil fields toward the small command post. Marines guarding the post raced forward, firing every weapon they had— rifles, machine guns, and hand-held antitank weapons. Ordnance from both sides ripped through the command post as the task force's own security detail, confused in the fog, fired through the circle of vehicles. After a fierce ten-minute firefight, most of the Iraqi vehicles retreated into the mist. The Marines had destroyed one tank and several armored vehicles. Turner was amazed that none of his men had been hit.

When the shooting subsided, Papa Bear's Kuwaiti liaison officer and a Marine intelligence officer climbed inside one of the Iraqi personnel carriers surrendered by its crew. It was crammed with radio equipment crackling with orders shouted in Arabic.

The Arabic-speaking Kuwaiti officer stepped up to the Iraqi officer, who identified himself as Major Adai. "Give us the code words so we can talk to them." The Kuwaiti officer hoped to infiltrate Iraqi communications and issue enough false instructions to halt a further attack or misdirect its commanders.

"No, I fear for my life after the war!" he declared. He'd lost a finger on his right hand during the Iran-Iraq war, and he did not want to risk execution for aiding the enemy in this one.

Undeterred, the Kuwaiti lieutenant began shouting orders in Arabic into the radio. The chatter of Iraqi voices abruptly ceased as they recognized the accent of an intruder. At least now they couldn't talk among themselves, the U.S. commanders thought. Papa Bear's intelligence officer combed the captured Iraqi vehicles and scored another coup: an overlay of the Iraqi III Armored Corps's troop positions for their entire sector of the desert.

8:25 a.m., Monday, February 25, 1991, G-day Plus One, Boomer's Mobile Command Post, Inside Saudi Arabia Near the Kuwaiti Border

Our convoy pulled into a small campsite on a barren patch of desert just short of the Kuwaiti border. The cluster of tents and vehicles was the rear headquarters for the 2nd Marine Division.

Boomer was greeted by a tall one-star general with a bald head and a glass eye—Brigadier General Russell Sutton, the number two man in the division, who was known as "Cyclops." Each year, at the Marine birthday ball, a big formal affair, Sutton delighted in startling people with his special-occasion glass eye: a red iris in the shape of an eagle perched atop a globe, the Marine Corps symbol.

"The Iraqis reorganized part of their defenses last night," he told Boomer, leading him to a large tent bustling with activity. No one tried to stop me, so I trailed them inside.

The Iraqis, according to morning intelligence reports, were struggling to regroup. Five of the eleven Iraqi divisions in the Marine sector were considered "ineffective" and two others were badly damaged after yesterday's pounding by the Marines. Three Iraqi brigades had established new defensive positions near Al Jahra, a stronghold west of Kuwait City, and the main armored units in the III Armored Corps were struggling to hold blocking positions between Al Jahra and Kuwait International Airport south of Kuwait City. Meanwhile three Iraqi infantry divisions and three special forces brigades remained along the beachfront inside Kuwait City, focused on the sea in anticipation of a Marine amphibious attack.

"I don't think he has a good idea of what we're doing," Cyclops said, shouldering his way through the crowded tent to a large map leaning against the far wall. "His communications is kinda broke. He can't get a good picture of the battlefield."

"What about your casualties?" Boomer asked.

I could barely hear. Boomer and Sutton stood with their backs to me, peering at the map. I pushed my way through the crowd of hangers-on and squeezed beside Boomer.

"We've got reports of two KIA and thirteen WIA for the division. Lost two plows and a few other things. We had to rebreach one of the lanes in the minefields because of equipment failures."

"We'll continue to run into armored units," Boomer warned. "We could have better weather." He paused. "One of my guys this morning said, 'I've never seen a plan hold together this long.' Neither have I."

"Sir, we're ready to do it again today," Sutton replied. "You never want to underestimate the enemy."

Our convoy picked up some additional insurance before we left the 2nd Marine Division's rear command post: two humvees equipped with TOW missiles. Even though the Marine armored troops had blazed through the minefields more than twenty-four-hours earlier, Iraqis could still be hiding in the front-line trenches, bypassed and undetected by the allied forces. What better target than the commanding general of the Marine forces?

To the untrained eye, we looked like just another caravan of trucks, humvees, and armored vehicles. But to the schooled eye, the forest of radio antennas swaying atop Boomer's vehicle was the dead giveaway of a command post.

At 8:35 a.m. we rumbled back into the desert, bound for the Kuwaiti border and the minefields beyond. Boomer had crawled through the hatch on top of the command vehicle and was perched on the edge, his face reddened by the biting wind. As his war wagon lurched forward, he adjusted a green helmet equipped with a radio headset. "BOOMER" had been stenciled in large black letters on the back. For the trip through the desert, he'd traded his contact lenses for gold-rimmed glasses, which he wore beneath wide goggles.

As we zoomed past the sentries guarding the perimeter of the camp, Boomer flashed a victory sign to a Huey crew lounging against their chopper. Our guides estimated it would take three hours to cross the minefields and reach our next destination, the 2nd Marine Division's forward command post, about eighteen miles inside Kuwait.

The route was marked by a neon-red plastic garbage can with a black arrow painted on its side. The arrow pointed to the Berm, a massive sand wall dividing Saudi Arabia and Kuwait that stretched from Horizon to horizon. On the far side was no-man's-land, where Iraqi troops crouched in trenches ready to attack at any moment—or so I imagined.

Most reporters, including myself, originally believed the Berm was constructed to slow an attack by Iraqi tankers. Not so. It had been bulldozed into place years before as part of Saudi Arabia's war against alcohol smugglers and other would-be desert trespassers.

Military bulldozers had eaten large gaps in the wall, and lines of trucks now churned through the gates. American and Saudi sentries stood atop the wall. Orange flags marked the road ahead.

My heart leapt into my throat as we crossed the border. The radio next to me crackled. "We are into Kuwait." I looked at my watch. It was 9:35. I leaned forward as we cleared the sand piles, straining to see the battlefield.

It looked no different than the desert we'd just left behind. Hundreds of tanks and trucks had chewed ruts into the desert floor. Slivers of tire treads littered the road, much like the shoulder of an interstate highway in the United States. We passed cardboard food cartons, a cot which had fallen off someone's caravan, empty water bottles. It looked more like the litter of Memorial Day weekend at the beach than the spoils of war.

Minutes later I spotted orange flames roaring skyward from three oil wellheads to our right. The sand was blackened by spewing petroleum. The sky was smudged with purple-black clouds of smoke. The air was acrid with the smell of burning oil.

A group of Marines, faces blackened by the charcoal lining of their chemical suits, leaned against a parked truck. An American flag flapped in the wind overhead. It was the first American flag I'd seen flying on a vehicle since the buildup had begun in August. Troops were forbidden from displaying the flag openly in one of the many deferences to Saudi sensibilities. The men waved, wide grins on their grimy faces.

Major Chris Weldon looked at his boss, who was sitting atop the bouncing command post, waving at the cluster of troops below him.

"The Old Man is in hog heaven," he said with a chuckle.

It looked like a staged scene from a Hollywood war flick: Boomer, sitting atop the command wagon, surveying the battlefield with an air of absolute authority.

Boomer believed very deeply that commanders should lead from the front, not from a protected office in the rear. He thought the sight of a commanding general sharing the hardships and dangers of the battlefield had a major psychological impact on troops, giving them greater confidence in their leader. He also believed he could not adequately judge events on the battlefield by listening to a radio twenty-five or more miles away.

But there was another, simpler explanation for his decision to command from the front: This part of the job epitomized the reason people made careers of the military. Boomer knew there was not a general in the Pentagon who wouldn't trade places with him. It was easy to see, even from inside the Blazer seventy-five yards behind him, that Boomer had waited most of his career for this moment.

After passing the first few American troops, I noticed something missing among the members of our command convoy: We were the only ones not wearing chemical suits. Boomer thought the risk of chemical attack was slim, since the Iraqis had missed their chance to strike while the Marines were most vulnerable—crossing the minefields just after H-hour. He knew the Marines on the battlefield were more frightened by chemical warfare than by bullets or missiles, and he hoped that if they saw him without a chemical suit, they might be less fearful themselves. And, as much as anything, Boomer simply didn't want to wear one of the grimy, uncomfortable suits unless it was absolutely necessary.

As we approached the first minefield, the convoy slowed to a four-mile-per-hour crawl. Barbed wire marked the narrow passageway through the mine belt. Sand on either side was scorched black from explosive line charges used to detonate the mines. Only a few yards from the road, I could see the tops of exposed mines. American bombs—many of them unexploded—littered the desert in every direction.

We passed the front-line Iraqi defenses: camps of sand bunkers with corrugated-metal tops, sandbags surrounding buried fuel tanks, the remnants of bombed artillery guns, their barrels broken. Gaping craters pocked the sand. Charred tanks lay buried in their berms. The skeletons of cars and jeeps that had attempted to escape Kuwait in the first days of the Iraqi invasion were strewn across the desert.

A pair of cheap green shoes lay in the sand a few feet from the lane. "That Iraqi was running so fast he left his shoes," Weldon cracked.

I was simultaneously excited about being on the battlefield and profoundly disturbed by what I saw around me. This did not look like a high-technology war against a formidable foe, as advertised by the Pentagon. This battle looked like the aftermath of a war from decades past, with tanks and artillery guns that looked as if they predated their American counterparts by more than a generation.

The deeper we drove into Kuwait, the more evidence we saw of the devastation to its oil fields. The horizon was ablaze with flames from dozens of burning wells. Some were so close to our path I could feel the heat. Each wellhead burned in a different pattern. One spewed a geyser of flames. Another sent a spike of fire skyward, topped with a mushroom cloud of smoke. One blaze slithered across the ground like a fiery serpent.

9:30 a.m., Monday, February 25, 1991, G-day Plus One, 1st Marine Division Forward Command Post, South of the Burqan Oil Field

Brigadier General Tom Draude was busy monitoring the 1st Marine Division's chaotic tank battles on the edge of the Burqan oil field when one of his radio operators shouted, "Our security battalion is falling back!"

That could mean only one thing, Draude thought. We're under attack! He composed himself, trying to exude calmness. The last thing I need, Draude said to himself, is for my staff to fall apart on me.

"Hey, listen," he said to the young radio operator in the most casual Midwestern tone he could muster. "This is nothing to worry about. In football you lose yardage to get a better shot at the end zone. That's all that's going on."

Five T-54 tanks and thirty-three armored troop carriers barreled out of the oil field, bearing down on the command post. It wasn't enough that he'd been wrong about the Iraqi forces gathered in the oil field. As he worked the radios, another thought flashed through Draude's mind: He was liable to go down in history as the officer who allowed the division command post to be overrun by Iraqis.

Captain Ed Ray, who'd been cursing his bosses the night before for dispatching him to babysit the generals, scrambled to assemble his security team, mobilizing every man he could find, including Draude's personal driver.

Outside Draude's command tent, the security teams unleashed shoulder-fired antitank rockets at the approaching Iraqi column. Inside the tent, Draude tried to keep his young radio operators calm.

Draude tried to ignore the thunder of rocket launchers and guns as He worked the radio. The division headquarters dispatched a terse message to the Marines; rear command post in Saudi Arabia: "Enemy tanks and troops flushed from Burqan area. Much confusion." The smoke and fog were so thick that Iraqi forces were becoming intermingled with Marine armor on the battlefield. Air power was useless—neither helicopter nor bomber pilots could see well enough to fly through the black clouds, much less distinguish good guys from bad guys.

Just before 10 a.m., however, the skies suddenly lightened. Draude heard Cobra helicopters thumping overhead.

"Hey, Spank, man, I got tons of tanks out here!" declared an excited voice over Captain Randy "Spanky" Hammond's headset. "They're out of our main gun range right now. You're cleared hot in front of us."

His choppers were free to fire on any enemy vehicles they could find. *God, I've got all the luck in the world,* Hammond thought, leading his four Cobra helicopters into the smoke of the burning Burqan oil field, where the 1st Marine Division was battling Iraqi armor. *Right place, right time.* He'd been begging the air controllers all morning to unleash his four Cobras.

Finally, Hammond had persuaded the air controllers to let his Cobras go on a hunting expedition, looking for breaks in the thick ground cover. "Let us see what we can find out there," he'd pleaded.

Now, the mist and smoke were beginning to lift, and Hammond could see Iraqi tanks ahead of him, roaring toward the Marines on the ground. His cobras lit the desert with Hellfire and TOW missiles. One of Hammond's pilots watched as his TOW missile streaked toward an Iraqi tank. The tank commander saw the missile blazing toward him and jumped from his open hatch. Just as his feet cleared the opening, the TOW slammed into the armor, blowing the tanker into the air like a circus stunt man.

Hammond spotted a Soviet S60 artillery gun surrounded by Iraqi troops. They weren't shooting at him, but they weren't surrendering either. He edged closer, hovering so near the ground that he could see an Iraqi officer cowering in the corner of a foxhole, clawing at the sand in an attempt to make himself invisible. *God, wouldn't it be a great bar story to open my canopy, pull out my 9 millimeter Beretta, and shoot this guy,* Hammond thought. He resisted the urge.

By now many of the Iraqi tanks and personnel carriers were retreating deep into the burning oil field, seeking safety under the smoky black blanket. Hammond pushed his Cobras deeper into the clouds. He dialed radio frequencies trying to make contact with a Marine scout on the ground who could help direct the helicopters to their targets.

Corporal Bryan R. Freeman, a twenty-three-year-old scout from Olympia, Washington, who'd joined the Marine Corps looking for college tuition money and a war, answered Hammond's call from his humvee.

Freeman had led his three-man scout team through the fog and smoke of the Burqan oil field as soon as he'd heard that Papa Bear's command post was under attack, almost one and one-half hours earlier. Freeman was angry and distressed that the enemy tanks had gotten past him in the fog. After all, he was supposed to be the forward eyes of the task force. It was his job to spot the enemy and warn the commanders. The commanders weren't supposed to be telling him they'd spotted the enemy first.

Freeman heard machine-gun fire echo through the smoky fog as his men stole toward the sound of tanks on the left flank of Papa Bear. The noise was deafening: Papa Bear's tanks to his right, gunfire from Iraqi tanks somewhere ahead of him, burning oil wells all around, Cobras thundering overhead, and shrapnel pinging off his humvee.

The cloud of smoke above had turned day into night, but for several dozen feet above the ground, the air was clear enough for him to make out Iraqi tanks through his night-vision goggles. He carried a laser target designator in a suitcase-sized box called a mule. He pointed the laser toward the tanks and shouted into his radio at the pilots he could not see above him, "Two thousand meters, 100 bearing 100. Laser's on good spot. Fire when ready!"

Boom! A Hellfire missile from one of the Cobras streaked through the fog and followed Freeman's laser beam into the tank. Freeman pointed the laser at a second tank and radioed the direction and distance. "Fire when ready!" A second tank exploded in flames.

While Freeman searched for more targets on the ground, Hammond edged slowly toward a tank he's spotted from the air, angling for the best shot. Suddenly a wave of humanity rose from the ground. Several clusters of men held up white flags, others raised their arms.

"Man, I don't feel good about this," Hammond hissed into the radio. "But let's keep going."

He flew over the troops, sent a Hellfire missile into the tank, then began pushing his chopper higher above the desert floor. A dozen or more Iraqi troops lay sprawled in the sand below him. Without warning, they sprang to life, grabbled AK-47s, and began firing at the Cobras. Hammond jerked his chopper skyward.

No more Mr. Nice Guy, he told himself, racing toward another column of Iraqi tanks to his east. Dozens of Iraqi soldiers leaped out of a trench line on the ground in front of him. They weren't waving white flags, and Hammond was still smarting from the troops who'd fooled him playing possum.

He positioned the sight of his 20 millimeter machine gun in front of his eye, adjusted the gun, and pulled the trigger. The barrel spit out bright red flashes of 635 rounds a minute, sending shudders through the helicopter. Iraqi soldiers pitched forward into the sand, as though stumbling over a trip wire.

The other three Cobras in Hammond's group were having mechanical problems with their guns, leaving Hammond with the only working machine gun. He fired round after round, adrenaline pumping. I'm the only bubba out here with a gun, he thought, and I'm eating this up. He stopped shooting. Two Iraqi soldiers continued to flee across the sand. Hammond squeeze the trigger again. One man fell, the other turned and waved his arms in the air.

The trench suddenly erupted with gunfire, and Hammond saw tracer flashes streaking toward his chopper and whistling past his canopy.

"Hey, Spanky's taking small arms! I got tracer fire!" He jerked the stick and shot skyward.

A surface-to-air missile streaked past the copters. Hammond looked down and spotted four Iraqi soldiers running toward an antiaircraft artillery gun, a WEP4, which Hammond knew could fire 4,000 rounds per minute.

God, here we go, he thought, desperately trying to pull away. The pilot next to him, Corn-fed, was also jerking his bird upward. Hammond glanced out the cockpit to see a third pilot—Steve Rudder—blazing his Cobra across the battlefield, spitting rockets. Rudder slipped between Spanky and Corn-fed and the Iraqi artillery gun, shooting rockets into the ground as the Iraqis returned fire.

The Cobras pulled away to regroup. Hammond later spotted some Iraqi vehicles milling around an old Kuwaiti police post and saw Iraqi troops in a nearby trench. Adrenaline and emotion seized control, and he raced forward in a killing frenzy, pushing harder and harder, firing left and right. Can't stop. Over there, hit 'em. Keep pushing, keep pushing. Yeah!

Two massive black bursts rattled the helicopter. He heard a loud whoom over the sound of his own shooting. Another burst, as big as a house, exploded behind him, then another in front. Antiaircraft artillery was bracketing him, getting closer with every shot,

A rocket-propelled grenade sliced through the sky inches from Hammond's wingman. Rudder jerked his helicopter back.

"Hey, Rudder, where're you going!" Hammond shouted.

"I'll be right with you, Spank," replied the pilot. "I've got to clean out my underwear. Give me a minute, okay?"

"All right, pal. Whatever you need."

Hammond realized that in the heat of the moment, he'd pushed his men far too deep into the danger zone. Adrenaline was pushing him to make stupid decisions. He pulled back.

At the end of a three-and-one-half-hour battle, the Cobras, tanks, and other armaments of Task Force Papa Bear's 1st Tank Battalion had destroyed fifty tanks and twenty-five armored personnel carriers and captured more than 300 prisoners. The Iraqis, whose armor and artillery crews could not respond quickly enough to the combined air and ground assault of the American forces, scored no American casualties.

★ ★ ★ ★ ★

After only one hundred hours of ground combat, the Iraqis called for a cease-fire. President George H. W. Bush agreed and by February, Kuwait had been liberated. Saddam Hussein remained in power, brutally ending the Shiite uprising in southern Iraq and a Kurdish revolt to the north. The overthrowing of Hussein that the Americans hoped for failed to materialize. Molly Moore joined the foreign staff for the *Washington Post* in 9991 and is now living in Paris.

From Baghdad, with Love

JAY KOPELMAN

The fight to retake the Iraqi city of Fallujah from the control of insurgent forces in November and December of 2004 saw American forces in the heaviest urban combat since the battle for Hué in Vietnam. With the Marines in Fallujah were Lieutenant Colonel Jay Kopleman and his "Lava Dogs" of First Battalion, Third Marines. In an abandoned house in the middle of the fighting, Marines from Alpha Company discovered an orphaned puppy they adopted as their mascot "Lava." Kopelman would eventually break regulations to smuggle the dog out of Iraq back to the United States. The following chapter, taken from Kopelman's memoir, *From Baghdad with Love*, recounts the first days his unit adopted the mischievous puppy. It is a poignant human story from the chaos and blackness of wartime Iraq.

> So he sent the man out; and at the east of the Garden of Eden
> he put winged ones and a flaming sword turning everyway to
> keep the way to the tree of life.
> —Genesis 3:24

★　★　★　★　★

Prologue: November 2004
First week of the US invasion of Fallujah, Iraq

IN AN ABANDONED house in the northeast section of Fallujah, members of the First Battalion, Third Marines—known as the Lava Dogs—froze when they heard a series of clicks coming from the one remaining room of the compound.

Grenade pins?

Most of the military deaths in Fallujah during the first week of the US invasion happened inside buildings like this, where insurgents hid in upper rooms and threw grenades down at the Marines as they moved upward. There were a lot of head and face injuries, and while the Lava Dogs considered themselves some of the toughest Marines around—they named themselves out of respect for the jagged pumice they trained on back in Hawaii—just being a Lava Dog didn't shield you from a grenade's fancy special effects. Being careful did. Being focused did. Having your weapon locked and loaded when you inched around every corner did.

Click. Click. Click . . . Click.

If a grenade did detach your face from your skull, at least you would check out in the GPS coordinate closest to Heaven. Iraq was considered by most biblical archaeologists to be the location of the Garden of Eden—God's only hard copy of Heaven, his Paradise on earth. Not that you'd have adequate excuses prepared once you got there, because lines between good and evil here in the battle zone required more than reading glasses to see. But whether Abraham, Muhammad, or Jesus called your cadence, it's where it officially all started and where it officially all went bad.

Good marketing potential for the region at first, though, because it trademarked the birthplace of Abraham, the Tower of Babel, and the construction of Babylon in addition to agriculture, writing, the wheel, the zodiac, legal theory, bureaucracy, and urbanization. From the beginning, everyone wanted a piece of the place that went from the Mesopotamians to the Sumerians to the Akkadians to the Empire of Ur to the Babylonians to the Assyrians to the Persians to the Greeks to the Arabs to the Mongols to the Turks to the British.

None of these were polite handovers, either. By the time Saddam Hussein got to the land of milk and honey, it had been captured, pillaged, beaten, and raped by so many cultures over such a long period of time, there was little left except a whole lot of desert covering a whole lot of oil. That, and claims by locals living near the Tigris and Euphrates Rivers that the Garden of Eden and its Tree of Life stood in the middle of their very town. They built a wall around the area, constructed the Garden of Eden Hotel, and tourism flourished for a short while. Then the Americans came, and because the folks living in the area supported the newest invasion, Hussein drained all their water. Soon the Tree of Life died, members of the Supreme Council for the Islamic Revolution in Iraq took over the Garden of Eden Hotel, and DOWN WITH AMERICANS was painted all over the walls of Paradise.

Clickclickclickclick.

Maybe timed explosives.

If this country was Paradise, then the Marines weren't taking any bets on Hell. Outside the building they searched, gunships prowled the skies looking for hiding insurgents as pockmarked Humvees patrolled what was left of the streets. Every driving car in the city was targeted because of bomb risks. Every loose wire was suspect. Every building was searched, and JIHAD, JIHAD, JIHAD plastered every wall.

Throughout the first days of the invasion of Fallujah, the Marines discovered weapons caches, suicide vests, and large amounts of heroin, speed, and cocaine apparently used to bolster suicide bombers' courage. They found dead bodies of fighters from Chechnya, Syria, Libya, Jordan, Afghanistan, and Saudi Arabia. They walked into human slaughterhouses with hooks hanging from the ceilings, black masks, knives, bloody straw mats, and videos of beheadings. They freed emaciated prisoners shackled and insane with fear.

Fallujah, near the center of where it all began, was now a city cordoned off from the rest of the world, inhabited only by invisible snipers and stray dogs feasting on the dead.

Click. Snuffle. Snuffle. Click.

The Lava Dogs tightened their jaws and clenched their weapons as they ran through the rules in their heads: Cover danger areas, stay low, move stealthily, be prepared to adapt, and eliminate threats.

Snuffle. Clickclickclick. Snufflesnuffle.

An insurgent strapping a bomb to his chest?

They should have prepped the room first with a grenade—tossed it in and just let it do all the dirty work. Instead, for reasons still obscured by war and fear and things just destined to be, they backed up to the walls on either side of the doorway and positioned their weapons to fire.

Then they thrust their rifles around the corner, squared off, and zeroed in on the clicks as their target rushed to the other side of the room.

"Holy shit."

The puppy turned at the sound of their voices and stared at them.

"What the hell?"

He cocked his head, trying to interpret their intent rather than their words.

"You gotta be kidding."

Then he yipped, wagged his tail, and clicked his toenails on the floor as he pranced up and down in place, happy it seemed someone had found him at last.

Part I

> "In toil you shall eat of it all the days of your life."
>
> —Genesis 3:17

November 2004—Fallujah

I don't remember exactly when I got to the house that served as our command post in the northwest sector of Fallujah, and I don't remember exactly how I got there. It was a couple of days after the Lava Dogs arrived and took over the compound, I do know that much, and I remember that after four days of dodging sniper fire, sleeping on the ground, and patrolling Fallujah with wide-eyed Iraqi soldiers in training who shot at anything that moved, including their own boots, I walked up to the building with a sense of having escaped an abstract rendition of the wrong hereafter.

I remember being exhausted, the tiredness weighing more heavily on me than the sixty-pound rucksack I lugged around, and as I walked through the front door and shrugged what I could off my back, all I could think about was sleep.

That's when I saw Lava for the first time. Only it's not as if I walked in and saw a chubby puppy cuddled up on a blanket undefiled by the world like an overstuffed lamb. There were no squeaky toys, no baby yips, no eyes looking up at me with an artless blue-gray innocence.

Instead a sudden flash of something rolls toward me out of nowhere, shooting so much adrenaline into my wiring that I jump back and slam into a wall. A ball of fur not much bigger than a grenade skids across the floor, screeches to a halt at my boots, and then whirls in circles around me with the torque of a windup toy. It scares me, right? Like I'm tired and wired and anything quick coming at me jerked at my nerves, so I peel back off the wall and reach for my rifle even though I can see it's only a puppy.

Now, before you get all out of whack about me aiming a weapon at cute baby mammals, keep in mind that I just walked in from the streets. Out there, things were spooky, like a plague or a flood or dust from an atomic bomb had just rolled through. Most of the city fled before the US-led attack, and the quiet rang so loud after the bombardment, even windblown newspaper sent your nerves screaming for solid cover.

The day before the offensive started, we dropped leaflets over the city warning the few remaining citizens that we were on our way in, but insurgents inside spit back that they had hundreds of car bombs rigged, booby traps set, and suicide bombers with jittery fingers waiting to go. They'd already dug trenches in the city's cemeteries for the expected martyrs.

In the days prior to our march into the city, our warplanes pounded Fallujah with cannon fire, rockets, and bombs. Because the skies were so crowded, attack jets had only a three-minute window to unload their cargo and clear out before another jet swooped in. Hundreds and hundreds of pounds of 105mm shells, 25mm rounds, and 40mm rounds blasted into Fallujah that night with the impact of meteors from several galaxies away. The aerial bombardment was so spectacular, I—along with ten thousand other Marines waiting to advance on the outskirts of the city—doubted anyone inside would live through it. But plenty managed, and now that we were here, sniper fire came at us from nowhere like the screams from ghosts.

So when this unexpected thing, this puppy, comes barreling toward me in this unexpected place, I reach for my gun. I must have yelled or something, because at the sound of my voice, the puppy looks up at me, raises his tail, and starts growling this baby-dog version of *I am about to kick your ass.*

The fur gets all puffy around his neck like he's trying to make himself look big, and then he lets loose these wienie war cries—*roo-roo-roo-rooo*—as he bounces up and down on stiff legs.

I stomp my boot his way to quiet him down, but he doesn't budge and intensified the *roo-roo-roo-roooos* shooting in staccato from his lungs.

"Hey."

I shove the rifle to my back and bend down. The puppy bounces backward in time to the *roo-roo-roo-roooos* but doesn't take his eyes from my face.

"Hey. Calm down."

He looks like a bloated panda bear, and when he howls the last *rooooo* of the *roo-roo-rooooo*, his snout stretches skyward until his fat front paws lift off the floor.

There's fear in his eyes despite the bravado. He's only a puppy, too young to know how to mask it, so I can see how bravery and terror trap him on all sides while testosterone and adrenaline compete in the meantime for every ounce of his attention. Recognized it right away.

I reach into my pocket, *roo-roo-roo*, pull out a bullet, *roo-roo-roo-roo*, and hold it out toward him in hopes he'll think it's food. The puppy stops barking and cocks his head, which makes me feel manipulative but wise.

"Thatta boy."

He sniffs the air above his head, finds nothing, and then directs his nose toward the bullet. It interests him, and he leans forward for a better whiff of the metal, which surprises me until I notice how filthy my hands are, almost black from a week without washing, and I realize he's smelling accumulated dirt and death on my skin.

I lean forward, but fear gets the better of him and he tears off down the hall.

"Hey, come back."

I stand there and watch him career into a wall. I wince, that's got to hurt, but he gets up, shakes his head, and takes off again.

"Hey, come here."

The puppy stops and looks back at me, ears high, tiny tail rotating wildly, pink tongue hanging out sideways from his mouth like he's crazy. I realize he wants me to chase him, like he figured out he was bamboozled only he's too proud to admit it and now covers up with this *I-was-never-afraid-of-you* routine. I recognize that one, too.

He leaps in a circle on paws as big as his face, hits the wall again, and repels into a puddle of daze. I'm, like, mesmerized by the little guy. Wipes my windshield clean just watching him, so I scoop him up off the ground with one hand and pretend I didn't notice his wall slam.

"Tough guy, huh?"

He smells like kerosene.

"What's that aftershave you're wearing?"

He feels lighter than a pint of bottled water as he squirms and laps at my face, blackened from explosive residue, soot from bombed-out buildings, and dust from hitting the ground so many times.

"Where'd you come from?"

I have a pretty good idea where he came from and a pretty good idea where he's going, too. I've seen it before, Marines letting their guards down and getting too friendly with the locals—pretty girls, little kids, cute furry mammals, doesn't matter; it's not allowed. So as I'm holding the little tough guy and he's acting like he just jumped out of a box under the Christmas tree, I call my cool to attention,

It's not allowed, Kopelman.

But he keeps licking and squirming and wiggling around, and I remember this part pretty well, because I liked the way he felt in my hands, I liked that he forgave me for scaring him, I liked not caring about getting home or staying alive or feeling warped as a human being—just him wiggling around in my hands, wiping all the grime off my face.

The Lava Dogs told me they'd found the little outlaw here at the compound when they stormed the place, and the reason he was still here was that they didn't know what else to do with him. Since they'd decided to use the compound as the command post, and since this starving five-week-old puppy was already there, the choices were either to put him out on the street, execute him, or ignore him as he slowly died in the corner. The excuses they gave me were as follows:

"Not me, man, no way."

"Not worth the ammo."

"I ain't some kind of sicko, man."

In other words, they had enough pictures already from Fallujah to torture them slowly for the rest of their lives; they didn't need any more. Warriors, yes—puppy killers, no.

The puppy is named Lava, and while I'd like to say my comrades are creative enough to name him for symbolic reasons—like, you know, if they save him, they save themselves—I'm fairly sure they just couldn't come up with anything else.

Lave is the newest grunt, de-flea'd with kerosene, de-wormed with chewing tobacco, and pumped full of MREs.

Just so you understand how tough Lava really is: MREs, officially called "Meals Ready to Eat," but unofficially called "Meals Rejected by Everyone," are trilaminate retort pouches containing exactly twelve hundred calories of food, a plastic spoon, and a flameless heater that mixes magnesium and iron dust with salt to provide enough heat to warm the entrée. On the package, the meals state that "Restriction of food and nutrients leads to rapid weight loss, which leads to: Loss of strength, Decreased endurance, Loss of motivation, Decreased mental alertness," which supposedly coaxes us into at least opening the pouch to see what's inside.

Lava can't get enough of them, though, and learns real quick how to tear open pouches designed with three-year shelf lives that can withstand parachute drops of 1,250 feet or more.

Still, the best part is how these Marines, these elite, well-oiled machines of war who in theory can kill another human being in a hundred unique ways, become mere mortals in the presence of a tiny mammal. I'm shocked to hear a weird, misty tone in my fellow Marines' voices, a weird, misty look in their eyes, and weird, misty words that end in *ee*.

"You had yuckee little buggees all over you when we found you, huh? Now you're a brave little toughee. Are you our brave little toughee? You're a brave, little toughee, yessiree."

And the whole time Lava knows I've got him pegged, and he's stealing glances at me to make sure I see how he's soaking it all up.

The Marines brag about how the puppy attacks their boots and sleeps in their helmets and gnaws nonstop on the wires from journalists' satellite phones up on the roof. They tell me he can almost pick up an ammo belt. They tell me he loves M&Ms.

"Did anyone feed Lava this morning?" someone yells out as "I did" comes back from every guy in the room.

He's like a cartoon character on fast-forward, always chasing something, chewing something, spinning head-on into something. He stalks shadows and dust balls and pieces of balled-up paper. He can eat an entire cigar in less than two minutes and drag a flak jacket all the way across the floor. I mean, the little shit never stops. If you aren't dragging him along after you as he hangs on to your bootlaces with his teeth, he's up on the roof tangled in wires or lost and wailing in the bowels of somebody's backpack.

You can't yell at him, either, because even though you are an elite, well-oiled machine of war who in theory can kill another human being in a hundred unique ways, you'd still be considered a freak if you yelled at a puppy. He's completely pampered, kept warm, his sticks never thrown out of his sight range so his ego isn't damaged when he can't find them. I find it all pathetic. At first.

But the newest recruit already knows the two most important rules of boot camp by the time I come around: You don't chew on bullets and you only pee outside.

It's like Lava is everyone's kid. It gives them something to be responsible for above and beyond protecting their country and one another, and getting their brains blown out or worse in the process. He gives them a routine. And somehow, I become part of it.

Every morning we feed Lava his rehydrated Country Captain Chicken with Buttered Noodles and then pile out of the house to various posts across the city. Some Marines patrol the streets, some clear buildings looking for weapons, and some get killed and don't do much of anything after that.

Me, I have to patrol the streets with three wide-eyes Iraqi soldiers who, in their brand-new, US-issued, chocolate-chip cammies, wave their rifles around as if clearing the way of spiderwebs. Most still haven't figured out how to keep their rifles safely locked.

They are untrained, out of shape, and terrified. They're members of the Iraqi Armed Forces (IAF)—stouthearted doublespeak for "conquered and unemployed"—who were coaxed by the Untied States to help root out insurgents in Fallujah before the upcoming national elections.

Several days before we bombed the city, the new Iraqi recruits reported to Camp Fallujah, a few miles southeast of the city, with plenty of promising bravado. When Prime Minister Iyad Allawi made a surprise visit to the camp and urged them to be brave, to go forth and "arrest the killers" in Fallujah, the young Iraqi soldiers cried back with newly developed devil-dog gusto. "May they go to Hell!"

Things deteriorated quickly, though. First we built a tent camp for them just outside the walled safety of the main camp. We called it the East Fallujah Iraqi Camp and hoped the name and the handful of American advisers and liaison officers who also stayed there would boost their courage. The Iraqi soldiers endured both regular mortar shelling of their tents by insurgents and verbal bombardments from the Americans who only had one week to prepare them for their first-ever combat experience. So they were prone to the jitters and often woke up in the middle of the night shooting their unsafed rifles wildly. Thank God they didn't know how to aim.

It didn't help that influential Iraqi clerics publicly threatened the IAF soldiers with banishment to Hell, and the insurgent council that controlled Fallujah promised to behead any one of them who entered the city to "fight their own people." In a statement issued by the council just before we attacked, the insurgents stated: "We swear by God that we will stand against you in the streets, we will enter your houses and we will slaughter you just like sheep."

More than two hundred Iraqi troops quickly "resigned," and another two hundred were "on leave." My job now is to baby sit some of the few who remain.

One afternoon about a week after I arrived at the compound, a few other Marines and I are patrolling one of the main streets with them. We're in front of a mosque, right? And they're all bug-eyed and waving their guns around and I'm a little strung out myself about what's going on around us only I can't let on, because I'm their example of what they're supposed to do and feel and be. But they're so freaked out, they're clearly about to shoot me or one of the other Marines by accident, so I figure the best thing is to make them more afraid of me than they are of the streets—you know, take their minds off it for a little while—so I start yelling.

"Knock that shit off."

And I keep yelling.

"Safe your weapons."

And they keep jerking their eyes one way and their rifles another way.

"I *said* knock that shit off!"

Until I see they've gone into another zone of fear that even I don't have access to, and one of the other Marines, I don't remember who, Tim

O'Brien, Dan Doyle, or Mark Lombard, says to me, "Take is easy on them, man, they don't understand English," which kind of ruins my whole show.

"Yeah, well they *better* learn fast." But I stop yelling and give them a look instead.

Then something rips past us in the air and we freeze. Just like that. It comes from nowhere but explodes a few yards away. Now we're moving fast. Fast.

A second rocket-propelled grenade (RPG) comes screaming our way, and I assess the situation in staccato—taking fire from two directions; small arms, medium machine gun, and rocket-propelled grenades; two men wounded; Iraqi soldiers running for cover; outnumbered in more ways than one.

I maneuver behind the hood of the Humvee to direct the men as Tim O'Brien, up in the turret, opens up with the MK-19 turret gun laying down a base of covering fire so the rest of us can position to fight.

Dan Doyle picks up a squad automatic weapon and fires toward the southwest.

Tim's a primary target in the turret, especially when his MK-19 jams and he has to fight with his M4—a shortened version of the M16A4 assault rifle—while he's trying to clear the MK-19 and make it ready to fire again. But it's Dan who gets hit. Blood runs down the inside of his left leg.

"Dan, get into that mosque," I order, but he ignores me and takes off running to get the Humvees positioned so we can evacuate the rest of the wounded, including Mark Lombard, who's bleeding all over the place but is on the radio calling in our situation report anyway.

Bullets and shrapnel ricochet from the hood of the Humvee inches to my right. Blood soaks Dan's pant leg.

"Get you ass into that mosque," I yell again, but he, get this, looks over at me and grins.

"Just a flesh wound."

Two armor-piercing rounds hit the vehicle and tear through its quarter-inch steel plate easier than needles through skin. I fire my M16A2 and yell for the Iraqi soldiers to direct their fire to the south.

Only I don't see them. Where the hell are they? I have to get the wounded to safety, so when I see them from the corner of my eye crouched numb between two overturned vehicles, I realize we're on our own.

I abandon my M16A2 for a more powerful squad automatic weapon, then run in front of the Humvee and fire away to the south. This apparently inspires one of the Iraqi soldiers to stick his head out, fire two rounds quickly—using me as his cover—and then duck back in. It's the last I see of the Iraqis for the rest of the thirty-minute fight.

At night we all gather back at the compound, where we cover the windows with blankets and sandbags, clean our weapons, and make sure Lava has something for dinner that he didn't have the night before.

Then the time comes when you have to put back on all your gear, ready your weapon, and sneak out to the portable toilets down the block. We call them porta-shitters. One of my greatest fears during the weeks I stay at the compound is the possibility of being blasted by an RPG in a porta-shitter.

If you survive that, then you bed down and smoke cigars and review the day's events with everyone else who made it.

"We found a weapons cache in that old UN food-for-oil place . . ."

"Yeah, well, we got caught in an alley . . ."

"Yeah, well, we had to transport wounded and they actually fell out of the Humvee onto the street when we got hit with an RPG or something we never saw coming."

They have nothing on me, though.

"Yeah, well, my Iraqi guys decided to take their naps during a fire-fight . . ."

As we talk, Lava climbs up and over our boots, destroys packages of M&Ms, and paws through our blankets for prey.

"They don't have a clue out there . . ."

Then the puppy finds my lap and sits between my crossed legs staring out at the other Marines.

"I mean, how do DC brass ever expect to get these guys to secure their country if we're doing it all for them?"

I untie my boots, and Lava bites at the laces.

"I swear I am going to accidentally shoot the whole group of them if they don't shape up."

As I pull a boot off, the puppy grabs hold of the lace and tugs. I tug back. The puppy growls. I growl back.

"Hey, what's with this puppy anyway?" I ask. "What are you guys planning on doing with him?"

No one answers. Then one of the Marines stretches and yawns and says he's turning in. Others grunt. Lava crawls out of my lap and turns a few circles, flops down, and falls asleep with his nose buried in my empty boot.

Meanwhile, outside on the streets, psychological operations teams blast AC/DC and Jimi Hendrix through loudspeakers, with the additional sound effects of crying babies, screaming women, screeching cats, and howling dogs, in hopes of turning the insurgents' nerves to shreds. They broadcast insults in Arabic, including "You shoot like goatherders" and "May all the ambulances in Fallujah have enough fuel to pick up the bodies of the mujahideen," which, along with the mortar, grenades, ceaseless rumbling of Humvees, and twenty different kinds of aircraft flying in precise layers over the city including helicopters, attack jets, and small, pneumatically launched spy drones that roam the skies beaming back images to base from automatic video cameras, create a kind of white noise that allows us all to sleep pretty soundly through the night.

I guess they didn't want to answer my question about Lava that night, because like everything else in Fallujah during the invasion, nothing but the immediate was worth thinking about. Really, there wasn't room in your head for anything but what was right in front of your or right behind you or right around the next corner. The future spanned one city block at most. Your dreams consisted of RPGs that missed; lifelong goals were met if you made it back to the compound at night.

So the guys probably weren't avoiding the subject of what would happen to Lava so much as they were ignoring it. There just wasn't any room. But jeez, when a puppy picks your boots to fall asleep in, you do start to wonder how he'll die.

See, I've been a Marine since 1992 when I transferred from the navy, and I know that the little guy is going to die. I knew it right away when I saw him in the hall—*this one won't make it*—just like you could look at some of the other guys and think *This one won't make it, because his one eye twitches* or *This one won't make it, because he parts his hair on the right instead of the left*—superstitious stuff like that, which you know doesn't make sense but oils your engine anyway. I was thinking *This one won't make it, because he's too damned cute.*

I'm also a lieutenant colonel, which means I know military rules as well as anyone, and every time I picked Lava up, they darted across my brain like flares: *Prohibited activities for service members under General Order 1-A include adopting as pets or mascots, caring for or feeding any type of domestic or wild animals.*

★　★　★　★　★

With the help of a journalist and some conspiring friends, Kopelman was able to have Lava flown back to the United States where he was reunited with Jay and his family. Kopelman's book, *From Baghdad With Love* went on to be a best-selling story.

Endnotes

Introduction

Dispatches from the Mexican War

[1] These gates defended the southern entrances to the city.

[2] This meeting followed several days of reconnoitering by Scott's engineers to determine which routes through the marshy land around the city were most suitable for maneuvering artillery and infantry units. Discussions focused on the approach to San Antonio Garita on the capital's south side and a route from the west to the Belén and San Cosmé gates. After hearing presentations that featured the views of Lee and Beauregard, Scott chose the latter approach, which required the taking of Chapultepec and which he had probably favored from the outset.

[3] Scott sent Quitman's division toward La Piedad on the city's southwest corner to prevent Santa Anna from strengthening Chapultepec and at the same time to direct heavy artillery fire on the castle in hopes of forcing the Mexican defenders to evacuate. By nightfall on September 12, the Mexicans had lost the use of two cannons but still held their ground. Meanwhile, Scott prepared for an infantry assault.

[4] The *Picayune* published the first news of Scott's victory on September 25, 1847, having received sketchy reports of the fall of Mexico City from the American customs official F. M. Dimond in Vera Cruz. This dispatch by Kendall, along with one authored by the *Delta*'s Freaner, arrived in New Orleans on October 13, providing the first confirmation of the American victory.

[5] With heavy artillery fire and hand-to-hand fighting, the Americans overwhelmed the less than 1,000 men commanded by Nicolá Bravo in the undermanned fortification. Mentioned is José Mariano Monterde.

[6] Kendall was slightly wounded during this action.

[7]

Miracle at Belleau Wood

1 Catlin, *"With the Help of God and a Few Marines,"* p. 114.

2 Catlin, *"With the Help of God and a Few Marines,"* p. 114.

3 Gibbons, *"And They Thought We Wouldn't Fight,"* p. 303.

4 Gibbons, *"And They Thought We Wouldn't Fight,"* pp. 303–4.

5 Marine Corps Legacy Museum, "Sergeant Major Daniel J. Daly, USMC," www.mclm.com/tohonor/ddaly.html (accessed January 25, 2007).

6 Medal of Honor, "Double Congressional Medal of Honor Recipient Sergeant Major Daniel Joseph Daly," www.medalofhonor.com/DanDaly.htm (accessed January 25, 2007).

7 Catlin, *"With the Help of God and a Few Marines,"* p. 126.

8 Catlin, *"With the Help of God and a Few Marines,"* p. 114; Mattfeldt, *Records of the Second Division*, 5, quoted in Asprey, *At Belleau Wood*, p. 172; Catlin, *"With the Help of God and a Few Marines,"* p. 114.

9 Gibbons, *"And They Thought We Wouldn't Fight,"* pp. 310–11.

10 Gibbons, *"And They Thought We Wouldn't Fight,"* pp. 310–11.

11 Gibbons, *"And They Thought We Wouldn't Fight,"* pp. 311–12.

12 Gibbons, *"And They Thought We Wouldn't Fight,"* p. 312.

13 Gibbons, *"And They Thought We Wouldn't Fight,"* p. 312.

14 Gibbons, *"And They Thought We Wouldn't Fight,"* p. 313.

15 Gibbons, *"And They Thought We Wouldn't Fight,"* pp. 313–14.

16 Gibbons, *"And They Thought We Wouldn't Fight,"* p. 314.

17 Gibbons, *"And They Thought We Wouldn't Fight,"* p. 314.

18 George V. Gordon, *Leathernecks and Doughboys* (Chicago: privately printed, 1927), cited in Asprey, *At Belleau Wood,* p. 173.

19 Catlin, *"With the Help of God and a Few Marines,"* p. 115.

20 Catlin, *"With the Help of God and a Few Marines,"* p. 115.

21 Leatherneck, "Oldest Marine Found Living in Syracuse, NY," www.leatherneck.com/forums/showthread.php?t=10334 (accessed January 25, 2007).

22 Catlin, *"With the Help of God and a Few Marines,"* pp. 115–16.

23 Catlin, *"With the Help of God and a Few Marines,"* p. 116.

24 Catlin, *"With the Help of God and a Few Marines,"* p. 117.

25 Catlin, *"With the Help of God and a Few Marines,"* pp. 117–18.

[26] Catlin, *"With the Help of God and a Few Marines,"* p. 119.

[27] Catlin, *"With the Help of God and a Few Marines,"* p. 119.

[28] Catlin, *"With the Help of God and a Few Marines,"* p. 119.

[29] Catlin, *"With the Help of God and a Few Marines,"* pp. 120–21.

[30] Catlin, *"With the Help of God and a Few Marines,"* p. 121.

[31] Louis F. Timmerman, *War Diary, 1917–1919* (unpublished manuscript in private collection), quoted in Asprey, *At Belleau Wood* , p. 179.

[32] Timmerman, *War Diary*, quoted in Asprey, *At Belleau Wood*, p. 179.

[33] Timmerman, *War Diary*, quoted in Asprey, *At Belleau Wood*, pp. 179–80.

[34] Timmerman, *War Diary*, quoted in Asprey, *At Belleau Wood*, p. 180.

[35] Timmerman, *War Diary*, quoted in Asprey, *At Belleau Wood*, p. 181.

Henderson Field

[1] John Field, *Life*, 7 June 1943.

[2] Ben Finney, *Feet First*, foreword by John O'Hara (New York: Crown Publishers, 1971).

Credits

The Pirate Coast

From *The Pirate Coast: Thomas Jefferson, the First Marines, and the Secret Mission of 1805*. Copyright © 2006 Richard Zacks. Reprinted by permission of Hyperion. All rights reserved. Available wherever books are sold.

Gamble of the Marines

Albert Whitman & Company, Chicago, from the original manuscript by Captain Raymond J. Toner, U.S.N. © Copyright 1963 by Raymond J. Toner.

The Battle of Bladensburg

John Brannan, ed. *Official Letters of the Military and Naval Officers of the United States During the War with Great Britain in the Years 1812, 13, 14, & 15* With Some Additional Letters and Documents Elucidating the History of that Period. (Washington: 1823), pp. 405-407. Public domain.

Dispatches from the Mexican War

Reprinted with the permission of The University of Oklahoma Press. Edited with an introduction by Lawrence Delbert Cress. Copyright © 1999 by the University of Oklahoma Press, Norman, Publishing Division of the University.

A Civil War Marine at Sea

From *A Civil War Marine at Sea": The Diary of Medal of Honor Recipient Miles M. Oviatt*, Mary P. Livingston, Ed., Copyright © 1998. Reprinted by permission of White Mane Publishing Company, Inc.

Miracle at Belleau Wood

Alan Axelrod. Lyons Press. Copyright 2007.